*Garland English Texts*

Stephen Orgel
*Editor*

Jerome McGann
*Associate Editor*

# The Poems of Charlotte Brontë
## A New Text and Commentary

edited by
*Victor A. Neufeldt*

Garland English Texts
*Number 9*

GARLAND PUBLISHING, INC.
NEW YORK & LONDON
1985

**Library of Congress Cataloging-in-Publication Data**

Brontë, Charlotte, 1816–1855.
　The poems of Charlotte Brontë.

　(Garland English texts ; no. 9)
Bibliography: p.
Includes index.
1. Neufeldt, Victor A.　II. Title.　III. Series.
PR4166.N48　1985　821'.8　84-48884
ISBN 0-8240-8742-9 (alk. paper)

Cover Design by Alison Lew

Printed on acid-free, 250-year-life paper
Manufactured in the United States of America

For Audrey

# CONTENTS

## Acknowledgements

This work could not have been undertaken without the cooperation and generous assistance of many persons and agencies, whose help I acknowledge with pleasure.

For their generous financial assistance in the form of various research grants and a Leave Fellowship I wish to thank the Social Sciences and Humanities Research Council of Canada and the Office of Research Administration of the University of Victoria.

For permission to reproduce the texts of manuscripts, transcriptions, and letters held by them it is my pleasure to acknowledge the following libraries and individuals: the family of the late Mr. C. K. Shorter; the Council of the Brontë Society; Miss Agnes Hatfield; the British Library, Department of Manuscripts; the Brotherton Collection, Brotherton Library, University of Leeds; the Council of Newnham College, Cambridge University; Mr. Roger W. Barrett; Beinecke Rare Book and Manuscript Library, Yale University; the Houghton Library, Harvard University; the Humanities Research Center, the University of Texas at Austin; the Huntington Library, San Marino, California; the University of Missouri Library and Press; the Henry W. and Albert A. Berg Collection, the New York Public Library; Astor, Lenox and Tilden Foundations; the Carl and Lily Pforzheimer Foundation, Inc., and the Carl H. Pforzheimer Library; the Pierpont Morgan Library; Special Collections, Rutgers University Library; Mr. William Self; the Poetry/Rare Books Collection of the University Libraries, State University of New York at Buffalo; Mr. Robert H. Taylor; Special Collections Division, University of British Columbia Library; Wellesley College Library.

For their assistance in locating and making available various materials and answering various queries, I wish to thank the following individuals: Sally Stonehouse, former Librarian, and Juliet Barker, Librarian, Brontë Parsonage; Charles Lemon and Albert H. Preston, Brontë Society Council; the Keeper and staff, Department of Manuscripts, British Library; C. D. W. Sheppard and staff, Brotherton Collection, University of Leeds; A. Phillips, Newnham College Library; Edward Chitham, Wolverhampton Polytechnic; Brian Wilkes, Leeds University; Tom Winnifrith, Warwick University; Roger W. Barrett; Marjorie G. Wynne, Beinecke Rare Book and Manuscript Library; Rodney G. Dennis and staff, Houghton Library; Ellen S. Dunlap, Humanities Research Center; Virginia Renner and Sara S. Hodson, Huntington Library; Lola L. Szladits and staff, Berg Collection; Mihai H. Handrea, Pforzheimer Library; Verlyn Klingenborg, Herbert Cahoon, Edith W. Semler, Pierpont Morgan Library; Charles Greene, Princeton University Library; Clark L. Beck Jr., Rutgers University Library; William Self; Robert J. Bertholf, Poetry/Rare Books Collection, SUNY at Buffalo; Nancy N. Coffin, Robert H. Taylor Collection; George Brandak, University of British Columbia Library; staff of the McPherson

Library, University of Victoria; Eleanor L. Nicholes, Wellesley College
Library; Lionel Adey, William Benzie, Anthony Edwards, Brian Gooch, John
Greene, Odean Long, and Henry Summerfield, University of Victoria.

Finally, for their help in preparing the manuscript I wish to thank
Pamela Dalziel, Colleen Donnelly and Louise Laforest for their patient
work on the word-processor, Susan Cripps for her meticulous proof-
reading, and above all my wife, Audrey, the unpaid assistant editor for
this project.

## List of Abbreviations

The following abbreviations for frequently cited works are used throughout:

Alexander

**A Bibliography of the Manuscripts of Charlotte Brontë**, by Christine Alexander, The Brontë Society in association with Meckler Publishing, 1982.

Alexander EW

**The Early Writings of Charlotte Brontë**, Oxford: Basil Blackwell, 1983.

Benson 1915

**Brontë Poems, Selections From the Poetry of Charlotte Brontë**, edited by Arthur C. Benson, London: Smith Elder Co., 1915.

BPM

The Brontë Parsonage Museum Library.

BST

**Brontë Society Transactions** 1895-1983.

Christian Census

"A Census of Brontë Manuscripts in the United States," by Mildred Christian, **The Trollopian** II (1947) and III (1948).

Dodd Mead 1902

**Poems by Charlotte, Emily, and Anne Brontë**, New York: Dodd, Mead and Co., 1902.

Gérin CB

**Charlotte Brontë. The Evolution of Genius**, by Winifred Gérin, Oxford: Oxford University Press, 1967.

Gérin Five Novelettes

**Five Novelettes**, by Charlotte Brontë, ed., Winifred Gérin, London: Folio Press, 1971.

Hatfield Papers

The papers of the late C. W. Hatfield at the BPM, containing notes, transcriptions, and correspondence.

Poems 1846

**Poems by Currer, Ellis, and Acton Bell**, London: Aylott and Jones, 1846.

Ratchford Legends

**Legends of Angria: Compiled from the Early Writings of Charlotte Brontë**, by Fannie E. Ratchford, with the collaboration of William Clyde DeVane, New Haven: Yale University Press, 1933.

| | |
|---|---|
| Ratchford Web | **The Brontës' Web of Childhood,** by Fannie E. Ratchford, New York: Columbia University Press, 1941. |
| SHB C and B | **The Poems of Charlotte and Patrick Branwell Brontë** (The Shakespeare Head edition), ed. Thomas J. Wise and John Alexander Symington, Oxford: Basil Blackwell, 1934. |
| SHB LL | **The Brontës: Their Lives, Friendships, and Correspondence** (The Shakespeare Head edition), ed., Thomas J. Wise and John Alexander Symington, 4 volumes, Oxford: Basil Blackwell, 1932. |
| SHB Misc | **The Miscellaneous and Unpublished Writings of Charlotte and Patrick Branwell Brontë** (The Shakespeare Head edition), ed., Thomas J. Wise and John Alexander Symington, 2 volumes, Oxford: Basil Blackwell, 1936 and 1938. |
| Shorter 1923 | **The Complete Poems of Charlotte Brontë,** ed., Clement Shorter, with the assistance of C. W. Hatfield, London: Hodder and Stoughton, 1923. |
| Shorter EJB 1910 | Volume I, **Poetry,** of **The Complete Works of Emily Jane Brontë,** ed., Clement Shorter, London: Hodder and Stoughton, 1910. |
| Shorter 1918 | **Latest Gleanings: Being a Series of Unpublished Poems Selected From Her Early Manuscripts,** by Charlotte Brontë, Privately printed by Clement Shorter, 1918. |
| Symington Collection | The papers of John Alexander Symington in Special Collections, Rutgers University Library, containing transcriptions made by Davidson Cook of Brontë manuscripts in the library of Sir Alfred Law. |
| Winnifrith | **The Brontës and Their Background,** by Tom Winnifrith, London: Macmillan, 1973. |
| Winnifrith PCB | **The Poems of Charlotte Brontë,** ed., Tom Winnifrith, Oxford: Basil Blackwell, 1984. |

Wise Collection          The Stockett-Thomas J. Wise Collection, Special
                         Collections Division, Library of the University
                         of British Columbia, containing, along with
                         works by and about Wise, Hatfield's proof copy
                         of Shorter 1923, and correspondence concerning
                         the Brontës by Hatfield, Davidson Cook, Alice
                         Law, and J. A. Symington.

Wise Orphans 1917        **The Orphans and Other Poems,** By Charlotte,
                         Emily, and Branwell Brontë, London:    Printed
                         for Thomas J. Wise, 1917.

Wise RCK 1917            **The Red Cross Knight and Other Poems,** By
                         Charlotte Brontë, London:   Printed for Thomas
                         J. Wise, 1917.

Wise Saul 1913           **Saul and Other Poems,** By Charlotte Brontë,
                         London:  Printed for Thomas J. Wise, 1913.

Wise SER 1917            **The Swiss Emigrant's Return and Other
                         Poems,** By Charlotte Brontë, London:    Printed
                         for Thomas J.  Wise, 1917.

## List of Manuscript Locations

A  The Houghton Library, Harvard University

B  (1) The British Library:  Ashley Collection
   (2) The British Library:  Additional Manuscripts

C  Library of William Self, Los Angeles, California

D  (1) Brontë Parsonage Museum:  Bonnell Collection
   (2) Brontë Parsonage Museum:  Bronte Society's Collection
   (3) Brontë Parsonage Museum:  Seton-Gordon Collection

E  Library of Roger W. Barrett, Chicago, Illinois

F  (1) Pierpont Morgan Library, New York:  Bonnell Collection
   (2) Pierpont Morgan Library, New York:  General Collection

G  Princeton University Library:  Robert H. Taylor Collection

H  New York Public Library:  Berg Collection

I  Carl H. Pforzheimer Library, New York

J  Wellesley College Library:  Special Collections

K  Brotherton Library, University of Leeds:  Brotherton Collection

L  Humanities Research Center, University of Texas at Austin

M  University of Missouri Library--Columbia:  Special Collections

N  Henry E. Huntington Library, San Marino, California

O  Beinecke Rare Book and Manuscript Library, Yale University

P  University Library, State University of New York at Buffalo:
   Poetry and Rare Books Collection

R  Newnham College Library, Cambridge University


In addition there are the manuscripts held by the descendants of Sir
Alfred Law, transcriptions of these manuscripts by Davidson Cook in the
Symington Collection and the Hatfield papers, and transcriptions by C. W.
Hatfield in the Hatfield papers.

## Editions Containing Previously Unpublished Poems by Charlotte Brontë

The following publications, listed in chronological order, contained previously unpublished verse by Charlotte Brontë. Where a poem has first been partially, then completely published, both publications are included.

**Poems by Currer, Ellis, and Acton Bell**, London:   Aylott and Jones, 1846.

**Jane Eyre. An Autobiography.**  Edited by Currer Bell, London:   Smith, Elder & Co., 1847.

**The Manchester Athenaeum Album**, 1850.

**The Life of Charlotte Brontë**, E. C. Gaskell, London:   Smith, Elder & Co., 1857.

**The Professor, A Tale.**  By Currer Bell, London:   Smith, Elder & Co., 1857.

**The Cornhill Magazine** (December 1860).

**The Cornhill Magazine** (August 1861).

**Scribner's Monthly**, II (May 1871).

**Whitehaven News**, February 17, 1876.

**The Cornhill Magazine** (February 1893).

**The British Weekly**, March 28, 1895.

**The Adventures of Ernest Alembert:   A Fairy Tale.**  By Charlotte Brontë, ed., T. J. Wise, London:  Privately printed, 1896.

**The Woman at Home** (December 1896).

**Poet Lore**, IX (Spring 1897).

**Poet Lore**, IX (Autumn 1897).

**Poems by Charlotte, Emily, and Anne Brontë**, New York:   Dodd, Mead & Co., 1902.

**Meditations of An Autograph Collector**, Adrian H. Joline, New York:  Harper & Bros., 1902.

**TLS**, January 4, 1907.

**The Complete Poems of Emily Brontë**, edited by Clement Shorter, London: Hodder and Stoughton, 1910.

**Cosmopolitan Magazine** (October 1911).

**Richard Coeur de Lion and Blondel: A Poem by Charlotte Brontë**, London: Printed for T. J. Wise, 1912.

**Saul and Other Poems** By Charlotte Brontë, London: Printed for T. J. Wise, 1913.

**Brontë Poems. Selections from the Poetry of Charlotte, Emily, Anne and Branwell Brontë**, edited by Arthur C. Benson, London: Smith, Elder & Co., 1915.

**BST** (1916) 5:26.

**The Cornhill Magazine** (August 1916).

**The Violet. A Poem written at the Age of Fourteen by Charlotte Brontë**, London: Privately printed by Clement Shorter, 1916.

**A Bibliography of the Writings in Prose and Verse of the Members of the Brontë Family** By Thomas J. Wise, London: Privately printed, 1917.

**The Orphans and Other Poems** by Charlotte, Emily, and Branwell Brontë, London: Printed for T. J. Wise, 1917.

**The Red Cross Knight and Other Poems**, By Charlotte Brontë, London: Printed for T. J. Wise, 1917.

**The Swiss Emigrant's Return and Other Poems**, By Charlotte Brontë, London: Printed for T. J. Wise, 1917.

**Voltaire's "Henriade," Book I Translated from the French** by Charlotte Brontë, London: Privately printed by Clement Shorter, 1917.

**The Four Wishes. A Fairy Tale.** By Charlotte Brontë, London: Privately printed by Clement Shorter, 1918.

**Latest Gleanings: Being a Series of Unpublished Poems Selected from Her Early Manuscripts**, by Charlotte Brontë, London: Privately printed by Clement Shorter, 1918.

**BST** (1919) 5:29.

**Napoleon and the Spectre: A Ghost Story,** By Charlotte Brontë, London: Privately printed by Clement Shorter, 1919.

**Darius Codomannus. A Poem by Charlotte Brontë,** London: Printed for T. J. Wise, 1920.

**The Complete Poems of Charlotte Brontë,** edited by Clement Shorter, with the assistance of C. W. Hatfield, London: Hodder and Stoughton, 1923.

**BST** (1924) 6:34.

**The Bookman** (November 1925).

**The Twelve Adventurers and Other Stories,** by Charlotte Brontë, edited by Clement Shorter, with the assistance of C. W. Hatfield, London: Hodder and Stoughton, 1925.

**The Bookman** (December 1926).

**BST** (1926) 7:36.

**BST** (1931) 7:41.

**Legends of Angria: Compiled from the Early Writings of Charlotte Brontë,** by Fannie E. Ratchford, with the collaboration of William Clyde DeVane, New Haven: Yale University Press, 1933.

**BST** (1934) 8:44.

**The Poems of Charlotte Brontë and Patrick Branwell Brontë** (The Shakespeare Head Brontë), edited by Thomas James Wise and John Alexander Symington, Oxford: Basil Blackwell, 1934.

**The Miscellaneous and Unpublished Writings of Charlotte and Patrick Branwell Brontë** (The Shakespeare Head Brontë), edited by Thomas J. Wise and John Alexander Symington, 2 volumes, Oxford: Basil Blackwell, 1936 and 1938.

**The Brontës' Web of Childhood,** Fannie E. Ratchford, New York: Columbia University Press, 1941.

**BST** (1942), 10:52.

**Five Novelettes,** by Charlotte Brontë, edited by Winifred Gérin, London: Folio Press, 1971.

**Jane Eyre,** ed. Margaret Smith, Oxford:    Oxford University Press, 1975.

**Two Tales by Charlotte Brontë:** **"The Secret"** & **"Lily Hart,"** transcribed and edited by William Holtz, Columbia:    The University of Missouri Press, 1978.

**BST** (1980) 17:90.

**Something about Arthur,** by Charlotte Brontë, transcribed and edited by Christine Alexander, The University of Texas at Austin:    Humanities Research Center, 1981.

**Studies in Romanticism,** 20 (Winter 1981).

**The Early Writings of Charlotte Brontë,** by Christine Alexander, Oxford:    Basil Blackwell, 1983.

**The Poems of Charlotte Brontë,** edited by Tom Winnifrith, Oxford: Basil Blackwell, 1984.

# INTRODUCTION

> It is one of the hateful characteristics of a degenerate age,
> that the idle world will not let the worker alone, accepting
> his offering of work and appraise it for itself, but must
> insist upon turning him inside out, and knowing all about him,
> and really troubling itself a great deal more about his little
> peculiarities and personal pursuits, than his abiding work.[1]

One might well wish to quarrel with James A. H. Murray's equation of a
strong interest in biography with degeneracy, and with the implication
that the critic and scholar ought to restrict himself solely to an
author's work. Yet, when one surveys the history of Brontë scholarship,
Murray's condemnation of an undue emphasis on biography is justified.
Because the Brontë story is deeply moving in both its tragedy and its
pathos, it has lent itself to sensationalism, sentimentality and myth-
making. "Their lives are so literally improbable," writes R. B. Martin,
"as to tease one into considering the lives of the Brontë's themselves as
some wild metaphorical statement of the Romantic conception of the
world."[2] As a result, the line between fact and fiction has often
become fatally blurred, and Charlotte in particular has suffered from
"The Purple Heather School of Criticism and Biography."[3] Yet when one
heeds Murray's advice and turns from the Brontës' lives to their works,
one is confronted with a major anomaly: more than a century after their
deaths the text of their work is still not available in its entirety. In
fact, as both Mildred Christian and Herbert Rosengarten have pointed out,
there is still no complete bibliography of the writings of the Brontë
family.[4] Thus the torrent of biographical and critical activity that
began with Mrs. Gaskell's **Life** has far too often been based on
unreliable and incomplete texts, or none at all. Even the most recent
biographies still contain highly erroneous statements. For example,
Winifred Gérin attributes 400 lines of poetry to Charlotte for 1834 (CB,
p. 87); the actual figure is approximately 1,350. Clearly the definitive
biography of Charlotte Brontë has not yet been written, and cannot be
until we have complete and reliable texts of her works and
correspondence.

The availability of reliable texts of primary materials has improved
recently, but the task is far from finished. With the completion of the
Clarendon edition we will have a reliable text of all the novels.
Emily's poetry was quite well edited by C. W. Hatfield in 1941, and a new
edition which will correct errors in Hatfield's text is being prepared by
Edward Chitham, who produced the first complete and reliable edition of
Anne's poems in 1979. This edition of Charlotte's poems, though not
"complete" (see **Appendix B**), provides a reliable text of all of her
available verse. Christine Alexander is at present editing Charlotte's
juvenilia, and soon, one hopes, we will also have reliable editions of
Branwell's work and of the letters.[5]

# THE TEXT

The obvious question is why it has taken so long to produce a reliable edition of Charlotte's poems. Much of the answer to that question is contained in the activities of two men--Clement K. Shorter and Thomas J. Wise. Of the 206 poems, fragments, and verse translations in this volume,[6] only twenty-two were published in Charlotte's lifetime (Nos. 185-203; 208-209; 215). After her death in 1855, two additional poems appeared in 1857 (Nos. 110, 205) and one poem in each of 1860, 1861, 1871, 1876, 1895 (Nos. 148; 128; 104, 177; 98). Not until after 1895, when Shorter, acting on behalf of Wise, purchased a large collection of Brontë manuscripts from Charlotte's husband, The Reverend A. B. Nicholls, did Brontë readers even begin to get some sense of the extent of Charlotte's poetic activity.[7] Although Wise did not obtain all the Brontë manuscripts, as he had hoped, the subsequent activities of Shorter and Wise so confused and muddled the situation that only after the painstaking efforts of such scholars as Fannie Ratchford, Davidson Cook, C. W. Hatfield and Mildred Christian has it become possible to prepare this edition. In the meantime, the reader has had to rely for the most part on printed texts of Charlotte's poems produced by Shorter and Wise. Yet Wise's bibliographies in 1893, 1917 and 1929 were incomplete and inaccurate, sometimes attributing material to the wrong author. Similarly, the expensive limited editions produced by both Wise and Shorter between 1896 and 1920 (see pp.xvii-xix) grouped poems in a random piecemeal fashion, and were textually inaccurate, with poems sometimes incomplete and attributed to the wrong author. The same strictures also apply to Shorter's biographies in 1896 and 1908, his editions in 1923 and 1925, and to the Shakespeare Head edition (1931-38), edited by Wise and J. A. Symington. For a discussion of the reasons for the poor editing, see pp. xxvii-xxxii below. The Shakespeare Head included all of Charlotte's previously published poems as well as much new material and has remained the closest thing we have to a definitive edition, yet it contains only 141 of the 206 items in this edition, spread over three volumes, with some poems in facsimile reproduction only. As recently as 1964, Mildred Christian lamented, "The authoritative air of the publications by Wise continues to mislead students who do not go directly to the Brontë manuscripts."[8] Unfortunately, for reasons that will be explained shortly, going directly to the manuscripts has been extremely difficult, if not impossible. Since the publication of the Shakespeare Head edition thirty-four additional poems (in whole or in part) by Charlotte have appeared in various journals and books, twenty of these in 1984 in Winnifrith PCB. Even so, this new edition contains twenty-seven items never before printed or only partially printed, and that total does not include earlier variant forms included in the **Commentary**.

Because of the unreliable nature of existing texts of Charlotte's poems, any new edition had to be based on new transcriptions of all available manuscripts. In addition to the manuscripts noted in

**Appendix B**, manuscripts for seventeen items I have included are lost or inaccessible. Of these, eleven were last known to be in the library of Sir Alfred Law of Honresfeld. After Sir Alfred's death in 1939, his descendants moved to Jersey, and scholars have been denied all access to the manuscripts for many years now.[9] Fortunately, Davidson Cook visited Sir Alfred's library in 1925 and 1926, and was able to make meticulous transcriptions, which are preserved in the Symington Collection and among C. W. Hatfield's papers at the BPM,[10] and provide the texts for Nos. 44, 58-61, 100-101, 169-172. The location of the manuscripts for the remaining six items is unknown; their texts are based on the photograph of a manuscript preserved at the BPM (No. 68), transcriptions made by Nicholls (No. 67) and Hatfield (Nos. 50, 148, 150), and the most reliable published version (No. 177). Of the remaining 207 items, 22 are based on Charlotte's published text, 174 on my own transcriptions of the manuscripts, and 11 on transcriptions made from high-quality photographic reproductions (Nos. 3-5, 18, 104, 107-112).[11] Making these transcriptions necessitated visits to fifteen libraries and private collections in the U. S. A. and Britain. When one adds the three locations I was unable to visit (see n. 11) and the Law Collection, the number of known repositories of manuscripts of Charlotte's verse alone totals nineteen. Clearly, this edition would have been impossible without the generosity of librarians and collectors in granting me ready access to their manuscripts, some of which are in very fragile condition.

The majority of Charlotte's manuscripts are in a minute printed script which must in many cases be read with a magnifying glass. The difficulty of transcribing such minute script, often badly blotted, has been compounded not only because the known manuscripts are spread over nineteen locations, but also because leaves of single poems (see Nos. 51, 54, 120) or of related poems (see Nos. 51-57, 65-66, 87, 94, 99, 104, 105) have been scattered over various locations on two continents, as have different drafts of the same poem (see Nos. 94, 104, 166, 192, 193, 195, 196, 197, 199, 201, 202, 205, 209, 216). Naturally these factors have exacerbated problems of establishing complete texts, of making correct attributions, of dating, and of defining interrelationships. The responsibility for the unreliable editions and for the fragmentation and dispersal of the manuscripts rests primarily with T. J. Wise.

On the death of Charlotte in 1855, all the manuscripts and letters in her possession passed to her husband. The only items Nicholls did not have were letters and autographs she had sent to her friends, the manuscripts of novels and letters she had sent to her publishers, and the manuscripts she had left in Brussels, which Professor Ernest Nys discovered and sold to the British Library (see Nos. 91, 92, 98, 102, 103).[12] In August 1856 Nicholls allowed Mrs. Gaskell to carry away "a whole heap of those minute writings" (Gérin, CB, p. 579) in preparation for her life of Charlotte. In her biography Gaskell recorded: "I have had a curious packet confided to me, containing an immense amount of manuscript, in an inconceivably small space; tales, dramas, poems, romances, written principally by Charlotte" (Chapter V). Just what was in the packet we do not know; with the exception of the one poem Gaskell transcribed, all of the samples she included date from 1829-30. The poem, **The Wounded Stag** (No. 110), was probably composed in January 1836.[13] In 1861 Nicholls returned to Ireland and took all the manuscripts with him, where they remained until Shorter purchased a large portion of them in 1895.

Sometime between Charlotte's death and Shorter's purchase, Nicholls transcribed some of the poems of all three sisters, including twenty-four of Charlotte's (see Alexander, items 12 and 13). In all likelihood these transcriptions were made before his departure for Ireland.[14] Unfortunately, Nicholls was not only a careless copyist, he also 'edited' poems at times. For example, he copied Nos. 136 and 137 as one poem, and in a letter to Davidson Cook, Hatfield wrote: "I was able to point out [to Sir E. A. Brotherton] that not only had Mr. Nicholls omitted two stanzas (without indicating the omission) doubtless because he found them undecipherable, but that he had inserted a most unsuitable word in one line where the author [Anne] had left a blank space." In another letter to Cook, Hatfield notes that many of the errors in Shorter's 1910 edition of Emily's poems resulted from his use of Nicholls' transcriptions.[15] Unwittingly, therefore, Nicholls himself became the source of some of the unreliable texts Brontë scholars have had to deal with, and one has to view the text of No. 67 with reservation.

Thus the manuscripts had not rested undisturbed in Nicholls' possession, as Shorter believed.[16] Not only had Nicholls made transcriptions, he had also given a number of manuscripts to at least two of his cousins. One of them, a Mrs. Bolster, sold Mr. Henry H. Bonnell "nineteen scraps of manuscript in an envelope marked 'C. Brontë.'" Some of the scraps, Hatfield had to point out to Bonnell, were in fact Anne's and Branwell's.[17] Nor did Nicholls sell Shorter all the manuscripts in his possession, as the latter believed.[18] At least thirty-three of Charlotte's manuscripts, some of them manuscript volumes containing collections of poems, were sold after Nicholls' death at Sotheby's in 1907 and 1914.[19] Hatfield notes that the Nicholls family disposed of one long poem (No. 116) "in three separate parts and fortunately all three were bought (at separate times) by Mr. Bonnell who did not discover that they were parts of the same poem until he had made transcripts of them for me" (Letter to Cook, April 7, 1926, Wise Collection). Thus, again unwittingly, Nicholls also bears some of the responsibility for the scattering of the Brontë manuscripts.

The details of Shorter's negotiations and purchase have been well covered, as have the discrepancies over the price he paid, and need not be repeated here.[20] Whatever the actual sum paid, the more important question here is what happened to the manuscripts once they were in the hands of Shorter and Wise. According to Shorter, Wise became the actual possessor of the documents, while Shorter retained the copyright. Tom Winnifrith's indictment of Wise is scathing:

> Once it has been established that financial gain rather than the disinterested pursuit of knowledge was the mainspring behind Wise's activities, a whole area of uncertainty is opened up, since Wise exercised such a monopoly in Brontë affairs . . . . By selling Branwell's manuscripts as Charlotte's, by selling manuscripts which he had promised to bequeath to the nation, by binding manuscripts together which had no connection, but which might result in a more profitable sale, and by editing inefficiently the Brontë manuscripts he had squandered Wise has surely won himself an immortal place in Brontë studies.[21]

These are serious charges indeed, yet when one pieces together information supplied by Shorter, Hatfield, Christian, and Wise himself, they are justified. In a letter to Hatfield in 1917, Shorter wrote, "Mr. Wise obtained the whole collection, which he distributed from year to year, doubtless to his own great commercial advantage."[22] As early as 1899 Wise himself wrote to J. H. Wrenn:

> This MS. [one of Charlotte's] was once my property. At $48 you got it very cheaply . . . . I had them [manuscripts purchased in 1895] all arranged and bound, and they are detailed in Shorter's book [**Charlotte Brontë and Her Circle,** 1896]. When that book had been published, and the MSS. finished with, I selected a series for my own library. From the remainder I let all my friends have a representative series, and some of the rest I sold. Those which turned up in New York were among those I sold, and I don't think they brought enough . . . . But the demand for such things as MSS of the Brontë sisters can only increase . . . . and you'll find your purchase good enough even at $48.[23]

Some of the remaining unbound manuscripts Wise used for exchanges or gifts; the rest he sold through London booksellers, among them Herbert Gorfin. Clearly, then, Wise's dispersal of the manuscripts was already well under way by the turn of the century, within five years of his purchase. It was further augmented by the Sotheby's sales of Nicholls' property in 1907, 1914, and 1916, at which Wise was also a purchaser, and one has to assume that he continued his previous practices with these purchases. Thus all but one or two of the many editions produced by Wise and Shorter in the first two decades of this century, including Shorter's **Life and Letters,** 1908, were based on the highly unreliable transcriptions (see p. xxiii) Wise had made before he dispersed the manuscripts. He retained some manuscripts for his own collection, but in

xxv

the case of Charlotte, the manuscripts for only seven of the poems published by Wise and Shorter were in the Ashley Library at the time of Wise's death. In his 1924 letter to the **TLS** Shorter could state that the manuscripts were "scattered all over the world among Brontë enthusiasts."

But the wide-spread dispersal was only a small part of the problem, and Wise's comments require a certain amount of interpretation. In having the manuscripts "arranged" and expensively bound, he not only misattributed authorship, but also broke up manuscripts. Some of the results, which have frustrated and confused Brontë scholars ever since, are:

(a) manuscripts divided and sold in parts to different collectors (see p. xxiii). By 1926 Hatfield was already commenting to Cook:

the Harvard catalogue mentions that one of the above manuscripts is incomplete and I have just discovered among Mr. Bonnell's transcripts what I am fairly certain is a copy of the missing fragment. If that is so, I shall try to get Mr. Bonnell to present the missing part of the MS to Harvard. I doubt whether he will for I have always been unsuccessful in attempting to get different parts of the Brontë manuscripts brought together. That is one of the reasons why I look upon my collection of transcripts as of particular value, because they contain complete copies of manuscripts obtained from fragments in different collections and of manuscripts which have been divided and sold in sections.[24]

(b) manuscripts attributed to the wrong author or leaves from various Brontë manuscripts bound together and attributed to one author (see Nos. 18, 62, 90, 116, 120, 153, 179, 211, and **Appendix C**). Both Branwell's and Charlotte's manuscripts were ascribed to Emily, and Branwell's to Charlotte.[25] At the end of the final volume of the Shakespeare Head edition, produced after Wise's death, even Symington hinted his unease about the accuracy of some attributions in the earlier volumes, and included many facsimiles in the final two volumes.[26]

(c) collections of unrelated manuscript leaves, all by the same author, randomly bound together (see Nos. 11, 12, 20, 22, 23, 64, 72, 97, 118, 119). Hatfield wrote to Cook in 1926, "I now learn from him [Bonnell], and am not at all surprised, that his Branwell Brontë manuscripts, which are beautifully bound and which he thought to be complete, are really made up of odd sheets from various manuscripts" (November 17, 1926, Wise Collection).

(d) bound collections in which the leaves have been cut and tipped in with few or none of the poems dated; although it is clear that the leaves belong together, one cannot be sure what their original order was (Nos. 107-112, 154-160, 163-164, 167-168).[27]

(e) dealers and collectors deceived and defrauded, among them the greatest American collector of Brontë manuscripts, H. H. Bonnell. As early as 1926 Hatfield warned Bonnell that parts of manuscripts had been sold to him as complete, "so I sent him copies of all the complete transcripts which I had as a check upon possible future purchases. He had bought a lot of Branwell's poems as Emily's, but both the dealers and he were deceived."[28]

By 1916, ten years before Hatfield's letters to Cook, Shorter already understood the likely implications of scattering the manuscripts in this fragmented and incoherent fashion--"vandalism for the sake of profit."[29] He wrote:

> One has to go to all these four volumes, in many of which the poems are repeated in Emily Brontë's handwriting, to get at the real text of Emily's work; and a reason why there cannot be a perfectly satisfactory edition of Emily Brontë's poems is due to the circumstance that no editor will ever manage now to obtain access to all the original manuscripts. The bulkiest of all the volumes of manuscript poems is that owned by Mr. Reginald Smith, the other three having been originally in the possession of Mr. Wise and by him taken to pieces and rebound.[30]

Fortunately, because of the meticulous detective work of such scholars as Cook, Ratchford, Christian, Alexander, Chitham, and especially Hatfield, Shorter's predictions have not been fulfilled. As far as the poetry is concerned, after many decades of locating, unraveling, and piecing together, the canon of each Brontë is now, with a few minor exceptions (see Appendix C), established, and sound editions have become possible if funds for all the traveling required are available. Nevertheless, every Brontë editor, for obvious reasons, uses the word "complete" with trepidation.

Before leaving the sad tale of Wise and Shorter, however, one further source of confusion must be dealt with. The last of Winnifrith's accusations cited earlier is that Wise edited the manuscripts "inefficiently." Winnifrith's term is more than kind. Before Wise arranged, bound, and sold the manuscripts, he had many of them transcribed in part or in whole. The quality of those transcriptions is apparent from Shorter's description of them as "rough typewritten copy" and Hatfield's comment that "none of them is in the handwriting of either Mr. Shorter or Mr. Wise. They are in half a dozen different kinds of handwriting and it is clear that some of the scribes exercised great care and that some were careless and inefficient" (Letter to Cook, January 9,

xxvii

1926, Wise Collection). Shorter, who also made some transcriptions, seems to have been more conscientious. After obtaining transcriptions of Charlotte's **The Search after Hapiness** from both Shorter and Wise, Hatfield commented: "That from Mr. Shorter is almost an accurate transcript of the manuscript in the possession of Mr. Wise, while the transcript from the latter contains so many differences that it seems impossible for it to have been made from the same manuscript" (Letter to Cook, December 10, 1925, Wise Collection). Hatfield's comment is quite consistent with Partington's description of Wise's carelessness and irresponsibility as an editor.[31] Not only were Wise's transcriptions full of errors, but there were also blank spaces for words and phrases his scribes had been unable to decipher (Hatfield letter to Cook, January 12, 1926, Wise Collection), and in some instances manuscripts were only partially transcribed (Hatfield letters to Cook, January 25, February 19, May 18, 1926, Wise Collection). Even worse, in some cases the scribes had conflated manuscripts. Hatfield wrote to Cook that he was "particularly pleased to get the photograph copy of Arthuriana because I knew the transcript I had was incomplete and I now find that it also includes one poem which is not in the manuscript, and does not include one of the poems that is" (July 25, 1927, Wise Collection).

Yet it was from these transcriptions that Wise and Shorter prepared their expensive limited editions, with poems in some cases attributed to the wrong author (Nos. 18, 62, 120, 179, 211 and **Appendix C**). Until Shorter's 1923 edition of Charlotte's poems, prepared with Hatfield's assistance, these editions provided the only printed text available for twenty-six of Charlotte's poems. These "manufactured rarities" certainly contributed to Wise's commercial advantage,[32] and there is evidence that he printed more than the number of copies he had certified for his limited editions.[33]

Although Shorter's transcriptions were more reliable, he made only a few; for the most part he relied on Wise's transcriptions, seemingly without question, and, as he indicates in his 1924 letter to the **TLS**, did not publish them "until long years afterwards." In 1925 Hatfield wrote to Cook about **The Twelve Adventurer's**, just published by Shorter:

> I welcome your suggestion to send your copy of THE TWELVE ADVENTURERS to me when you have made it agree with the manuscripts which we know <u>do</u> exist . . . . The fact is the whole book was prepared from transcripts made thirty years ago and sent to me six years ago by Mr. Wise and Mr. Shorter. I sent the transcript of the book five years ago to Mr. Shorter as he had long before promised to publish a volume of Brontë juvenilia . . . . When the proofs came along I was prepared with the necessary corrections in the text of two of the stories, the manuscripts of which I had in the meantime traced;

the others are copies of the old transcripts (December 10, 1926, Wise Collection).

When one examines the various editions prepared by Shorter it becomes clear that his editorial practises also contributed much to the unreliability of published texts of Charlotte's poems. Shorter was a journalist, and he was not overly concerned with accuracy and completeness.[34] Hatfield complains to Cook that the version he (Hatfield) printed of Anne Brontë's **Last Lines** in 1920 "came to me from Mr. Shorter and was supposed to be complete, but it was not" (May 18, 1926, Wise Collection). When Shorter prepared his error-filled 1910 edition of Emily's poems, he used the text in the privately printed edition issued by Dodd Mead in 1902 without checking the text against his own transcriptions made years earlier (Hatfield letter to Cook, January 12, 1926, Wise Collection).[35] Shorter, in the name of efficiency, obviously preferred any existing printed text over manuscripts and transcriptions, yet because of his status as a Brontë scholar his text was accepted by other editors. A. C. Benson's 1915 edition includes most of the errors in the 1910 volume, in addition to poems by Charlotte, Branwell, and Anne in the Emily section.

After helping Shorter prepare the 1923 editions of Emily's and Charlotte's poems, Hatfield complains of various problems he encountered:

(a) Shorter refused to make use of available manuscripts to check the accuracy of his transcriptions, including manuscripts in the British Museum (letter to Cook, April 7, 1926, Wise Collection), and even neglected to inform Hatfield of the existence of manuscripts--"With regard to that manuscript and the Honresfeld manuscript I find that Mr. Shorter knew of both of them, but he never mentioned them to me and I think he ought to have done so when he asked me to prepare the poems volumes" (letter to Cook, June 7, 1927, Wise Collection).

(b) Shorter refused Hatfield access to manuscripts in his possession--"Your news about the sale of the MS. of 'The Violet' is the first definite information I have been able to get about it since 1916. When I prepared the book of Charlotte Brontë's poems at the suggestion of Mr. Shorter I asked him to let me have the loan of the MS. and he sent me the poem in print. I asked him again, and again he sent me a printed copy. With that I came to the conclusion that he had probably sold the MS. and did not care to say so. Now I find that it must have been in his possession all the time and he could have let me satisfy myself as to the true text it contains" (letter to Cook, June 2, 1928, Wise Collection).[36]

(c) Shorter handled typescript sent to him by Hatfield carelessly, resulting in serious losses and delays--"You can imagine what an immense task it was to prepare the Charlotte Brontë poems volume. It took me several months to arrange and type. I sent it to him and he lost it and so far as I know it has never been found. So I set to work and made another, and he managed not to lose that" (letter to Cook, January 9, 1926, Wise Collection). In another letter to Cook (October 29, 1926) he complains about his inability to get any word from Shorter about a typescript volume of Branwell's poems he had sent to Shorter, which it had taken him two years to prepare.

Thus, while Shorter was very industrious indeed in making Brontë materials available to the general public, that industry was governed by a principle noted in the **DNB**--"Shorter's biographies of the Brontës and of George Borrow were compilations of facts, governed much more by the novelty of their discovery, than by their importance, set forth with no literary grace, and with hardly any attempt at literary appreciation." Yet, despite their shortcomings, Shorter's contributions to Brontë scholarship were more scrupulous and more useful than Wise's.

But Shorter died in 1926, well before what should have been the great edition of the works of the Brontës, the Shakespeare Head, was begun. The intriguing question is why the editors, T. J. Wise and J. A. Symington, with a full knowledge of the problems inherent in the existing published texts of the poems, produced so little improvement.[37] Knowledgeable Brontë scholars were already raising that question before the final volume appeared in 1938 (see Helen Brown's letter to Hatfield, February 5, 1938, Hatfield Papers). That Wise and Symington decided to regularize spelling, punctuation, line length, and stanza form is not surprising. But why, one has to ask, did this edition repeat so many of the known errors of previous editions, and add new ones:

(a) poems for which the manuscripts were known to be extant omitted;

(b) poems attributed to the wrong author and misdated;

(c) words, lines, and whole stanzas omitted;

(d) many serious misreadings;

(e) uncanceled variants ignored completely or inconsistently noted--i.e. sometimes Charlotte's first version is given as the preferred reading, sometimes the later variant;

(f) notes referring to non-existent alternate drafts, or confusing the chronological sequence of alternate drafts.

These problems were further complicated by the decision to spread Charlotte's poems over three volumes: **The Poems of Charlotte and**

Patrick Branwell Brontë, 1934; **The Miscellaneous and Unpublished Writings of Charlotte and Patrick Branwell Brontë**, 2 vols., 1936 and 1938. Shorter's 1923 edition contained every poem by Charlotte previously printed, and forty-nine new ones. The SHB 1934 volume was to contain all of the poems in Shorter's edition (except those that were part of the Angrian manuscripts which were to be printed in the two later volumes), three poems recently printed in the **BST**, and twenty-eight new poems. However only a selection of the Angrian manuscripts was included in the Miscellaneous volumes, some in facsimile only, and the 1934 volume still contained a number of poems which had been lifted out of a prose context without any indication thereof. Nor is the "Bibliography of the Poems of Charlotte Brontë" at the end of the 1934 volume accurate. It does not contain at least three publications between 1923 and 1934 which contained previously unpublished poems by Charlotte,[38] although the poems were included in the two later volumes.

The failure to include poems for which manuscripts were known to be extant rests with both the editors of the SHB and with C. W. Hatfield. The editors of the SHB note that the manuscript of **The Wounded Stag** is included with several other poems in a small manuscript volume entitled **The Wounded Stag and Other Poems.** That volume, they note, is signed "C Brontë," and is dated January 19, 1836. Yet of the five other poems and fragments in the manuscript volume, only one, **Reason,** is included--in the "Undated Poems" section (in one of his earlier private editions, Wise dated it 1834). One has to assume that Symington simply accepted whatever text Wise provided. The manuscripts for the bulk of the omitted poems were at Harvard and in the Bonnell Collection, and Hatfield, who eventually assisted Wise and Symington, knew of them. In a letter to Cook, Hatfield had indicated that because of his lack of faith in Shorter's editorial policies, he had not revealed to Shorter in 1923 a large number of Charlotte's poems "only known to Mr. Bonnell and myself" (April 7, 1926, Wise Collection). In a letter to Helen Brown, March 9, 1938 (Hatfield Papers), he indicates that he similarly withheld material from Wise and Symington, again because he was disgusted with editorial policy. Wise, it was clear, wanted to produce an edition in the quickest and easiest manner possible--i.e. to rely without question on existing printed texts where possible. He simply reproduced Shorter's 1923 text, including Shorter's annotations. Anne's poems, Hatfield points out, were reprinted from Shorter's 1920 edition, with the addition of three poems found among Shorter's papers, purchased by Wise. "If I remember rightly the errors and omissions revealed by the Honresfeld manuscript (printed in facsimile in the volume) were disregarded by the editors" (Letter to Helen Brown, May 7, 1938, Hatfield Papers).[39] But Hatfield's most damning comment concerns the editing of the letters:

> Whether I made that correction for the Shakespeare Head Life
> and Letters I do not remember--I made many hundreds--perhaps

thousands--of corrections and additions to the galley proofs of the four volumes. It surprised me to find the editors following so closely Shorter's two volumes of 1908, and if I had not added the material he and I had gathered from 1908 up to the time of his death, and what I had collected later, the volumes would have been almost a copy of the 1908 edition except for the previously unprinted parts of the letters of C. B. to Miss Wooler. My additions and corrections must have caused a good deal of trouble and expense; but I was very dissatisfied with the result. The 'editing' is as poor as in the other volumes; and I was disgusted to find the spurious Hartlepool letter in the finished volumes although I had cancelled it heavily in the proofs (letter to Helen Brown, March 1, 1938, Hatfield Papers).

In his "Conclusion" to the 1938 volume, published after Wise's death, even Symington expresses his discomfort over the unreliability of the edition.

How, one might well ask, in the face of this textual history, is it possible to produce reliable editions today? The answer is by a good bit of luck and much hard work by many people. Even though the known manuscripts of Charlotte's poems are scattered among nineteen locations, this represents considerable consolidation; many of the manuscripts originally in private collections have moved to major collections and institutions: Harvard, Princeton, the Pierpont Morgan, the New York Public Library, SUNY at Buffalo, the Huntington, the University of Texas, the Brontë Parsonage.[40] Then there has been the detective work of the scholars mentioned above, especially that of Hatfield. Not only do we have his bibliography of Charlotte's manuscripts in the BST (1922-24) and his many other publications, but when one goes through his papers at the Parsonage, one comes to realize what an enormous amount of Charlotte's and Branwell's manuscript material he had managed to piece together and transcribe with great care as a result of his access to the major collections of manuscripts and transcriptions, including the Bonnell Collection, the University of Texas, Harvard, the British Library, the Law Collection, the transcriptions of Shorter and Wise, and the Parsonage. From his papers it is clear that but for his untimely death in 1942, shortly after the publication of his edition of Emily's poems, he was in a position to add major editions of Charlotte and Branwell. He was "one of the most accurate of all students of the Brontë's [sic]."[41] Finally, four recent works appeared just in time to corroborate and supplement the research that went into the preparation of this edition: **Index of English Literary Manuscripts**, Vol IV, 1800-1900, ed., Barbara Rosenbaum and Pamela White, New York: Mansell, 1982; **A Bibliography of the Manuscripts of Charlotte Brontë**, ed., Christine Alexander, The Brontë Society: Meckler Publishing, 1982; **The Early Writings of Charlotte Brontë**, by Christine Alexander, Oxford: Basil Blackwell, 1983; **The**

**Poems of Charlotte Brontë**, ed., Tom Winnifrith, Oxford: Basil Blackwell, 1984. With these resources it is possible to establish Charlotte's poetic canon with only a few very minor exceptions (see Appendix C). Despite Charlotte's collaboration with Branwell, Alexander is quite correct when she says that it is possible to distinguish between their early miniature script, and that problems of attribution have been largely resolved (p. xv). Thus while Rosenbaum and White are technically right when they state, "No study has . . . systematically corrected the traditional attributions, and the canon is not yet definitely established" (p. 46), those corrections have in fact been made through a process of accretion of which this edition is the end product.


CHARLOTTE'S POETIC CAREER

That it has taken so long to have a full picture of Charlotte's poetic career is ironic, for in 1830, at the age of fourteen, Charlotte was convinced that she was called to be a poet. Eighteen-thirty was the most productive single year of her poetic career and marked the culmination of her first period of intensive poetic activity (see pp. xxxiv-xxxv). Many of her 1830 poems dealt with such subjects as the nature of genius, the nature of art, and the craft of poetry. She wrote poems about the sort of inspiration she drew from nature, and the poor quality of her own verse, and lampooned Branwell's poetic posturings. In short, it was a year of self-conscious exploration of the conception of herself as poet and artist, culminating in a kind of Wordsworthian call to the divine vocation of poet, albeit not of the first rank. In **The Violet**, November 10, 1830 (No. 51), the speaker, stirred into thought by "Aeolian music," reviews the accomplishments of the great classical writers-- Homer, Sophocles, Euripides, Aeschylus, Tasso, Virgil--and laments the decline of the glory that once was Greece. But, all is not lost, for the "holy nine," though having forsaken Parnassus, "now in fair Britannia shine." There the "sons of Albion in that rank/ Shine crowned with honours they have won" because they have drunk deeply of "the sacred fount of Helicon." The speaker prays that he too might be allowed to march beneath the banners of that "army of immortals."

> Yet joy deep joy would fill my heart
> Nature unveil thy awful face
> To me a poet's pow'r impart
> Thoug[h] humble be my destined place

His prayer reaches the "Mighty Mother's ear," and after a series of portentous natural disturbances,

> Now dawned upon my awe-struck eyes
> A shape more beauteous than the morn

When radiant with a thousand dyes
The pearls of night her brow adorn

A woman's form the vision wore
. . . . . . . . . .
A gracious smile illumed her face
As throned she sate on clouds of light
In attitude of heavenly grace
Beneath an arch like rainbow bright

The visionary figure grants the speaker's "high request" with the proviso
that "in humbler sphere thy fate is set." Little did the fourteen-year-
old Charlotte realize how prophetic her modest disclaimer to poetic
greatness was. In one of those ironies not altogether uncommon in the
world of literature, she became famous as author of one of the best-
known novels in English literature, but her poetry has been largely
ignored and neglected, receiving almost no critical attention.

Yet over a span of twenty years (1829-49), she produced over 200
poems and verse fragments which in bulk exceed those of Emily and Anne
combined by approximately 3,000 lines. Charlotte's earliest known poem
is "in this fairy land of light" (No. 2)[42] from **The Search after
Hapiness,** dated July 28-August 17, 1829. It was her first "published"
poem in that the manuscript of sixteen pages is stitched in brown paper
covers, has a title-page and a Preface, and is "Printed by Herself and
Sold by Nobody." Already she saw herself as an editor--**The Young Mens
Magazine**--a publisher, and a writer. Her last poem is No. 224 on the
death of Anne, June 21, 1849, but she really ceased writing poetry with
the publication of the 1846 volume of poems; other than the poems in
**The Professor** and **Jane Eyre,** begun before 1846, there are only
six poems and fragments between 1846 and 1849, three of them on the
deaths of her sisters in 1848 and 1849. Her last two novels contain no
poetry of her own.

Her poetic career is marked by three periods of intensive
composition: 1829-30; 1833-34; 1837-38. The first of these commenced
with her assumption of the editorship in July 1829 of **Branwell's
Blackwoods Magazine,** now renamed **Blackwoods Young Mens Magazine,**
and ended with her departure for Roe Head School in January 1831. During
this period she produced sixty-five poems (twelve in collaboration with
Branwell; the figure includes ten missing poems--see **Appendix B)** and
seven other verse items including a verse translation of Voltaire's
**Henriade.** Twenty of the sixty-five poems were included in the twelve
issues of the **Young Mens Magazine** Charlotte edited, seventeen in
"published" (as defined above) volumes of poems (see Nos. 34, 51-57, and
**Appendix B),** and seven in a volume of fair copies (see Nos. 19, 21,
24, 25, 28, 32, 33). She also wrote a play entitled **The Poetaster,**
in which, while mocking Branwell's literary posturing, she demonstrated

her sense of wit through her use of literary allusions to Elizabethan drama.[43] Charlotte was very much concerned with gathering poems that were not part of a larger prose context, and one would have to describe the manuscripts of her poems during this period as fair copies, for there are no uncanceled variant manuscripts, uncanceled variant readings in only four poems, and relatively few canceled readings. The poems range in length from 12 to 276 lines, and encompass a wide variety of stanza forms and rhyme schemes, including a pindaric ode and a blank verse drama. In 1829 all but two of the available poems are in quatrains, but even here Charlotte uses three different rhyme patterns. The two exceptions are wholly or partially in blank verse, perhaps reflecting her reading of Shakespeare and Milton.[44] Eighteen-thirty, however, was a year of great experimentation. In addition to the usual quatrains, one finds open and closed couplets; five, six, and eight-line stanzas; and poems with mixed stanza forms. Similarly there is a variety of rhyme patterns and line lengths, ranging from trimeters to a seven-foot line (No. 56), and the ballad stanza.

Alexander's statement (EW, p. 66) that all Charlotte's early poems relate to the Glass Town saga needs to be qualified, for not all the poems signed by Charles Wellesley or Douro are directly related. In fact, only just over half of the poems of this period relate directly to the activities of the genii and the development of Glass Town. Significantly, most of the "gathered" poems noted above are distinctly non-Glass Town, including Charlotte's two earliest "collected" volumes. It would seem that she was intent on setting up a "non-Glass Town stream" to provide the necessary flexibility for poetic experimentation.

From January 1831 to May 1832, while a student at Roe Head, Charlotte wrote only three poems, all during vacation time, and all concerned with the imaginary world of the genii and Glass Town. During her absence, Emily and Anne decided to branch off on their own to create Gondal;[45] their decision is reflected in the dissolution of the imaginary kingdom the four had shared as recorded by Charlotte in No. 63. While her next poem expresses her sense of regret, Charlotte seems to have taken this dissolution seriously, for although she returned home in May 1832, she produced only two Glass Town poems that year, and those not until July and August. Her two other poems for 1832, one in August and one in November, seem to be determinedly non-Glass Town: one is on a Biblical subject, the other on the death of Bewick, whose work she was so fond of. Winifred Gérin records that at Roe Head Charlotte was determined to make the most of her educational opportunity and quotes Ellen Nussey's recollection "that she [Charlotte] must use every moment to attain the purpose for which she was sent to school i.e. to fit herself for governess life." "The twilight hour," continues Gérin, "had been for her a time of poetic imaginings and extravagant invention; it was now dedicated to the ideal of learning" (CB, p. 66). For a time at least,

after her return home, she seems to have maintained her
dedication.[46]

However, in 1833-34 Charlotte returned to the development of the
Glass Town saga in collaboration with Branwell. With the creation of the
Kingdom of Angria, Arthur Wellesley, Marquis of Douro, became the Duke of
Zamorna and King of Angria, and the focus of Charlotte's creative
energies. She began the development of all his domestic infidelities--
the casting off of his first wife (Marian Hume) and his marriage to Mary
Percy--and of the political intrigues centering on Zamorna and his
father-in-law, Alexander Percy, Earl of Northangerland. This return
marks the second period of intensive poetic activity: thirty-two poems
and three other bits of verse totaling over 2,200 lines. All but four
of the poems are related to the Glass Town/Angrian saga, and the great
majority are embedded in prose narratives. Thus there is a greater
narrative emphasis in the verse and a general increase in length.
Charlotte's handling of verse form and meter becomes much surer and more
sophisticated, with much less reliance on the quatrain, and much greater
use of more complex five, six, seven, and nine-line stanzas, including
the Spenserian (Nos. 94-96). There is also a poem in Yorkshire dialect.
The manuscripts are still fair copies--most carefully signed and dated,
with only minor uncanceled variants in two poems--but in two instances
(Nos. 88, 94) we have earlier uncanceled drafts of the poems, providing
the first opportunity to see something of Charlotte's process of
composition. However, it is not until 1837-38 that we begin to get substantial numbers of uncanceled variant readings and manuscripts; until
then Charlotte seems to have left behind only fair copies, and to have
destroyed whatever earlier drafts existed.

The only non-Angrian poem Charlotte wrote in 1833, **Richard Cour de
Lion & Bondel** (December 27) presents an intriguing puzzle. Although
now bound separately by Rivière, the poem was originally the first in a
manuscript volume of poems, for across the top of the page, above the
title, appear the words "1833 All that is written in this book, must be
in a good, plain and legible hand. P B." There are four other poems
written on the same distinctively lined paper and in the same regular
script rather than the usual miniscule print: **Death of Darius
Codomanus** (May 2, 1834) again bound separately by Rivière; **Saul**
(October 7, 1834) and **Memory** (August 2, 1835)[47] bound together by
Rivière; and **Morning**, undated, but probably the last in the series as
it is in pencil, has two uncanceled variant readings, and is followed by
three blank pages. All of these poems must originally have been part of a
single manuscript volume of distinctly non-Angrian poems. It would seem
that the Rev. Mr. Brontë became aware of his daughter's feverish writing
activity during 1833, saw something of the miniscule print, and demanded
material written in a hand he could read. Charlotte continued the volume
through 1834 and into 1835 until after her second departure for Roe Head,
this time as a teacher. It served, one has to speculate, to show to

xxxvi

those who wanted to know what she was writing, and to keep prying eyes away from compositions that would have shocked them. But the last two poems also strike an intensely personal note, quite new in Charlotte's poetry, reflecting something of the loneliness and despair she experienced at Roe Head and the solace provided by escape into imaginary worlds.

Perhaps the poems in this volume were also a sop to a conscience that was still telling her to put her time and energy to more constructive use, for with her departure for Roe Head in July 1835, the composition of poems slowed noticeably, especially, ironically, of ones related to Angria, for matters there had reached a state of crisis (Alexander EW, p. 135). The three poems Charlotte produced in 1835 consist of the two personal poems just noted and the closely-linked, well-known "We wove a web in childhood" (December 19, 1835), in which she reviews the creation of her fantasy world, and recalls the solace it has provided her in the past in times of loneliness and despondency, only to be reminded of the debilitating division that exists between the life of her imagination and the demands of her teaching duties. The departure of Emily from Roe Head in October 1835, Branwell's failure in London, the drudgery of teaching, and the lack of time for writing produced in Charlotte a sense of desolation, guilt, and mental depression[48] that led to an agonizing reappraisal of her situation and purpose in life, reflected in a manuscript volume of six poems and fragments (bound by Rivière as **The Wounded Stag and Other Poems**) dated at the end January 19, 1836 (Nos. 107-112). In No. 108 we get the only overt reference in Charlotte's poems to the religious turmoil she was undergoing as described in her letters to Ellen Nussey between May and December 1836. The speaker in the poem laments the loss of childhood faith and piety and the bliss they brought, recalls the "grinding tyranny" of religious doubt and terror, then proceeds to describe those "other visions" that have replaced the dreams of infancy, visions that are comforting yet delusory and obsessive. But the most significant element in these poems is the conflict over the need to accept the dictates of "Duty" and "Necessity," and to abandon those imaginary worlds. In **Reason** (No. 111) the speaker dedicates her heart to "Reason-Science-Learning-Thought," and in the final poem (No. 112) a frantic note of panic builds as the speaker returns to her old comrades one more time, "For ancient friendship's sake," then bids "Farewell! & yet again farewell."

Not surprisingly, Charlotte's farewell to her old comrades was short-lived. By the spring of 1836 she was once more composing Angrian poems, and during the summer vacation she produced the longest, most ambitious narrative poem of her career (No. 116). Although perhaps more reminiscent of **Childe Harold**, it is in the Don Juan stanza, a verse form she was to use with some frequency over the next few years. With the addition of the last six stanzas to intensify the sense of Byronic anguish and despair, this is the most Byronic of all her poems. It also marks the beginning of the third and last period of intensive poetic composition.

In December of 1836 Charlotte wrote to Southey to enquire about the possibilities of a woman earning her living by writing. His reply was not encouraging:

> The day-dreams in which you habitually indulge are likely to induce a distempered state of mind and, in proportion as all the ordinary uses of the world seem to you flat and unprofitable, you will be unfitted for them without becoming fitted for anything else. Literature cannot be the business of a woman's life, and it ought not to be. The more she is engaged in her proper duties, the less leisure will she have for it, even as an accomplishment and a recreation.

Charlotte replied, and received in turn a reply which again was not encouraging. This letter she endorsed "Southey's advice to be kept forever. My twenty-first birthday. Roe Head. April 21, 1837" (SHB LL, I, 154-59). Yet when one looks at the number and dates of poems she wrote in 1837, it is clear that she was already breaking her resolution as she wrote it. During the second school term in 1836, Charlotte produced only one short poem seemingly confirming her complaint that teaching left her no time for writing. Yet between January 1837 and July 1838 (she left Roe Head in December 1838) she produced sixty poems and fragments, with more than one draft extant in many cases. Approximately two-thirds are Angrian; but there is a decided shift from the long narrative to the short lyric, and in the latter the boundary between the fictional and the autobiographical is frequently blurred. A large number of the 1837 poems, a proportion that increased as the year went on, are personal recollections, often interior monologues, filled with a sense of loneliness, loss, regret, and frustration (see, for example, Nos. 121, 122, 128, 129, 121-37, 143, 144, 147, 153, 155, 156, 158).[49] Charlotte began 1837 with another long verse narrative in the Don Juan stanza (No. 118), closely linked to the one she had composed the previous summer, yet three-quarters of the way along, after an unfinished stanza, meter and stanza form change, altering the poem from a narrative to a personal lyric of longing and regret. In No. 133 one senses Charlotte's growing fear of the fantasy world she has delighted in, perhaps linked to continuing religious qualms she is experiencing over her obsession with Angria (No. 133-37). In contrast to the "finished quality" of the earlier poems, many in 1837 are fragmentary and unfinished; there are many more uncanceled drafts, trial lines, variant readings, and blank spaces, and the majority of the poems are undated and unsigned. Also many of the manuscripts are in pencil, consistent with the general pattern in Charlotte's manuscripts of fair copies in ink, early drafts, unfinished poems, etc. in pencil. Twelve of these poems and fragments were later reworked for the 1846 volume to constitute ten of her nineteen poems. Significantly, only three poems (Nos. 148-150) are part of a prose narrative, written during the summer vacation, where previously most of the Angrian poems were embedded in prose narratives. In part, the change can be attributed to the lack of time and energy her teaching duties left her, but one also senses a rift developing between poetry and prose, and a waning of the poetic impulse as Charlotte came to realize more and more that prose fiction was her real métier. The quality of her poetry seems to me to decline noticeably from about mid-1837 on.

In 1838 the pattern becomes more regular again. The emphasis on the short lyric remains, but a great majority of the poems are relatively finished, signed and dated. All but one is Angrian and seven are part of prose narratives. But there are only eleven poems in all, composed during Christmas and summer vacation, and the spurt of writing during the summer shows a clear shift of emphasis from poetry to prose. Of the eight summer poems, all Angrian, six are embedded in prose narratives, as are all the 1839 poems. Winifred Gérin suggests that 1838-39 marks a change in Charlotte's work from unself-conscious dreaming to critical artistic composition and self-critical evaluation (CB, p. 118). It would seem that with the growth of critical awareness, the urge to write verse declined.

Over the next three years, before her departure for Brussels in February 1842, Charlotte produced only six poems and bits of verse. Four of these, all part of Angrian prose narratives, were composed in 1839, before Charlotte wrote her **Farewell to Angria**. In 1840, despite time and leisure at home, she produced only the "valentine" poem (No. 177). In 1841 there is also only one poem, but it suggests a bit of an Angrian relapse. In this early draft of **Passion** Charlotte returns to the Napoleonic Wars in Spain from which she had years ago taken the name of Douro for her hero. The speaker is a tyrannical male who very much resembles the Zamorna she has supposedly left behind.[50]

While she was in Brussels Charlotte did not entirely forego the composition of verse. In the fall of 1842 she wrote a poem on the death of her friend Martha Taylor. In addition to the manuscripts discovered by Ernest Nys (p. xxiii) she seems to have taken to Brussels the "Copy Book" in the Bonnell Collection at the Pierpont Morgan Library, into which she had been copying revised versions of earlier poems. Two of the poems (Nos. 164, 174) are signed "Copied at Bruxelles 1843." In addition, she translated poems from French and German into English and from English and German into French (see **Appendix A**).

On her return home from Brussels in January 1844 Charlotte was convinced that her writing career was over, and there is no evidence of any poetry composed that year. In July she wrote to Heger:

Formerly I passed whole days and weeks and months in writing
. . . but now my sight is too weak to write. Were I to write
much I should become blind. This weakness of sight is a
terrible hindrance to me . . . . The career of letters is
closed to me--only that of teaching is open (SHB LL, II, 13).

Thus when in October she and her sisters abandoned the project of setting
up their own school for lack of pupils, Charlotte did not have the consolation of either teaching or writing. To add to her frustration, Heger
was not answering her letters, creating a growing sense of betrayal and
anger, and a growing conviction that the enmity of Madame Heger was at
least partially responsible. On January 9, 1845 she wrote the angriest
of all her letters to her former teacher and colleague:

I have a hidden consciousness that some people, cold and
common-sense, in reading it [Charlotte's letter] would
say--'She is talking nonsense.' I would avenge myself on such
persons in no other way than by wishing them one single day of
the torments which I have suffered for eight months. We should
then see if they would not talk nonsense too.
    One suffers in silence so long as one has the strength so
to do, and when that strength gives out one speaks without too
carefully measuring one's words (SHB LL, II, 24).

Her anger and sense of betrayal seem to to have stirred her into a final
flurry of poetic activity, culminating in the preparation of the 1846
volume of poems.

    Although the dating of the poems ascribed to 1845 has to be tenta-
tive because the manuscripts are undated, the disjointed, head-long
quality, the fervent declaration of love, the tone of anger and betrayal,
and the presence of a hostile, scheming female rival in No. 180 all
suggest that the poem was written soon after the January letter. The
similarity of content and tone suggest that the revision of an Angrian
fragment into what was to become **Francis** in the 1846 volume also
belongs to this period. Sometime in the spring or summer of 1845
Charlotte composed the partial draft of **Gilbert,** the early draft of
"I gave at first attention close," and the two other fragments (Nos. 183,
184) in the partially used exercise book retained from her Brussel's
studies. The theme of vengeance wreaked on Gilbert for his betrayal of
Elinor, who

. . . loved me more than life;
    And truly it was sweet
To see so fair a woman kneel,
    In bondage, at my feet

> There was a sort of quiet bliss
>    To be so deeply loved,
> To gaze on trembling eagerness
>    And sit myself, unmoved

suggests that the poem must have been completed, at least in draft form, before June 26, when Charlotte left to visit Ellen Nussey for three weeks, and returned to find Branwell distracted and in disgrace after his dismissal by the Robinsons, unless one speculates that the poem reflects her sense of having been betrayed by Branwell. Certainly the tone of Charlotte's last letter to Heger in November is much more calm and controlled perhaps, in part, because she was writing again.

In the autumn she made the now well-known discovery of Emily's manuscript volume of poems, that led, at Charlotte's insistence, to the publication of the 1846 volume of poems. The final revisions of the nineteen poems she included must have been largely completed by the end of 1845, for the approach to Aylott and Jones was made on January 28, 1846, and the manuscript was dispatched on February 7. The task must have been formidable; although she used nine items from her Copy-Book, in which the last item is dated August 30, 1845, some of the poems underwent substantial revision. For three poems--**Preference, The Missionary,** and **The Wood**--there are no manuscripts extant. The subject matter of the first two, with their themes of haughty defiance and submission to God's will, suggests that they may have been composed earlier in the year when **Gilbert** was completed, although **Preference** has enough Angrian overtones to suggest it may be a revision of an earlier draft no longer extant. This is certainly the case with **The Wood**. **Pilate's Wife's Dream** is likely also a revision of a longer manuscript of which only a small scrap now remains. Thus fifteen years after Charlotte decided that she was called to be a poet and "published" some of her little volumes, she actually became a published poet.

True to her prophecy in 1830, she was a very minor one. The volume attracted little attention and her career as poet had come to an end. By June 1846 she had revised the poem in **The Professor**; by August 1847, the poems for **Jane Eyre**. It is fitting, therefore, that her last four poems were all about endings: "He saw my heart's woe" (December 1847) in which she exorcised the ghost of Heger, two poems on the death of Emily in 1848, and one on the death of Anne in 1849.

In later life Charlotte did not hold her poetry in high regard. She commented that her poems in the 1846 volume were written "before taste was chastened or judgement matured--accordingly they now appear to me very crude" (SHB LL, III, 86). To Mrs. Gaskell, she described her 1846 poems as "chiefly juvenile productions; the restless effervescence of a mind that would not be still. In those days the sea too often 'wrought and was tempestuous,' and weed, sand, and shingle--all turned up in tumult" (SHB LL, III, 162). With this edition it becomes possible for posterity to judge how accurately Charlotte evaluated her own work.

THE LAYOUT OF THE TEXT

For the twenty-two poems published by Charlotte the primary text given is her printed text. In all other cases the text follows the manuscripts as closely as possible. Her spelling, punctuation, and verse format have been reproduced, but canceled words, lines, etc., have been omitted. Where uncanceled variant readings occur, the primary text gives the latest variant, with earlier variants noted at the end of the poem. Similarly, where more than one draft exists, the primary text gives the latest; the earlier drafts appear in the commentary. Only titles provided by Charlotte are included. Editorial insertions appear in [ ], uncertain readings in < >.

The poems are arranged in chronological order, and Charlotte's signature and date have been reproduced when given. Where the date appears in square brackets, either the poem is undated but part of a dated manuscript, or the manuscript is undated. In the first case, the date and signature on the manuscript are provided in the commentary; in the second case, the reasons for the placement of the poem are given in the commentary. Although the last item in **Appendix A** is numbered 224, for the convenience of the reader eighteen early drafts of poems in the 1846 volume and **The Professor** have been included in the numbering at the chronologically appropriate place; thus the actual number of items is 206, excluding **Appendixes B** and **C**.

In the notes at the end of each poem the reader will find:

(a) The coded location of the manuscript(s) (for the key, see p. xv ). Where more than one location is listed, either the manuscript has been split or more than one version is extant. In the latter case, the locations appear in chronological order and the copy text is the last one noted.

(b) The first publication of the poem keyed to the **List of Abbreviations**, pp. xi-xiii.

(c) Variant readings and other textual matters.

In addition to information about dating and variant drafts, the commentary includes other relevant information about the manuscripts, information about the context of the poems, and some glossing of literary and Biblical references and sources. For Angrian references, a glossary of Glass Town/Angrian names is provided in **Appendix D.**

# Notes

1 K. M. Elizabeth Murray, **Caught in the Web of Words** (Oxford: Oxford University Press, 1979), p. 2.

2 **Charlotte Brontë's Novels: The Accents of Persuasion** (New York: W. W. Norton & Co., Inc., 1966), p. 16.

3 **Ibid.**, p. 18. See also chapter one of Winnifrith.

4 "The Brontës," **Victorian Fiction: A Guide to Research**, ed. Lionel Stevenson, Cambridge: Harvard University Press, 1964; "The Brontës," **Victorian Fiction: A Second Guide to Research**, ed. George H. Ford, New York: The Modern Language Association of America, 1978. Two most welcome recent publications are Christine Alexander's **A Bibliography of the Manuscripts of Charlotte Brontë**, The Brontë Society in association with Meckler Publishing, 1982, and **The Early Writings of Charlotte Brontë**, Oxford: Basil Blackwell, 1983.

5 For good discussions of the inadequacy of existing editions of the letters, see Rosengarten, "The Brontës," Winnifrith (chapter two), and BST (1982). Tom Winnifrith's recent editions of Branwell's and Charlotte's poems (Oxford: Shakespeare Head Press, 1983 and 1984), though an improvement over the SHB, still do not provide a complete text in either case.

6 For an explanation of how this figure is determined, see **The Layout of the Text** at the end of the Introduction.

7 **A Reference Catalogue of British and Foreign Autographs and Manuscripts.** Part I. "The Autograph of Charlotte Brontë," London, 1893; **A Bibliography of the Writings in Prose and Verse of the Members of the Brontë Family,** London, 1917; **A Brontë Library. A Catalogue of Printed Books, Manuscripts and Autograph Letters By the Members of the Brontë Family,** Collected by Thomas James Wise, London, 1929.

8 "The Brontës," p. 215.

9 In the early part of this century Sir Alfred Law of Honresfeld, Lancashire, acquired a number of Brontë manuscripts, including at least twelve of Charlotte's poems, the eleven listed on p. xix, and a draft of **Mementos.** Some of the manuscripts were in the collection of Shorter purchased from Nicholls; therefore Law must have acquired them from Wise; others Law purchased in the Sotheby's sale of 1907, after Nicholls' death. Neither Shorter nor Hatfield seem to have known of the Law collection at the time they prepared the 1923 edition of Charlotte's poems, nor when Hatfield prepared his Bibliography of Charlotte's manuscripts in 1922-24 (BST 6: 32-34). For a more detailed discussion of

the collection see "Brontë Manuscripts in the Law Collection" by Davidson Cook, **The Bookman**, November 1925, pp. 100-104. It was Cook (see n. 10) who drew Hatfield's attention to the existence of the collection. Just how many manuscripts remain in the possession of the Law family it is impossible to say; sometime after Sir Alfred's death in 1939 all further access was closed off, and scholars' pleas for information continue to go unanswered. Apparently Sir Alfred did offer some manuscripts for sale in 1933. C. W. Hatfield notes in a letter to Helen Brown (June 23, 1938) "It is interesting to know that Sir Alfred Law is still in possession of some of C. B.'s early mss. They were in the sale rooms of Hodgson and Company on 31$^{st}$ March 1933 and were supposed to have been sold as follows: Two Romantic Tales, L250 to Rolleston; Characters of Celebrated Men, Ŀ270 (no record of name of purchaser); Visits in Verreopolis, Ŀ400 to Robson. I was informed soon afterwards that there was a doubt about the manuscripts having really been sold. According to the catalogue a number of other early manuscripts from the same collection were sold" (Hatfield Papers). The doubt seems to have been accurate, for Helen Brown states in a letter dated June 21, 1938 that she visited Honresfeld and saw the three manuscripts listed above, but at least one manuscript listed by Cook, **Mina Laury** (see No. 162), is now in the Taylor Collection in Princeton.

10 That Cook made meticulous transcriptions of the Law manuscripts is clear from the Hatfield-Cook correspondence, 1925-28, in the Wise Collection. On the fly-leaf of one of Cook's transcriptions in the Symington Collection, Symington has noted: "Davidson Cook--a man of great Literary Research achievement: He was an authority on R. Burns, Sir W. Scott, and did work on the Brontës. He was trusted by Sir Alfred Law to copy the Burns and Scott MSS & Letters, which led him to getting access to the Brontë MSS. The Brontë MSS in the Law Collection had not been previously copied [actually Wise had copied some and Shorter had used the transcripts]. D. C.'s transcripts and editing have been followed by writers on the Angrian Stories of the Brontës, including Hatfield, Ratchford, & J A S."

11 By the time I discovered the existence of the three manuscripts containing these items, time and money for travel were no longer available.

12 See BST (1916) 5:26, 137-43.

13 Mrs. Gaskell's dating of "before 1833" is incorrect and may well have resulted from the fact that the manuscript is undated, and may not have been combined with a dated manuscript as it now is (see comment for No. 110).

14 See Clement Shorter, **The Brontës: Life and Letters** (London: Hodder and Stoughton, 1908), I, 19-20, and Shorter's letter in the **TLS**, April 3, 1924, p. 208.

15 May 8, 1926; November 17, 1926, Wise Collection.   In another letter to Cook, dated April 21, 1926, Hatfield discusses some of Nicholls' errors in dating Emily's poems.

16 See n. 14.

17 Letters to Helen Brown, March 1, 1938 and May 23, 1938, in the Hatfield papers.  According to J. A. Symington's catalogue of the Bonnell Collection, prepared for Mrs. Bonnell after the death of her husband (Symington Collection), Bonnell purchased at least one manuscript of Charlotte's (Nos. 40 and 41) from Miss Bell--"a niece of Mr. Nicholls"-- and eight poems and fragments (Nos. 121, 122, 124-125, 135, 142) from Mrs. Bolster.

18 Shorter, **Life and Letters**, I, 19.

19 The total does not include a number of exercise books from Charlotte's Brussels' period.

20 For the various versions of the purchase, see Shorter, **Life and Letters**, I, 19-20; "The Four Wishes," ed. Shorter, **Strand Magazine**, LVI (December, 1918), 461; **TLS**, April 3, 1924, p. 208; Christian, Census, pp.  180-81; Fannie E.  Ratchford, ed., **The Letters of Thomas J. Wise to John Henry Wrenn** (New York:  Knopf, 1944), pp. 471 and 484.

21 Winnifrith, pp. 200-01.

22 Christian, Census, p. 180.   See also Wilfred Partington, **Thomas J. Wise In The Original Cloth** (London:  Robert Hale Ltd., 1946), pp. 101, 104-5, 116-17, 164-65, for some of Wise's other commercial trans- actions concerning manuscripts.

23 Ratchford, **Letters of T. J. Wise**, pp. 162-63.

24 September 9, 1926, Wise Collection.   See also Christian, Census, p. 181 n. 16.

25 In letters dated June 15, 1926 (Wise Collection); March 9, April 12, April 16, August 6, 1938 (Hatfield Papers), Hatfield cites examples of Wise's deliberate attempts to pass off the work of Charlotte and Branwell as Emily's, in one case even after Hatfield had sent to Wise evidence to the contrary.

26 SHB Misc, II, 472-73.

27 Although I have confined my remarks to the effects on the manuscripts of Charlotte's poems, all these problems apply to the other manuscripts as well, including the letters. Christian notes that one type of "representative series" Wise prepared for his friends consisted of "taking a sample among the letters . . . of each type of signature that Charlotte used: 'C Brontë,' 'C B,' 'C Bell,' 'Charlotte Brontë,' and 'C. B. Nicholls'" (Census, p. 182).

28 Letter to Cook, December 24, 1926, Wise Collection. See also Hatfield's letter to Helen Brown, March 15, 1938 (Hatfield Papers).

29 The phrase is Partington's, p. 117.

30 "A Literary Letter," **The Sphere**, January 1, 1916.

31 See pp. 96-101, 257.

32 See Christian, Census, p. 181 n. 13, and Partington, **Thomas J Wise**, pp. 101-105.

33 "There must surely have been plenty of subscribers for such a small number of a purported Charlotte Brontë first edition. Yet we find Wise still selling the edition in 1910--disposing of a bundle of fifteen copies for only six pounds nineteen shillings, fourteen years after the production of '30 copies only'." Partington, **Thomas J Wise**, p. 108.

34 According to J. M. Bulloch, Shorter was too impatient to learn to collate and depended completely on Wise in editorial matters (**C.K.S. An Autobiography** (Privately printed, 1927), p. xvii).

35 In fact, all the new poems of Emily's in the 1902 edition were based on transcriptions made by Nicholls which had been bound and sold by Wise as original manuscripts. Shorter printed 67 of Emily's poems from the 1902 edition (Hatfield letter to Helen Brown, March 1, 1938, Hatfield Papers).

36 A similar problem obtained in the preparation of the 1920 edition of Anne's poems, which did not contain Anne's three earliest poems, yet the manuscripts for them were found among Shorter's papers after his death (Hatfield to Helen Brown, May 7, 1938, Hatfield Papers).

37 My remarks are restricted to the poetry volumes. For a discussion of the shabby treatment of the letters, see Winnifrith, pp. 7-27; 195-210.

38 **The Bookman**, 1925 and 1926; **The Twelve Adventurers and Other Stories**, 1925; **Legends of Angria**, 1933.

39 On Emily's poems, he comments, "I corrected a number of errors in the proof-sheets, errors fairly well known to the reviewers; but I left the others for the editors and other proof-readers to correct. When I saw the completed book, I came to the conclusion that I had been the only one to make any corrections in the text of the poems!" (Letter to Helen Brown, February 9, 1937, Hatfield Papers).

40 For more detailed information, see Alexander, p. xvii.

41 Christian, "The Brontës," p. 217.

42 I exclude No. 1 because it was written in collaboration with Branwell. Because of the collaboration with Branwell on the early poems, the number of lines can only be approximate.

43 For a discussion of Charlotte's use of allusion, see Melodie Monahan, "Charlotte Brontë's **The Poetaster**: Text and Notes," **Studies in Romanticism** 20 (Winter 1981), 475-96.

44 Gérin, CB, pp. 24-25.

45 Alexander (EW, p. 63) points out that the separation may have been underway by mid-1830.

46 See Charlotte's letter to Ellen Nussey, July 21, 1832 (SHB LL, I, 103), and Alexander EW, pp. 87-88.

47 Three versions of the poem are extant (see comment for No. 104). Wise had the second and third versions bound separately by Rivière, another example of how he "arranged" manuscripts.

48 Gérin, CB, p. 98.

49 Clearly, many of these poems relate to the hypochondria Charlotte suffered from in 1837-38--see Gérin, CB, pp. 113-15.

50 As late as May 1, 1843 Charlotte wrote to Branwell: "It is a curious metaphysical fact that always in the evening when I am in the great dormitory alone, having no other company than a number of beds with white curtains, I always recur as fanatically as ever to the old ideas, the old faces, and the old scenes in the world below" (SHB LL, I, 197).

THE POEMS

**1**
O when shall our brave land be free
when shall our castles rise
in pure & glorious liberty
before our joyful eyes

How long shall tyrants ride in state          5
upon the thundercloud
the arbiters of Englands fate
and of her nobles proud

Thou sun of liberty arise--
upon our beauteous land                        10
terrible vengeance rend the skys
let tyrants feel thy hand

let tyrants feel thy hand we cry
& let them see thy gaze
for they will shrink beneath thy eye          15
& we will sing thy praise

the song of vengeance shall arise
before the morning sun
illuminates the arched skys
or its high course doth run                    20

the song of vengeance shall not cease
when midnight cometh on
when the silver moon shines out in peace
to light the traveler lone

---

July the 24          U T

---

MS:   A
Not previously published

**2**
in this fairy land of light
no mortal ere has been
and the dreadful grandeu[r] of this sight
by them hath not been seen

t'would strike them shudering to the earth     5
like the flash from a thunder cloud
it would quench their light & joyous mirth
and fit them for the shroud

3

the rising of our palaces
like visions of the deep                                 10
and the glory of their structure
no mortal voice can speak

the music of our songs
and our mighty trumpets swell
& the sounding of our silver harps                       15
no mortal tongue can tell

of us they know but little
save when the storm doth rise
and the mighty waves are tossing
agains[t] the arched skys                                20

then oft they see us striding
oe'r the billows snow white foam
or hear us speak in thunder
when we stand in grandeur lone

on the darkest of the mighty clouds                      25
which veil the pearly moon
around us lightning flashing
nights blackness to illume

chorus    the music of our songs
          and our mighty trumpets                        30
          swell & the sounding of our silver
          harp[s] no mortal tongue can tell

                              [August 1829]

Ms:  B(1)
First Publication:   Shorter 1923


**3**            Lo our mighty cheiftains come
                 clothed in glory infinite
                 with the sound of harp & drum
                 loud pealing their might

                 on they march in splendour            5
                 to their adamantine thrones
                 & there they sit in grandeur
                 while our high melodious tones

                              4

are peeling to the arched roof
making the palace ring
making the mountains echo
& the desert wild to sing

    10

O may they reign eternally
in the glory of their might
may their armies be victorious
while they like stars of light

    15

illuminate the darksome world
<while> their sceptres might
changes the present state
into a glorious day

    20

[August 1829]

MS:  D(3)
Not previously published


**4**          **Interior of A Pothouse By Young Soult**

the cheerful fire is blazing bright
& cast[s] a ruddy glare
on beams & rafters all in sight
& on the sanded floor

the scoured pewter on the shelf
glitters like silver pure
& all the ware of stony delf
doth like to Gold allure

    5

and where this fire so magical
doth spread its light around
sure many scenes most magical
are acted on that ground

    10

about that oaken table
in the middle of the floor
are sat those who are able
to play one card or more

    15

and now behold the stakes are set
now watch the anxious faces
of all who have laid down a bet
scarce can they keep their places

    20

5

but see the teller holds the card
above the silent crowd
look at his meagre visage hard
& list' his accents loud

he says the card is number one                                            25
look at that fellow there
I think he has his buisness done
Behold his ghastly stare

now he has drawn his sword
and plunged it in his side                                                30
look at his dying struggle
while rushes forth the tide

of red & streaming blood
the current of his life
pouring a crimson flood                                                   35
while all within the strife

of racking pain of body
& torturing pain of mind
doth rend his heart in peices
& will no freind mos[t] kind                                              40

wipe from his brow the <clamy> swet
& cheer his dying hour
promise to aid his orphans dear
with all within his power

no there they'll alway let him lay                                        45
& pass unheeding by
unless the[y] find him in their way
when theyll kick him all awry

or tearing up a flag
in the neatly sanded floor                                                50
theyll throw him in & leave him there
& think of him no more

& now I've done my verses
you may read them if you choose
or throw them in the fire                                                 55
as Ive nought to gain or lose

                            Young Soult
                            August the <23> 1829

MS:   D(3)
Not previously published

**The Glass Town by U T**
   **the Glass Town***

            1
tis sunset & the golden orb
has sunk behind the mountains far
& rises now the silver moon
& sparkles bright the evening star

            2
but in the west an crimson light                    5
above the horizon glows
tinting all nature with the bright
gay colours of the rose

            3
and over all the eastern sky
the robe of twilight gray                           10
is heaving up the heavens nigh
while the pale milky way

            4
<gets> clearer still & clearer
as vanishes the light
till it arches all the firmament                    15
like a rainbow of the night

but the sound of <murmuring> waters
from distance far I hear
like the rushing of a cataract
it fall[s] upon my ear                              20

tis the roaring of the multitude
within those mighty walls
whose noise is like to rageing
or rushing waterfalls

tis that great & glorious city                      25
whose high ruler doth defy
the might[i]est of the a[r]mies
who their strength against <her try>

only he ever reign[s] in glory
may his glittering sword be dyed                    30
in the lifeblood of his enemies
though on the clouds they ride

O may he bring them to the <seat>
with fearful scorn and shame
may they bow their heads before him                    35
& dread his mighty name

but now the roaring sound has ceased
the citys sunk to sleep
& oe'r the world nights curtain falls
mid silence still & deep                               40

but yet the silver moon shines out
& the brilliant sparkling stars
are wheeling down the firmament
their <shining> pearly <cars>

no sound doth break the silence                        45
save the merry nightingale
as it pours its sweet warbling
dow[n] the still & <lonely> vale

U T   August the 24 1829

MS:  D(3)
Not previously published
Text:  title:  the first line appears at the bottom of a manuscript page;
      the second at the top of the next page.  Line 44 has been heavily
      amended and is virtually unreadable
*For  a  glossary  of  Glass  Town/Angrian  person  and  place  names,  see
**Appendix D**


**6**                    **on seeing A beautiful statue
                         & a rich golden vase full of wine lying beside
                         it in the desert of Sahara**

                         ――――――――――

                         see that golden goblet shine
                         decked with gems so starry bright
                         crowned with the most sparkling wine
                         casting forth a ruby light

                         Emerald leaves its brim encircle            5
                         with their brilliant green
                         and rich grapes of saphire purple
                         twined with these are seen


                                    8

near a majestic statue
of purest marble stands
rising like a spirit
from the wilderness of sand's

but heark unto that trumpet swell
which soundeth long and loud
rivalling the music
of the darkest thunder cloud

tis the signal that from hence
we both of us must go
so come my brother dear
let it be even so

10

15

20

U T  Sep<sup>t</sup> 2 1829

MS:   A
Not previously published
Text:   A canceled stanza following stanza three reads:
        but see a flash of lightning
        has darted from that glass
        now listen to that thunder peal
        so crashing long and loud


**7**         **THE SONG of THE ANCIENT
                  BRITON'S
          ON LEAVING THE GENILAND by U T**


Farewell O thou pleasant land
rich are thy feild's and fair
thy mighty forest's they are grand
but freedom dwells not there

thy rugged mountains rise sublime
from the barren desert wild
and thou wouldst be a pleasant land
if freedom on thee smiled

our hearts are sad as we turn from thee
and thy pleasant smiling shore
to think that not again shall we
Behold thee ever more

5

10

9

ere many day's are passed away
the sea will between us lie
and when in freedoms land we dewll 15
for thee we'll heave a sigh

because that oer thee triumph
those tyrant's of the air
who dwell in halls of thunder
& robes of lightning wear 20

but now we're bound afar off
to our fathers land we go
swift foaming billows roll us
and winds of heaven blow

there rises freedoms palace 25
like a tower of burning gold
around it roars the ocean
with its world of waters rolled

up to the glorious castle
where mighty freedom dewells 30
while round her like a tempest
sea music sweetly swells

U T
Sep^t 7 1829

But now were bound afar off
to our father's land we go
swif[t] foaming billows roll us 35
and winds of heaven blow

U T
Sep^t 7 1829

MS:  A
Not previously published


8          **ON seeing the Garden of**
           **A Genius by U T**

How pleasant is the world
where mighty Geni dwell
like a vision is the beauty
of wild forest stream & fell

their palaces arise                                      5
from the green and flowry ground
while strains of sweetest music
are floating all around

their castles of bright adamant
all mortal strength defy                                10
encircled round with geni
towering like rocks on high

& now behold that verdant plain
spa[n]gled with star like flowers
watered by purest silver lakes                          15
& crowned with emerald bowers

in the midst appear[s] a palace
of yellow topaz bright
from which streams forth a glory
of sunny golden light                                   20

O if the dwellers in this land
heeded their dreadful name
how all the mortal world would sing
their bright & quenchless Fame

But now the eye of hatred                               25
follows where ere they go
in the sea or in the firmament
it tries to work them woe

they may robe themselves in darkness
themselves with lightning crown                         30
they may weild the sword of vengeance
but to them we'll not bow down

they may frame in the dark ocean
high palaces of pearl
mid the silver orbs of heaven                           35
their dragon wings unfurl

& throned on the star's of night
while thunder rolls around
may bid the earth to <wait on> them
but vain shall be the sound                             40
                              U T
                              Sep^t 9 1829

11

how pleasant is the world
where mighty geni dwell
like a vision is the beauty
of wild forest stream & fell &c &c

MS:  A
Not previously published


9              **Found in the Inn belonging to you**


Thou art a sweet & lovely flower
planted in a fairy's bower
cherished by a bright sunbeam
watered by a silver stream

Thou art a palm tree green & fair                    5
rising from the desert plain
thou art a ray of silver light
streaming o'er the stormy main

When the mighty billows mix
with the hanging cloud                              10
when the light[n]ings flashes
& the thunder roaring loud

Then when some pale star sends out
a gentle pearly ray
the mariners all hail it                            15
as the herald of the day

When the sun shall rise in splendour
ting[e]ing the coursing foam
with the colours of that gorgeous bow
Which arches heavens dome                           20

When the rocking ship shall rest
on the glassy ocean calm
its red flag stirred by the gale
whose breath is sweetest balm

Blowing from Brita[i]n's shore's                    25
& her roses red and white
O'er Scotia's thistle wild
and Erin's emerald bright

While the music of the harp
and the music of the song                          30
are borne upon the passing wind
in solemn strains along.

U T
Sep<sup>t</sup> 28. 1829

MS:  C
First Publication:  SHB C and B


**10**              **Addressed to 'the tower of all nations[']**


O thou great thou mighty tower
rising so solemnly
o'er all this splendid glorious city
this city of the sea

thou seeme'st as silently I gaze             5
a pillar of the sky
so lofty is thy structure
so massive & so high

the dome of heaven is oer thee
hung with it's silver star's              10
the earth is round about the[e]
with it's eternal bars.

& such a charming dogge[re]l
as this was never wrote
not even by the mighty               15
& high Sir Walter Scott

U T   October 7 1829

MS:  C
First Publication:  BST 1920


13

1    Beneath a shady tree I sat
     Through which with wondrous lustre gleamed
     The rays of the departing sun
     Which in its golden glory beamed

2    Among the shady verdant boughs                    5
     Ting[e]ing with crimson light
     The beauteous emerald foliage
     Now like the ruby bright

3    All still & peaceful was the scene
     And silence reigned around                        10
     Save the music of a murmuring stream
     Which with its gentle sound

4    Filled the shady valley where I sat
     With a low melodious tone
     In concert with the nightingale                   15
     And zephyrs gentle moan

5    At length the robe of twilight spread
     O'er all the dark'ning earth
     And still & peaceful were the sounds
     Of sorrow & of mirth                              20

6    And silently the little stars
     Looked from the azure sky
     While Orions golden belt
     Shone gloriously on high

                              C B  Oct^{br} 8. 1829

MS:  D(1)
First Publication:  Dodd Mead 1902


12                  **SUNRISE**

1    Behold that silvery streak of light
     Circling the heavens grey
     Encroaching on the reign of night
     And heralding the day

2  Now of a richer deeper tint
   The sunny glory grows
   Until a stream of heavenly light
   Along the horizon flows                          5

3  Rising it melts into the pale
   Soft azure of the sky
   How beautiful how glowing bright                 10
   Is its ethereal dye

4  Hung in the saphire arch of heaven,
   Above this golden light
   The silver crescent of the moon                  15
   Seems to the wondering sight

5  A world in which fair spirits dwell
   So pure & fair it beams
   So gentle is the pearly light
   That softly from it streams                      20

6  But rises now the glorious sun
   Casting the clouds aside
   And in his burning chariot forth
   Triumphantly doth ride

7  And at his flaming presence bright               25
   All nature doth rejoice
   Earth sky & sea join in his praise
   With one united voice

8  Sweetly the little birds do sing
   Warbling their notes in air                      30
   While flowrets in their tiny cups
   Bright gem like dewdrops bear

          Charlotte Bronte   Oct<sup>br</sup> 9 1829

MS:  D(1)
First Publication:  Dodd Mead 1902

**13**            **On the great Bay of the glass Town**

1  tis pleasant on some evning fair
   after a sumers day
   when still the breeze & calm the air
   & seawaves gently play

15

2   to veiw the bay o'er whose still breast       5
white sails do softly glide
how peacefully its waters rest
like to a sleeping child

3   when the blue concave of the sky
is clear without a stain                    10
& the bright arch of heaven on high
imparts to the wide main

4   its beautiful & saphire glow
while the suns golden light
makes all the western sky to flow     15
with streams like ruby bright

5   then like fair piles of burnished gold
those marble pillars stand
palaces of imortal mould
& castles tow'ring grand             20

6   while mur'm'ring sounds of pomp & mirth
rise from the mighty walls
& wildly mingleing sweep forth
like thundring waterfalls

7   till softened into echo's &lt;vapour&gt; tone   25
on the calm sea they die
or rising with the deaths moan
on winds of heaven fly

8   to play with them amid the strings
of harps whose magic voice           30
in the long dark'nd rest sings
while fairies round rejoice

9   as through tall trees the wild winds moan
& silver moonbeams glance
the harp peals forth with triumphs tone   35
& spirits mirthful dance

U T November 2
1829

MS:  D(2)
First Publication:  BST 1919
Text:  There are two undecipherable words above "Bay" in the title

**14**          **lines spoken by a lawyer on the occasion of the
          transfer of this magazine**

All soberness is past & gone
the reign of gravity is done
frivolity comes in its place
light smiling sits in every face

gone is that grave & gorgeous light                              5
which every page illumind bright
a flimsy torch glare in the stead
of a bright golden sun now fled

Foolish romances now employ
each silly senseless girl & boy                                 10
O for the strong hand of the law
to stop it with its powerful claw

at night I lay my weary head
upon my sofa or my bed
in the dark watches of the night                               15
does flash upon my inward sight

visions of times now pass'd away
when dulness did the sceptre sway
then to my troubled mind comes peace
would those bright dreams did never cease                       20

thus sang a lawyer in his cell
when suddenly the midnight bell
rang out a peal both loud & deep
which told it was the hour of sleep

                        W T   Nov 20   1829

MS:   D(2)
First Publication:   BST 1919


**15**          **lines written by one who was tired of dullness
          upon the same occasion**

Sweep the sounding harp string
all ye winds that blow
let it loudly swelling
make sweet music flow

17

let the thundring drum roll                          5
gladness fly around
merry bells peal & toll
ringing trumpets sound

let the mighty organ
play & peal & swell                                 10
roll its floods of sound on
till echos every dell

sweetly sweetly breath[e] flute
pour thy gentle strains
let thy music rise lute                             15
no more Dullness reigns

sweep the sounding harp string
all ye winds that blow
let it loudly swell & ring
make sweet music flow                               20

in your splendid cloud halls
princely Geni dance
till from the vapour walls
bloody lightnings glance

your music is black thunder                         25
therefore let it sound
tear the earth asunder
shake the sky around

faires of the greenwood
Sing amid the trees                                 30
pour of joy a bright flood
dance upon the breeze

drink from the bright flower
crowned with crystal dew
<furnish> with <the green> bower                    35
<buds> of snowy hue

no longer hid your name is
ye spirits of the air
for now your mighty fame is
set forth in coulours fair                          40

sweep the sounding harp string
all ye winds that blow
let it loudly swelling
make sweet music flow

U T
Nov 27 1829

MS:  D(2)
First Publication:  BST 1919
Text:  Alexander dates the poem "Nov 21" (item 267), but the manuscript
reads "Nov 27"


**16**        **HARVEST IN SPAIN**


Now all is joy & gladness, the ripe fruits
Of autum hang on every orchard bough
The living gold of harvest waves around
The festooned vine empurpled with the grape
Weighed to the ground by clusters rich & bright          5
As precious amethyst, gives promise fair
Of future plenty.  While the almond tree
Springs gracefully from out the verd[ant] earth
Crowned with its em'rald leaves its pleasant fruit
and waveing in the gentle Fragrant breeze                10
which sweeps o'er orange groves mid myrtle bowers
& plays in Olive woods drinking the dew
which falls like crystal on their russet leaves
hid by luxuriant foliage from the beam
of the great glorious sun which shines on high           15
In bright & burning strength casting its rays
to the far corners of the mighty land
enlightning & illuminating all
making it glow with beauty and with joy
& raising songs of gladness and of praise                20
To God the Father & the king of all

December 9  [C. Brontë deleted]  UT 1829

MS:  B(1)
First Publication:  **The Bookman,** December 1926

**17**        Merry England, land of glory
plenty on thee fall
joy dwell on thy castles hoary
gladness in each hall

might be on thy stately towers        5
beauty in each dell
in thy blossomed vernal bowers
may peace ever dwell

when wars trumpet fierce is sounding
Brit[ain's] lion roars        10
Oer the mighty waters bounding
to The foes dark shores

When in battle he stands warlike
And his meteor sword
Gleams amid the fight more starlike        15
Round him blood is poured

Till his mane is red and gory
And his flashing eye
As he springs to future glory
Is of crimson dye        20

Now when victory hath assuaged him
Of his thirst for blood
'Neath his oak tree he hath laid him
While around the flood

Of the raging mighty ocean        25
Guards his own fair land
Standing mid the wild commotion
All serene and grand

        Marquis of Duro & Lord C Wellesly
Now that will do (amids[t] loud cheering
        the curtain falls

[December 1829]

MS:  B(1)
First Publication:  **The Bookman,** December 1926

**18**
Ive been wandering in the greenwoods
And mid flowery smiling plains
I've been listning to the dark floods
To the thrushes thrilling strains

I have gathered the pale primrose                          5
And the purple violet sweet
Ive been where the asphadel grows
And where lives the red deer fleet

I've been to the distant mountain
to the silver singing rill                                 10
by the crystal murm'ring fountain
and the shady verdant hill

I've been where the poplar's springing
From the fair enameled ground
While the nightingale is singing                           15
With a solemn plaintive sound

> December 14. 1829
> C. Brontë

MS: E
First Publication: Shorter EJB 1910


**19**    **The Churchyard  A Poemn of my  my**


'Twas one fair evening, when the closing day
Shines lustrous in Apollos' parting beam;
Who as he sinks within his azure palace
And draws the splendid curtains ruby red,
Of his sublime pavillion; casts a glance                   5
O'er this round g[l]obe terest[r]ial, then bids
A bright farewell, and drops the veil which hides
His glories in its cloud like crimson folds.
'Twas in that hour I entered the high gates
Of consecrated ground; there stood a Church,              10
Whose grey and ruined form seemed to have felt
The storms and blasts of centuries; It was
Enrobed with ivy and its pillared portals
All wreathed with green young tendrils, seemed in their
Massive grandeur, t'have been formed in ages             15
When the British chivalry rode forth with might
To meet the Saracen: And free the land;

21

The sacred land of Palestine, from their
Unhallowed presence. Through the dark yew trees
Gloomy cypresses and high black firs;                              20
Which grew around a soft & faint light stole
Investing with a holy solemness,
The ancient building and illumining,
The tombs and grave-mounds, where the still dead slept.
Among those monuments there stood a figure                         25
Clothed in deep mourning from whose dark eye beamed
The sad and wild light of insanity
And as she stood she poured a thrilling strain
Which echoed mid the churchyard from whose walls
A soft response came forth as thus she sang                        30

---

I know my sister thou art gone
For the mild peaceful light;
Which ever in they fair eye shone
Has vanished from my sight.
And when black midnight cast her pall                              35
O'er the reposing earth,
I heard a faint voice on thee call
And bid thy soul come forth.
I saw thee in a glazed shroud
Within the chamber lie;                                            40
And when with greif my heart was bowed
A whisper from on high;
Has told me that thou dwell'st among
Bright bands of Seraphim
Who with a sweet eternal song                                      45
The triune Godhead hymn.
One night when silence reigned around
I heard sweet music rise
Whose harplike & harmonious sound
Came from the star-hung skies                                      50
And when had dyed each soft sweet tone
Thy spirit passed away
And left me a sad mourner here
On this dark earth to stay.

Then ceased the requiem and the figure moved                       55
With slow and noiseless step from the dark grave
Amid grey mantled twilights deep'ning gloom
Now hov'ring over all the silent earth.

                    Charlotte Brontë   December 24 1829

MS: F(1)
First Publication: partial Benson 1915; full SHB C and B
Text: In the right-hand margin opposite l. 5 appears the word "my"

20         **Written upon the ocasion of the dinner given to
           the literati of the Glass Town which was attended
           by all the Great men of the present time Soldier
           Sailor Poet & Painter Architect Politician novelist
           & Romancer.**


           1   The Splendid Hall is blazing
               With many a glowing light
               And a spirit like effulgence mild
               A flood of glory bright

           2   Flows round the stately pillars                      5
               Nor dimly dyes away
               In the arched roof of solid stone
               But there each golden ray

           3   Shines with a brightened splendour
               A radiance rich & fair                              10
               And then falls amid the palace vast
               And lightens up the air

           4   Till the atmosphere around
               Is one continued flow
               Of streaming lustre, brilliant light                15
               & liquid topaz glow.

           5   All beneath this gorgeousness
               There sits a chosen band
               Of genius high & courage bold
               The noblest of the land                             20

           6   The feast is spread & brightly
               The purple juice doth shine
               In the yellow gold magnificen[ce]
               The sparkling gen'rous wine

           7   And all between the thunders                        25
               Of patriotic cheers
               Is heard the sounding orchestra
               While the inspiriting tears


                              23

8   Of a rich southern vineyard
    Are quaffed to wish the health                    30
    Of some most noble warrior feirce
    A nations powr & wealth

9   And then arises slowly
    An orator of might
    And pours a flood of eloquence                    35
    Upon this festal night

10  The gentle stream flows dimpling
    'Mong rethorics bright flow'rs
    Poise[s] in wild sublimity
    On eagles wing high towers                         40

11  And lost amid the cloudy
    Curtains of his might
    Far beyond the common vulgars ken
    His spirit hath ta'en flight

12  For a while it dwells in glory                     45
    Within the solemn veil
    Then returns upon the smoother seas
    Of beauty fair to sail

13  The scene this night is joyous
    Within these palace walls                          50
    But ere ten passing centuries
    Are gone these lofty halls

14  May stand in darksome ruin
    These stately pillars high
    May echo back far other sounds                     55
    Than those which sweetly fly

15  Among their light bold arches
    And mingling softly rise
    In a wild enchanting melody
    Which tremulously dies                             60

16  The yell of the hyena
    The bloody tigers howl
    May be heard in this magnificence
    Mixed with the lions growl

17    While in the cold pale moonlight                          65
      May stand the ruins gray
      All these marble columns mouldering
      And gladness fled away

                    C. Brontë  January 8 1830

MS:  D(1)
First Publication:  Dodd Mead 1902


21          **Written on the Summit of A High**
            **Mountain in the north of England**


      ─────────────────────────────────────


      How lonely is this spot, deep silence reigns,
      For ceased has ev'ry human stir and sound;
      But Natures voice is heard in gentle strains
      Which, with a stilly noise float softly round.
      Each leaf which quivers in those giant elms               5
      Falls audibly upon the list'ning ear;
      As if it came from distant spirit realms
      A warning of some death or danger near.
      And now strange thoughts & mournful, slowly rise
      Each after other in a gloomy train,                       10
      Each quickly born, and each as quickly dies;
      Drunk by the whirlpool, of oblivions main.
      But sudden bursting from a thick dark cloud,
      Lo! the bright sun illumines all the earth,
      Tinting with amber light, that wat'ry shroud:             15
      Radiant with beauty as he now walks forth
      Behold the valley glows with life and light,
      Each raindrop bears a glory in its cell
      Of Saphire, ruby, or fair em'rald bright
      Rejoicing in its palace clear to dwell.                   20
      A wilderness of sweets yon wood appears;
      Before a forest full of darksome gloom:
      But now a smilling face of joy it wears;
      Not such as would befit the churchyard tomb.
      But all unseemly mid the gladness stands,                 25
      That ancient castle, mossed and grey with age;
      Once the resort of warlike feudal bands:
      Where oft was heard the battles bloody rage
      Now an unbroken stillness reigns around:
      No warriors step rings through the arched halls;          30
      No hunting horns sweet thrilling mellow sound,


                          25

Or bloodhounds yell reverb[e]rates mid those walls.
The gladsome sunshine suits not with this place,
And golden light seems but to mock the grey
And sorrowing aspect, of its furrowed face;                    35
Too time worn to be joyous with the day.
But when black night o'ershadows with her wing
The prospect; and the solemn nightingale;
Sings while the moon her silver light doth fling
In trem'lous lustre o'er the sleeping vale.                    40
Then awfully that ancient castle tow'rs,
From out its grove of venerable trees;
Amid whose scathed and withered leafless bow'rs,
Howls mournfuly the peircing winter breeze.
Or on some day, when dark and sombre clouds,                   45
Veil dismally the blue etherial sky:
When the deep grandeur of their blackness shrouds,
The sun with all its majesty on high.
When fitful shadows hurry o'er the plain;
And curtain round this mountain's hoary brow:                  50
Rolling voluminous, a misty train;
Or curled in floating vapours ev'n as now;
Those light soft clouds piled in the ambient air,
Of gentle lustre and of pearly hue:
Calm in the summer twilight, mild, and fair;                  55
Distilling from their pureness, crystal dew.

                    Charlotte Brontë.  January 14. 1830

MS:  F(1)
First Publication:  Shorter 1923


**22**      **A wretch in prison by Murry**


O for the song of the gladsome lark
For the morning suns fair beam
Instead of this dungeon deeply dark
Where n[e]'er its light doth gleam
O for the breath of the fragrant vale                          5
For the woodlands bracing breeze
Blowing like Arabys spicy gale
Amid the stately forest trees
O for the light & elastic spring
For the swift unwearied step                                   10
When the sound of the horn makes the high hills ring
With the bounding hunter[s] leap


                              26

O for the noise of freedoms voice
Heard in the hunters cry
When the deer has fled like an arrow sped                    15
Or a lightning flash on high
O for the rush for the bold free rush
Of the mighty mountain breeze
Down the rocks away to the dashing spray
Of the roaring rolling seas                                  20
O for the light most feirce & bright
Of the heavens cloudy gloom
O for the <dreadful> sound like an earthquake bound
Of the thunders hollow boom

O! that the glad stars through my dungeon bars               25
Would shed their lustre clear
That the solemn moon would lighten the gloom
Which reigns in silence here
O for some fair light to illume this night
With a swift & silver glance                                 30
Through these grates to play, with a pearly ray
And lightly here to dance

                              C Bronte   February 1
                              1830

MS:  D(1)
First Publication:  Dodd Mead 1902


**23**     Of College I am tired I wish to be at home
           Far from the pompous tutors voice & the hated
              schoolboys groan

           I wish that I had freedom to walk about at will
           That I no more was troubled with my Greek & slate
              & quill

           I wish to see my kitten to hear my ape rejoice         5
           To listen to my nightingale & parrots lovely voice

           And England does not suit me it's cold and full of snow
           So different from Black Africa's warm sunny genial glow

           I'm shivering all the day-time & shivering all the night
           Im called a poor startled withered wretch & miserable
              wight                                              10


                              27

And O! I miss my brother I miss his gentle smile
Which used so many long dark hours of sorrow to beguile

I miss my dearest mother I now no longer find
Ought half so mild as she was so careful and so kind

O I have not my father's my noble fathers arms                    15
To gaurd me from all wickedness and keep me safe from
      harm[s]

I hear his voice no longer I see no more his eye
Smile on me in my misery to whom now shall I fly

                          C B  C W  February [2] 1830

MS:  D(1)
First Publication:  Dodd Mead 1902


**24**        **Winter A Short Poem, by C Bronte;**

    1   Autumn has vanished with his train
        Of ripened fruits and golden grain
        Now the white hoar frost spreads the feilds
        Grim Winter now the sceptre weilds

    2   Lowring clouds deface the sky                             5
        Veil the solemn worlds on high
        Many a storm portending blast
        Sweeps with mournful cadence past

    3   And the lonely traveller
        Now sees the tempest from afar                          10
        Benighted on some desert moor
        He hears the distant sullen roar

    4   Sent by the spirit of the storm
        From the dark bosom of a cloud
        It floats & sounds more near & loud                     15
        As in the heavens, black he sees an awful form

    5   It rears its huge & ghastly head
        Around which plays an halo red
        From out the battlements of air
        All gilded by the moonlight fair                        20


                              28

<pre>
6   Which suddenly as if unbound
    Flings a radiance around
    Bright'ning with a fitful glory
    The grim cloudy giant hoary

7   Lost again in dessert gloom                              25
    It sinks within a vapoury tomb
    Meantime the swift descending snow
    Comes with one continuous flow

8   Whitening all the earth around
    From the heavens black and louring                       30
    Ceaseless & incessant pouring
    Till in its winter robe is clothed all the ground

9   Dismal & deathlike is the scene
    But soon arrayed in robes of green
    Spring will come, the budding bower                      35
    & the snowdrops humble flower

10  Heralding her coming step
    From the verdant earth will peep
    While the little birds will sing
    At the approach of gentle spring                         40

11  Soon the rose will ope her bud
    And each fair flowret of the wood
    The violet dark the primrose pale
    The cowslip of the sweeping vale

12  Will all unfold their fragrant leaves                    45
    Purple, crimson and bright gold
    A wreath for meadow waste & wold
    Their rich united sweets harmoniously weaves
</pre>

Charlotte Brontë, Feb<sup>ry</sup> 3 1830

MS:  F(1)
First Publication:  SHB C and B
Text:   Between the title and the first stanza appear the following un-
        canceled trial lines divided from the first stanza by a heavy
        line:
        1   Autumn has vanished, with his sickly train
            Of withering forests & falling leaves
            No more wide waving o'er the fruitful plain
            Stands the ripe corn or bound in sheaves
            Mixed with the vine A harvest garland weaves

----------------------------------------

1   True Pleasure breathes not city air
    Nor in Arts temples dwells
    In palaces and towers where
    The voice of Grandeur swells

    No, Seek it where high nature holds          5
    Her court mid stately groves
    Where she her majesty unfolds
    And in fresh beauty moves

3   Where thousand birds of sweetest song
    The wildly rushing storm                     10
    And hundred streams which glide along
    Her mighty concert form

4   Go where the woods in beauty sleep
    Bathed in pale Luna's light
    Or where among their branches sweep          15
    The Hollow winds of night

5   Go where the warbling nigh[t]ingale
    In gushes rich doth sing
    Till all the lonely quiet vale
    With melody doth ring                         20

6   Go sit upon a Mountain steep
    And view the prospect round
    The hills and vale's the valleys sweep
    The far horizons bound

7   Then view the wide sky overhead              25
    The still deep vault of blue
    The sun which golden light doth shed
    The clouds of pearly hue

8   And as you gaze on this vast scene
    Your thoughts will journey far               30
    Though hundred years should roll between
    On times swift passing car

9   To ages when the earth was young
    When patriarchs grey & old
    The praises of their God oft sung            35
    And oft his mercies told

10    You see them with their beards of snow
      Their robes of ample form
      Their lives whose peaceful gentle flow
      Felt seldom passions storm                              40

11    Then a calm solemn pleasure steals
      Into your inmost mind
      A quiet amen your spirit feels
      A softened stillness kind

              Charlotte Brontë  February 8. 1830.

MS:  F(1)
First Publication:  SHB C and B

## 26    **Verses by Lord Charles Wellesley**

1    Once more I view thy happy shores
         O England bold & free
     Round whom the guardian ocean roars
         Fair flowret of the sea
2    And starlike thou dost gently rest                       5
         Arrayed in living green
     Upon the black waves gloomy bre[a]st
         A bright gem thou art seen
3    Those oft dark curtain'ning vapours veil
     Thy clear cerulian sky                                   10
     And often loud winds wildly wail
     Or sorrowfully sigh
4    Among thy oaken forests vast
     All robed in misty gloom
     Which by the lightnings fire scathed                     15
     Bend neath the thunders boom
5    Yet still bold hearts within thee dwell
     The brave the free the feirce
     Inspired by the battles <knell>
     Rush forthe their foes to peirce                         20
     But Africa to me is dear,
     I love its sunny clime
     Its skies for ever blue & clear
         And now Ive done my rhyme

              C Bronte  Feb[r]uary 11 1830

MS:  G
First Publication:  Winnifrith PCB

31

27        O blessed mildly rising morn
            I feel thy sweet fresh breeze
        I see thee wave the springing corn
            & the tops of the green young trees

        When thou com'st stately from the hills        5
            Thy flowry mantle o'er thee
        Thy praise is sung by a hundred rills
            And all the woods adore thee

        They bend their mighty branches so low
            To kiss the sparkling dews        10
        Or dip them in the streams which flow
            'Mong flow'rets of all hues

        Thou art welcomed by the feilds & plains
            & the lark with gladsome song
        & with joy pours forth his matin strains        15
            On the soft clouds borne along

        The heavens rejoice at thy approach
            The blue arch with fresh glory
        Spans the earth spread beneath like an emerald couch
            And brightens the mountains hoary        20

                            [February 1830]

MS: A
Not previously published

28     **The Vision  A Short Poemn**

        The gentle, Show'ry Spring had passed away
        And no more breathed the fragrant breath of June
        Summer had clad in glorious array
        Each hill and plain & now the harvest moon
        Shone on the waving corn brown Autumn's golden boon        5

        In that glad time, as twilight softly crept
        Over the earth; I wandered to a place
        Where stillness reigned As if the whole world slept
        For here of noise remained no wearying trace
        But deepest silence sat on all nature's face        10

It was a wild glen near it frowned huge rocks
Which hung their dark beams o'er its stony bed
And in their caverned sides faint echo mocks
When rolls some fragment down, with rumbling dread
And horrid noise launched from the mountains head.          15

The valley now was still a midnight calm
Fell on it; as I sat beneath a tree
Whose leaflets glistened with the dew's mild balm
Wept by the evening stir so freshly free
And filling all the air with soft humidity                 20

'Mong the huge trees which canopied that glen
I saw the sky with many a bright star hung
And through the midst alone sailed glorious gem
The moon who still her trembling lustre flung
Unchanged as when her spheres together tuneful-sung         25

At intervals her light fell through the trees
And with mild glory silvered all the vale
While Through all those branches whispered not a breeze
No hollow blast did sad and mournful wail
But solemn silence walked beneath the moonbeams pale        30

Yet black the gaunt rocks rose before my eyes
And their black caverns filled the heart with dread
They stood in grand releif from out the skies
Whose clear vaults arched oer each shaggy head
And from those quivering stars a radian[t] light was shed   35

I gazed upon this scene till slumber fell
Upon my eyelids, then methought I saw
On my entranced sight a vision swell
Whose glory passed the bound of Natures law
And filled the spirit with a mingl[e]d joy & awe            40

A land was spread before me where the trees
Formed woods of emrald clearness and high bowers
Through which the[re] whispered many a murmuring breeze
Perfumed with incence of a hundred flowers
Wat[e]red by clouds of light which fell in fragrant showers 45

I heard sweet voices not like human sound
But tuneful of artic'late harmony
I saw no shape but oft there floated round
A zephyr soft & breathing from the sky
As if some unseen form in light wings flitted by            50

33

At length the air 'gan brighten faint there shone
A rainbow path through all the expanse of blue
And music of a soft melodious tone
Subdued by distance through hea'vens wide arch flew
Falling upon the ear calm as the twilight dew                      55

Louder it rose, sweep harp & timbrel clear
Rang tunefully to many a sweeter voice
These mingling fell upon the list'ning ear
While all the echo's answered to the noise
And Nature seemed united to rejoice                                60

Then a bright chariot glided through the air
Attended by a glorious company
Of beings radiant surpassing fair
Around them rolled of light a mighty sea
And now the music played with loudest melody                       65

And while this scene slow passed before my eyes
Dazzled with splendor suddenly I woke
& Lo the light dawn tinged the easterns skies
Showing the rugged front of many a rock
And faintly gilding each wide branching oak                        70

                    C. Bronte   April the 13 or April 13 1830

MS:  F(1)
First Publication:  Shorter 1923
Text:  Between the title and the first stanza appear the following
       uncanceled lines:

       Sweet Spring had passed away,
       The balmy breath,
       of June, had breathed on all the rising corn
       which waved in sumer pride on fertile plains
       Or robed in green array, the sloping side
       of many a cultured hill


**29**                  O Where has Arthur been this night
                          Why did he not come home
                        For long the suns fair orb of light
                          hath shone in heavens dome
                        Beneath the greenwood tree he's slept        5
                          his tester was the sky
                        O'er him the midnight stars have wept
                          bright dewdrops from on high


                                   34

And when the first faint streak of day
    did in the east appear                       10
His eyes touched by the mornings ray
    shone out with lustre clear
He rose & from his dark brown hair
    He shook the glit'ring gems
Which natures hand had scattered there           15
    as on the forest stems
The flowers sent up an odour sweet
    as forth he stately stept
The stag sprang past more light & fleet
    the hare through brushwood crept              20

                    [May 1830]

MS:  H
First Publication:  **Cosmopolitan Magazine,** October 1911


**30**            To the forest to the wilderness
                  Ah let me hasten now
                  Wher'ere I go I still shall see
                  My masters lowering brow

                  The Woods black shade won't hide my greif   5
                  No influence now I have
                  But th[e] stream will give me quick releif
                  I'll seek a watry grave

                  Unto the shore I'll swiftly fly
                  I'll plunge into the sea                    10
                  The foam bells will ascend on high
                  When drowning sets me free

                  From all the ills which life doth give
                  O mis'ry in me dwells
                  When no longer I shall live                 15
                  The tide of sorrow swells

                  Suspended from an elm tree tall
                  I'll end my mournful life
                  My soul more bitter is than gall
                  My heart is full of strife                 20

I'll cut my neck with some sharp blade
I'll swallow poison dire
<With> now my resolutions made
I'll set myself on fire

[May 1830]

MS:  H
Not previously published
Text:  l. 15:  "shall" was initially canceled, but "when shall" appears
       above the line, uncanceled

31          "Proudly the sun has sunk to rest
            "Behind yon dim & distant hill
            "The busy noise of day has ceas't
            "A holy calm the air doth fill

            "That softning haze which veils the light          5
            "Of sunset in the gorgeous sky
            "Is Dusk, grey harbinger of Night
            "Now gliding onward silently

            "No sound rings through the solemn vale
            "Save murmurs of those tall dark trees            10
            "Who raise eternally their wail
            "Bending beneath the twilight breeze

            "And my harp peals the woods among
            "When Vesper lifts it's quiet eye
            "Comingling with each night birds song             15
            "That chants its vigils pensively

            "And here I sit until nights noon
            "Hath gemed the heavens with many a star
            "And sing beneath the wandring moon
            "Who comes high journeying from afar              20

            "O sweet to me is that still hour
            "When frown the shades of night around
            "Deep'ning the gloom of forest bower
            "Filling the air with awe profound

            "I hush my harp and hush my song                   25
            "Low kneeling 'neath the lofty sky
            "I heark the nightingale prolong
            "Her strain of wondrous melody

36

"Forth gushing like a mountain rill
"So rich so deep so clear & free                              30
"She pours it forth o'er dale & hill
"O'er rock, and river, lake and tree.

"Till morn comes, & with rosy hand
"Unbars the golden gates of day
"Then as at touch of magic wand                              35
"The earth is clad in fair array

"Then from its couch the skylark springs
"The trembling drops of glittering dew
"Are scattered as with vigorous wings
"It mounts the glorious arch of blue                         40

[May 1830]

MS:  I
First Publication:   **The Adventures of Ernest Alembert:  A Fairy Tale.**  By
Charlotte Brontë, ed., T. J. Wise, London:  Privately
printed, 1896


32          **Fragment**


Now rolls the sounding Ocean
'Neath nights tenebrious wing
How wild is that eternal motion
That sullen slow unceasing swing
Of waves & billows loudly roaring                             5
Under cloud-becurtained skies
Up the scattered foam-bell flies
While down the dashing torrent's pouring
And rejoicing in the storm
Glides through all the aeriel form                           10
Of some snow [w]hite sea-bird fair
Borne on sleek wings light as air
Now the dull uncertain sound
Of rising wind moans oft around

May 29 1830

MS:  F(1)
First Publication:   SHB C and B


37

33
    Now sweetly shines the golden sun
    The howling wind is still
    The glorious light of day is flung
    O'er every vale & hill

    On yonder bank myself I'll rest          5
    A blue stream wanders by
    In whose smooth wavy liquid breast
    Inverted glows the sky

    The sweet wild flower's are loosely cast
    In wreaths & clusters round         10
    I'll watch the waves meandering past
    To far off regions bound

    I'll gaze upon the world below
    The clear translucent sky
    The shrubs & trees that downward grow    15
    The swift clouds sailing by

    Each shines with dim and wat'ry gleam
    A pale & gentle light
    Encircles them with solenn beam
    Like glory of the night         20

    The Willow waving o'er my head
    Waves also neath my feet
    Reflected in the rivers bed
    The heavens & branches meet.

    Lone drooping to the azure deep      25
    They seem to touch the cloud
    & there unmoved they calmly sleep
    Not e'en by Zephyrs bowed.

                    C Bronte
                    May 31 1830

MS:  F(1)
First Publication:  Shorter 1923

34       **THE EVENING WALK:**
**AN IRREGULAR POEM:  BY THE**
**II MARQUIS OF DOURO**

When August glowed with fervid summer pride
And noon had faded into eventide
A fresh breeze through my unclosed lattice playing
Amid a vines young tendrils wanton straying
Asked me with voice more sweet than harp or lute       5
Or merry dulcimer or gentle Flute
To walk abroad & taste the balmy air
Which violets of the vale & lillies fair
Had filled with fragrance, as it o'er them breathed.
Upon the green grass in rich clusters wreathed      10
They lay--when the wind passed each raised its head
And o'dorous perfumes softly calmly shed
Pouring delights upon the sweeping gale
E're twiligh[t] came their beauties bright to veil
Their loveliness in sheltering leaves to fold      15
While clouds of night high o'er the skies are rolled
& shadows blacken meadow plain & wold

    Not unheeded spoke the wind
    Murm'ring in my ear
    Soon I saw afar behind      20
    The thund'rous city peer

Above its girdling green-robed hills
Above its forests wild & high
And the tower which with wonder fill[s]
Each stranger--clave the sky      25

    No mist slept on it's head
    N[o] cloud begirt it round,
  & the majesty about it shed
With awe my spirit bound.
Then I turned away opprest      30
Toward the glories of the west
    I could gaze for aye
    On the proud array
Of the sunset heavens at close of day
    At the radiant dyes      35
    Which paint the skies
When Appollo to his haven hies
And bathed in seas of golden light
Diving he leaves the world to night
There the roses crimson blend      40
With purple bright that soft ascend

39

To the stainless blue
Whose heavenly hue
Robes the vault which distills translucent dew
On the thirsty earth                                    45
Giving joyous birth
To the signs of vegetable mirth
& while each clear drop is lit with glory
The pearl-strew[n] plains like a frost looks hoary

On splendour of the gorgeous west                      50
At length I ceased to gaze
& my dazzled eyes sought in the east
The soft restoring haze;
That dusky dun-clad twilight brings
Ever on it's rosy silent wings                         55
There a belt of paleest red
All th' horizon circled
Dimly it did wane & fade
With indistinctly melting shade
Into the cerulean sky                                  60
As it calmly rose on high
Rivalling the rainbows hue
When it blended with the blue

Eastward I took my lonely way
Attracted by that aspect mild                          65
And as the last transcendant ray
Of the sun o'er verdant nature smiled

    I came to a pile of high gaunt rocks
    Whose Giant plumes were the shaggy oaks
        Now grimly waving                              70
    And a mighty stream went howling by
    Whose voice arose to the lofty sky
        As wildly raving
    It chafed its bounds of solid stone
    And the desert rung with the ceaseless moan        75
    While the caverned rocks sent back the sound
    Which through all that region echoed round--

A while by that impetuous flood
Wrapped in thought I silent stood
    Till splashed with spray                           80
    I turned away
& Aided by the sinking day
Emerging from that chasm wild
Where in solitude the rocks were piled
I ent[e]red a grassy plain                             85
Embosoned in mountains towring aloft

40

It smiled with a garb of green herbage soft
Like emeral[d] circlets which fairies trace
When their morrice dance they merrily pace
The enormous gloom was round it cast                    90
Of a forest of frowning Pine-wood vast
     Which stretched o'er every mountain grey
     Was closed all the night long
     & even in meridian day
     Night reigned those hills among                     95
          For blackened there a shade
          By nodding branches made
And in the solemn twiligh[t] mirk
[A] hundred noisesome reptiles lurk
The matted grass or bushy brake                         100
Conceal the slyly creep[ing] snake
While hemlock rears its baleful head
Where thickest is the darkness shed


     But no loathsome creature crept
     Through that flowry plain                           105
     There 'mid sweets the sk[y]lark slept
     Chanting in dreams the strain
Which soon the morning skies should thrill
The air of dawn with music fill
     When on its spotted breast                          110
The first light gleamed amid some cloud
While far below in misty shroud
     The earth is laid at rest


Now above the horizon bar
The quiet moon rose o'er the world                      115
Nights banner decked with many a star
     Was silently unfurled


In one continuous sheet of light
& yellow lustre swathed
Meek nature lay & faintly bright                        120
Her hills & tree's were bathed
          With floods of glory
          Gushing from on high
          On rocks made hoary
          By splendour of the sky                       125


The plain, I wandred o'er
          Uncertain w[h]ere to go
Until I heard before - - -
          A warbling streamlet flow

41

Soon I crossed the narrow brook                            130
& my onward way I took
Till I reached a haunted dell
Down the green sides sloping fell
'Broidering moss spread o'er each bank
'Neath my footsteps softly sank                            135
Purple violet's frequent pept
From where with closed buds they slept
    Nestling in their leaves
Coming night had deepened round
On the solitary ground                                     140
And the bottom of the dell
As it far receding fell
From the fair moons silver light
Which peirced the gath'ring gloom of night
Indistinct & dark appeare[d]                               145
Covered with a dusky veil
Through whic[h] no fair object peered
Star illumined faint & pale

From the gloom methought I heard
    Music sweet ascend                                     150
Like the voice of singing bird,
    Sweetly did it blend

Strain of Thrush & nightingale
In one superhuman song
Pensive as a wind-harp's wail                              155
    It poured the air along

Fairies were in the hollow green
    Feasting amid wild flowers
And the harmony came from them unseen
    Passing in joy the hours                               160
I knew the trip of their little feet
    By the rustling grass far down
As o'er it they flew elastic fleet
    Where it waved in that region lone

I heard the song of the elves arise                        165
    And O twas sweetly flung
On the breeze as it mingled with whose signs
    Thus the tiny spirits sung

Come fill with sparkling dew
Each gold & crystal cup                                    170
Let the clarion and the horn
Full joyously resound
Lo the lamps of eve are twinkling

And the stars of night are up
And the music of the night-bird                               175
Is gushing all around
The flowers close their leaflets
And listen to the tone
Dull howling through those ancient trees
'Tis the hoarse wild winds moan                              180

That blast has broken from its hold
    With might of thunders roar
O'er the trembling vault of heaven rolled
    O'er the mountains sumits hoar
        Heark how it rushes                                 185
        And furiously gushes
    Adown that narrow vale--
        The stern oaks bend
        their strong roots rend
    'Neath that triumphant gale                             190

    Now feirce tumult cease
    Loud wind rest in peace
    Restrain thy wearying
    Tumultuous breath
    And let a silence come                                  195
    Frozen & fast as death

Now stopped the merry danceing
    I heard it no more
Yet by light moon beams glancing
    I saw the fairies soar                                  200

On soft & noiseless silken wing
The calm air gently winnowing
    They swiftly rose on high
Then slowly disappeared
    And melted in the sky                                   205

Now the hush of moonlight lay
    On all the hills around
& no murmuring sign of lightsome day
Peirced the still night profound

I yet walked on unheeding                                   210
Over the lonely plain
The stars of heaven reading
Like wand'rer on the main

Whe[n] sudden the sound of a torrent fell
   Loud rushing on my ear 215
& I saw through trees a cat'ract swell
   That roared impetuous near

Strangely that ceaseless thunder broke
   Those vast solitary woods
In silence dead that eloquent spok[e] 220
   It ever rolled its floods

Eagles that shoot on wings athwart the sky
Or soar sublimely wrap[t] in solemn cloud
That build their inaccessible nests on high
Mid oaks, whose knarled trunks in homage bowed 225
Conceal the erie in their leafy shroud

Sleep sometimes & the Lion doth also rest
In forest den couching till close of day
Till the sun sinking in the crimson west
Shall call him forth again to hunt for prey 230
& for his royal food the subject beasts to slay
Huge Behemoth shakes not for aye the ground
At night he lays his vast bulk under trees
Whose thick leaves lull him to repose with sound
Of hoarsely murm'ring waters of the seas 235
When swell the azure waves unswept by wind or breeze.

   But running brook & river
      Still rush along their way
   They stop their courses never
      By midnight or noonday 240

   Though stars to soothe their raving
   May sweetly o'er them play
   Yet still their green bank laveing
   They hold the chanelled way

   Though quiet moonlights streaming 245
      Unmindful that still ray
   Through emerald foliage gleaming
      They churn the silver spray

How weary seems that lasting task
Still in motion on to pour 250
Ne'er in fixed calm to bask
Like mirror by the sounding shore

Then the trees might droop unshaken
Round the quiet bay
And the silence then might waken                    255
Birds to chant their lay

Inarticulate anthems hymning
Perched on slender twig & bough
Their music o'er the surface skimming
While the stream rests from it's flow              260
& no longer past meandering
    Doth eternal go

When again the river glides
From Binding chains set free
Each majestic wavelet rides                         265
Laden with melody
Bearing it's tribute waters
    Towards the boundless sea
Then in awful billows heaving
    With its own loud harmony                       270

These were my thoughts as home my steps I turned
By clouds which sailed along the horizon warned:
I cast one last glance at the lovely moon
To see if yet In the wide heavens she shone
Lo! curtaining mists o're all the sky were spread    275
& weary with nightly watching she'd veiled her beauteous head.

            Marquis of Douro    C. Brontë    June 28 1830

MS:  D(2)
First Publication:  Shorter 1923

**35**           **Miss Hume's Dream**

            One summer's eve as Mariane stood
            In pensive melancholy mood
                By lattice of her room
            Gazing with wrapt and solemn eyes
            And oft' repeated mournful sighs           5
                And face which spoke of gloom

            Towards w[h]ere a tow'ring palace peered
            Bove a wide extending wood
            Its high head statelily upreared
            O'er tall trees stretching many a rood.    10

She gazzed & gazed till tears 'gan start
From sad deep fountain of her heart
   Then slowly turned away
She sat her down to think alone
And by herself to mourn and moan                    15
   And weep till close of day

Then she took a net-work veil
To 'Broider graceful flowers thereon
But O! her face turned deadly pale
The While she laboured all alone                     20

To think That Arthur was not there
The mighty work with her to share
   And wind the cobweb silk
On ivory bobins beautiful
Or for her flow'r-vase wreaths to cull              25
   Of lillies white as milk

But suddenly she heard a voice
From the green shady lane below
Which made her starting to rejoice
And down the stairs she swift did go                30

And when the pleasant walk she gained
Bright tears of joy her blue eyes rained
   For <u>he</u> was standing there
Forward she sprang, but sudden stopped
& from her tongue no welcome dropped               35
   Arthur like empty air

Full fast before her, noiseless flies
With an upbraiding ghost-like look
Fixed were his dark & lustrous eyes
No sigh or murmur from him broke                    40

He raised his hand & beckoned Her
No sound was heard no rust'ling stir
   As swift he glided on
Until they reached the churchyard gate
The hour now had waxed late                         45
   Had set the golden sun

The moon had risen and many a star
Looked from the windows of the sky
Like lamps bright beaming from afar
They glowed in the blue arc on high                 50

A hollow breeze blows o'er the grav[es]
And in the blast <all> wildly waves
    The unmown whistling grass
Each monument in moonlight sleeps
Their sides the tall-grown rank weed <sweeps>                55
    As on the loud winds pass

Now the church in ruins bowed
They ent[e]red soft & silently
And lo! enwraped with snowy shroud
In the midst did form of Arthur lie                         60

Marianne trembling with the shock
Sent forth a loud & peircing scream
By which the spell of midnight <broke>
She raised her head it was a dream

                Islander lord C Wellesley    June 29 1830

MS:  F(1)
First Publication:  Winnifrith PCB
Text:  ll. 51, 55, 63:  the right-hand edge of the page has been torn
    off


**36**                   Silver moon how sweet thou shinest
                         In the midnigh[t] sky
                         Hollow wind how wild thou whinest
                         Through the vault on high

                    Very pretty especially the third          5
                    line I declare  (writes again
                    seems puzzled--reads) -----

                         The heavens how beautiful they are
                         Majestically dark
                         They are bedecked with many a star   10

                    Oh! dear (I can't get on--
                    (stamps & seems in a passion)
                    shark--clark bark stark--
                    mark lark.  Ah that'll do
                    (writes again.  then reads)               15

                         Fit sojourn for the lark.


                              47

Capital. how lucky to find it
but--it came quite apropos.
Writes for about half an hour
then reads again)                                    20

        When he comes to the realms
        On high
        Like wandring Savoyard
        To teach the people of the sky
        The music of nature's bard              25

        How lightly sail the clouds along

        While he continues there
        Electrified by his sweet song
        He even charms the air
        Presumptuous it would be of me          30
        To tell his magic deeds
        For he enchants the very sea
          & spell-binds even reeds
        And the nightingale he has his Powers
          When singing neath the moon           35
        In those soft melancholy hours
        Held sacred to nights moon

                              [July 1830]

MS:  A
First Publication:  Ratchford, Web, partial; **Studies in Romanticism,**
                    20 (Winter 1981)


**37**                    I obey your gentle call ye
                          pearly threads of light & Oh!
                          like g[u]ardian spirits
                          watch by my couch this night

                              [July 1830]

MS:  A
First Publication:  **Studies in Romanticism,** 20 (Winter 1981)


48

**38**     4 volume of the Plays of Islands,
           That is Emily's Branwell's Ann's and my lands;
           And now I bid a kind and glad good-bye
           To those who o'er my book cast indulgent eye.

                                              [July 30 1830]

MS:  H
First Publication:  Alexander EW


**39**              **Lines To The Aragua a river of the**
                    **x CAUCASIAN MOUNTAINS     BY D**


           Mighty river bold gushing
           From the mountains snow clad heigh[t]
           Wildly furious onward rushing
           As nought could they wrath abat[e]
               Soon shall thy anger cease                    5
               Soon Thy waves in peace
           Soft subsiding still & slow
           Calmly gliding gently flow

           Lovely valleys sleeping mildly
           In the frozen hills embrace                       10
           Icerocks round them soaring wildly
           Give their beauty fairer grace
               There let thy waters glide
               Verdure on each side
           Shall brighten, as the azure wave                 15
           Peacefully its banks does lave

           When the soft moonbeams are playing
           On thy deep & rapid stream
           All in web of light arraying
           Dyed with their own pearly gleam                  20
               Dost see Elborous
               Flit forth in winged hosts
           While with hoarse tumults might
           Trembles the ebon car of night


                              49

Or doth music breathed from heaven                25
Serenade <each> giant hill
Pierce the yawning chasms riven
E'en stern rocks with sweetness fill
    Solemnly & slow
    Heard the melodios flow                30
Soon awful Gara listning bends
& Kasibeck on high attends

Now in storms of grandeur pealing
Faintly now it dies away
Then again terrific swelling                       35
Listen to the music play
    On thy foaming tide
    The last calm note hath died
Like the strain of skylark tone
The giants are into silence gone                   40

August 13 1830     Douro

x  The Aragua rushes at times with violence amid masses of ice & snow And
then glide[s] gently through the Green vales of Georgia . . . . . .

MS:  D(1)
Not previously published
Text:  The note at the end is Charlotte's

**40**       **MORNING BY MARQUIS DOURO**

Lo! the light of the morning is flowing
    Through radiant portals of gold
Which Aurora in crimson robes glowing
    For the horses of fire doth unfold

See Apollo's burnished car                         5
Glorifies the east afar
As it draws the horizon nigher
As it climbs the heavens higher
Richer grows the amber light
Fairer, more intensely bright                      10
Till floods of liquid splendor roll
O'er all the earth from pole to pole

```
Hark! the birds in the green forest bower
   Have beheld the suns chariot arise
And the humblest the stateliest flower                          15
   Are arrayed in more beautiful dyes

   Now while the woodland choir are singing
   Opening buds fresh odours flinging
   And while natures tuneful voice
   Calls on all things to rejoice                               20
   I cannot join the common gladness
   'tis to me a time of sadness
   All these sounds of mirth impart
   Nought but sorrow to my heart

But I love eve'nings still quiet hour                           25
   The whispering twilight breeze
The damp dew's invisible shower
   Conglobing in drops on the trees

   Then is heard no sound or tone
   But the night-bird singing lone                              30
   Peacefully adown the vale
   It passes on the balmy gale
   Ceases oft the pensive strain
   Solemn sinking & again
   Philomela sends her song                                     35
   To wander the night winds along

While silver-robed Luna is beaming
   Afar in the heavens on high
And her bright train of planets are gleaming
   Like gems in the dome of the sky                             40

   From the firmament above
   Down they gaze with looks of love
   On the minstrel all unheeding
   Still their ears entranced feeding
   With <the> notes of sweetest sound                          45
   Gushing forth on all around
   Music not unfit for heaven
   But to earth in mercy given
   Thou dost charm the mourner[s] heart
   Thou dost pensive joy impart                                 50
   Peerless Queen of harmony
   How I love thy melody

            August 22 1830     Marquis of Douro
```

MS:  D(1)
First Publication:  Wise RCK 1917

**41**
O spirits of the sky were there
Strange enchantmen[t] filled the air
I have seen from each dark cloud
Which in gloom these vales did shroud
White robed beings glance & fly                      5
& rend the curtain from the sky
I have seen their, wings of light
Streaming o'er the heavens height
I have seen them bend & kiss
Those eternal vales of bliss                          10
& I've seen them close the cloud
& I've seen them fast enshroud
The edens of unfading bloom
All in mist & all in gloom
O the darkness of that night                          15
O the grandeur of that sight
None can speak it none can tell
Heark I hear the thunder swell
Crashing through the firmament
'tis by wrothful spirits sent                         20
Warning me to say no more
Now hath ceased the dreadful roar
Now a calm is all around
Not a breath & not a sound
That frozen stillness stirs to break                  25
This is natures silent sleep
Sudden night above me springs
Sudden music round me rings
Now again the spirits dance
Again the sunbeams glance                             30
This is light & this is mirth
All of heaven not of earth
Up hath risen purple morn
Love & joy & life are born
I veil my eyes with a holy fear                       35
For the coming visions no mortal may bear

[August 1830]

MS:   D(1)
Not previously published

52

Some love sorrows dismal howls
Write verses on her sighs & scowls
  And rant about her mourning dress
Her long black funeral array
Her veil which shuts out light & day                    5
  And love her not the less

Although she sits with woful face
On some old monumental tomb
Where yellow skulls & bones have place
Where corpses rot in churchyard gloom                   10

I wish some eve as thus she's weeping
While sober men are soundly sleeping
Amid the obscurity of night
From out its grave a ghost woul[d] start
And make her throat receive her heart                   15
  And give her sore affright

Or catch her by the long black gown
No matter how the lady screams
Into the damp vault drag her down
Where sun or moonlight never beams                      20

But cheerfulness full well I know
& oft Ive' seen her ruddy face
Her lips whence streams of pleasure flow,
Wher[e] tones of joy have place

One morn as the skylark tuned his song                  25
Afar in the heavens on high
I walked forth the green fields & the uplands among
To list' the sweet tones from the sky

    Onward I sprang
    While light music rang                              30
Above & below & around.
For the black-bird the linnet the dove & the thrush
Filled the air with a warbling sound

The fresh breeze of dawn passed o'er the hills
  Laden with insence of flowers                         35
It sung with the fountain & rippled the rills
  & sighed softly throug[h] the green bow[e]rs

53

Joy was in earth & joy was in heaven
   And joy was also in me
I felt gladness & health & strong might given          40
By the wind of the morning free

While I brushed the dew with hasty feet
From golden cups & clover sweet
I felt on my arm a touch like light
Or the downy wings of some gentle sprite               45
& e're I could turn myself around
I heard the sweet tones & the silvery sound
   Of an oft-heard well-known voice
& one stood by in a robe that shone
As the soft fair clouds which array the moon           50
Her radiant eyes were of lucid blue
& her crown of flowers rich odours threw
   It was her whom all lands & nations bless
   & her welcome name is cheerfulness

She gave me a sign with winning grace                  55
While dimpled smiles illumed her face
   I followed as she led
On we passed by moor and lea
   Plain & vale & stream and Tree
Over hills w[h]ere torrents rushed                     60
Down deep glens where whirlwinds gushed
   Nought could stop our way

Now Apollo reached the west
   Diving in the oceans wave
Thetis' bowers afford him rest                         65
Billows vast his coursers lave

When we gained a mighty plain
   Stretching to the horizons bound
Verdant as the robe of spring
Flowers of summer strewed the ground                   70
Gloomy silence held her reign
& the skys exalteded dome
Shone with glory of the stars
Beauteous gems of twilights throne

Suddenly a song arose                                  75
Through the obscurity of night
On my sight fair visions grew
Lovely forms all swiftly flew
Upsprang a golden light

Then merry music rang                                          80
And bright lamps radiance flang
On thousand burning gems
Who sent back the dazzling streams
& the green grassy earth & the mild ambient air
Glowed with the strong insufferable glare                      85

I viewed it for an instant then night in double gloom
Fell around on the world with the silence of the tomb
The moon no more her pale light shed
No glimmering stars were o'er my head
    For I lay asleep in a curtained bed                         90
& when I had awakened
The apparitions all were fled

Instead of the musics heavenly strain
I heard the fast-descending rain
Rattle against my window pane                                  95
I tossed about & strove in vain
To sleep or slumber once again

So, At length I rose
& put on my clothes
The whole house slept                                         100
So I softly crept
Down the long winding stair
& passed the gate by bribing the guard
& I bent my steps to the poultry yard
    When who should I meet                                     105
    At a turn of the street
But Tree, with a cock & hen
I collared the theif & bade him say
Why he was at this time o' day
But Tree got free & skulked away                              110
    & I never caught him again

            August 27 1830      Charles Wellesley

MS:   D(2)
Not previously published
Text:  l. 12:  "while" is preceded by an almost undecipherable but
       uncanceled word that looks like "when"


**43**          Death is here I feel his power
                Here Are trophies of his might
                Ruthless warrior that fair flower
                    Hath fallen beneath thy blight

He hath cast his dart at thee                          5
Sister thou art gone for aye
He hath set thy spirit free
    & it hath fled away

Soon the grave will be thy bed
Tears no more shall dim thine eye                      10
Thou wilt rest that weary head
    All calm & peacefully

Undisturbed will be thy sleep
Nought can break its still repose
Though the worm may o'er the[e] creep                  15
    It cannot raise thy woes

I have shut thy glazed eye
I have heard thy funeral knell
Now I hush the struggling sigh
    Sister fare thee well                              20

[August 1830]

MS: D(2)
First Publication: BST 1942


**44**     **ON SEEING AN ANCIENT DIRK IN THE ARMOURY
OF THE TOWER OF ALL NATIONS BLOODSTAINED
WITH THREE DISTINCT SPOTS, OF WHICH MARKS
NONE HAVE YET BEEN ABLE TO ERASE, BY THE
M. DOURO.**

---

Dagger what heart hath quivered neath thy blow?
Whence fell these three dark spots to stain the steel.
All else is bright:  was it a human Foe
Who did the rankling of thy strong blade feel?
Or has some ruffian grasped that jewelled hilt         5
And Peirced of innocense the quiet breast.
Hast thou the glorious blood of martyrs spilt
Or torn the mighty warrior's lofty crest.

Perhaps in gloomy Forest thou hast slain
The tiger or the Lion,--horrid thing--                    10
Till hot blood from his heart thy brightness stain.
Didst thou from him loud roars of anguish wring.
Why midst each glancing sword and shield and spear
Which dart around insufferable day
Dost thou alone tarnished and marked appear              15
Not sending forth an undefiled ray.

Ages on Ages long have passed away
Since thou wast ruthless in the battle plain,
Since chieftains clad in polished war array
Have with thee triumphed o'er the bloody slain.          20
Thou hast not yet forgot the purple streams
That slaked of old thy savage thirst for gore.
Black mid the radiance which around it gleams
Appear those remnants of the days of yore.

What spell pronounced by the unholy tongue               25
O wizard or magician gave command
That those three drops in wrath or treachery wrung
For rolling years untold would steadfast stand
Irraseable by power of mortal hand.
Dagger thou knowst not; voiceless is the crowd           30
Of ancient arms that clothe this spacious wall.
Voiceless and speechless are those nobles grand
Who bore ye once:  now each in gloomy pall
Lies deaf even to his own shrill battle call
Which erst had roused him from the slumber deep          35
And girt him with a giant's vigorous might
Sent him like thunder or the whirlwind sweep
To death or victory in the glorious fight
Victry's reward and death's eternal night.

                    August 30 1830    DOURO.

MS:  Unlocated:  last known to be in the library of Sir Alfred Law
First Publication:  **The Bookman,** November 1925


45        **A TRAVELLER['S] MEDITATIONS**
          **BY the Marquis of Douro**

          This wide world I have compassed round
             Beheld each verdant state & shore
          I have been where nought but the sullen sound
             Was heard of oceans roar

Where boundless liquid plains were spread                5
Bright in the tropic solar beam
From the blue arch overhead
    Rushed down a burning stream

Oh I have lain while twilights robe
Wraped the heavens & wraped the globe                    10
Stretched on the deck for a lonely pillow
Listning the wind & the rolling billow
Watching each wavelet sink & rise
Neath the gold light of the evening skies
While whispered around me the Zephyr calm               15
Sweeter than music & softer than balm
Each breeze seemed the voice of a spir[i]t on high
Speaking of peace in the tones of the sky
    Some went past with rushing swell
    Others more mild on the waters fell                  20
    Scarce heaving with their gentle breath
    The rippling wavelets snowy wreath
    Subsiding as the moon arose
    & threw her light on their liquid snows
    Which melted away & appeared again                   25
    Checked by the restless main
    As if when they saw her silver beam
    They loved to sport in the pearly gleam
    A ceaseless murmur went up from the Ocean
    Which told of his never ending motion                30
    Of the waves that eternally roll & rage
    War against the <solid> caverns wage
        Sinking & swelling
        Like sea monster yelling
Unseen in tenebrious night                               35
    Loud roars the dull thunder
    That old still surface under
Far hid from the regions of light
    That fathomless tomb
    That kingdom of gloom                                40
Where darkness aye reigns in his night

& I have been on icy hill
    Awe at the thought my soul doth fill
Unrivalled mid Alps it towers
Sternly its form o'er Gallia towers                      45
    Clad in robe of purest white
    Radiant as the lunar light
    Rearing its bald head on high
    To a clear unclouded sky
    Cold & chill imensity                                50
    Subject giants stand around

Wastes of snow its limits bound
Save where far below is seen
Golden fields & vineyards green
<Tis> Ausonias's fruitful plains                         55
Where all-giving Ceres reigns

O'er all the earth I've wandered long
In every land of every tongue
Now I come to my own loved home
Ne'er again from its bounds to roam                      60
What though those I knew are dead
Though my kin from earth are fled
Yet the same woods & rills & trees
Murmur & sing in the same sweet breeze
& I can sit in the forest bower                          65
& solace my heart with some wild flower
That looks from the green grassy ground
At the dead leaflets strewn around
Speaking thought voiceless & empty of sound
Bidding all gloomy care depart                           70
Soothing the passions & calming the heart

                    September 3 1830      Douro

MS:   D(1)
Not previously published


**46**     Haste bring us the wine cup
           & let it be full
           Fully fill it to the brim up
           't will make e'en the dull
           Set his feet a-dancing                        5
           Twinkling & glancing
           While the tabor the pipe & the lute
           The thundering drum & the flute
                Are ringing around
                Hark the merry sound!                    10

           Arise I say Arise guests
           Dismiss care from your quests

```
     See the wine trembles
       In purple light
Its radiance resembles,                                          15
     The amethyst bright
     Sip guests sip
     Raise it to your lip
Fear not the harmless cup
     Drink the sweet nectar up                                   20
       List to my song
     It is like as the nightengales singing among
       Old forest trees
       Where murmurs the breeze
     & bears the rich music the calm air along                   25
       Nature is my dearest mother
       I will never own another
         And I am her child
         Untameable wild
Like the strong mountain eagle my royal brother                  30
I was c[r]adled like him in a cloud
     & the winds as they rushed <or swept>
Rocked our cold misty shroud
     Till the two innocents slept
         < > his strong beak and talons                          35
       & the golden ring in his eye
     Methinks I see him now
A speck in the azure sky
     He is soaring to the thunder
     Or swiftly swe[e]ping under                                 40
Arched rocks & mountains majestically high
     Whose bright silver fountains
     Spring up to the sky
Eagle farewell I shall see thee no more
From my sight thy wings have borne thee, to Appollo's            45
         chariot soar.
     Unwinking may'st thou gaze
       Fearlesly aspire
       Thy circlet of fire
May bear the sun's most ardent blaze                             50
```

                                          [Sept 1830]

MS:   D(1)
Not previously published
Text:  l. 35:  the first word is undecipherable

60

**47**     CONCLUDING AD[D]RESS

```
Reader farewell
   Hark my note of
      triumph swell
   my labour finished
      my trouble diminished          5
though twas tedious & long
   Heres my last
      Concluding
         Song
```

[September 1830]

MS:  D(1)
First Publication:  Ratchford Web


**48**          I think of thee when the moonbeams play
                   On the placid water's face
              For thus thy blue eyes lustrous ray
                   Shone with resembling grace

              I think of thee when the snowy swan           5
                   Glides calm[l]y down the stream
              Its plumes the breezes scarcely fan
                   Awed by their radiant gleam

              For thus I've seen the loud winds hush
                   To pass thy beauty by                    10
              With soft caress & playful rush
                   Mid thy bright tresses fly

              And I have seen the wild birds sail
                   In rings thy head above
              While thou hast stood like lily pale          15
                   Unknowing of their love

              O for the day when once again
                   Mine eyes will gaze on thee!
              But an ocean vast a sounding main
                   An ever howling sea                      20
              Roll us between with their billows green
                   High tost tempestuously.

[October 1830]

61

MS: J
First Publication: Shorter 1918

**49**

        Long my anxious ear hath listend
          For the step that neer returned
        And my tearful eye hath glistened
        And my heart hath inly burned
                But now I rest                    5

        Natures self seemed clothed in mourning
          Even the starlike wood[l]and flower
        With its leaflets fair adorning
          Pathway of the Forest Bower
                Drooped its head                  10

        From the Cavern of the mountain
          From the groves that crowned the hill
        From the stream & from the fountain
          Sounds prophetic murmured still
                Betokening greif                  15

        Boding winds came fitful sighing
          Throug[h] the tall & leafy trees
        Birds of omen wildly crying
          Sent their yells upon the breeze
                Wailing round me                  20

        At each sound I paled & trembled
          At each step I raised my head
        Hearkening if it his resembled
          Or if news that he was dead
                Were come from far                25

        All my days were days of weeping
          Thoughts of grim despair were stirred
        Time on leaden feet seemed creeping
          Long heart-sickness hope deferred
                Cankered my heart                 30

                [October 1830]

MS: J
First Publication: Shorter 1918

Murk was the night: nor star, nor moon,
   Shone in the cloud-wrapped sky,
To break the dull, tenebrous gloom
   Of the arched vault on high,

When Naughty, with his dog and gun,                    5
   Walked lonely o'er the moor;
True the shooting-season had not begun,
   But poachers commence before.

The howling winds blew fierce around,
   The rain drove in his face,                 10
And as Naughty heard the hollow sound
   He quickened his creeping pace;

For, as each hoarse, sepulchral blast
   Drew slow and solemn near,
It seemed like spirits sailing past              15
   To his affrighted ear.

For he was on a dreadful errand bent
   To the ancient witch of the moor:
A delegate by his comrades sent
   To consult the beldam hoar.                 20

Now yelled the wind with more terrible din,
   Now rattled the rain full fast,
And, noiselessly gliding, forms were seen
   As around his eyes he cast;

When a rustling sound in the heather he heard:   25
   Starting, he turned about;
Was it a spirit?  Was it a bird?
   No, a hare sprang trembling out!

The shot went 'Whizz!' and the gun went 'Bang!'
   A flash illumed the air;                    30
Far and wide the moor with echo rang
   As down dropped the luckless hare.

He ran to the spot, and, lo! there lay
   A woman on the hard heath bed,
Whose soul had left its breathless clay,         35
   For the witch of the moor was dead!

       Charlotte Brontë.  October 14, 1830

MS: Unknown
First Publication: Shorter 1923

**51**      **THE VIOLET BY CHARLOTTE**

1   One eve as all the radiant west
    Far-beaming with the liquid gold
    Of sunset, gilt the mountains crest
    Girdling the sky with outlines bold

2   & flung a broad & mellow light                    5
    Around the rocks that rose on high
    As pillars for the throne of night
    Then shading soft the eastern sky

3   I stood amid a desert vast
    Nor golden feild nor mead was there          10
    No tree or grove their shadow cast
    Or shook their tresses on the air

4   But one wide solemn wilderness
    Whose aspect filled the mind with fear
    Showed Nature in her sternest dress           15
    With rugged brow & Face severe.

5   Winds o'er that land have come & gone
    But voiceless & unblent with sound
    Of living song or human tone
    They ceaseless sigh & murmur round            20

6   Yet oft the lonely traveller hears
    A sugh* as of some distant stream
    And lo! far off in gloom appears
    A mighty waters azure gleam

       *This most expressive word is surely more worthy
       of being adopted into the English language than
       many of the foreign phrases we delight in.

7   No white sail glideth o'er its breast            25
    No snowy seamew cuts the waves
    But all unburdened & at rest
    The passing surge that lone shore laves

8    Life in these wilds has ceased to be
      Not e'en the eagles royal wing             30
      Waves in the sky.  No red-deer free
      Make[s] with his cry this desert ring

9    My heart quaked at the silence dead
      The utter silence reigning there
      An incubus, an awful dread              35
      With leaden pow'r oppressed the air

10   At length a gentle breeze up-sprang
      With low wild moaning on it swept
      It seem[ed] AEolian music rang
      As softly on the ear they crept        40

11   And wakened by that harp-like blast
      Thoughts rose within my spirits cell
      Of those who in long ages past
      Attuned the muses hallowed shell

12   *Of him, the Bard that swept the lyre     45
      Whose sounding strings were stained with gore
      Whose aged eyes shot heavenly fire
      Beaming beneath his forehead hoar


    *Homer


13   All honour, to that mighty one
      Let earth with his great praises ring     50
      Child of the self illumined sun
      How didst thou strike the trembling string

14   While music like a mountain flood
      Rolled forth as swept thy hand along
      Wars, horrid wars & streaming blood     55
      Ensanguined deep thy martial song

15   Greece thy fair skies have flung their light
      On mightiest of this sunlit world
      Genius enthroned in glory bright
      O'er thee her banner hath unfurled      60

16   Now desolate by time decayed
      Thy solemn temples mouldring lye
      While black groves throw Cimerian shade
      Beneath a still transparent sky

17    Degenerate are thy sons & slaves          65
      Athens & Sparta are no more
      Unswept by swans Eurotas laves
      As yet its laurel shaded shore

18    Parnassus now uplifts her head
      Forsaken of the holy nine               70
      They from her heights for aye have fled
      And now in fair Britania shine

19    If rising from the silent tomb
      Thy tragic bards could see thee now
      What solemn clouds of greif & gloom      75
      Would shade each spirits lofty brow

20    How would the haunted air resound
      With moanings of each shadowy lyre
      How would earth tremble at the sound
      And quake before the wailing dire        80

21    He* that with soft but stately tread
      Passed solemn o'er the Grecian stage
      What tears of Pity would he shed
      At sight of thy base vasallage


      *Sophocles


22    The tender* & the terrible**             85
      Commingling each their notes of woe
      One strain with rage divine would swell
      The other sadly sorrowing flow


      *Euripides           **Aeschylus


23    Though fair Ausonia too hath sunk
      And fallen from her high estate          90
      Though deeply she the cup hath drunk
      Of vengeance from the hand of Fate

24    Yet mid her mighty ruins oft
      Some beauteous flow'r is seen to bloom
      Peircing with radiance mildly soft        95
      Her crumbling cities cloudy gloom

25  Such he* that sang Jerusalem
    In strains as sweet as ever flow'd
    From harp of Mantuas glorious swain**
    Though heavens own fire within him glow'd          100

    *Tasso           **Virgil

26  But no faint star on thee hath shone
    O Greece since set those orbs of light
    Each in itself a quenchless sun
    Refulgently, divinely bright!

27  And said I set?  No still they beam                105
    With dazeling lustre far on high
    Aye sending forth a golden gleam
    O'er azure of the vaulted sky

28  And sons of Albion in that rank
    Shine crowned with honours they have won           110
    For deeply of the fount they drank
    The sacred fount of Helicon

29  Hail army of immortals hail!
    O Might I neath your banners march!
    Though faint my lustre faint & pale                115
    Scarce seen amid the glorious arch

30  Yet joy deep joy would fill my heart
    Nature unveil thy awful face
    To me a poets pow'r impart
    Thoug[h] humble be my destined place               120

    'Twas thus arose my ardent prayer
    Amid the desert solitude
    It reached the "Mighty Mothers" ear
    She saw me where I lowly stood

    And first a voice went sweeping by                 125
    On the wild wind that murmured round
    From the deep bosom of the sky
    Seemed to proceed that solemn sound

    Then shadowy vapours gathered fast
    Which shut from veiw the pale moon-light           130
    Swelled louder the triumphant blast
    High pealing with tumultuous might

67

The river's voice from distance far
Proclaimed some prodigy was nigh
Clouds veil'd from sight each glimmering star          135
And waned their splendour from the sky

I trembled as a brighter ray
Unknown from whence, illumed the air
Transforming twilight into day
As luna's beam of silver fair                          140

Now dawned upon my awe-struck eyes
A shape more beauteous than the morn
When radiant with a thousand dyes
The pearls of night her brow adorn

A womans form the vision wore                          145
Her lofty forehead touched the sky
Her crown, a rugged mountain hoar
Where plume-like trees waved solemnly

Down fell her mantle white as snow
An azure river girt her round                          150
That liquid belt did circling flow
With faint but never ceasing sound

The heavenly & the terrene globe
In lines of light were pictured fair
On foldings of her spotless robe                       155
Wide floating on the ambient air

Her dusky tresses dark as night
With crescent moon & stars were bound
As through black clouds shone out their light
In rays of glory beaming round                         160

A gracious smile illumed her face
As throned she sate on clouds of light
In attitude of heavenly grace
Beneath an arch like rainbow bright

& Sweet as the echos of the hill                       165
At length her voice the silence broke
In accents calm serene & still
Thus Nature condescending spoke

"Thy prayre hath reached me where I dewll
"In river or in sounding cave                          170
"By woodland bower by hidden dell
"Or under Oceans foamy wave

"Thou Would'st be one of that bright band
"The favoured children of the sky
"The chosen from each shore & land                      175
"Of deathless fame & memory

"Mortal I grant that high request
"(But dim thy beam & faint thy ray)
"Partake the glory of the blest
"Son of Apollo King of day                               180

"Laurel thy temples may not bind
"& In humbler sphere thy fate is set
"That for the more exalted mind
"But take yon lowly violet

"And press it mortal to thy heart                        185
"And wreath the floweret round thy brow
"O! never from that token part
"Till death thy energies shall bow

Thus spoke the glorious deity
Then passed in dazzling light away                       190
The mighty sovereign of the sky
Shone never with so bright a ray

I plucked the violet where it grew
Beside a stone, green moss amid
Its lovely leaflets bright with dew                      195
Like modest worth half seen half hid

Years have rolled o'er me since that night
Still doth the flower its perfume shed
Still shall it free from withering blight
Till I lie with the silent dead                          200

                              Marquis of Duro
                              Charlotte
                              Bronte

November 10 1830

MS:  G & D(2)
First Publication:  **The Violet.  A poem Written at the Age of Fourteen
            By Charlotte Brontë,** London:   Privately printed by
            Clement Shorter, 1916
Text:  All the notes are Charlotte's

## Lines on seeing the portrait of
### _____ Painted by De Lisle

Radiant creature is thy birth
Of the heavens or of the earth?
For those bright & beaming eyes
Speak the language of the skies
And methinks, upon thy tongue                    5
Dwells the songs by angels sung
Still & tranquil is the beam
That doth from those blue orbs stream
Like the azure moonlight sky
Like the lucid stars on high                     10
Rays of mind are darting thence
Mild & pure intelligence

Art thou then of spirit birth
Not a denizen of earth
No thou'rt but a child of clay                   15
Simply robed in white array
Not a gem is gleaming there
All as spotless snow is fair
Symbol Angel of thy mind
Meek benevolent & kind                           20
Sprightly as some beauteous fawn
Springing up at break of dawn
& Graceful bounding o'er the hills
To the music of the rills

What bright hues thy cheeks adorn                25
Like the blushes of the Morn!
How thy curled & glossy hair
Clusters o'er thy forehead fair
How the sportive ringlets deck
(golden Snow) Thy ivory neck
And thy hands so smooth & white                  30
Folded while the rosy light
Of a summer sunset sky
Gleams around thee gloriously
All the west one crimson flood
Pouring light o'er mount & wood                  35
Beauteous being most divine
I am thine & thou art mine

November 10            Marquis of Douro
                            1830
                        Charlotte
                         Bronte

MS: D(2)
First Publication: Shorter 1923

## 53     VESPER

I'll hang my lyre amid these ancient treess
And while the sad wind moans the chords among
Sweet forest music of the harp & breeze
Shall steal the circumambient air along
And I will sing meantime a low responsive song                5

What shall I sing?  wilt thou O! rising moon
Like a broad shield suspended in the east
Wilt thou attend some melancholy tune
While sleeps thy light upon the rivers breast
Whose swelling wavelets sink when by thy beam carest          10

No beauteous as thou art thy gentle ear
Would call my music rugged & mid clouds
Thou might'st offended hide thy silver car
And draw o'er heaven dark & sombre shrouds
Concealing all its hosts, marshalled in radiant crowds        15

What shall I sing then?  hark that sudden swell!
That rose in the old forests glimmering light
How like the tone of some old convent bell
Borne to the travellers ear at dead of night
Sounding in utter silence with a tenfold might               20

The rising wind hath stolen it from the strings
Of my sweet lyre suspended in yon tree
And now the wild wood with rich music rings
And thrilling cadences most bold and free
Are pealing round with heavenly melody                       25

I need not sing, the armies of the skys
Nights empress, & the dryad wood-nymphs fair
Would rather list the tones that now arise
And fill with harmony the twilight air
Sweet sounds for all the winds beneath the stars to bear     30

Then I will sit & listen, not a voice
Disturbs the unbroken stillness of this hour
No nestling bird, with faintly rustling noise
Raises the leaflets of the vernal bower
OR bends the spray where blooms the fruit betokning flowr     35

71

Even the chorister of night is still
Sweet Philomel restrains her customed song
Hushed are the murmers of the unseen rill
Creeping through matted grass & weeds along
Silent I too will be these solemn shades among                    40

                                                    Marquis of Douro

                    Novemtion 11           Charlotte Brontë
                    1830

MS:  B(1)
First Publication:  Shorter 1923


**54    MATIN**


Long hath earth lain beneath the dark profound
Of Silent-footed, planet-crested night
Now from the chains of slumber soft, unbound
She springs from sleep to hail, the glorious birth of light

A solemn Hush lay on her hills and woods                           5
Now as the day approaches, fast dispelling
For at the touch of the bright orient floods
Thousands of voices rise, in mingled murmurs swelling

First the suns glories tip the lofty hill
Then roll impetuous down the dusky vale                            10
Sings sweet in light the pebbled crystal rill
And joy expands the buds, of flowers that woo the gale

O! I might sing of pastures meads & trees
Whose verdant hue is tinged with solar beams
And I might sing of morns fresh bracing breeze                     15
That with awaking breath, riples the glassy-streams

And of the merry lark who 'soar's on high
Aye rising in his course toward the sun
Of his descending from the vaulted sky
To the expectant nest, when that sweet song is done               20

These I could sing, if thou wert near me now
Thou whom I love, my souls most fair delight
If the fair orbs that beam beneath thy brow
Shed on my darkling page their ray divinely bright

72

But no, great waters of the mighty deep                                          25
Howling like famished wolves roll us between
O! sad & bitter drops I mournful weep
To think of those vast leagues, of tossing billows green

Come from the fairy valley where thou dwellest
Shady and green, in Britains favoured isle                                        30
Come for all gloom & sadness thou dispellest,
And chase away my greif, with one sweet-sunny smile

Methinks I see thee sitting calm & lonely
Beneath th' umbrageous elm upon the lawn
Naught near thee but the woodland warblers only                                   35
Singing their matin song, and perhaps some gentle fawn

Or pearly dews, with thy light footstep brushing
Tripping as cheerful as the lambkin gay
Beside the cataract that thunderous rushing
Covers its shaken bank. with white churned bells and spray        40

Hark! Africa unto her desert calls thee
Where the bright sun pours his most fervid beams
Alas! the chain of love for aye enthrals me
My prisoned heart still pants in shifting dreams

I hear thy voice I see thy figure nightly                                         45
Thou; comest to me in midnight slum[b]er deep
And through the dark thy blue eyes glimmer brightly
Beaming upon me in, unquiet haunted-sleep

O! How I loved to hear thy low sweet singing
When evening threw her quiet shades around                                        50
The moon her mild light through the casement flinging
Seemed from the sky to list the half-angelic-sound

Thou to the scene a calmer beauty lending
With eyes steeped in the lingering light of song
And o'er the harp thy form so graceful bending                                    55
What melting notes then stole the dusky air along

O! when within thy still retired bower
Shall I once more hear that entrancing strain
Could I bring back the oft desired hour
My sad bereaved heart might beat with joy again                                   60

May I still hope for thy long-wished returning?
Come swiftly o'er the dark & raging sea
Come for my soul with hope deferred is burning
Then will I sing a song worthy of morn and thee.

Marquis of Douro
November 12 1830     Charlotte Brontë

MS:  B(1) & G
First Publication:  Wise RCK 1917

55       **Line[s] addressed to lady ZE sent with my portrait
         which she had asked me to give her.  By Marquis Douro**

Lady this worthless gift I send
    Obeying your command
Now to my poor request attend
    And give with willing hand

You have an aspect passing fair                     5
    A form of beauteous guise
A Juno-like majestic air
    And peircing, radiant eyes

And you have locks whose jetty light
    Is like the ravens wing                          10
And O! when from your forehead bright
    Those glossy locks you fling;

How down your shoulders fair they stream
    And down your stately neck
How richly with their dusky gleam                   15
    Your queen-like form they deck

Now from those ample treasures take
    One little sportive ring
And I will keep it for your sake
    And oft its praises sing                         20

I'll set it round with orient pearl
    Inclosed in case of gold
More I shall prize that single curl
    Than precious gems untold

Memmorial though frail yet fair                                    25
    Of one whose genius bright
Hath glorified our age with glare
    Of its unsetting light

And O! if ghastly Death should break
    The tie that binds us now                                      30
That token unto me shall speak
    Of the imperial brow

O'er it gracefully did stray
    And bright & burnished shone
Like the vine tendrils wanton play                                 35
    In times long past & gone.

                                        Marquis of Douro
                                        Charlotte Bronte
                                        November 12 1830

MS:  G
First Publication:  SHB C and B


**56**        **Reflections on the fate of neglected Genius**


        Mighty winds that sing on high
        Wildly, sweetly, mournfully,
        Bear my song through heavens dome
    Add from your stores some sweeter tone
    To fit it for its passage in the sky.                          5
        None can tell the bitter anguish
        Of those lofty souls that languish!
        With Grim Penury still dwelling
        Quenched by frowns their sacred fire
        All their powers within them swelling                      10
        Tortured by neglect to ire
    And inly conscious that the radiant light
    Of Genius is around them ever shed
    What marvel if their high poetic might
        Should burst to rage                                       15
        When hope is vanished
    And for the golden haired & bright-eyed queen
    A Ghastly band of brooding cares are seen


                                 75

Genius enthroned in light
Dost thou for those who at thine altars kneel                    20
One passing cloud of greif to dim thy radiance feel
    Speak from thy dwelling bright!
Hark! came that voice from thee
Omnipotent and great Divinity
    No 'twas but the breeze drew near                           25
    And seemed articulate to my ear
Answer thou that Dwell'st on high
Answer from the azure sky
O! this utter silence break
But do I to an unseen shadow speak                              30
A spiritual essence pure divine
Which the hearts of men enshrine
    And that sheds a holy ray
    Over animated clay
And for him in whom it dwells                                   35
Whose heart with generous feeling swells
    Clears <the> film from his eyes
    And his vision purifies
    Of that dim & earthly haze
Through which less favoured mortals gaze                        40


And O! what strange sensations gush
    To his expanding soul
With wild & overwhelming rush
    & onward silent roll
When some fair scene of nature breaks                          45
    At once upon his eye
And to his heart though voiceless speaks        ₋
    Sweetly and solemnly
Some huge and hoary mountain
A shade tremendous flinging o'er the land                      50
Like a dark cloud that natures mighty hand
Hath piled aloft, cumbering the earth with gloom
And ominous, blackness as the last great day
Were hasting fast & dreadful signs of doom
Tokens of coming terrors, upon the great world lay             55


    Or the blue moonlight heaven
        Bathed in a mystery of light
    By myriads of glorious planets given
    Moving in orbits vast around the central light
Then when the high cerulean vault                              60
    Quivers & trembles with their lustre stranqe
Genius thou dost thy votarys thoughts exalt
To other, mightier worlds, that never, never change!
    And winged forms flit rapid o'er his brain
    Floating in radiance still and silently                    65



76

And on his ear swells some celestial strain
Sounding from regions far beyond the sky
None hear the unearthly song save him
And e'en to his entranced ear
Fitful dreamlike and dim                                              70
Those midnight sounds appear!

These are the joys of Genius but the grief
The sting of cold neglect, unheeded merit
No cheering ray no balsam of releif
Soothe the heart-peircing pains that rack His spirit                  75

Thousands on Thousand[s] pass the mourner by
Nor heave a sigh nor one kind tear drop lend
In sorrow for his woeful agony
And for the pangs that all his bosom rend

The love of fame the love of deathless glory                          80
Inspires alike the feeble & the strong
The vigourous stripling & the ancient hoary
Would each his nam[e] to future years prolong

Far brighter burns the universal fire
Within his breast whom now I feebly sing                              85
Possessing but that high, and sole desire
That after times should with his praises ring

And thus mid greif & strife he yeilds to death
Then slow & solemn tolls his funeral knell
And broken hearted he resigns his breath                             90
Unhappy child of Genius fare the[e] well

November 13 1830                    Marquis of Douro
                                    Charlotte Bronte

MS:  G
First Publication:  SHB C and B
Text:  l. 38:  "darkness" changed to "film"; neither is canceled


**57 SERANADE**


Awake! Awake! fair sleeper, Awake and view the night
For the armies clad in diamond mail, now shed abroad their light
Come forth! with me fair sleeper, & perchance upon our ears
While we walk may fall the solemn chime of the music of the
    spheres

We will go to the huge forest & hearken to the sound            5
Like the voices of a hundred streams, that ever rushes round
Of nodding boughs & branches, great plumes--that wave on high
And hide with their thick darkness. the star bespangled sky

And haply as we tread beneath, that black embowred shade
Full on our sight may sudden burst, some moon illumined glade        10
Where with crowns of radiant adamant, & robes of vernal green
The morrice dancing fairy train, in other times were seen

Or shall we wander by the side, of ancient oceans shore
Where dull thunder of the billows is sounding evermore
And gaze into the mighty depths, whence comes that wildring
    sound                                                          15
On the swift winds of heaven, dispersing all around

There dwell great dragons of the deep, & issuing from their caves
Our eyes may view them gliding amid the liquid waves
Or solemnly withdrawn into tenebrious gloom
With noiseless movement ent[e]ring their coral shaded tomb          20

While still sad music rises from regions far beneath
At which the winds hush every sound of sigh & murmured breath
Unseen the sweet musician, but still the tones--ascend
And e'en the everlasting rocks, their cloud-veild summits bend

It is the maiden of the sea, that sings within her cell            25
Where she with gold & orient pearl, in glimering gloom doth
    dwell
And when her, monstrous form is seen swift gliding o'er the deep
The Blood within the sailors veins, in frozen streams doth creep*

For mighty winds behind her fly and clouds are round her shed
And lurid lightnings flashing, wreath the green locks
    on her head                                                    30
But she shall bode no storm for us to rack the lucid skies
Then awake! Awake fair sleeper, & unclose thine azure eyes

                                          Marquis of Douro
            November 14 1830                Charlotte Brontë

                    FINIS; FINIS.

*the appearance of the mermaid, is said by sailors to be a sign of
approaching tempest, I have heard many an experienced mariner confidently
assert his beleif in the existence of such a creature.

MS:  G
First Publication:  Wise Orphans 1917
Text:  The note on mermaids is Charlotte's

                          78

**58**

The pearl within the shell concealed
    Oft sheds a fairer light
Than that whose beauties are revealed
    To unrestricted sight.

So she who sweetly shines at home,                    5
    And seldom wanders thence,
Is of her partner's happy dome
    The blest intelligence.

The highest talents of her mind,
    The sunlight of her heart,                        10
Are all t' illume her home designed,
    And never thence they part.

[December 1830]

MS: Unlocated: last known to be in the library of Sir Alfred Law
First Publication: Shorter 1918


**59**


Scene: thick forest, under the trees of which Lady Zenobia
    Ellrington is reposing, dressed in her usual attire of a
    crimson-velvet robe and black plumes. She speaks:

'Tis eve; how that rich sunlight streameth through
The inwoven arches of this sylvan roof!               5
How those long lustrous lines of light illume
With trembling radiance, all the aged boles
Of elms, majestic as the lofty columns
That proudly rear their tall forms to the dome
Of old cathedral or imperial palace!                 10
Yea, they are grander than the mightiest shafts
That e'er by hand of man were fashioned forth
Their holy solemn temples to uphold;
And sweeter far than the harmonious peals
Of choral thunder, that in music roll                15
Through vaulted aisles, are the low forest sounds
Murmuring around: of wind and stirred leaf,
And warbled song of nightingale or lark,
Whose swelling cadences and dying falls
And whelming gushes of rich melody                   20
Attune to meditation, all serene,
The weary spirit; and draw forth still thoughts

Of happy scenes, half veiled by the mists
Of by-gone times. Yea, that calm influence
Hath soothed the billowy troubles of my heart                        25
Till scarce one sad thought rises, though I sit
Beneath these trees, utterly desolate.
But no, not utterly, for still one friend
I fain would hope remains to brighten yet
My mournful journey through this vale of tears;                       30
And while he shines, all other lesser lights
May wane and fade unnoticed from the sky.
But more than friend e'en he can never be
                                    (Heaves a deep sigh)
That thought is sorrowful, but yet I'll hope.                         35
What is my rival? Nought but a weak girl
Ungifted with the state and majesty
That mark superior minds: her eyes gleam not
Like windows to a soul of loftiness;
She hath not raven locks that lightly wave                            40
Over a brow whose calm placidity
Might emulate the white and polished marble.
                          (A white dove flutters by)
Ha! what art thou, fair creature? It hath vanished
Down that long vista of low-drooping trees.                          45
How gracefully its pinions waved! Methinks
It was the spirit of this solitude.
List! I hear footsteps; and the rustling leaves
Proclaim the approach of some corporeal being.

(A young girl advances up the vista, dressed in green,               50
with a garland of flowers wreathed in the curls of her
hazel hair. She comes towards Lady Zenobia, and says:)

Lady, methinks I erst have seen thy face:
Art thou not that Zenobia, she whose name
Renown hath borne e'en to this far retreat?                          55

            Lady Ellrington:

Aye, maiden, thou hast rightly guessed. But how
Didst recognize me?

            Girl:

                    In Verdopolis                                     60
I saw thee walking mid those gardens fair
That like a rich embroidered belt surround
That mighty city, and one bade me look
At her whose genius had illumined bright
Her age, and country, with undying splendour.                        65

                        80

The majesty of thy imperial form,
The fire and sweetness of thy radiant eye
Alike conspired to impress thine image
Upon my memory; and thus it is
That now I know thee as thou sittest there                    70
Queen-like, beneath the over-shadowing boughs
Of that huge oak-tree, monarch of this wood.

      Lady Ellrington: (smiling graciously)

Who art thou, maiden?

      Girl:                                                  75

        Marian is my name

      Lady Ellrington (starting up: aside):

Ha! my rival! (sternly) What dost thou here alone?

      Girl (aside):

How her tone changed! (Aloud) My favourite cushat-dove,       80
Whose plumes are whiter than new-fallen snow,
Hath wandered, heedless, from my vigilant care.
I saw it gleaming through these dusky trees,
Fair as a star, while soft it glided by.
So here I come to find and lure it back.                      85

      Lady Ellrington:

Are all thy affections centred in a bird?
For thus thou speakest, as though nought were worthy
Of thought or care, saving a silly dove?

      Girl:                                                  90

Nay, lady, I've a father, and mayhap
Others whom gratitude or tenderer ties,
If such there be, bind my heart closely to.

      Lady Ellrington:

But birds and flowers and such trifles vain                   95
Seem most t' attract thy love, if I may form

A judgment from thy locks elaborate curl'd
And wreathed around with woven garlandry,
And from thy whining speech, all redolent
With tone of most affected sentiment!                    100
    (Seizes Marian, and exclaims with a violent gesture)
Wretch, I could kill thee!

                Marian:

                Why, what have I done?
How have I wronged thee?  Surely thou'rt distraught!     105

            Lady Ellrington:

How hast thou wronged me?  Where didst weave the net
Whose cunning meshes have entangled round
The mightiest heart that e'er in mortal breast
Did beat responsive unto human feeling?                  110

                Marian:

The net?  What net?  I wove no net; she's frantic!

            Lady Ellrington:

Dull, simple creature!  Canst not understand?

                Marian:                                  115

Truly, I cannot.  'Tis to me a problem,
An unsolved riddle, an enigma dark.

            Lady Ellrington:

I'll tell thee, then.  But, hark!  What voice is that?

            Voice (from the forest):                     120

Marian, where art thou?  I have found a rose
Fair as thyself!  Come hither and I'll place it
With the blue violets on thine ivory brow.

                Marian:

He calls me, I must go:  restrain me not!                125

            Lady Ellrington:

Nay!  I will hold thee firmly as grim death.
Thou need'st not struggle, for my grasp is strong.

```
Thou shalt not go.  Lord Arthur shall come here,
And I will gain the rose despite of thee.                        130
Now for my hour of triumph:  here he comes!

    (Lord Arthur advances from among the trees, and
    exclaims on seeing Lady Ellrington):

        Lord Arthur:

Zenobia!  How cam'st thou here?  What ails thee?                  135
Thy cheek is flushed as with a fever glow,
Thine eyes flash strangest radiance, and thy frame
Trembles like to the wind-stirred aspen tree!

        Lady Ellrington:

Give me the rose, Lord Arthur, for methinks                      140
I merit it more than my girlish rival.
I pray thee now grant my request and place
That rose upon my forehead, not on hers,
Then will I serve thee all my after-days
As thy poor hand-maid, as thy humblest slave,                    145
Happy to kiss the dust beneath thy tread,
To kneel submissive in thy lordly presence.
Oh! turn thine eyes from her and look on me
As I lie here imploring at thy feet,
Supremely blest if but a single glance                           150
Could tell me that thou art not wholly deaf
To my petition, earnestly preferred.

        Lord Arthur:

Lady, thou'rt surely mad!  Depart, and hush
Those importunate cries.  They are not worthy                    155
Of the great name which thou hast fairly earned.

        Lady Ellrington:

Give me that rose, or I to thee will cleave
Till death these vigorous sinews has unstrung.
Hear me this once and give it me, Lord Arthur!                   160

    Lord Arthur (After a few minutes deliberation):

Here, take the flower, and keep it for my sake.
    (Marian utters a suppressed scream, and sinks to the ground)
```

Lady Ellrington (assisting her to rise):

Now I have triumphed! But I'll not exult.                              165
Yet know, henceforth I'm thy superior.
Farewell, my lord; I thank thee for thy preference!
              (Plunges into the wood and disappears)

        Lord Arthur:

Fear nothing, Marian, for a fading flower                              170
Is not symbolical of constancy.
But take this sign! (gives her his diamond ring) enduring
    adamant
Betokens well affection that will live
Long as life animates my faithful heart.
Now, let us go, for see the deepening shades                           175
Of twilight darken our lone forest path;
And, lo! thy dove comes gliding through the mirk,
Fair wanderer, back to its loved mistress' care.
Luna will light us on our journey home:
For see her lamp shines radiant in the sky,                            180
And her bright beams will pierce the thickest boughs.
              (Exeunt, curtain falls).

                          [December 1830]

MS:  Unlocated:  see No. **58**
First Publication:  **The Twelve Adventurers and Other Stories**, ed., C.
              K. Shorter, London:  Hodder and Stoughton, 1925


**60**        Now fall the last drops of the shower,
              And sunshine rests on every hill;
              The liquid diamonds in each flower
              Their cups with trembling radiance fill.
              Lo! from Apollo's golden light                            5
              The fertilizing vapours fly,
              And reappears in splendour bright
              The calmly lustrous sky.
              A clearer azure paints the robe
              Spread gloriously on high;                               10
              A fresher verdure decks the globe
              That far beneath doth lie.
              How glad and sweet the murmurings
              That from blue streams ascend,
              While around cool shade the woodland flings              15
              As its boughs to the waters bend.


                              84

But now the clouds with densest gloom
Have gather'd in the north,
And methinks I hear the thunders boom
From their dark recess roll forth.                    20
Hushed in heaven and hushed in earth
Every sound of joy and mirth;
For upon that mighty cloud,
Huge and black as Nature's shroud,
Faint appears a vision fair                           25
Pil'd upon the ambient air;
From its darkness breathes a light,
Softly lustrous, dimly bright.
More distinct the glory grows:
Lo! a shade of light it throws,                       30
And upon the vaulted skies
Now a second arch doth rise.

And as they span the heavens,
Each gleaming like a star,
They seem as some fair vision                         35
That cometh from afar,

With transitory light
Flashing on our mortal sight,
And upon our slumbers stealing,
Strangest scenes in sleep revealing;                  40
At the dawn of daylight, flies
Swift before the opening eyes,
Scarce leaving mem'ry's shade,
As away they flit and fade.
Never they return again;                              45
Now I close my lightsome strain."

                              [December 1830]

MS:   Unlocated:   see No. **58**
First Publication:   SHB Misc I


**61**              Hearken, O! mortal! to the wail
                    Which round the wandering night-winds fling,
                    Soft-sighing 'neath the moonbeams pale,
                    How low! how odd! its murmuring!
                    No other voice, no other tone,          5
                    Disturbs the silence deep;
                    All saving that prophetic moan,
                    Are hushed in quiet sleep.

                              85

The moon, and each small lustrous star,
That journeys through the boundless sky,          10
Seem, as their radiance from afar
Falls on the still earth silently,
To weep the fresh, descending dew
That decks with gems the world,
Sweet teardrops of the glorious blue          15
Above us wide unfurled.

But, hark! again the solemn wail
Upon the rising breeze doth swell;
O! hasten from this haunted vale,
As mournful as a funeral knell!          20
For here, when gloomy midnight reigns,
The fairies form their ring,
And unto wild unearthly strains
In measured cadence sing.

No human eye their sports may see,          25
No human tongue their deeds reveal;
The sweetness of their melody
The ear of man may never feel.
But now the elfin horn resounds,
No longer mayst thou stay;          30
Near and more near the music sounds,
Then, Mortal! haste away.

[December 1830]

MS:  Unlocated:  see No. **58**
First Publication:  **The Four Wishes.  A Fairy Tale**, London:  Privately
                printed by C. K. Shorter, 1918

## 62  A Fragment


    Overcome with that delightful sensation of lassitude which the
perfect repose of nature in the stillness of such an evening
occasions I dropped the oars and falling listlessly back allowed my
light-winged pinnace to float as chance might lead.  For about an
hour I lay thus gazing on the calm ungemed & unclouded sky above me
from which breathed a sweet balminess that scarcely fanned my temples
at length my boat lay perfectly motionless & I raised myself & found
that as if soul-taught it had wafted itself into a little willow
fringed bay disembarking I fastened it to a decayed larch and
following a pleasant path embroidered with moss & wild flowers I

presently entered the twilight shadow of a wood ere I emerged from
the darkness of its impending boughs the moon & hesperus had set
their watch in heaven. the soft light which fell from them & was
reflected from the calm fading glories of the west showed me that I
was now in a wild, winding glen embosomed in lofty percipitous fells
barren of all ornament save the purple heath flower. a chill wind
now rose and as it sigh'd around or murmured mournfully in the heart
of the forest a sudden burst of sweet sad music mingled with its
wailing. I looked up and saw by the clear moonlight a figure clad in
white sitting on a overhanging cliff and bending over a harp with
whose tones this sorrowful strain was blent.

Lo! stretched beneath the clust'ring palm
   The stately noble lies
Around him dwells a holy calm
   Breathed softly from the skies

The zephyrs fan with sweet caress         5
   Recumbent majesty
And loud winds of the wilderness
   All silently pass by

The Lion from his desert lair
   Comes forth to fierce foray         10
His red eyes fired by hunger glare
   In eager search of prey

He spies him in his dreamless sleep
   All on the moonlit ground
And away as with a whirlwind sweep         15
   Behold the monster bound

For holy, holy, is thy rest
   Though in the desert laid
A spirit's spell is o'er thee cast
   Amid that palmy shade         20

O clouds come o'er that vision bright
   And soft it fades away
The witchery of mem'ry's might
   Inviting still it's stay.

But vainly, where my warrior slept         25
   The cold sad moonbeams lie
And where sabean odours wept
   The winds of midnight sigh

But while the ocean wilder'd spreads
    Afar her thundring plain                          30
And while the light of heaven sheds
    Still splendour on the main

I'll ne'er forget that stately form
    That eye's entrancing light
Whence oft the wildest passion storm                  35
    Flashed forth in sudden might

Or in those dark orbs lustre lay
    Borne from the worlds of thought
But brightest shone that wondrous ray
    From holy regions brought                          40

Where spirits of the favoured few
    Alone may ever dwell
Where clearer than Parnanssian dew
    A hundred fountains well

The fountains sweet of poesy                           45
    That nectar of the sky
Where wreaths of imortality
    In hallowed beauty lie

But Lo Diana's silver bow
    Hath quitted human ken                             50
And the chill night winds coldly blow
    Adown this lonely glen

O happy may his slumber be
    This night in lands afar
Beneath the desert plaintain tree                     55
    Beneath the silver star

Or in his gorgeous Indian home
    On slave-surrounded bed
All underneath some glorious dome
    Whence lamps their glories shed                    60

His dreams are are of some other world
    His mighty soul is free
His spirits pinions all unfurled
    rise high in radiancy

And music all on earth unknown                        65
    Floats solemnly around
And sweeter swells each following tone
    With clear seraphic sound

No being of this low earth born
    Is worthy of his love                    70
Doth the royal rider of the storm
    E're look upon the dove

Then farewell each rebellious thought
    And welcome peace again
Adversity hath wisdom taught             75
    But who shall break the chain

The long long chain, of memory
    Which leads to other hours
To other days when happily
    I dwelt 'mid Indian bowers              80

And from the dim clouds of the past
    Sweet smiles & glances glide
From those bright lips & dark eyes cast
    Where dwells the light of pride

Smiles faded from his lofty brow         85
    Sweet glances past away
For fell upon another now
    Their all desired-ray

And now my rivals hated form
    Salutes my mental eye                   90
And envys dark unhallowed storm
    O'ercasts the tranquil sky

Methinks I see her ringlets play
    In the starlight soft & fair
Methinks I see her eyes still ray        95
    Illume the dusky air

O she was fairer than the rose
    With morning dew All bright
She shone among a hundred foes
    The central orb of light               100

Their spirit's were of kindred mould
    From the same sweet fountain sprung
And melody of heaven rolled
    In music when she sung

How oft beneath the orange grove         105
    By Gambia's rolling tide
While shone on high the star of love
    He wandered with his bride

89

And while faint light fell on the wave
     And fainter music rung                                  110
From the green banks which their waters lave
     How sweet that lady sung

Between each pause so still & calm
     The whispering leaflets spoke
Or wandering Zephyr's soft as balm                           115
     Her harps wild echos woke

All winged minstrels of the vale
     Now silently repose
And voiceless is the dewy gale
     That breathing flower-scents blows                      120

Slow sailing through the clear wide sky
     Earths handmaid journeys free
Tracking to all eternity
     An ever shoreless sea

The solemn airs of evening sigh                              125
     Throug[h] wood & grove & bower
Charged with the mystic harmony
     Which thrills this hallowed hour

O once this happiness was mine
     When came still even-tide                               130
How often in that balmy time
     I've wandered by his side.

And while I heard his eloquence
     And watched his kindling eye
I saw a lustre beaming thence                                135
     Bright as the stars on high

It was as though his spirit lay
     Far in those wells of light
As though his souls irradiate day
     Shone bright as heaven is bright                        140

But never more O never more
     That lustre may I see
A thousand waves between us roar,
     Howl, thunder heavily.

And might that distant orient land                           145
     Again salute mine eye
And might I walk its burning strand
     Beneath its burning sky

                Yet cold as sunbeams on the snow
                    That light would fall on me                          150
                Then raging waters ever flow
                    & thunder heavily

                But dim dawn rises in the east
                    The air with matins rings
                I'll seek my wild, lone place of rest                     155
                    W[h]ere the stream in silence sings.

                                            [July 11, 1831]

MS:  D(1)
First Publication:    Lines 1-64 as Emily's in Wise Orphans 1917; lines
                      65-156 not previously published


**63**    The trumpet hath sounded, its voice is gone forth
          From the plains of the south to the seas of the north
          The great ocean groaned & the firm mountains shook
          & the rivers in terror their channels forsook
          The proud eagle quailed in her aerial dome                      5
          The gentle dove flew to her bowery home
          The antelope trembled as onward she sprung
          When hollow & death-like the trumpet-blast rung
          It was midnight deep midnight & shrouded in sleep
          Men heard not the roar of the terror struck deep                10
          Nor the peal of the trumpet still sounding on high
          They saw not the flashes that brightened the sky
          All silent & tomb-like the great city lay
          And fair rose her towers in their moonlight array
          'Twas the ruler of Spirits that sent forth the sound            15
          To call his dread legions in myriads around

                They heard him & from land & wave
                    The genii armies sprung
                Some came from dim green ocean cave
                    Where thousand gems are flung                         20

                Some from the forests of the west
                    'Mid dark shades wandering
                A giant host of winged forms
                    Rose round their mighty King

                Some from the chill & ice-bound North                    25
                    All swathed in snowy shrouds
                With the wild howl of storms came forth
                    Sailing on tempest clouds

                                    91

```
The gentler fays in bright bands flew
    From each sweet woodland dell                              30
All broidered with the violets blue
    & wild-flowers drooping bell

A sound of harps was on the blast
    Breathing faint melody
A dim light was from distance cast                             35
    As their fair troop drew nigh

And mingling with stern Giant forms
    Their tiny shapes are seen
Bright gleaming mid the gloom of storms
    Their gems & robes of green                                40
```

The hall where they sat was the heart of the sky
And the stars to give light stooped their lamps from on high
The noise of the host rose like thunder around
The heavens gathered gloom at the hoarse sullen sound
No mortal may farther the vision reveal                       45
Human eye cannot peirce what a spirit would seal
The secrets of Genii my tongue may not tell
But hoarsely they murmured bright city farewell
Then melted away like a dream of the night
While their palace evanished in oceans of light               50
Far beneath them the city lay silent & calm
The breath of the night-wind was softer than balm
As it sighed o'er its gardens & mourned in its bowers
And shook the bright dew drops from orient flowers
But still as the breeze on the myrtle groves fell             55
A voice was heard wailing bright city farewell
The morning arose o'er the far distant hill
And yet the great city lay silent & still
No chariot rode thunderous adown the wide street
Nor horse of Arabia impetuous & fleet                         60
The river flowed on to the foam-crested sea
But unburdened by vessel its waves murmured free
The silence is dreadful.  O city arise!
The <sun> is ascending the arch of the skies
Mute mute are the mighty & chilled is their breath            65
For at midnight passed o'er them the angel of Death
The King & the peasant the lord & the slave
Lie entombed in the depth of one wide solemn grave

```
Now Ruin daemon of the wild
    Her shadow round hath flung                                70
And where the face of beauty smiled
    & Where sweet music rung
```

The tigers howl shall oft' be heard
   Sounding through tower & dome
And to the moon the desert bird                     75
   Shall make her thrilling moan

The murmur of the myrtle bowers
   The voice of waving trees
The fragrance of the sweet wild flower[s]
   Shall mingle with the breeze                     80

Unheard that gentle wind shall sweep
   The wide campaign of air
Unfelt the heavens their balm shall weep
   The living are not there.

                C Bronte͏̈ Dec<sup>br</sup> 11, 1831

MS:  A
First Publication:   Shorter 1923


**64  December 25 1831**


O There is a land which the sun loves to lighten
   Whose bowers are of myrtle whose forests are palm
Whose shores the pure rays of the amethyst brighten
& Whose winds as they murmur are softer than balm

The streams of that land spring in might from their fountains    5
Rush through the deep valley & o'er the vast plain
Pass swiftly the cloud-crested sky-girdling mountains
As onward bright-bounding they meet the wide main

The boughs of the willow-tree gracefully drooping
Hang over their borders in shadowy gloom                        10
And on the green banks to the clear waters sloping
Flowers bright as the rainbow eternally bloom

There silence asserts not her solemn dominion
There the bird of the wilderness evermore sings
Still tunes the sweet pipe & still waves the soft pinion        15
While Echo her tribute from far distance brings

      But though fair as bright Elysian dreams
         These vernal Eden bowers
      Yet O this land hath other scenes
         Than woods & streams & flowers                         20


                        93

High hills that woo the winds of heaven
    To breathe upon them from the skies
Rocks tempest shaken, thunder-riven
    Whose cliffs like giant turrets rise

Great cataracts rolling down the steep                          25
Shaking the sky & steady shore
Rousing all Nature from her sleep
With hoarse, rebounding, thunderous roar

Trees shaken by the wailing blast
Wave in the dim air mournfully                                  30
While sullen sounds float fitful past
Like the dull moaning of the sea

There rubys shed their blood-red ray
There orient em'ralds softly gleam
There diamond[s] flash forth transient day                     35
And emulate the solar beam

But vainly the diamond sheds light thro that land
    As though formed by the might of some dark wizards wand
And vainly the rivers flow forth to the sea
In brightness & beauty and sweet melody                        40
And the hills lift their tall stately summits on high
And the winds are called forth from the heart of the sky
And vainly the cataracts roll swift down the steep
To a murmur is softened the roar of the deep
The bright sun in vain to this far land is given               45
And the Planets look forth from the windows of heaven
The birds sing unheeded in woods fresh & green
And the flowers grow unscented ungathered unseen
The Lion rules the forest & the eagle the air
Mankind is dominionless portionless there                      50
His voice never rung through those wide spreading woods
His bark never stemmed the wild rush of those floods
His foot never trod on the green flowery sward
No beast of these deserts acknowledged him lord
His hand never gathered those gems rich & rare                 55
Mankind is dominionless [portionless there]

MS:   D(1)
First Publication:  Dodd Mead 1902
Text:   1. 56:  the last two words are conjectural; the corner of the page
        is torn off.

1    O! there is a wood in a still and deep
     And solitary vale
     Where no sound is heard save the wild wind's sweep
     And the lay of the nightingale

2    And far in the depth of the leafy trees                    5
     An elm grows fair and high
     Where ever the voice of the solemn breeze
     Sighs with soft harmony

3    And far beneath its tremb'ling shade
     Soft moss and green grass grow                             10
     There the violet & wild-rose bud & fade
     There the lily & hare bell blow

4    A ripp'ling streamlet wanders near
     Unseen in the flow'r-blent grass
     But a murmur is heard full sweet & clear                   15
     As its silver waters pass

5    Twas night, a pearly lustre fell
     On mountain, wave, & tower
     Now spirits wove their magic spell
     In many a hidden bower                                     20

6    I lay within that calm retreat
     The green wood shade among
     And soon I sunk to slumber sweet
     Lulled by the streamlet's song.

7    A strange dream o'er my spirit crept                       25
     As in that shady dell
     In silent peace I lay and slept
     While the balm of heaven fell

     Methought I saw a wild deep sea
     And heard a sullen roar                                    30
     As its mighty waves broke heavily
     On the bleak & lonely shore

     I saw two forms of human mould
     Beneath a tall rock's shade
     Watching the long bright rays of gold                      35
     Far in the bright west fade

95

One was a young and noble Knight
    Stately, in plumed pride
The other was a lady bright
    And she stood by the warrior's side           40

I saw the dark light of the noble's eye
    As he leaned on his white war-steed
But her's was as blue as the sapphire sky
    And frail was her form as the reed

The young knight made a solemn vow           45
    Of constancy till death
Truth's light beamed fair on his brow
    While he pledged his knightly faith

The lady smiled a heavenly smile
    Which showed nor doubt nor fear           50
But their stood in her radiant eye the while
    A bright and tender tear

She took one lock of her golden hair
    From all those clust'ring curls
Bound with a garland of Flow'rets fair           55
    And a string of orient pearls

Then gave that token tremblingly
    To the soldier by her side
And he swore again by earth & sky
    That she should be his bride           60

---------------------------------

Now changed the scene. upon my sight
    A lofty palace grew
And a sun-like splendour a golden light
    High lamps & torches threw

The juice of the scorched grape was sparkling bright    65
    With ruby radiance & bloodred light
That nectar which lightens the weary soul
    Gleamed in the wine-cup & wassail bowl

The music of harps & of trumpets rung
And The strings of the wild guitar were strung    70
Full soft were the breathings of viol and lute
While the clear clarion answered the tones of the flute

Now white robes fluttered and tall plumes glanced,
While nobles and ladies in bright rings danced
    Gracefully gliding the pillars among            75
    To the sound of the harps and the joyous song

I knew 'twas a bridal, for under a bower
Of the rose & the myrtle & fair lily flower
Stood that that stately noble in plumed pride
And that sweet fair lady his plighted bride       80

With the mystic ring on her finger fair
And the nuptial wreath in her radiant hair
They are joined & for ever the mingled name
Of Marina and Albion is hallowed to fame

C. Brontë  July 14<sup>th</sup>
1832

MS:  F(1)
First Publication:  Shorter 1923

**66**      He is gone and all grandeur has fled from the mountain
All beauty departed from stream and from fountain
    A dark veil is hung
  O'er the bright sky of gladness
    And where birds sweetly sung      5
There's a murmur of sadness
The wind sings with a warning tone
  Through many a shadowy tree
I Hear in every passing moan
  The voice of destiny      10

Then Oh lord of the waters! the great and all-seeing
Preserve in thy mercy his safety and being
    May he trust in thy might
  When the dark storm is howling
    And the blackness of night      15
  Over Heaven is scowling
But may the sea flow glidingly
  With gentle summer waves
And silent may all tempests lie
  Chained in vast Eolian caves      20

Yet though e're he returns long years will have vanished
Sweet Hope from my bosom shall never be banished
    I'll think of the time
    When his step lightly bounding
        Shall be heard on the rock                    25
    Where the cat'ract is sounding
When the banner of his Fathers host
    Shall be unfurled on high
To welcome back the pride & boast
    Of England's chivalry                             30

Yet tears will flow forth while of hope I am singing
Still Despair her dark shadow is over me flinging
    But when he's far away
    I will pluck the wild flower
        On bank & on brae                             35
    At the still moonlight hour
And I will twine for him a wreath
    Low in the fairy's dell
Methought I heard the night wind breathe
    That solemn word farewell                         40

                                    [August 1832]

MS:  D(1)
First Publication:  Wise RCK 1917


**67      St. John in the Island of Patmos**

                    ─────────────

    The holy exile lies all desolate,
        In that lone island of the Grecian sea.
    And does he murmur at his earthly fate,
        The doom of thraldom and captivity?

    No, lulled by the rushing of th' unquiet breeze,       5
        And the dull solemn thunder of the deep
    Under the hanging boughs of loftiest trees,
        Behold the Apostle sunk in silent sleep.

    And is that slumber dreamless, as the lone
        Unbroken, frozen stillness of the grave?          10
    Or is his soul on some far journey gone
        To lands beyond the wildly howling wave?

                        98

Where Zion's daughter views with tear dimmed eye
    Her proud, all-beauteous temple's lofty form,
Piercing with radiant front the blue bright sky,                    15
    And mourns with veiled brow the coming storm.

Haply his spirit lingers where the palm
    Upspringing from the flow'ry, verdant sod
Throws a dark, solemn shade, a breezeless calm
    Over the home where first he spoke with God.                    20

Or to his freed soul is it once more given,
    To wander in the dark, wild wilderness?
The Herald of the lord of Earth and Heav'n,
    Who came, in mercy came; to heal and bless

No: from his eyes a veil is rent away,                              25
    The will of God is gloriously revealed;
And in the full light of eternal day,
    Jehovah's fix'd decrees are all unsealed.

The armed hosts of God, in panoply
    Of splendour most insufferably bright,                         30
Rush forth triumphant from the parting sky,
    Whose wide arch yawns before those floods of light.

He hears the voices of Archangels tell
    The doom, the fiery, fearful doom of Earth;
And as the trumpet's tones still louder swell,                     35
    On the dark world red plagues are poured forth.

At once ten thousand mighty thunders sound,
    With one wild howl the sea yields up her dead;
A flaming whirlwind sweeps the trembling ground,
    The skies are passed away in fear and dread.                   40

All earth departs, at God's supreme behest
    Sinners are bound, in the black depths of hell;
The souls of righteous men for ever rest,
    Where angel harps in sounds harmonious swell.

And now the new Jerusalem descends,                                45
    Beaming with rainbow radiance, from on high;
In awe and fear the holy Prophet bends,
    As that bright wonder rushes on his eye.

He hears the last voice, ere Heavens gates are sealed,
    Proclaim, that all God's works are consuminate;                50
That unto him, th' Almighty hath reveal'd
    Th' unfathomed mysteries of Time and Fate.

He wakes from his wondrous trance and hears
    Faint distant warblings, from the morning sky;
Floating, like tuneful music of the spheres,                    55
    Sweet as the voice of Angel harmony
Sounding Jehovah's praise to all eternity--

                              Aug^t. 30^th 1832.  C. Bronte

MS: Unknown
First Publication:  Winnifrith PCB


**68        Lines on the Celebrated Bewick**


The cloud of recent death is past away
But yet a shadow lingers o'er his tomb;
To tell that the pale standard of decay
Is reared triumphantly o'er life's sullied bloom.

And now the eye bedimmed by tears may gaze            5
On the fair lines his gifted pencil drew
The tongue unfalt'ring speak[s] its meed of praise
When we behold those scenes to Nature true

True to the common Nature that we see
In England's sunny fields, her hills, and vales       10
On the wild bosom of her storm-dark sea
Still heaving to the wind that o'er it wails

How many winged inhabitants of air
How many plume-clad floaters of the deep
The mighty artist drew in forms as fair               15
As those that now the skies and waters sweep

From the great Eagle, with his lightning eye
His tyrant glance, his talons dyed in blood
To the sweet breather-forth of melody
The gentle merry minstrel of the wood                 20

Each in his attitude of native grace
Looks on the gazer life-like free and bold
And if the rocks be his abiding place
Far off appears the winged marauder's hold

But if the little builder rears his nest
In the still shadow of green tranquil trees
And singing sweetly 'mid the silence blest
Sits a meet emblem of untroubled peace

A change comes o'er the spirit of our dream
Woods wave around in crested majesty
We almost feel the joyous sunshine's beam
And hear the breath of the sweet south go by.

Our childhood's days return, again in thought
We wander in a land of love and light--
And mingled memories joy and sorrow fraught
Gush on our hearts with overwhelming might

Sweet flowers seem gleaming 'mid the tangled grass
Sparkling with spring-drops from the rushing rill
And as these fleeting visions fade and pass
Perchance some pensive tears our eyes may fill

These soon are wiped away, again we turn
With fresh delight, to the enchanted page
Where pictured thoughts that breathe and speak and burn
Still please alike our youth and riper age

There rises some lone rock, all wet with surge
And dashing billows glimmering in the light
Of a wan moon whose silent rays emerge
From clouds that veil their lustre cold and bright

And there 'mongst reeds upon a river's side
A wild bird sits, and brooding o'er her nest
Still guards the priceless gems her joy and pride
Now ripening 'neath her hope-enlivened breast

We turn the page, before the expectant eye
A traveller stands lone on some desert heath
The glorious sun is passing from the sky
While fall his farewell rays on all beneath

O'er the far hills a purple veil seems flung
Dim herald of the coming shades of night
E'en now Diana's lamp aloft is hung
Drinking full radiance from the fount of light

O, when the solemn wind of midnight sighs
Where will the lonely trav'ller lay his head
Beneath the tester of the star-bright skies
On the wild moor he'll find a dreary bed

25

30

35

40

45

50

55

60

Now we behold a marble Naiad, placed                              65
Beside a fountain on her sculptured throne
Her bending form with simplest beauty graced
Her white robes gathered in a snowy zone

She from a polished vase pours forth a stream
Of sparkling water to the waves below                            70
Which roll in light & music while the gleam
Of sunshine flings through shade a golden glow

A hundred fairer scenes these leaves reveal
But there are tongues that injure while they praise
I cannot speak the rapture that I feel                           75
When on the work of such a mind I gaze

Then Farewell Bewick genius' favoured son
Death's sleep is on thee all thy woes are past
From earth departed, life and labour done
Eternal peace and rest are thine at last                         80

Nov<sup>br</sup> 27<sup>th</sup> 1832

$$\text{Nov}^{br} \ 27^{th} \ 1832$$
C Bronte

MS:   Unknown
First Publication: **TLS,** January 4, 1907


**69**            Last Branch of murdered royalty
                       How calmly thou are sleeping
                  While the storm that bowed thy parent tree
                       Is still around the[e] sweeping

                  Dost thou not hear in that wild moan           5
                       Mid the tall palm branches dying
                  A kindred an ancestral tone
                       For blood for vengeance crying

                  Dost thou not hear faint mingled cries
                       In the murmurs of the river                10
                  Like those which death's last agonies
                       From flesh and spirit sever

                  Dost thou not hear in every sound
                       A sign a warning token?
                  Thou dost not for thy soul is bound             15
                       In slumber most unbroken.

102

Awake my child lift up thine eyes
    And ere our souls are sundered
Swear by the silence of those skies
    Where late the war-storm thundered                    20

Swear by our altars overthrown
    Swear by our death-swept dwelling
And by thy father's dying moan
    When the battle round was swelling

Swear by our Halls now desolate                           25
    Where the desert born are crying
Swear by inexorable fate
    By the wild wind round thee sighing

By the river flowing past thy feet
    By all that moves around thee                          30
That when the shroud an[d] winding sheet
    In icy fold[s] have bound me

And when the warm and full-orbed light
    Of youth is o'er thee beaming
Thoult take thy holy sword of right                        35
    Through blood-stains redly gleaming

And swift and bright as wand'ring star
    Go piling heaps of dead
Nor stay till shines thy scymitar
    Deep deep empurpled                                    40

May'st thou thy father's mind [and] form
    His kingly soul inherit
When he's a banquet for the worm
    And Im a fleshless spirit

Farewell I see a tomb-like shade                           45
    Come darkly-creeping o'er me
And Earth in light and life arrayed
    Is fading from before me

Look child where Hyla's waters lie
    I hear a deep tone breathing thence                    50
A voice a sound of prophecy
    Which speaks of bloody recompense

Tyrants a dying woman's moan
    An orphan infant's wailing cry
Shall rise to the eternal throne                           55
Shall send us final victory


103

'When she had finished her song her eyes closed
and she slipped from the tree against which she had
supported herself, to the ground.  Life was extinct.
I afterwards caused her to be interred under the palm
tree where she died, and I took the child under my
protection.  I afterwards found that his name was
Quashi and that he was the son of the Great Sai
Too-Too Quamina.

February 12<sup>th</sup>, 1833

MS: D(1)
First Publication:  SHB Misc I


**70**     O Hyle thy waves are like Babylon's streams
       When the daughters of Zion hung o'er them in woe
       When the sad exiles wept in their desolate dreams
       And sighed for the sound of thier calm Kedron's flow

       The palms are all withered that shadowed thy shore          5
       The breezes that kiss thee through sepulchres sweep
       For the plume of the Ethiop, the lance of the moor
       All under the sods of the battle-field sleep

       O Hylle! that mo[o]nlight shines colder on thee
       Than afar of it shines on the salt lake of graves          10
       And drear as the voice of its wild waters be
       'Tis joy to the sound of thy desolate waves

       O Hylle! thy children are scattered afar
       All gone is their glory all faded is their fame
       Crushed Broken their banner-staff, vanished is their star          15
       Unburied their ashes, Forgotten their name.

[February 1833]

MS:  D(1)
First Publication:  Shorter 1923
Text:  l. 9:  "is" uncanceled precedes "shines"; Charlotte probably first
       intended to write "is shining"


104

**71**  Justine upon thy silent tomb the dews of ev[en]ing weep
Descending twilight's wings of doom around & o'er thee sweep
The flowers closed on thy grave Justine & the fern-leaves bend
    & fade
And the fitful night-wind dies & swells as it ushers in the shade
A lonely light in heaven smiles one pale star in the west          5
The night-clouds rise in giant-piles, far along Gambia's breast

I am come, & come alone Justine, to spend one hour with thee
But the turf with its flowers & fern-leaves green doth hide
    thee jealously

O long & still hath been thy sleep beneath that grassy grave
Years have rolled on their billows deep & time its whelming wave   10
Yet still I do remember my young nurse ere she died
Ere the gloom of dark December had quenched the summers pride

Long lay she in the latticed room, which crowns that turret grey
And I used to think its death-bed gloom prophetic of decay
In the placid sunny, summer eves when the light of sunset fell     15
Through the checquering play of those ivy-leaves, with smiles
    of sad farewell    /

How did I love to climb the stair, which to her c[h]amber led
That I might drop a childish tear on Justine's dying bed
I felt she was not long for earth her pale cheek told me so
She who had loved me from my birth, I knew was soon to go          20

How wearily her eye would turn to the lattice & the sky
Within a wild wish seemed to burn that yet she might not die
As golden clouds went sailing on & the sound of winds & trees
Came as unto a mariner, comes the deep moan of the seas

Then her daughter & her foster-son she'd to her bosom press        25
And say with such a bitter moan may God my children bless
And then I called her mother & weepingly I said
I would be Mina's brother when she was cold & dead

That vow has since been broken as when lightning shivers trees
Those words in anguish spoken have been scattered to the breeze    30
Justine if God has given a glance of earth to thee
Thou hast even wept in heaven--my withering crimes to see

But let me not remember those hours of darkness past
Nor blow the dying ember, to light with such a blast
I do not know repentance, I cannot bend my pride                   35
nor deprecate my conscience even at thy cold graves side

Lifes fit-ful fever over thou sleepest well Justine
pale flowers thine ashes cover, & grass-mounds ever green
The fox-glove here is drooping its silent peal of bells
And the shadowy yew-tree stooping of rest eternal tells                40

O might I find a dwelling but half so calm as thine
When my life-storm stills its yelling when my comet-fires decline
But the wild the raging billow is a fitter home for me
The coral for the willow, for the turf, the tossing sea

                                                    [February-March, 1833]

MS:  D(1)
First Publication:  Winnifrith PCB


72          Fair forms of glistening marble stand around
            Whose fixed & sightless eye-balls chill the soul
            As they stand cold & silent while a sound
            Is heard without of the deep thunder roll
            And wild swift wind-blasts sweep the moonless sky            5
            Now with a faroff wail now howling sternly nigh

            Stretched on that couch I see an old mans form
            Whose head is hoary with a century's snow
            He shudders while he lists the sullen storm
            And the cold death-sweats trickle from his brow            10
            As his high palace echos to a yell
            Loud as a hundred tempest's mightiest swell

            There lies Lord Rowan all his eye's dark light
            Quenched in the lapse of time.  his raven hair
            Which once in grape-like clusters thick & bright           15
            Hung o'er his temples now so wan & bare
            Falls down in meagre locks of hoary grey
            Which turn to silver where the torch-beams play

            A cloud of costliest inscence fills the room
            The wealth of nations shines resplendent round             20
            But shadowy horrors cast o'er him their gloom
            And near his death-bed fien[d]ish whispers sound
            Calling his soul with awful summonings
            To stand e're morn before the King of Kings


106

Now that dark contract, which in years gone by          25
He sealed with solemn oaths, weighs on his breast
A fiery burden that eternally
Will shut his spirit from the heaven of rest
And claim it where the wicked ceaseless cry
And where' the pangs of torture never die          30

He hath lived long the terrible the feared
Of all that journey on the sounding sea
And long hath in the storm of battle reared
His blood-red pirate flag triumphantly
His name is known to all the sons of men          35
O'er hill & plain & far-off mountain glen

And ever it was rumoured through the land
That he was guarded by a spirit's might
For still a shield borne by some unseen hand
Hovered around him in the raging fight          40
And still when fiercest tempests swept the sea
His stately ship sailed on unscathed & free

But now he feels the ghastly King draw nigh
The life blood turns to ice in evry vein
As through the black night sounds that solemn cry          45
Rising above the howling storm again
Strongly he struggles.  Death will have his prey
And 'mid responsive shrieks his spirit bursts away

Mar 26<sup>th</sup> 1833                    Charlotte Bronte

MS:  D(1)
First Publication:  Dodd Mead 1902

**73**          Almighty hush the dying cries
That sound so sadly in mine ear
The sobs, the groans, the soul-breathed sighs
And wipe away the burning tear
That now wets many a gallant cheek          5
While pain wrings forth the wild death-shriek
From brave hearts steeled to fear

Voice of the solemn trumpet sound
Rend your dark mist-veil from the sky
Peirce through the war-shouts bursting round                    10
And swell again triumphantly
For I would leave this mangl'ed clay
And pass to regions far-away
    'Mid tones of victory

List to that sweet, heart-stirring strain                      15
That clear, but martial harmony
It peals above the battle plain
Like music o'er a stormy sea
Soothes the wild waves of fear to rest
And wakes in ev'ry fainting breast                             20
    A sudden energy

All the dark pageantry of war
Is fading swiftly from my sight
The clash of arms sound faint & far
Death's wing's spread o'er me the blackest night               25
Yet still that music floats around
And mingles with its harp-like sound
    A more than trumpet night

A flood of light bursts from the skies
While higher swells that symphony                              30
I see the Isles of Paradise
Rise beauteous from a golden sea
And now I feel the fragrant breeze
Borne from sweet Eden's bowers & trees
    Which bloom eternally                                      35

Bretheren in arms a long farewell
To other brighter scenes I go
Where joys unmixed and endless dwell
And where undying waters flow
There I shall bathe in seas of life                           40
Unharmed by war unvexed by strife
    Far from this world of woe

                                    [May 1833]

MS:  L
First   Publication:  **Something   About   Arthur**,   by   Charlotte   Brontë,
                transcribed  and  edited  by  Christine  Alexander,  The
                University  of  Texas  at  Austin,  Humanities  Research
                Centre, 1981

**74**
```
            Let us drive care away
            And laugh while we may
        And sing though it be in the valley of Death
            And still let us drink
            And from wine never shrink                    5
        So long my rare lads as our bodies hold Breath

            I'd far rather die
            In good company
        Than live a long life with the solemn and sad
            Then let all the world know                   10
            That from toppin to toe
        I'm a roaring fellow a proper, rare lad
```

                                        [May 1833]

MS:  L
First Publication:  See previous poem


**75**
```
        Eamala is a gurt bellaring bull
        Shoo swilled and swilled till shoo drank her full
            Then shoo rolled abaat
            Wi' screeaam and shaat
        And aat of her pocket a knoife did pull          5

        And wi'that knoife shoo'd a cutt her throit
        If I had'nt gean her a strait-waist coit
            Then shoo flang & jumped
            And girned & grump'd
        But I did'nt caare for her a doit                10

        A sooin shoo doffed her mantle of red
        And shoo went and shoo ligged her da'an aent bed
            And theere shoo slept
            Till' th' haase wor swept
        And all the gooid liquar wor gooan fro her head  15
```

                                        [June 1833]

MS:  B(1)
First Publication:  SHB Misc I

Long I have sighed for my home in the mountain
Far have I wandered & sadly I've wept
For the land of the stream & the sweet-singing fountain
The land which the torrent for ages has swept

Back to the rock with its bosom of snow                           5
Back to the wild rushing river I come
Still may its waters in melody flow
With moan & with murmur, with ripple & hum

List to the voice of the far tempest yelling
Darkly it broods o'er that white icy hill                        10
Yet its dread music is deepning & swelling
Sounds the loud wind-blast more hollow & shrill

Stern is the welcome & haughty & high
Which greets my return to the land of my birth
Thunder peals speak from the heart of the sky                    15
Pine Forests bow to the storm-smitten earth

Yet to my spirit more sweet is the sound
Than the music which floats over vine-covered France
When the soft winds of twilight sigh soothingly round
When stars in the firmament tremble & glance                     20

And fairer those snowy peaks flash on my sight
Beneath the black veil of that wild heaven above
Than Italy's sky ever cloudless and bright
than the sun which shines over that region of love

There stands the hut where my first breath I drew                25
Perched like the nest of an eaglet on high
Under that lone roof in childhood I grew
And now I return neath it's shelter to die

                                              [June 1833]

MS:  B(1)
First Publication:  Wise SER 1917

Gently the moon-beams are kissing the deep
Soft on its waters the yellow rays light
Waken my love from the visions of sleep
Bend from thy casement and gaze on the night

Now Heaven is all clear, not a cloud flecks its blue          5
Like a bow of bright sapphires it arches the main
While the cinnamon-perfumed & balm-breathing dew
Wafts scents of Arabia o'er valley and plain

The bird of the night hath forgotten her song
But hark how the tall trees are whispering on high          10
As a soft Zephyr passes their branches among
And wakes as it wanders a tremulous sigh

Stars o'er our path-way resplendently shine
Dian is leading the hosts of the sky
Haste then & meet me my fair Geraldine          15
Come we will walk where the silver sands lie

Whence came that whispered voice through the still night
Faintly it sounded yet sweet in mine ear
Do thine eyes bend on me their soft dewy light
Oh say my beloved art thou wandering near          20

The leafy boughs rustle in yonder dark grove
A white garment glances & floats on the breeze
And lo! like a vision of beauty & love
She glides from the shadow of wide-waving trees

[June 1833]

MS:  B(1)
First Publication:  Wise SER 1917


78              O wind that o'er the ocean
                Comes wafted from the west
                And fans with gentle motion
                The deep's unquiet breast

                Say hast thou passed a stately ship          5
                    On the broad & boundless sea
                Did the crimson flag of England float
                    From her main-mast gallantly

111

Did the pleasant sound of singing
   Rise from her gentle gale?                                          10
Were harps in concert ringing
   With the trumpets hollow wail

And as she breasted the waters blue
   And severed the mighty main
Didst thou see upon her lordly deck                                    15
   Some prince or noble's train

Was snowy plumage streaming
   Were rich-robes waving free
Were jewels brightly beaming
   'Neath a purple canopy                                             20

Spirit of the western breeze
Silent sweeper of the seas
If thou hast seen that gallant ship
Sailing the unfathomed deep
Soon my doom shall sealed be                                         25
Fixed my future destiny
Soon in saddest, wildest woe
I shall mourn my hapless love
Yes 'ere heaven's crescent bow
Shall light again this cedar grove                                   30
I shall stand a weeping bride
At the altars hallowed side
But though lost to me for-ever
Worshipped, cherished of my heart
I can still forget thee never                                        35
   Though on earth we part
Loved one we may meet again
   In a land uncursed by pain

                                                    [June 1833]

MS:  B(1)
First Publication:  Shorter 1923


**79**    Sound a lament in the halls of his father
          Waken the harp-string & pour forth a wail
          The caves of the hill the sad echoes will gather
          The chant will be sung by the wandering gale
          Damp lies his corpse in the folds of the shroud             5
          & low to the dust his bright forehead is bowed

Weep in thy chambers where music is sighing
Weep in thy palace fair bride of his heart
Thy love with the worms of corruption is lying
Thou from his bosom for ever must part                           10
For ever, For ever, how sad is that word
When by the lone grave of the buried 'tis heard

Shake from thy tresses the flower-wreath of gladness
Scatter its bloom to the winds of the sky
Cover thy brow with a mantle of sadness                          15
Weep for thy moment of mourning draws nigh
And leave that bright robe of the youthful & gay
For the grief-darkened weeds, of a widow's array

But longer & louder uplift a shrill wail
For the parent of him who sleeps low with the dead               20
His eye shall grow dim & his cheek shall turn pale
And the plumes shall droop low on that proud warrior's head
When he treads the lone isle of the desolate shore
When he fears that his loved one, his son is no more

He fell not in battle, he fell not in war                        25
Where conquest & carnage have followed his might
No, suddenly, silently vanished his star
At noonday fell on him the darkness of night
A murderer's voice bade his spirit depart
The hand of a traitor brought death to his heart                 30

O! why was the morn of his young being clouded
By darkness so solemn, by horror so deep
And why was that fair form all fettered & shrouded
So early laid down for its long dreamless sleep
What hand can dispel that dense shadowy gloom                    35
Which hides from our vision that volume of doom

[June 1833]

MS:   B(1)
First Publication:   Wise SER 1917


**80**            The night fell down all calm and still
                  The moon shone out o'er vale & hill
                      Stars trembled in the sky
                  Then forth into that pale, sad light
                  There came a gentle lady bright                5
                  With veil & cymar spotless white
                      Fair brow & dark blue eye

Her lover sailed on the mighty deep
The Ocean wild and stern
And now she walks to pray & weep                    10
    For his swift & safe return

Full oft she pauses as the breeze
Moans wildly through those Giant trees
    As startled at the tone
The sounds it waked were like the sigh             15
Of spirits voice through midnight sky
So soft, so sad so drearily
    That wandering wind swept on

    And ever as she listened
    Unbidden thoughts would rise                    20
    Till the pearly tear-drop glistened
    All in her star-like eyes

She saw her love's proud battle ship
Tossed wildly on the storm-dark deep
By the roused wind's destroying sweep              25
    A wrecked & shattered hull
And as the red bolt burst its shroud
And glanced in fire o'er sea & cloud
She heard a peal break deep [and] loud
    Then sink to echoes dull                        30

And as that thunder died away
She saw amid the rushing spray
    Her Edwards Eagle plume
While thus that deathly scene she wrought
And viewed in the deep realms of thought           35
    His soul['s] appalling doom
A voice through all the forest rang
Up like a deer the lady sprang
    'Tis he 'tis he she cried
And ere another moments space                       40
In time's unresting course found place
By heaven! & by our ladys grace
    Lord Edward clasped his bride

                        [July-August 1833]

MS: L
First Publication: **Poet Lore,** Autumn 1897, partial; Shorter 1918

**81**    A quarter of an hour had scarcely elapsed before a sweet yet
solemn strain of music rising at a distance came stealing
gradually in until it appeared to be almost within the apartment
& then a feminine voice rich deep & melodious rose chanting the
following wild stanzas

O who has broke the stilly hush
Which hung around the spirits tower
What strange wild tones & voices rush
Through the lone silence of their bower

Who bade the builders hammer ring                     5
Through chambers dedicate to gloom
Who dared his household gods to bring
Where wander dwellers of the tomb?

here the song ceased but the music still continued & in a
little while another voice softer & sweeter than the
previous one but not so rich adopted the strain &
proceeded thus

O thou who lists the spirit's song
O thou who broke the spirit's rest                10
Long shall their terrors deep & long
Wake torture in thy guilty breast

I bid thee by the spectral light
Of the wan moon that sails the sky
And by the sunshined glad & bright              15
Whence dim night-loving spectres fly

I bid thee quit these haunted halls
'Ere morn emits one golden ray
Haste leave to us our ruined walls
& speed thee on a brighter way                20
Heark to the wind so wild & dying
Through the black solemn Fir grove sighing
List to th' unearthly voice that calls
The tongue that summons thee away

Harp and song were now hushed but a sepulchural voice
like the echo of a vault took up the last word & in
hollow far receding tones muttered thrice away, away,
away.

                                  October 1, 1833

MS:  F(2)
First Publication:  Shorter 1918

To the desert sands of Palestine
    To the Kingdoms of the East
For love of the cross & the holy shrine
    For hope of heavenly rest
In the old dark times of faintest light            5
Aye wandered forth each Red-cross Knight

Warmed by the Palmer's strange, wild tale
    Warmed by the minstrel's song
They took plumed helm & coat of mail
    And sabre keenly strong                        10
Then left O high and gallant band!
For unknown shores, their own sweet land!

The cross was still their guiding star
    Their weapon and their shield
In vain the lance & scymitar                       15
    Opposing squadrons wield
For still victorious from the Fight
Came back each noble red-cross Knight

In vain shrill pipe and timbrel's swell
    Rose from the turbaned host                    20
For still the bloody infidel
    The wreath of conquest lost
And still that garland's hallowed light
Crowned gloriously the red-cross Knight

The lion King of Christendom                       25
Was gathered where his fathers rest
And ne'er again did battle-hum
Sound from the deserts of the East
And on Britannia's Island shore
The red-cross Knight was seen no more              30

Six hundred circles of our Earth
Moved round the God of light
When lo! a great and glorious birth
    Broke forth on Afric's night
Now flow my strain more swiftly flow               35
Drink Inspiration's spirit glow

For Gifford is thy wonderous theme
The bravest and the best of men
Whose life has been one martial dream
One war against the Saracen                           40
Reviver of the holy sign
Which whelmed with slaughter Palestine

Hail great Crusader! lift the cross
Call kingdom's to thy banner's shade
And heedless of all earthly loss                      45
Through blood, through fire, through carnage wade
Led by that high & heavenly gem
The living star of Bethlehem

Wade to the city of renown
    And ransom Zion from her Foe                      50
Take to thyself a radiant crown
    And pour on him eternal woe
Then shall earth's mightiest bless thy name
And yield to thee the palm of Fame.

        C. Brontë                      Oct$^{br}$ 2$^{nd}$ -33

MS:  F(2)
First Publication:  Wise RCK 1917


**83**        **Lines written beside a fountain in the ground's of
              York Villa.**

                      _____

Dear is the hour, when freed from toils & care
I wander where this lonely fount is singing
And listen to the sounds which fill the air
        From its sweet waters springing

O! who can tell how welcome is that hour             5
How deeply tranquil, how divinely blest
None but the wearied know the hallowed pow'r
        Of one sweet pause of rest

My burning brow, pressed to the cool green grass
Freshened with spray-drops from the murmuring well   10
What strange, wild musings through my spirit pass
        What transient fancies swell


                        117

High soars my soul from it's chilled earthy bed
I hear the harmonius gates of heaven unfold
I see around me all the silent dead                    15
    Great ones who lived of old

But these bright shadows fade full soon away
The wood with all its twilight shades returns
Again the fount springs in the moon's dim ray
    Again the night-breeze mourns           20

O 'God of heaven! what now is Earth to me
What all the pow'r the grandeur she can give
But for the joys of sweet Tranquility
    I care not now to live

Aye! by this lonely fount on this hushed night          25
I would amid untroubled silence die
Expire in stilly darkness, wake to light
    And heavenly melody

           C B Oct$^{br}$ 7$^{th}$ 33

MS:  F(2)
First Publication:  BST 1931

**84**        On the shore of the dark wild sea
Alone I am roaming
While sounds its voice mournfully
Through the dim gloaming

O those deep hollow tones                               5
Sad thoughts inspire
They swell like the thrilling moans
From breeze swept lyre

Echos from rock & cave
Solemnly dying                                          10
Answer the howling wave
Mock the wind's sighing

Far in the silent sky
Wandering worlds quiver
Thus they shall beam on high                            15
Changeless for ever

But ere another moon
Silvers the billow
Ocean will be my tomb
Sea-sand my pillow                                    20

Then my unhallowed name
None shall remember
Gone like the dying flame
Quenched like the ember

[November 1833]

MS:  M
First  Publication:  **Two  Tales  By  Charlotte  Brontë:    "The  Secret"  and
**"Lily  Hart"**,  transcribed  and  edited  by  William
Holtz,  Columbia:    The  University  of  Missouri  Press,
1978


**85**        Dark is the mansion of the dead
                  Dark desolate and still
            Around it dwells a solemn dread
                  Within a charnel chill

            O mother! does thy spirit rest                   5
                  In fairer worlds than ours?
            'mid tranquil valleys ever-blest
                  And ever-blooming bowers?

            I trust it doth for thy pale clay
                  Hath found no fair abode                    10
            Shut from the happy light of day
                  Pressed by the cold earth's load

            Yet mother! I would rest with thee
                  In thy long dreamless sleep
            Though dread its mute solemnity                   15
                  All voiceless, still & deep

            And I would rest my weary head
                  Upon thy lifeless breast
            Nor feel one shuddering thrill of dread
                  At what my temples prest                    20

119

Earth is a dreary void to me
Heaven is a cloud of gloom
Then mother! let me sleep with thee
Safe in thy stilly tomb

[November 1833]

MS: M
First Publication:  See previous poem


86  Each, sound of woe has dyed away upon the summer air
    The sob of sharp impassioned grief the sigh of calm despair
    And now on the decaying brieze no human accent swells
    But oft at intervals sweeps by the hallowed sound of bells
    As ever in the village church a solemn peal they toll                    5
    A requiem of soft harmony to rest the parted soul
    The dove-like wings of Sacred Peace are brooding o'er the scene
    No troubled wind goes murmuring through grove & alley green
    No cloud sits in the tranquil sky or flings a fitful shade
    Upon the bosoms shadowless of forest walk or glade                       10
    But calmly the descending sun smiles through a halo bright
    And joyously the sportive deer bound in his setting light
    Amid these huge ancestral trees how merrily they leap
    Through the alternate bursts of light or gloom profoundly deep
    They know not that the might of death hath borne that form away          15
    That angel form of innocence round which they loved to play
    They heard not the lament which rung through yonder lordly hall
    The hymn of woe which late was sung o'er sable bier & pall
    And little know they of the grief that darkens Percy's brow
    And weighs a bitter burden on his haughty heart even now                 20
    Alone he stands & motionless in that small cemetery
    No paleness on his brow or cheek no moisture in his eye
    With arms enfolded on his breast mute as a sculptured stone
    He utters not a whispered word he murmurs not a moan
    His eyes are on his Mary's tomb, fresh mid surrounding waves             25
    But his thoughts are wandering far amid a raging world of waves
    He thinks upon that bygone time, when with his Rover free
    All bright with beauty dark with crime he swept the
        earth-wide sea
    The conquering, the invincible, the angel-like in form
    The fiend in heart he heeded not the moaning of the storm               30
    He loved the voice of ocean strife the thunder of the flood
    Where he quenched his thirst for glory in war's wine-red cup
        of blood
    But not on conflicts of the deep dwells his dark spirit now
    No other actions other scenes within his memory grow


                              120

The wild waves of the Genii deep                          35
Roll dark before his mental eye
And waken from their silent sleep
_Thoughts that can never, never die
That barren shore, that, briny sea
That sound of saddest harmony                             40
Which still o'er those green waters wailed
_All in their ancient might return
Again they roll again they mourn
    While half in mist-wreaths veiled
Arise high rocks, sweep up steep Fells                    45
Cliffs where the monarch Eagle dwells
Hill beyond Hill receding swells
And all between lye wildest dells
    Where not a green herb grows
Where no sweet floweret droops its bells                  50
    And no bright streamlet flows
Afar off the dim Spirits throne
Towers in it's haughtiness alone
    _   Clouds on its brow repose
And nearer soars the Robbers Hill                         55
Where deeds that might the heart's blood chill
And every nerve with horror thrill
    _   Have cursed the light of day
Whose were those deeds?  he knows full well
No need for other tongue to tell                          60
    Since Percy's soul can say
How once their came to that dark land
    Across that stormy water
The dread scourge of a Pirate band
    Stern ruthless sons of slaughter                      65
And not a hearth on hill or vale
    Round all that salt lake's border
But echoed to the long death wail
    Or bore the stain of murder
He was the leader of that band                            70
He led those hell-hounds to the land
Yes he it was the, Fair the young
From a proud line of nobles sprung
A race by bard & minstrel sung
    That passed with them the Flood                       75
And while sharp death-shrieks round him rung
    Smiled at the scene of blood

But yet at times the Corsair had far other moods than these
He still within his bosom held some human sympathies
His heart yet answered to the thrill of loves all conquering
    power                                                 80


121

Here first he saw his Mary's form, that sweet but faded flower
It was about the set of sun when heaven blushed crimson bright
And the Great Lake from east to west rolled on in waves of light
When he in melancholy thought paced slow beside the sea
Soothed by the sound of surge and wave which murmured mournfully    85
When sudden through the evening sky, a strain of music stole
So sweet, so sad its melody thrilled through his inmost soul
And then a voice most silver sweet joined in that vesper song
And woke the laughter of the arch those caverned rocks among
O! still that voice is in his ear, its tones will never die          90
But low & faint they murmur on like some wild harp's last sigh
          Thus while the answering echoes rung
          That lyre was swept that strain was sung

          There are lands where scents of flowers
               All the air with fragrance fill                        95
          Where Fountains spring in myrtle bowers
               But I love my native hill

          There are lands where birds are singing
               Ceaselessly their notes they trill
          Till the earth with song is ringing                        100
               But I love my native hill

          There are lands where woods are waving
               Under skies for ever still
          Lands which golden streams are laving
               But I love my native hill                             105

          Though its barren stony wildness
               Every heart with dread might chill
          Though beneath no heaven of mildness
               Yet I love my native hill

Slowly lord Percy raised his head, when ceased that gentle          110
     strain
Before him rose a giant rock far beetling o'er the main
And at his foot a maiden sat so young so mildly fair
She seemed a vision of the deep, a spirit of the air
Beside her on the silvery sand a ivory lyre was laid
Her plume was from the eagle's wing her robe a rainbow plaid        115
Soft parted on her placid brow like gloss her tresses beamed
And down the neck of stainless snow in sunny ringlets streamed
Her eyes were on the wandering waves that murmured at her feet
And the dark drooping lashes hid their lustre calm & sweet
But as the pirate's stately step along the beach drew nigh          120
The lids were raised & showed beneath an azure like the sky
Up sprung the lady with a shriek faint tremulous with dread
She knew the robber of the deep by his girdle bloody red

Fear not said he in gentlest tones fear not sweet mountain rose
I would not by one word or deed break thy pure hearts repose          125
Look on me lady am I one whom thou hast cause to fly
Is aught of Rapine on my brow of fierceness in my eye

    She looked, a figure stood beside
    Formed in the very mould of pride
       Almost of Giant height                                         130
    His curled lip wore a winning smile
    But his dark raidiant eye the while
       Shone with a haughty light
    Needs not to tell what feelings stole
    O'er that young mountain maiden's soul                         135
    When she beheld that noble form
    Needs not to tell the mortal love
    That soon a passion wild & warm
    Bound the proud Eagle to the dove
    Full oft in many an after night                                140
    They met upon the sea swept shore
    While o'er them sailed the stars of light
    And round them rang the wild wave's roar
    Oft in the time of Star & dew
    When winds fall low & skies gleam blue                        145
    When all the sounds of discord cease
    And balmiest breezes whisper peace
    When moonlight sleeps on hill & vale
    So soft & soothing pure & pale
    Would these two faithful lovers wander                        150
    Beside the dark lakes ceaseless thunder
    Or far away through some wild glen
    Stony & dark as cavarned den
    Which seldom heard the voice of men
       And seldom felt their tread                               155
    And there the silence stern & deep
    Was dreary as the dreamless sleep
       Of the unwaking dead
    O How their accents low and calm
    Went murmuring on the night-wind's balm                       160
       Through each dark rock recess
    How happy then each lover's heart
    How sad when morning bid them part
       O those were hours of bliss
    And now on Percy they return                                  165
    With such a might from memory's urn
    That heart & spirit kindled burn
       To think that what has been
    Can never while the clear stars shine
    While man is sinful God divine                                170
       Can never be again

For her sweet form is dust to dust
Her holy spirit with the just
    The pure the sanctified
And Hell's own pangs rend Percy's breast            175
To see her in the heaven of rest
    To know himself denied
He feels they never may meet more
For Death's wide sea without a shore
    Rolls boundlessly between                       180
Then corpse-like grew his cheek & brow
And from his eyes came rushing now
Hot tears like burning rain
O! is their peace for him in heaven
Can all his crimes be yet forgiven                  185
He lifted to the moonbeams bright
A face & forehead ghastly white
    Pale lips that moved in prayer
But ere the mute petition rose
Again his softened feelings froze                   190
    Dryed on his cheek his tear
Again the infidels black night
Closed o'er that glimpse of heaven's own light
    Lord Percy turned away
He left with death his buried bride                 195
And filled with the storm fiend of pride
    Went on his homeward way

                        C. Brontë Nov^{br} 20^{th} -33

 F(2)
st Publication:   Shorter 1923 partial; SHB Misc I

## Richard Cour de Lion & Blondel


The blush, the light, the gorgeous glow of Eve
Waned from the radiant chambers of the west;
Now, twilight's robe of dim, orient shadows weave:
One star; gleams faintly lustrous in the east;
Far down it shines, on the blue Danube's breast,           5
As calmly, wavelessly its waters glide
On to th' appointed region of their rest,
The Sea, profound and hoary, waste and wide;
Whose black'ning billows swell in ever restless pride.

High o'er the river rose a rocky hill,                                    10
With barren sides, precipitous, and steep:
There, 'gainst the sunset heav'ns, serene, and still
Frown'd the dark turrets of a feudal Keep:
The folded flag, hung in the air asleep;
The breathless beauty of the Summer night                                15
Gave not that Austrian standard, to the sweep
Of fresh'ning Zephyr, or wild Storm-blast's might;
But motionless, it drooped, in eve's soft, dying light

In that Stern Fortress, there were arch, and tow'r,
And Iron-wrought lattice, narrow, deep-embayed;                          20
Where the gloom gather'd thick as night's mid hour
And round about it, hung a chilling shade,
Which told of dungeons, where the light ne'er play'd;
Of prison-walls, of fetter-bolt and chain;
Of Captives, 'neath a Tyrant's durance laid;                            25
Never, to view the sun's bright face again;
Never to breathe the air, of free, wild hill and plain.

The moon had risen, a host of stars among,
When, to th' embattled castle walls, drew nigh
A wand'ring minstrel, from his shoulder hung                             30
A harp, sweet instrument of melody.
He paus'd awhile, beneath the turret high,
Then took his harp, and all the sweet chords swept,
Till a sound swell'd beneath the silent sky,
And holiest music, on the charmed air crept,                            35
Waked from the magic strings, Where till that hour they slept.

O! how that wild strain o'er the river swelled,
And mingled with its gentle murmuring,
From the true fount of song divine, it welled;
Music's own simple undefiled spring;                                     40
Notes rose, and dyed such as the wild birds sing
In the lone-wood, or the far lonelier sky.
O! none but Blondel, but the minstrel king
Could waken such transcendent melody;
Sweet as a fairy's lute, soft as a passing sigh.                        45
The strain he sung, was some antique romance,
Some long forgotten song of other years;
Born in the cloudless clime of sunny France,
Where Earth, in vernal loveliness appears;
Where the bright grape distils its purple tears;                        50
And clear streams flow, And dim, blue hills arise
A gleaming crown of snows Each mountain wears;
And there are cities, 'neath her starry skies,
As fair as ever blest, with beauty, mortal eyes.

Blondel's Song

The moonlight; sleeps low, on the hills of Provence;                    55
The stars are all tracking, their paths in the sky;
How softly, and brightly, their golden orbs glance,
Where the long shining waves, of the silver Rhone lie.

The tow'rs of De Courcy rise high in the beam,
From sky to earth trembling, so lustrous and pale,                      60
Around them there dwells the deep hush of a dream,
And stilled is the murmur of River and gale.

There are groves in the moonlight, all sparkling with dew,
There are dim garden-paths, round that Castle of Pride;
Where the bud of the rose, and the hyacinth blue,                       65
Close their leaves, to the balm of the moist even-tide.

And long is the alley, dark, bowery, and dim,
Where sits a white form 'neath a tall chestnut tree
Which waves its broad branches, all dark'ling and grim,
O'er the young rose of Courcy, Sweet Anna Marie.                        70

And who kneels beside her? A warrior in mail.
On his helm there's a plume In his hand there's a lance
And why does the cheek of the lady turn pale?
Why weeps in her beauty The Flower of Provence?

She weeps for her lover, this night, are they met                       75
To breathe a farewell, 'neath love's own holy star;
For to-morrow the crest of the young Lavalette,
Will float highest, and first in the van of the war.

Thus far sang Blondel, when
A sudden tone, of quivering harp-strings, on his ear upsprung;          80
It sounded, like an echo of his own;
So faintly, that mysterious music rung,
So sweet, it floated, those dark towers among,
And seemed to issue from their topmost height:
Then there were words, in measured cadence sung.                        85
Now soft and low, then with a master's might,
Poured forth that varying strain, upon the stilly night

Who sings? the minstrel knows there is but one,
Whose voice has music half so rich, and deep--
Whose hand can summon from the harp a tone,                             90
So thrilling, that it calls from latent sleep
Heroic thoughts, dims eyes, that seldom weep,
With tears of extasy, and fires the breast,
Till listening warriors, from their chargers leap,
Assume the glittering helm, and nodding Crest,                          95
Unsheathe the ready sword And lay the lance in rest

126

But not of war, nor of the battle blast,
Sung now the kingly harper no his strain
Was mournful, as a dream of days long past:
At times it swelled; but quickly died again;                    100
And oh! the sadness of that wild refrain!
Suited full well with the lone, solemn hour,
Too sad for joy, too exquisite for pain,--
It touched the heart Subdued the spirit's power
Blent with the Danube's moan, and wailed around the tower       105


Richard's Song

Thrice the great fadeless lights of heaven
The moon, and the eternal sun
As God's unchanging law was given,
Have each their course appointed run.
Three times the Earth, her mighty way                           110
Hath measured o'er a shoreless sea;
While hopeless still from day, to day,
I've sat in lone captivity;
Listening the wind, and river's moan wakening
My harp's solemn tone,                                          115
    And longing to be free.

Blondel! my heart seems cold, and dead;
My soul, has lost its ancient might;
The sun of chivalry is fled,
And dark despair's, unholy night                                120
Above me closes still and deep;
While wearily each lapsing day
Leads onward, to the last, long sleep;
The hour when all shall pass away;
When King and Captive, Lord and Slave                           125
Must rest unparted, in the grave
    A mass of soulless clay.

O long I've listened to the sound,
Of winter's blast, and Summer's breeze,
As their sweet voices sung around.                              130
Through echoing caves, and wind-waved trees.
And long I've viewed from prison bars
Sunset, and dawn, and night, and noon:
Watched the uprising of the stars,
Seen the calm advent of the moon:                              135
But blast and breeze and stars, and Sun
All vainly swept, all vainly shone,
I filled a living tomb.

God of my Fathers!  Can it be?
Must I, the chosen of thy might?                    140
Whose name alone, brought victory,
Whose battle-cry was God my Right
Closed, in a Tyrant's dungeon cell,
Wear out the remnant of my life?
And never hear again, the swell                      145
Of high and hot and glorious strife.
Where trumpet's peal, and bugles sing,
And minstrels sweep the martial string,
And wars, and fame are rife.

No Bondel! thou wert sent by heaven,                 150
Thy King, thy Lion-King to free,
To thee, the high command was given
To rescue from captivity

Haste from the Tyrant Austrian's Hold,
Cross rapidly the rolling sea,                       155
And go, where dwell the brave, the bold,
By stream and Hill and greenwood tree.
Minstrel let Merry England, ring
With tidings of her Lion-king,
    And bring back liberty.                          160

Such was the lay, the Monarch Minstrel sung,
A few bright moons, waned from the silent heavens
And Albion, with a shout of Triumph rung;
As once again her worshipped King was given
Back to her breast, his bonds asunder riven          165
And the Sweet Empress of the subject Sea
Sent up her hymn of gratitude to heaven
Through all her coasts she hailed him crowned & free
The Champion of God's hosts The pride of liberty.

                            Charlotte Brontë
                        Dec<sup>br</sup> 27<sup>th</sup> --- 1833
                        Haworth nr Bradford

MS:  B(1)
First  Publication:  **Richard  Coeur  de  Lion  and  Blondel:    A  Poem  by**
                     **Charlotte  Brontë**,  London,  Printed  for  T.J.  Wise,
                     1912


**88**              The moon dawned slow on the dusky gloaming
                        Dimly beside it gleamed a star
                    Broken, they shone on the waters foaming
                        Of the rapid Calabar

                              128

The lustrous moon the wailing river                    5
    Woke in my breast the voice of thought
In that calm hour I blessed the Giver
    The Source whence ray & moan were brought
And while they gleamed & while they sung
I gave them life life & soul & tongue               10

I asked the river whence its stream
    Rushed in resounding pride
And a voice like whispers in a dream
    Thus solemnly replied

    From the caverned earth I rose              15
        Mortal like to thee
    Ever-more my torrent flows
        Sounding to the sea
    Even as thy career will close
        In vast eternity.                      20

I asked the rising crescent moon
    O'er what her bow was bent
And thus the sweet response came down
    From heaven Earthward sent

    Beneath my midnight wandering               25
        How widely lies the earth
    I view the streams meandering
        To the ocean from its birth
    I see the proud hill swelling
        Where foot has never trod              30
    The snows eternal dwelling
        Beheld alone by God

    Alike my rays are glancing
        On cities filled with life
    Where sounds of mirth & dancing             35
        And harp & song are rife
    And on the ruined tower
        The rifted arch & dome
    The fallen & trampled bower
        The still, the desert home             40

    Where fitful winds are sighing
        Through temple, arch & hall
    And slowly, calmly dying
        With many a mild, faint fall
    Sweet murmurs, sad decaying                 45
        Fill all the air with moans
    Sounds through the desert straying
        Blent, mingled, nameless tones

129

Sounds of the palm-tree shaken
        Sounds of the lonely well                          50
Whose fairy murmurs waken
        To the Zephyr's softest swell
The waving of a pinion
        The desert wild deer's tread
And heard in that dominion                                 55
        Of silence deep & dead

I see beneath me spreading
        Dark visions of the slain
For my orb it's light is shedding
        O'er many a battle plain                           60
Where hero's famed in story
        Their deeds of war have done
And gained a crown of glory
        For mighty conflicts won

Where sunless clouds are sweeping                          65
        Shades of eternal Gloom
Yet my beams in peace are sleeping
        Above the warriors tomb
My gentlest, mildest splendour
        Is poured above their dust                         70
Whence earth at last shall render
        The brave, the good, the just

If mid the desert dreary
        Far, far from war & strife
Should rest the heroic weary                               75
        Rest from the toil of life
Though no shade be o'er him given
        Though the pale sand be his shroud
Yet above him, bright in heaven
        My silver arch is bowed                            80

If to the wilds denying
        That high & holy trust
The warriors corpse is lying
        Amid ancestral dust
Still lovelier is the lustre                               85
        that lingers round his tomb
And lights the trees that cluster
        Above his last, dark home.

                        [January 1834]

MS: D(2)
First Publication: **Poet Lore,** Spring 1897, partial; **A Bibliography of the Writings in Prose and Verse of the Members of the Brontë Family,** ed., T.J. Wise, London: Privately printed, 1917, partial; Winnifrith PCB

**89**
        In whatsoever character
        The book of Fate is writ
        'Tis well we understand not it
        We should go mad with too much
        Learning there

Thus ends my leafe from the unopened volume of Destiny.

                        Charlotte Brontë
                        January 17th 1834

MS:  D(2)
First Publication: **Poet Lore,** Spring 1897

**90**    Gods of the old mythology, arise in gloom and storm
        Adramalec bow down thy head, reveal dark fiend thy form
        The giant sons of Anakim, bowed lowest at thy shrine
        And thy temple rose in Argob, with its hallowed groves divine
        And there was eastern incense burnt & their were garments spread    5
        With the fine gold decked & broidered & tinged with radiant red
        With the radiant red of furnace flames, that through the shadow
            shone
        As the full moon when on Sinai's top her rising light is thrown

        Baal of Chaldee, dread God of the Sun
        Come from the towers of thy proud Babylon                       10
        From the groves where the green palms of Media grow
        Where flowers of Assyria all fragrantly blow
        Where the waves of Euphrates glide deep as the sea
        Washing the knarled roots of Lebanon's tree
        Ashtaroth curse on the Ammonites rise                          15
        Decked with the beauty & light of the skies
        Let stars by thy crown & let mists round thee curl
        Light as the gossamer, pure as the pearl
        Semele soft vision come glowing & bright
        Come in a shell like the Greek Aphrodite                       20
        Come on the billowy rush of the foam

131

From thy gold house in Elysium roam
From the bright purple gloom of glory
Picture forth thy Goddess story

Come from thy blood-lit furnaces most terrible most dread                          25
From thy most black & bloody flames God Moloch lift thy head
Where the wild wail of infant lungs shrieks horribly alone
And the fearful yelping of their tongues sounds like a demons
    groan
There their heart-riven mother's haste with burdened arms
    raised up
And offer in their agony to thee thy gory cup                                      30
O Dagon from thy threshold roll on thy fishy train
And fall upon thy face & hands & break thy neck again:
Enormous wretch, most beastly fiend.  Plague of the Philistine
O'er the locked Ark Il bid thee come with its cherubim divine
And Belial loathsome where art thou? dost hear my rampant voice    35
I mean to be obeyed man when I make such a noise
My harp is screeching ringing out with a wild & fevered moan
And my lyre like a sparrow with a soar throat has a most
    unearthly tone
A bottle of brandy is in me & my spirit is upon high
& I'll make every man amongst ye pay the piper e're I die          40
And as for thee thou scoundrel, thou brimstone sulpherous mamon
Lets have no more of thee nor of thy villanous gammon
I'll be with you with a salt-whip most horrible for aye
And I'll lash you till your hair turns black as mine is grey
You shall dwell in the red range, while I blow the coals
    full fast                                                      45
And I'll make you feel the fury of a rushing furnace blast
Leap down the sweating rocks & the murderous caves of the pit
& stamp with your hoofs & lash with your tails & fire & fury spit
I'll be at you in a jiffey as fast as I can run
But I'm riding now on the horns of the moon & the back of the
    burning sun                                                   50
The wind is rushing before me & the clouds at a hand-gallop go
And they are getting it properly when they fly a stiver too slow
But the weed slimy lands of the earth send up such a stink to me
That I'm fain to go on in my mad career & soon shall I be with ye
I'm a noble fellow, flames I spew, I shall eat them if I'm
    spared                                                        55
I'm going to the pit of sulpher blue & my name is Thomas Aird.

                                                       [March 1834]

MS:  D(1)
First Publication:  Dodd Mead 1902

**91**    My lady turned her from the light
          Which filled her radiant halls
          To where through veil & shade of night
          The dying moon-beam falls
          Why does she leave the dance & song                     5
          The sweet harps's stirring tone?
          Why turns she from the glittering throng.
          To sigh & mourn alone?

          Mary turned round, took the hand which was now laid
          on her shoulder kissed it fondly & replied with         10
          admirable tact

          She dreamt she saw a glance of fire
          Shot forth from princely eyes
          And viewed the scarlet flush of ire
          To brow of marble rise                                  15
          The troubling dream is past & o'er
          Beloved, thy love, will sigh no more

                                            [February 1834]

MS:  B(2)
First Publication:  SHB Misc I



**92**    The light wings of Zephyr oppressed with perfume
          That sigh through the Gardens of Gul in their bloom

          "Light of my eyes" replied the Duke "my lovely Zulma,
          the breath of this wind is sweet but not like that which
          sweeps over the rose gardens of <Surisean>.  Life not    5
          luxury is the burden borne on this wind, vigour not
          voluptuousness.  I have been in Persia & felt that

          The gale that breathed from that blue sky
          The wind to Earth that fell,
          Had magic in its softest sigh                           10
          And in its lightest swell
          And every breath that wandered by
          And whispered still felicity
          Came o'er me like a spell

                                    133

From morn till the decay of light                          15
    I could have sat alone
And watched through all the silent night
    To listen to its tone
For sweetest when the moon was bright
And stars rose dancing on the sight                        20
    Fell down that dying moan.

                                          [March 1834]

MS:  B(2)
First Publication:  SHB Misc I


93          The day is closed, that spectral sun
            Whose mighty course so strangely run
            Will never die in Afric's story
            Will never lose its awful glory
            Dark solemn, hidden terrible                    5
            For not on earth its radiance fell
            From the first rising of the light
            To the dread drawing-on of night
            A dim eclipse before it hung
            A shadow o'er its disk was flung                10
            A shield of Gloom it passed through heaven.
            A One bloody ring around it drawn
            No joy with those red beams was given
                Earth under it looked cold & lorn
            That orb is sunk in death's chill river         15
                It went down darkly mid the waves
            Whose pitchy ridges seemed to quiver
                A voice rang through the world of graves
            When the great sun its last light quelled
            Where those deep stormy waters swelled          20
            The waves of death, when torch & plume
            Bore Percy to his shrine-like tomb
            When drum to drum all muffeled spoke
            When the wild wailing trumpet woke
            And many sounds of lordly mourning              25
            Came on the still, hushed, voiceless air
            And lamps but not of triumph burning
            Threw to the sky their ghastly glare
            When deep bells, pealed upon the night
            And requiem music poured its might              30
            And Holy fanes were filled of light
                Sepulchral, pale, & dim
            When the pall-bearers glided by


                        134

With foot-steps measured solemnly
       To the slow funeral hymn                         35
Sadly they bore him to his place
Not mid the fathers of his race
       The vault was void & lone
Arched like a palace wide & high
A mansion meet for royalty                              40
When comes the mandate "monarch die"
       To call him from his throne
He rested by the Calabar
His kindred dust reposed afar
       Where storied Gambia glides                      45
Trees waved above their tranquil homes
Cloud-shadows slept upon their tombs
Dew fell, soft sunlight came & went
       As free as in the Arab's tent
Winds kissed their marble sides                         50
And came no dream, with Death's dim sleep
       Of all those silent graves
Came there no memory sad & deep
       To moan of Gambia's waves
No murmur of the breeze that swept                      55
       Amid his native groves
No holy voice that long had slept
       To speak of ancient loves
Was there no strange, no haunting sound
       [To] wail his dying pillow round                 60
Of whispering woods & gliding streams
That o'er his soul brought wondrous gleams
Not like th' uncertain light of dreams
& not like wildering memory's beams
       But quiet & clear & bright                       65
Of what was once, but is no more
A glimpse of a retiring shore
       Fading as swift as light
But while it lasts, each well-known place
The sharpened eye may clearly trace                     70
As if between <no> surging sea
Rolled on in vast solemnity
As if no rush of surge & foam
Then bore the shuddering vessel home
As if the dark expanse before                           75
Showed mid its waves no other shore
A lone, dim, blue unbounded line
Which never yet could man define
And none have e'er returned to tell
What visions in its darkness dwell                      80
No home-bound <bark> has crossed those seas
To speak its hidden mysteries

Men say that sometimes wrapt in gloom
& fraught with tidings dread of doom
A spectral sail has wandered back                    85
& noiseless ploughed its ancient track
But when th' appointed work was done
Has past like mist-wreaths in the sun
And passed there o'er this phantom sea
No cherished shape of memory                          90
Through the dull rushing of its water
    Spoke no remembered tongue
Maria! bright Italia's daughter
    Was not thine image flung
In all its clear & kindling ligh[t]                   95
Before thy dying Percy's sight
Long had that star <set> quenched in gloom
    Long had that flower lain dead
And long beneath the heavy tomb
    That palm had bowed its head                      100
Mouldering, mouldering silently
Gambia's quiet waters by
Morning, evening vainly shining
Day light's rise & dusk's declining
Vainly on that calm grave fell                        105
Earth had heard her last farewell

Yet as the star once twinkled
    Again its ray might glow
And that flower with dews besprinkled
    Might sweetly breathe <below>                     110
And the palm so shrunk & wrinkled
    To stately stature grow

One momment reappearing
    One moment & no more
The light the glory wearing                           115
That erst on earth she wore
The smile the step, the bearing
    All known, all loved before

The eye so full of fire
    The brow so marked with pride                     120

                                    [May 1834]

MS:  F(2)
First Publication:  Winnifrith PCB, partial
Text:  1. 12:  "A" probably intended to be deleted, but left uncanceled
       1. 60:  "that" canceled at the beginning of the line and "wailed"
               changed to "wail"
       1. 104:  the first two words seem to be canceled

The muffled clash of arms is past, as if it ne'er had been,
The light'ning scymitar has sheathed its terrors bright and keen;
Once bright, once keen, dark spots of blood bedim its lustre now,
And the sharpness of the tempered edge, is dull'd by many a blow.
Dark windings of the valley's bed! deep gorges of the Hill!      5
Bear further off that hurried tread,
Which wakes your echoes, low, and dead;
It fails and all is still.

Seems now as if no voice, no sound
Had ever rung, or moaned around,                                 10
Save perhaps, some lone bird's plaintive song,
Dying those wild, vast woods among;
Unanswered, for there lingers there
No joyous denizen of air,
And that one wand'rer flitting by,                               15
Vainly, for sweet response might sigh,
Vainly might hope for some far strain,
To greet his warbled call again;
The breeze alone, shrill, dirge-like, sad,
Borne down those huge hills cedar-clad;                          20
Deep hid in gloom, the rivers rush,
Pouring unseen, through reed and bush,
And (sign of utter solitude
Strange sounds of alien rill, and wood;
Woods, that are murmm'ring far away,                             25
Rills, that glide off in foam and spray,
Through mist-like distance dim, and grey:
No other sounds erewhile were heard
Responsive to the lonely bird
But now, there is another tone,                                  30
Faint, as the river's faintest moan;
Low, as the West-wind's softest sigh,
Breathed sweet, from an unclouded sky;
Sad, as the last note's calm decay,
'Ere the wild warbler flits away;                                35
Yet heard through all, those tones belong
Neither to stream, nor wood, nor song:
They speak of life, they bear a thrill
Not native to the wordless grove;
The whisper'd echoes of the hill,                                40
The gushing waters, of the rill,
Have no such power to move
And there is life, a human form
Lies prostrate in the vale,
Like a reft victim of the storm,                                 45

Fall'n, bleeding, cold & pale
A stately form, though blighted now,
For grandeur dwells upon his brow,
And light shines in his lifted eye,
Which looks on Death unfearingly,                    50
And o'er him, rests that placid grace,
Sign of high blood, and noble race,
His forehead bears a diadem
Burning with many an orient gem,
Stained ruddy now in blood                           55
The starry robe, the flashing ring
The pearls in bright, and braided string
All speak of Persia's slaughtered King,
Stretched dying by the flood

Let not the glass be shaken                           60
Life's sands, are ebbing low,
Let no loud winds awaken
The tide is past its flow

The swords that gleamed around him
Are reddened with his gore,                           65
The traitor-hands that bound him
Will never bind him more

All Iran has forsaken
The God to whom she kneeled
This word no more can waken                           70
Life on the battle-field

Not one, of all the glorious host
That bowed to Mithra's beam
Ere Persia's crown, was won, and lost,
By Issus fatal stream.                                75
Not one, who by the Granicus
Poured forth their lives in blood;
Not one, who on Arbela's plain
In serried phalanx stood,
Not one remains to watch him now                      80
Not one, to wipe his death-damp brow;
A monarch, left without a throne;
Pomp, might, dominion, all are gone,
A Son bereaved, a childless sire,
A King slain in the traitor's ire;                    85
On the dark streamlet's wild bank lying,
Behold Darius lone, and dying.

Where, are now, his farewell dreams
Fading fast as daylight's beams?
O! where rests the monarch's heart                    90
Now, when life, and glory part?
Sees he, with that glazing eye
Susa's gorgeous majesty?
All the light of regal halls
Where the gushing fountain falls?                      95
All that rich, and radiant ring,
Once the Guard of Asia's king?
Gardens bright, where flower, and tree,
Waved in airs of Araby?
Whither, wings his spirit now?                          100
Whither do his last thoughts flow?
All his mighty Empire, lies
Round him, as he droops & dies,
Ancient Egypt's, storied pride
With the dark Nile's pondrous tide;                     105
India, rich in pearl and gem,
Hallowed by the Ganges' stream;
Syria with her tideless sea
Ever sleeping placidly
Desert lands, where wand'ring dwell                     110
Ishmael's sons invincible,
Fall'n Palmyra, ruined Tyre,
Where the Grecian's flood of ire
Burst so full, and fierce and strong,
Rolled so dark, and deep along,                         115
That no voice was left, to tell
How their sovereign city fell
As the prophet-doom was spoken,
Her robe is rent, her sceptre broken
Israel's God is Conqu'ror now                           120
Crown, and plume have left her brow,
She rests silent by the sea
And so shall rest eternally.

O! not to these the monarch turns,
Not to glories past away;                               125
Remembrance, in his spirit burns,
But not of power's decay.

A voice, still whispers in his ear
Of one his word betrayed,
And shadow-like, there lingers near                    130
A form that will not fade.

The warning words of one who died,
That victim to a Tyrant's pride
Th' Athenian voice of prophesy,
"King my Avenger's step draws nigh                                135
"The twilight of thy day is closing,
"And clouds are on its fall reposing.
"I hear the distant tempest sighing,
"In muttered murmurs, faint, and dying
"Asia, with sound of arms is shaken,                             140
"But who will to the conflict waken?
"On rolls the foe, in living thunder,
"Insatiate for the dazzling plunder
"The steeled bands of Macedon,
"The hosts of Ammon's haughty son                                145
"Shall crush thy pomp, shall spurn thy gems,
"Shall dye with blood, thine Empire's streams
"From Iran's throne, its Sovereign hurl;
"And Mithra's gorgeous standard furl:
"For ever furl, the sacred fire                                  150
"Shall never more to heaven aspire,
"Its light shall fade; its flames shall die,
"They own not immortality
"Another Altar shall arise
"Beneath the bright Earth's cloudless skies.                     155
"King of the Earth, my course is run,
"Remember me, and Macedon."
Thus boldly Caridemus spoke
Then sank beneath the tyrant's stroke:
But his last voice, to heaven ascends,                           160
And heaven, to hear its accent bends.
From the dark tomb Darius gave,
There comes, no murmur of a slave,
The hallowed blood of
Liberty, sends from the                                          165
Dust its thrilling cry
Makes to the Gods its stern appeal,
And summons Grecia's sons of steel.

They come!  They come!
A measured tread                                                 170
Heavy, and clanking, deep, and dread,
Breaks up the hush, profoundly dead,
Of that wild, rocky vale
And gleaming lance, and flashing shield,
Their blood-gilt light and glitter yield,                        175
And plumes are on the gale
Onward they come!
A noble host!
Now in the deep'ning valley lost,

Now through the wood-glade, glancing seen,                    180
All mailed, and burnished, bright, & sheen
At length, around the king they pour,
Of Grecia's host, the pride and power.
Darius, lifts again his eye,
He sees not now, the placid sky,                               185
For the green-wood, and lonely glen,
He views a throng, of steel armed men;
The hum, and clash swell stern, and loud,
And o'er him many a form is bowed,
And many an eye of eagle-light,                                190
Meets piercingly his failing sight.
Tall warriors, on their lances leaning,
Plume shadowed brows of darkest meaning,
Surround the dying king
Their shapes before his vision swim                            195
Ghost-like, and wand'ring, faint & dim,
Their voice, sounds like a sacred hymn,
     Low, solemn, murmuring.
One kneels beside, and props his head,
And from the river's crystal bed,                              200
     Sprinkles his ghastly brow
The cool, clear water as it falls,
A moment, sight and speech recalls;
     Darius knew his foe.
He clasped his hands, and raised his eyes                      205
Bright with forgiveness to the skies,
He blessed his conqu'ror in that hour,
He prayed for added might, and pow'r,
To follow Asia's alien Lord,
And strengthen, his resistless sword:                          210
Statira's shade is near him now
She lightens thus his kingly brow
And, with her calm, and holy smiles
Her Lord, and Captor reconciles
But soon, that gentle shade is gone,                           215
And Vengeance lingers there alone;
A sudden gloom falls round the King;
Stern thoughts within his bosom spring,
The Rebel-Satrap, and his band,
Men, of unhallowed heart, and hand,                            220
Before their slaughtered monarch rise,
His Curse falls on them ere he dies,
"Soldiers of Greece and Macedon
"For the dark deed, by Bessus done,
I leave revenge to Ammon's son.                                225
He before whom all Persia fell
The Glorious, the Invincible
The lord of Cyrus solemn throne

The crowned in haughty Babylon,
I charge him, by his power, and pride,                    230
To think how Iran's monarch died,
To turn the Traitor's blood stained sword,
Back to the bosom of its lord,
A bitter draught he gave his King,
His lips shall drain the same dark spring:               235
Warriors! I may not longer stay,
For Mithra calls my soul away!

He said, his pale lip ceased to quiver
His soul soared to its awful Giver,
The host stood round, all hushed, and still,             240
While dirge-like murmured, breeze, and rill.

May 2$^{nd}$ 1834                              Charlotte Brontë.

MS:  F(1) & D(1)
First Publication:  **Darius Codomannus.  A Poem by Charlotte Brontë**,
                    London:  Printed for T.J. Wise, 1920


**95  STANZAS ON THE FATE OF HENRY PERCY**


Lieutenant H Percy it is well [known], took a voyage to the
South sea-Islands on board the Mermaid, Commander--Captain
Steighton.  he was drowned off Otaheite, I have heard strange
reports respecting the manner of his death, many of them from
undeniably authentic sources.  to give the reader some insight
as to their nature I need only say they tend to fix another
crime of the darkest dye on the character of his terrible
father, Steighton was a minion of the elder Percy's men say he
served him but too faithfully in the matter now before our
notice.

The tropic twilight falls, the deep is still,
All turmoils of the busy day are past,
From the calm land no voice comes deep, or shrill,
No murmur from the world of waters vast,
Save its own ceaseless sound, that breeze, or blast       5
Now chafes not into dull & thunderous moan;
The faintest gleam of eve is o'er it cast
And O how sweet! how holy! is the tone
That swell[s] from each green wave, then trembling dies alone


142

There's not a boat upon the darkened billow,!                    10
Theres not an oar dips in the moonlight main
Each islander rests on his happy pillow
Each swift canoe has sought its home again
And neither ringing shout nor trem'bling strain
Comes from the shore to break the green sea's rest            15
All earth lies hushed to watch the gorgeous wane
Of that bright sunset, from her burning breast
To see the light of heaven die, dim, & soft, and blest

Fair, southern Islands! they are sweetly sleeping
While the stars gather, in their heav'n above,                   20
While sky-breathed airs, the deep dark woods are sweeping
In gales too low to wake the slumbering dove,
Almost too faint to bend the palmy grove:
Intenslier purple, grows that kindling dome,
And brighter flash those orbs of light & love                   25
Sweet, tropic Islands! ye are beauty's home
O! who from your bright shores to colder lands would roam.

Midnight is near, that bark upon the water
Has furled her sails and set her watch on deck;
She rides at anchor, Neptune's noblest daughter,                30
The very waves seem subject to her beck
They dare not dash her glory to a wreck!
How the pure foam, curls round her mighty bows!
As fair as braided pearls, on beauty's neck
How the wild wave more softly gliding flows!                    35
Where that proud Ocean-queen, far down, her vast shadow throws.

A wondrous Stranger! from afar appearing
Long as she walked the path that leaves no track,
And her brave crew, a thousand hazards daring,
Still scorned to turn their noble vessel back,                   40
No heart fell cold, no hand grew faint and slack,
As on with heav'n above and waves beneath,
And round a wild horizon, densely black,
They stretched before the trade-gale's fiery breath,
Looked full of joy to hope, and fearlessly to Death.            45

Now all is tranquil, they have gained their bourne
The far, blest Islands of the stormless sea
Those happy shores, where man may cease to mourn
Where, all is peace & bliss and harmony
Gardens, of many a wondrous flower and tree                     50
Homes, of strange birds with wings of rainbow light
Shapes formed by nature in her fantasie
Glowing, and fresh, and fair, and Eden bright
But these were now unseen, beneath the veil of night.

143

And one within that anchored bark is sleeping                           55
The youngest, fairest, bravest of her crew
O how the stars his brows with light are steeping!
The sails, to his lone berth they tremble through
He sleeps on deck; and many a pearl of dew
Gleams in his light-hair as unroofed he lies,                          60
And from th' abyss of pure, deep speckless blue
A sweet gale round him wildly sings & sighs,
A dirge, comes to the ear so sad each cadence dies

Would he might waken! some sad dream is on him
How heavily the breath flows from his breast!                          65
Some unseen influence, strangely dwells upon him,
Some mournful memory will not let him rest;
Whate'er it was, he calm's, th' unwelcome guest
Has passed away, with all its mystery
And now, his clasped hands, to his bosom prest                         70
He turns his fair face to the solemn sky,
His forehead woos again the low breeze wandering by

Yes, he has dreamed, of one now far away,
His own sweet Florence, she, who was his bride
E're thirteen summer suns had flung their ray                          75
With gentlest glow on her youth's springing pride;
O! often had he wandered by her side
Through woodland-walks and alleys dimly bright
Too happy to discern, how fast the tide
Of time, was lapsing into shadowy night;                               80
How swift, the gloaming veiled each parting ray of light

And now, he saw her in a lofty chamber
Solemn & grandly vast, he knew it well,
As as, a light stole down from lamps of amber
The veil of years, and distance, sundered fell                         85
Faintly there tolled her father's castle bell.
It spoke the midnight hour, then all was hushed
Round on the pannels, pictured visions swell
Where forms of buried beauty, voiceless blushed
And the rich silent light, more softly o'er them gushed.               90

Calm, tenderly and pure the moon was shining,
Through one vast window, its white lustre streamed;
On her it fell, her loveliness refining
To beauty, such as mortal never dreamed
Her blue eyes looked to heaven, how bright they beamed!                95
How their deep zones caught glory from the sky
And as the long fringe o'er them, trembling gleamed,
Their centered light was almost mystery
They shone like mirrored stars, that glassed in dark waves lie

Henry! she looks to Heaven, through that vast sea,                    100
That boundless o'cean, decked with Isles of light,
Are her thoughts travelling to their home in thee?
Wakes thy remembered form the radiance bright
That fills her eye? a touch of Love's own might
Has surely clothed her in such, living grace                         105
'Tis not the calm serenity of night
That brings the blood so swiftly to her face
Like the clear flush of wine, seen through a crystal vase

Yes, it is love, but not such love as thine,
Not that pure, young affection of the breast                         110
That used to breathe of peace and bliss divine,
And o'er her white brow fling a shade of rest
Oft' with his hand to her's in transport pressed
Henry has watched that calm fall on her cheek
And while his own heart felt most deeply blest                       115
Has wished a blush of bashfulness to break
What seemed to him, too, still, too sisterly, too meek.

She's not alone, there's one beside her, bending
Is it a fiend? the form is dark and high,
A magic to the solemn chamber lending,                               120
Flashes through darkness, that refulgent eye;
Its fixed gaze, calls that blush and wakes that sigh,
And well might timid maiden shrink and quail
For never yet, a shape on earth passed by,
So like a spirit in a mortal veil                                    125
The cheek that glows for it, will soon turn deadly pale.

At once the chamber fades, in slow decay,
The lights are quenched that erst so softly shone
The dream revolves, the vast hall melts away
And gleaming arch, and golden lamp are gone                          130
And all is dim, and imageless, and lone
But Trees are rustling in the darkened air
And mossy grass the pavement springs upon
And for the vanished tapers' dazzling glare
There dawns a gentle gleam, faint, mellow, mildly fair.              135

Now o'er the scene a mighty wood is sweeping
And long deep, glades, on through it glimmering go
Rays of the moon, the spectral boughs are steeping
They wave in winds whose voice sounds wild & low
And far, far off a river's dreary flow                               140
Swells ceaseless though the gale at times be still
And though the strange sighs wandering to & fro
Like spirit wailings cease, the heart to thrill
Yet the swift waves rush on, of that unpausing rill

The maiden & the shape, stand in the lustre                    145
Flung from the sky on that star-silvered glade,
Those mighty arching trees that round them cluster
The flood of glory, with their shadows braid,
And when a sudden wind amongst them played
They swung like giant-phantoms on the grass                    150
All their boughs trembled, all their foliage swayed
Ghosts such as they, in cloudy gloomy might pass
Amid the gleaming pomp, of some dread wizards glass.

The maiden weeps, clear, moonlit tears are sparkling
Upon her cheeks, fast from her eyes they gush                  155
She looks to him, his brow grows strangely darkling,
His cheek is shadowed, with a sudden flush
Of earnest, eager triumph, that rich blush
Fades not, before her mute and sad appeal,
Now passion's waves of conflict o'er her rush                  160
The sob, the tear, the pallid brow reveal
How wildly strong the love, her heart & spirit feel.

O! Henry knows his Florence loves him not,
Not as he would be loved, not as his bride
Their youthfulness tenderness is all forgot,                   165
All vanished in the rapid, burning tide
That flows, resistless from those eyes of pride,
Flashing into her heart so fixedly
The voice of that strange vision by her side
Brings with its deep, sweet music other joy                    170
Than that which erewhile woke to bless her fair-haired boy.

The token of their love is on her finger,
A golden circlet, like a thread of light
And round her small sweet, lip there seems to linger
Some saddenning touch of memory's holy might                   175
The tears too, glancing as the lamps of night
From their clear sources, are not tears of bliss
But almost e're they tremble into sight,
Her stately lover dries them with a kiss
And soothes her spirit's awe with some proud, warm caress.     180

Sudden a voice came to the dreamer's ear,
Mournful, and sadly murmured, low and dread
At first it wailed far off, then whispered near,
Percy, thy Marian deems her bridegroom dead!
Lover! She mourns not! when the rumour spread                  185
She strove to quench the joy that filled her breast
Yes when she heard, that the unfathomed bed
Of the wild Sea, was by her Henry prest,
She wept that she should feel, so deeply, truly blest.

146

And Percy! she shall be thy rival's bride,                              190
She from his hand shall take the marriage wreath
And standing at the altar side by side,
Each unto each resolves of faith shall breathe
Oaths of eternal fealty till death
And Hill, and plain shall with that bridal ring                        195
Breezes shall waft it with their balmiest breath,
Minstrels shall raise, the song, and strike the string,
And wide the fires of joy like beacon lights shall spring.

Full glad shall be her life, in bright Halls dwelling
Beneath the awful light of those loved eyes.                           200
The fount of perfect bliss for ever swelling
Deep, fathomless, exhaustless in the skies
Shall sparkling, to her very lip arise;
Yet there are warnings of an early end,
There breathes afar, a dreary sound of sighs!                         205
And cold the tears of lonely woe descend,
Shades of untimely death, how silently ye blend!

Percy! thy love, so strong, so unreturned,
Shall be avenged, on earth her time is brief
The radiant Form, for whom, her spirit burned                          210
Shall smile awhile then leave her bowed with grief
The reaper's sickle, shall cut down the sheaf,
While the young corn is budding, fresh and green
She shall be gathered like a springing leaf,
One year, and that fair plant is no more seen,                         215
Few ev'n shall know where once its sunny place has been

        And never from that vision woke
            The journeyer of the deep
        Ere the pale light of morning broke
            He slept his final sleep                                   220

        The coral banks, of those far Isles,
            Now pillow Percy's head
        Their blessed moon for ever, smiles
            Above his lonely bed

        And many a spicy Zephyr, sings                                 225
            Sweet from those radiant skies
        And many a bright bird waves its wings
            Around where Henry lies

        No more, his rayless eye-balls shine,
            No more his curls are fair                                 230
        For tangled sea-weeds wet with brine
            Are garlanding his hair

147

But how he died, no tongue may tell
    No eye was there to see
Yet the winds that were his requiem knell                    235
    They moaned him mournfully

Some say the deck was red with blood,
    And wet with trampling feet;
It recks not, he sleeps in the secret flood
    With surge for his winding-sheet                         240

Dark were the rumours, and faintly spoken
    That came to his native shore,
Less by speech, than by sign & token,
    The crew those rumours bore.

There was no sound of wail, and weeping                      245
    Heard in his own proud home
When the whisper came that he was sleeping
    Beneath the green sea-foam.

His father's brow, first lit then darkled,
    He smiled a demon's smile                                250
And in his piercing eye there sparkled
    A glimpse of hell the while.

Henry! thy name still lives in story,
    Where the Percies' dark woods swell,
And it will live, till time grows hoary                      255
    A talisman, a spell!

And where wild Wansbeck's waves are foaming
    In Grassmere's lonely vale,
At the dim, still hour of solemn gloaming
    I oft' have heard thy tale                               260

The peasant o'er his calm hearth bending,
    Will speak of Percy's fame,
The name of Lady Florence blending
    Young Sailor! with thy name.

Thy dreaded Sire! thine awful father!                        265
    Of him they seldom speak,
For then the clouds of horror gather,
    And words of mystery break

Thy rival! every spirit thrills
    When that proud name is heard                            270
And light each flashing eye-ball fills
    As at a battle-word

148

But not of hatred, not of scorn
They see him in his gorgeous morn
    Their country's living sword                          275
And wild, and wicked though he be
Though his sun rises stormily
    He is their own young Lord!

Yet Henry rest! his name can never
    Ring through thy tomb profound,                       280
And thou may'st sleep unmoved for ever
    By that enkindling sound.

Charlotte Brontë
June 15<sup>th</sup> 1834
282 lines

MS: N
First Publication:  Shorter 1923 partial; SHB C and B


**96**   O that thy own son, thy noblest born
        Should rise that tranquil vision to dispel
        & fresh and sparkling in his glorious morn
        should thunder forth to crush, destroy & quell
        that he should cause the trumpet strain to swell      5
        and wring so many bosoms with its wail
        & light the battle fire unquenchable
        Whose bloody glow the star of war might pale
        & Sirius' burning beams with shrouding halo's veil

        Gods of our land withhold the radiant scourge        10
        Chain the young lion in his darkling den
        Hush the proud storm, & soothe the wild white surge
        & call us back to peace & rest again
        Let the sweet sunlight shine in each green glen
        & light each shadowy mount with beams of peace       15
        & still the voice that stirs the breasts of men
        cause the dread Glory of our land to cease
        & from the strong, bright chain our fettered hearts release

        Now hush for evermore the minstrels shell
        Lay by the flashing sword, lay by its sheath         20
        Let many lands moan to a burial knell
        & skies grow dark above & seas beneath
        And lay the noble poet's withering wreath

149

with the young conqueror's o'er a regal tomb
& let all flower's from rose to moorland heath                    25
Scattered around the house of mourning bloom
While thousands, millions weep the hero's early doom

That were a glorious death so bright, so young
No spot in all the lustrous orb grown dull
the battle fought & gained, the rich strain sung            30
the cup of honour to o'erflowing full
the ship in harbour, not a shattered hull
but strong & swift & bounding as when first
with scarce a breeze to break the ocean's lull
She from her moorings with wild plunge burst              35
& as she walked the waves dared storms to do their worst

Think not upon the grave! the silent grave
think not upon the cold concealing earth
When there are lands & lives & souls to save
What is a single transient mortal's worth                       40
Though he be noble even of kingly birth
A very God for majesty & might
In time of war & peace of woe & mirth
the battle's guiding star the banquets light
the worshipped of the fair the idol of their sight          45

Yet crush remorse, & quell the starting tear
Grasp the sharp brand, look! Yonder towers his crest
Now Patriot rise o'er mercy, softness fear
Plunge to the red hilt in his noble breast
send the young Despot, to his last high rest                50
the hearts-blood spouts, he heaves no moan, no sigh
Now earth is by his blasted beauty prest
Behold the radiant victor silent die
Look on his fading brow, look on his closing eye

He's with the Dead that hand can lock no chain          55
that head can wear no diadem, that tongue
can give no mandate to his awe-struck brain
No all the chords of life are slacked unstrung
the flower is plucked the tree to earth is flung
Afric may triumph, let her drop no tear                        60
a hundred deaths would sprung from his life have sprung
He that lies powerless voiceless bleeding there
Held no man's life or good when classed with glory dear

Bless him & leave him, seal his Royal tomb
One kiss on the cold stone, one bursting sigh                    65
& then let darkness fold him in its gloom
then let corruption brood triumphantly
o'er what was once so proud, so bright so high
so like the imperial splendour of the sun
That men were dazzled as they passed him by                      70
But now his beauty's past, his glory gone
He slumbers in his shroud still desolate [al]one

                                        [June-July 1834]

MS:  D(2)
First Publication:  BST 1980


## 97  A National Ode for the Angrians


The Sun is on the Calabar, the Dawn is quenched in day
The stars of night are vanishing, her shadows flee away
The sandy plains of Etrei, flash back arising light
And The wild wastes of Northangerland, gleam bright as heaven
    is bright
Zamorna lifts her fruitful hills, like Edens to the sky,          5
And fair as Enna's field of flowers, her golden prairies lie
And Angria calls from mount, & vale from wood & heather dell,
A song of joy and thankfulness on rushing winds to swell
For Romalla has put his robe of regal purple on
And from the crags of Pendlebrow the russet garb is gone         10
And Boulsworth off his Giant sides rolls down the vapours dim.
And Hawkscliffe's bright & bowery glades uplift their
    matin hymn
The ancient hills of Sydenham have never felt the glow
Of such a dawn as that which burns their blushing summits now
The fields, the woods of Edwardston are full of song and dew     15
Olympia's waves glance clear, along their wandering line
    of blue;
Green Arundel has caught the ray upspringing from the east
Guadima rolls exultingly with sunshine on his breast
All Angria through her provinces to arms and glory cries
Her sun is up, and she has heard her battle-shout "Arise"!       20
My Kingdom's Gallant Gentlemen are gathered like a host;
With such a bold and noble band was never conflict lost


151

For they would fight till red blood burst in sweat-drops from
    their brow
And never to the victor's yoke their Lion-Souls would bow,
Enara on the Douro's banks his serfs is gathering                    25
From Hut and Hall on the highland heath the sons of Warner
    spring
And Howard o'er his breezy moors the bugle blast has blown
O! Leopard-swift are the ready feet that answer to that tone
The Gor-cock quailed at the summons shrill unconquered
    Agar sent
And a living whirlwind crossed the Tracks that marked the
    withered bent                                                    30
Proud Moray called from the Calabar his vassals to the fight
And the lord of Southwood joyously has raised the flags
    of light
Segovia's dark Italian eye is lit with high-born pride
And the Chevalier of Arundel has bade his horsemen ride
Young Stuart in the ranks of war uplifts his lofty plume            35
And Roslyn like a red-deer bounds from the depths of mountain
    gloom
And Seymour's heir, has heard a voice come from the
    ancient dead
At once th' ancestral dauntlessness through all his veins was
    shed
But the sullen flag of Percy swells most proudly to the breeze
As haughtily the folds unfurl as if they swept the seas:           40
Patrician Pirate! on each side his blighting glance is flung
The silent scorn that curls his lip can never know a tongue
Upon his melancholy brow, a melancholy shade,
Like snow-wreaths on Aornus' slope eternally is laid:
But The Son of that tremendous Sire amid the throng appears        45
His second self, unpetrified by the chill lapse of years;
A form of noblest energy, most sternly beautiful!
A scymitar whose tempered edge, no time can ever dull
A sword unflashed, a quenchless, flame, a fixed & radiant star
A noble steed caparisoned, which snuffs the fight afar             50
The Glory of his youthful brow the light of his blue eye
Will flash upon the battle's verge like arrows of the sky
With such a host, with such a train what hand can stop our
    path
Who can withstand the torrents strength when it shall roll in
    wrath
Lift, Lift the scarlet banner up! Fling all its folds abroad       55
And let its bloody lustre fall on Afric's blasted sod
For gore shall run where it has been & blighted bones shall lie
Wherever the sun-standard swelled against the stormy sky
And when our battle-trumpets sound & when our bugles sing
The vulture from its distant rock shall spread its glancing
    wing                                                            60

And the Gaunt wolf at that signal cry shall gallop to the feast
A table in the wilderness we'll spread for bird & beast
We'll sheath not the avenging sword till earth & sea & skies
Through all God's mighty Universe shout back "Arise! Arise"!
Till Angria reign's Lord Paramount wherever human tongue                65
The slave's lament, the conqueror's hymn in woe or bliss
   hath sung.

Arthur Augustus Adrian Wellesley

July 17<sup>th</sup> 1834    C Bronte

MS: D(1)
First Publication:  Dodd Mead 1902


**98**          The wave of Death's river
        Hides the rose in its bloom
    The Gift & the Giver
        Sleep low in the tomb
    The fresh fruit is shaken                5
        The bright blossom strown
    The flower lies forsaken
        And withered & lone
    Then upward to heaven
        The dim cloud shall swell                10
    The veil shall be riven
        And broken the spell
    But slowly the cloud must rise
        Faint is the gale
    That sighs through the muffled skies                15
        Breathes on the veil
    High was the wanderer's power
        Wondrous his spell
    It wrought in their natal hour
        Strongly & well                20
    A might is yet on them
        No mortal can quell
    A charm rests upon them
        Which none can dispel
The watch through the dark time of star & of shade                25
    The shadow shall vanish the starlight shall fade

[June-July 1834]

MS: B(2)
First Publication:  **The British Weekly,** March 28, 1895 partial; BST
               1916

'Neath the palms, in Elah's valley,
Saul with all his thousands lay;
Israel's mightiest nobles, rally
Round their own anointed stay;
This, has been a battle-day                          5
And the host, lie wearily
On the field of conflict won;
Where their slaughter'd foeman be,
Spear, and target stretched upon

Saul, within his purple tent                          10
Seeks for rest, and seeks in vain,
Still, a voice of sad lament
Mingles with the trumpet strain
Sounding o'er that war-like plain;
And the spirit of the King                            15
Darkens with a cloud of woe
Thicker, denser gathering
As the rapid moments flow

"Abner," thus the monarch said;
God has left me desolate;                             20
All my heart is cold, and dead,
Crushed amid my royal state;
Samuel, bid me ever mourn
Crown, and Kingdom from me rent
God is not a man to turn                              25
Israel's strength can ne'er repent

Abner! is it day's declining
Brings this hour of darkness on?
As the evening sun is shining
Then I feel most sad & lone;                          30
Lo! its beams are almost gone
How their kindled glories, burn
All along our tented field
Spear, and Helm their flash return,
Back, it beams from lance, and shield.                35

Palm, and Cedar catch the lustre
Shining on them bright, and sheen;
Where, those woods of olives cluster
Light has lit their fadeless green
Those far hills, are gem-like seen                    40

154

Sparkling through the crimson'd air
All with roseate light embued,
Abner! never scene so fair
Smiled, on Monarch's solitude.

Once I could have smiled again,                    45
Full of hope, and young and free,
Now its beauty turns to bane,
And my Spirit, wearily
Shrinks that sight of bliss to see
It hath no communion now                            50
With a fair, and sunny sky
Nature's calm, and stormless brow,
Wakes in me no sympathy

O! methinks, were heaven scowling,
Were those green hills black and hoar               55
Were the winds and billows howling
Dashed against a sunless shore,
Darkly cheerless evermore;
I should feel, less full of woe,
Full of God-cursed misery                           60
Than when breezes soft and low
Whisper round me peacefully;

Than when eve, and twilight meet;
Dawning star, and setting sun;
All that Earth has calm, and sweet,                 65
Resting her bright plains upon;
Toil, and strife, and battle done;
Silent dews around me weeping;
Gleaming on the warrior's brow
The weary warrior, hushed and sleeping             70
By his conquered foe.

But I'll cease my bootless sighing;
Bid the Son of Jesse come;
Let his music, soft and dying,
Win my spirit from her gloom,                       75
Call her exile sun-shine home;
He has many a sacred air,
Many a Song of Holiness
That perchance, may soothly bear
Even to me, one hour of bliss.                      80

C. Brontë.  Oct^br 7^th 1834

MS:  H
First Publication:  Wise Saul 1913

Text:   In the process of binding the manuscript, the edges of the pages
       have been cut off, making it impossible to determine much of the
       end punctuation.

**100**  The Crypt, the Nave, the Chancel past
His burial Aisle is gained at last
His burial Aisle Oh! what a moan
Comes mingled with that simple tone.
No proud roofs rise for Percy now,     5
For him no gleaming arches bow.
The bright saloon, the columned Hall
Is changed for shroud, and vault and pall.
The Palace lit with sunshine clear
Has passed for rayless grave and bier.    10
The Hearth of his Patrician-Home,
The concave of his gorgeous Dome,
Have long forgot his voice, his tread.
They like himself stilled and dead.
  Pass on; the hush is mournful,    15
And the air is faint and dim,
And we know that earth is tombed in sleep
And we feel that midnight's shadows deep
  Brood round us brown and grim.
  Yet fear not lady! fear not.     20
  Why dost thou tremble so?
I hear the beatings of thy heart,
I see thee at each murmur start.
  However faint and low.
  There is nothing here to harm thee  25
  The dead are stilled for aye.
And many a year has glided by
In calm, and storm, since living eye
  Shed on that bier its ray.
Let's stand awhile; all is most still,   30
Save when the vault dews, dank and chill,
Settled in drops on arch and wall,
Down tinkling, to the pavement fall,
And save, when some strange, transient sound
Just echoes far and faintly round,    35
Then dies away as it was born--
Vague, nameless, drearily forlorn.
The creaking of a coffin lid,
A tressel, 'neath its burden slid,
A louder blast of the night wind swelling. 40
The distant clock from its tower knelling,
Though feeble sounds, yet shrill and deep

They fall, in these lone cells of sleep
Where, void of motion, vision, breath,
Our Fathers lie, at rest, in death!                                          45

And is this Percy's dwelling-place?
Is this the Goal of his proud race?
After the mighty path he trode
Is this his fixed, and last abode?
Great Spirit! hast thou slumbered here                                       50
While round and onward rolled our Sphere?
Still measuring out the marks of time
With customed change of light and clime?
Hast thou lain stirless in this cell
While Kings and Empires rose and fell,                                       55
And War's shrill trumpet-blast has rung
So many startled lands among,
While anguished wail, and heart-wrung moan
Have followed that arousing tone
From those its parting echoes left                                           60
Of all they loved, for e'er bereft.
Sometimes that noble storm of sound
Burst almost o'er the hallowed ground
Where, Percy! thy cold ashes lie
Beneath their marble canopy;                                                 65
Where, journeying from their far-off home
The wandering feet of pilgrims come,
And worshipping, their forms they bow
To greet thy win with lip or brow.
Sometimes it murmured far away                                               70
As distant thunder peals decay.
Land unto land in answer spoke,
Defiance sounded, War awoke,
The very billows of the sea
Took up that awful harmony.                                                  75
The roar of thine own element
Was with its chords of thunder blent.
Great Rivers running to the deep
Its voice bore onward in their sweep,
    Yet thou didst not awake.                                               80
A hundred plains were strewed with dead,
A thousand Hills grew gory red:
Morn saw them blushing when she rose
And still they blushed at twilight['s] close.
The moon her rays of silver threw                                           85
To shine on drops of crimson dew,
And sleep and silence fell no more
As night looked down on wave and shore,
And battle's dogs of slaughter yelled,
Rolled her dread drums, her clarions swelled                                90

157

Naught could thy slumber shake.
No more thy voice the senate stilled,
No more thy taunt its victims chilled:
That voice was hushed, the harp unstrung
Where once its deep, clear accents rung,          95
And the taunt, the stern denouncing word
Forgotten, lost, in death, unheard.
But years the while have ceaseless flown;
Each after each has come and gone.
Thy crimes, thy deeds, thy glories be          100
Recorded themes of History.
Thy tomb has grown a mighty shrine,
Thy name a feared, yet worshipped sign.
The clouds that once around it lay
Frown faintly through the mellowing ray          105
That still from lapsing ages stealing,
The Grandeur, not the gloom revealing,
Has given a due solemnity
To every line that speaks of thee.
Oh Percy! can I now behold          110
The face that pall and shroud infold?
O can I raise that coffin-lid
And look at what is 'neath it hid?
Can I the awful forehead see
That cere-cloth hides so jealously,          115
And see it as at last it lay
When the sun went down on thy dying day,
When myself beside thy pillow bending
Felt the dim shade of death descending,
And knew by voiceless sign and token          120
That the Pitcher at the fount was broken,
That the cistern wheel had ceased its turning,
And the lamp of Being quenched its burning,
That the golden cord, just loosened, quivered,
And the silver bowl lay crushed and shivered.          125
Thy death, it was so calm and still
That but for the silence and frozen chill,
I should have thought a blessed sleep
Had fallen thy pangs in rest to steep,
But gathering shadow on shadow told          130
That nothing lay there save an ashen mould,
That soul from the eye and the forehead was gone,
And the seal of its grandeur left lingering alone;
The streams were exhausted in Life's deep well,
And gone was the mighty INFIDEL!          135

Bride of his living breast draw near,
Bend Lady o'er thy husband's bier:
For e'er the night-lamps farther wane
We'll look on Percy's face again!
       (Lifts the coffin lid, curtain drops.)

      C. BRONTË Oct<sup>br</sup> 8<sup>th</sup> 1834      138 lines

MS: Unlocated: last known to have been in the possession of Sir Alfred Law
First Publication: Shorter 1923


**101   HURRAH FOR THE GEMINII!**


    Hurrah for the Geminii!
    Blessed be the Star!
That shone on the stream of the blue Calabar
When the Hills of the East and the woods of the West
Bore light for their banner and flame for their crest       5
As the wind its glad tidings exultingly blew,
That if Rome had one monarch, our Angria has two!

    Sons of an imperial line!
    Welcome to your land and home.
    Not in daylight's dark decline,      10
    Princes! is your advent come,
    Not as the orb of Nations fades
    Not as the deepening evening shades

Gather in starless gloom,

But at morning's primal flush      15
Angria's bright, uprising day
When her hills have caught the blush
Of earliest, fairest ray
And the path of the untravelled skies
Before, in crystal clearness lies      20
A wide, a trackless way.

When her gilded woods are bending
To the morning's wind of might.
When her mountain floods descending
Catch the sunbeam, dazzling bright,      25
Flash the golden lustre given
Backwards to the breaking heaven
In richer rays of light.

159

Princes! then to life you woke,
Then your father clasped his own,                    30
Then the shout of welcome broke,
Harp was swept, and bugle blown,
Then the deep Atlantic rung
As its flashing waters sprung
To thunder back that tone.                            35

Angria's glad and bracing breeze
With your earliest breath you drew,
All her mightiest energies
Round and o'er your cradle blew.
Drink them children of a King!                        40
Up to noble beauty Spring
In heaven's fair light and dew.

With your God-like father's form,
Catch his spirit, catch his might.
Then, albeit the battle-storm                         45
Gather round us black as night,
Still its blasts we may defy,
Still our flag aloft shall fly,
Still shall Angria's burning sky
    Smile its living light.                           50
Conqueror, Ruler, shall she be,
Sovereign Queen by land and sea,
Her watchword shall be 'Victory,'
    Her Glory, ever bright!

Hurrah for the Geminii! Blessed be the star!          55
That shone on the streams of the blue Calabar,
When the hills of the East and the woods of the West
Bore light for their banner, and flame for their crest,
As the wind its glad tidings exultingly blew,
That if Rome had one Monarch! our Angria has two!     60

                                      Charlotte Brontë
        53 lines                      October 14th 1834

MS: Unlocated: see No. **100**
First Publication: Shorter 1923

**102**      Lament for the martyr who dies for his faith
             Who prays for his foes with his failing breath
             Who see's as his looks to the kindling sky,
             God & his captain the Saviour nigh

                        160

Who sees the mighty recompense                          5
When soul is conquering flesh & sense
Sees heaven and all its angels bright
At the very end of his mortal flight
At the black close of that agony
Which sets the impatient spirit free                   10
Then as in christ he sinks to sleep
Weep for the Dying Martyr, weep
And the Soldier laid on the battle-plain
      At the close of night alone
The passing off of some warlike-strain                 15
      Blent with his latest moan
His thoughts all for his father-land
His feeble heart, his unnerved hand
Still quiveringly upraised to wield
Once more her bright sword on the field                20
While wakes his fainting energy
To gain her yet one victory
As he lies bleeding cold and low
As life's red tide is ebbing slow
Lament for fallen bravery                              25


For the son of wisdom the holy sage
Full of knowledge and hoar with age
Him who had walked through the times of night
As if on his path a secret light
Lustrous & pure & silent fell                          30
To all save himself invisible
A secret ray from Heaven's own shrine
Poured on the spirit half divine
And making a single Isle of light
In the wide, blank Ocean of Pagan night                35
Lament for him as you see him laid
      Waiting for Death on the Dungon bed
The sickly lamp beside him burning
      Its dim ray falling on sorrow & gloom
Around him his sad disciples mourning                  40
      As they watch for the hour of awful doom
And he by coming death unshaken
      As if that slumber would soon be o'er
As if all freshened he should waken
      An see the light of morn once more                45


Ay on the sage's the soldier's bier
I could drop many an pitying tear
And as the martyr sinks to sleep
I could in love, in sorrow weep
But Percy for that Rose of thine                       50
Maria Stuart, bright divine


161

Divine & bright the mortal form
The eternal soul a venomed worm
For her I'd never heave a sigh
Unmoaned I'd let the fair fiend die                    55
Seductive in her treachery
    Most dazzling in her crimes
The flower of France should fade away
And Scotlands heather bell decay
    Her death mass lift its chimes                     60
And I could smile vindictively
To know the earth I walked was free
From her who kissed her lord to death
And poisoned him with kindness breath
One moment fondly o'er him bending                     65
The next her gentle spirit lending
To plots that well might wake a shiver
In bosom's crime has seathed for ever
Accursed woman o'er thy tomb
My scorn flings down its sternest gloom                70

                 unfinished    C Bronte
            70 lines    Nov<sup>br</sup> 28<sup>th</sup> 1834

MS:  B(2)
First Publication:  **Cornhill Magazine,** August 1916 partial; Winnifrith
                    PCB


**103**          Jeffry my turtle fare the[e] well
                 Thou liv'st, but liv'st no more for me
                 And neither time nor fate shall quell
                     The grief I feel for thee

                 Thy sandy locks are in my eye               5
                 Thy puckered features fill my heart
                 And Jeffry never till I die
                     Will thy sweet form depart

                 I was whiled away from thee my love
                 By the Arch-fiend in a shape of man        10
                 But Oh! I'll come back my turtle dove
                     As soon as ever I can

                     [November-December 1834]

MS:  B(2)
First Publication:  SHB Misc II

When the dead in their cold graves are lying
Asleep, to wake never again!
When, past are their smiles and their sighing,
Oh! why should their memories remain?

Though sunshine, and spring may have lightened      5
The wild-flowers that blow on their graves,
Though summer their tombstones have brightened
And Autumn have pall'd them with leaves;

Though winter have wildly bewail'd them,
With her dirge-wind, as sad as a knell;      10
Though the shroud of her snow-wreath have veiled them,
Still--how deep in our bosoms they dwell!

The shadow, and sun-sparkle vanish;
The cloud, and the light fleet away,
But man, from his heart may not banish      15
Ev'n thoughts that are torment to stay.

The reflection departs from the river,
When the tree that hung o'er is cut down
But on Memory's calm current for ever
The shade, without substance is thrown.      20

When, quench'd is the glow of the ember,
When the life-fire ceases to burn,
Oh! why should the spirit remember?
Oh! why should the parted return?

Because, that the fire is still shining,      25
Because, that the lamp is still bright,
While the body, in dust is reclining,
The soul, lives in glory and light.

C Brontë--Oct$^{br}$ 2$^{nd}$ --35

MS:   D(2); H; O
First Publication:   **Scribner's Monthly,** May 1871 partial; **Cornhill
Magazine,** February 1893

163

Morning was in its freshness still
Noon yet far off with all its stir
Cool early shade, calm leisure fill
The silent hall and summer room
Two hours I yet may number ere                          5
Full glaring day brings tumult near
And lets intrusive labour care
    Disturb my humble home

Two hours!--how shall they speed with me
In measured task, toil self-asigned?                    10
No, eager claim for liberty
Some sense now urges in my mind
Through Fancy's realm of imagery
Some strange delight is ranging free
Some joy that will not prisoned be                      15
    Fresh as the western wind

It hurries back and brings the Past
    Sweetly before my soul
It wings its way like rapid blast
    To the far Futures goal                             20
Pleasant the thoughts its pinions chase
And bright though vague the dreamy place
Where tends its winged and ardent race
    Farther than Ocean's roll

Each pleasant passage in my life                        25
    I now live o'er again
I pass the weary hours of strife
    Forget the scenes of pain
What Scorn has said and Hate has done
Oblivion's veil lies dimly on                           30
And tears by Woe from Weakness won
    Remembrance cease to stain

But every gift by Joy bestowed
    I count in numbers true
And every hour that smoothly flowed                     35
    This hour does well renew
And if Love's whisper ever yet
    My ear like note of music met
This summer wind seems to repeat
    The tones with cadence due                          40

164

'Tis bitter sometimes to recall
      Illusions once deemed fair
But in this golden moment all
      Doth fairy gilding wear
And fond and fast the pulses beat                    45
Departed Passion's shade to greet
Rising in transient vision sweet
      To colour empty air

[October-November 1835]

MS:  D(2)
First Publication:  BST 1926
Text:  l. 8:  "Disturb" written above "Enter"; neither is canceled
       l. 44:  "wear" written above "share"; neither is canceled


**106**   We wove a web in childhood
            A web of sunny air
      We dug a spring in infancy
      Of water pure and fair

      We sowed in youth a mustard seed             5
      We cut an almond rod
      We are now grown up to riper age
      Are they withered in the sod

      Are they blighted failed and faded
            Are they mouldered back to clay       10
      For life is darkly shaded
      And Its joys fleet fast away

      Faded! the web is still of air
      But how its folds are spread
      And from its tints of crimson clear         15
      How deep a glow is shed
      The light of an Italian sky
      Where clouds of sunset lingering lie
      Is not more ruby-red

      But the spring was under a mossy stone       20
            Its jet may gush no more
      Heark! sceptic bid thy doubts be gone
      Is that a feeble roar
      Rushing around thee lo! the tide
      Of waves where armed fleets may ride         25
      Sinking and swelling frowns & smiles
      An ocean with a thousand Isles
      And scarce a glimpse of shore

165

The mustard-seed on distant land
Bends down a mighty tree                                          30
The dry unbudding almond-wand
    Has touched eternity
There came a second miracle
Such as on Aaron's sceptre fell
And sapless grew like life from heath                             35
Bud bloom & fruit in mingling wreath
All twined the shrivelled off-shoot round
As flowers lie on the lone grave-mound

38

Dream that stole o'er us in the time
When life was in its vernal <clime>                               40
Dream that still faster o'er us steals
As the mild star of spring declining
The advent of that day reveals
That glows in Sirius fiery shining
Oh! as thou swellest and as the scenes                           45
Cover this cold worlds darkest features
Stronger each change my spirit weans
To bow before thy god-like creatures

When I sat 'neath a strange roof-tree
With nought I knew or loved around me                            50
Oh how my heart shrank back to thee
Then I felt how fast thy ties had bound me

That hour that bleak hour when the day
Closed in the cold autumnal gloaming
When the clouds hung so bleak & drear & grey                     55
And a bitter wind through their folds was roaming

There shone no fire on, the cheerless hearth
In the chamber there gleamed no taper's twinkle
Within neither sight nor sound of mirth
Without but the blast & the sleet's chill sprinkle              60

Then sadly I longed for my own dear home
For a sight of the old familliar faces
I drew near the casement & sat in its gloom
And looked forth on the tempests desolate traces

Ever anon that wolfish breeze                                    65
The dead leaves & sere from their boughs was shaking
And I gazed on the hills through the leafless trees
And I felt as if my heart was breaking
                    68

Where was I e're an hour had past
Still list'ning to that dreary blast                          70
Still in that mirthless lifeless room
Cramped, chilled & deadened by its gloom

No! thanks to that bright darling dream
Its power had shot one kindling gleam
Its voice had sent one wakening cry                           75
And bade me lay my sorrows by
And called me earnestly to come
And borne me to my moorland home
I heard no more the senseless sound
Of task & chat that hummed around                            80
I saw no more that grisly night
Closing the day's sepulchral light

The vision's spell had deepened o'er me
Its lands its scenes were spread before me
In one short hour a hundred homes                            85
Had roofed me with their lordly domes
And I had sat by fires whose light
Flashed wide o'er halls of regal height
And I had seen those come & go
Whose forms gave radiance to the glow                         90
And I had heard the matted floor
Of ante-room & corridor
Shake to some half-remembered tread
Whose haughty firmness woke even dread
As through the curtained portal strode                        95
Some spurred & fur-wrapped Demi-God
Whose ride through that tempestuous night
Had added somewhat of a frown
To brow's that shadowed eyes of light
Fit to flash fire from Scythian crown                        100
Till sweet salute from lady gay
Chased that unconscious scowl away
And then the savage fur-cap doffed
The Georgian mantle laid aside
The satrap stretched on cushion soft                         105
His lov'd & chosen by his side
That hand that in its horseman's glove
Looked fit for nought but bridle rein
Caresses now its lady-love
With fingers white that shew no stain                        110
They got in hot & jarring strife
122   When hate or honour warred with life
Nought redder than the roseate ring
That glitters fit for Eastern King


167

In one proud household, where the sound                    115
Of life & stir rang highest round
Hall within hall burned starry bright
And light gave birth to richer light
Grandly its social tone seemed strung
Wildly its keen excitement rung                            120
And hundreds mid its splendors free
Moved with unfettered liberty
Not gathered to a lordly feast
But each a self-invited Guest
It was the kingly custom there                             125
That each at will the house should share

I saw the master not alone
He crossed me in a vast saloon
Just seen, then sudden vanishing
As laughingly he joined the ring                           130
That closed around a dazzling fire
& listened to a trembling lyre
He was in light & licensed mood
Fierce gaiety had warmed his blood
Kindled his dark & brilliant eye                           135
And toned his lips full melody

I saw him take a little child
That stretched its arms & called his name
It was his own & half he smiled
As the small eager creature came                           140
Nestling upon his stately breast
And its fair curls & forehead laying
To what but formed a fevered nest
Its father's cheek where curls were straying
Thicker & darker on a bloom                                145
Whose hectic brightness boded doom

He kissed it and a deeper blush
Rose to the already crimson flush
And a wild sadness flung its grace
Over his grand & Roman face                                150
The little heedless lovely thing
Lulled on the bosom of a King
Its fingers 'mid his thick locks twining
Pleased with their rich & wreathed shining
Dreamed not what thoughts his soul were haunting           155
Nor why his heart so high was panting

```
I went out in a summer night
My path lay o'er a lonesome waste
Slumbering & still in clear moon-light
A noble road was o'er it traced                          160
Far as the eye of man could see
No shade upon its surface stirred
All slept in mute tranquillity
Unbroke by step or wind or word

That waste had been a battle-plain                       165
    Head-stones were reared in the waving fern
There they had buried the gallant slain
That dust to its own dust might return

And one black marble monument
Rose w[h]ere the heather was rank & deep                 170
Its base was hid with bracken & bent
Its sides were bare to the night-winds sweep

A Victory carved in polished stone
Her trumpet to her cold lips held
And strange it seemed as she stood alone                 175
That not a single note was blown
That not a whisper swelled

It was Camalia's ancient field
I knew the desert well
For traced around a sculptured shield                    180
These words the summer moon revealed
    "Here brave Macarthy fell!"
The men of Keswick leading on
There first their best their noblest one
    He did his duty well"                                185
                195
```

I now heard the far clatter of hoofs on the hard & milk-white
road, the great highway that turns in a bend from Free-Town
and stretches on to the West. two horsemen rode slowly up in
the moonlight & leaving the path struck deep into the moor
galloping through heather to their Chargers breasts.. Hah!..
said one of them as he flung himself from his steed "& walked
forward to the monument  'Hah Edward here's my Kinsman's
tomb, now for the bugle sound! he must have his requiem or he
will trouble me-- the bell tolled for him on Alderwood on the
eve of the conflict, I heard it myself & though then but a
very little child I remember well how my mother trembled as
she sat in the drawing-room of the manor house & listened while
that unaccountable & supernatural sound was booming so horribly

through the woods Edward begin" Never shall I Charlotte Bronte
forget what a voice of wild & wailing music now came thrillingly
to my mind's almost to my body's ear, nor how distinctly I
sitting in the school-room at Roe-head saw the Duke of Zamorna
leaning against that obelisk with  the mute marble Victory above
him the fern waving at his feet his black horse turned loose
grazing among the heather, the moonlight so mild & so
exquisitely tranquil sleeping upon that vast & vacant road & the
African sky quivering & shaking with stars expanded above all, I
was quite gone I had really utterly forgot where I was and all
the gloom & cheerlessness of my situation I felt myself
breathing quick & short as I beheld the Duke lifting up his
sable crest which undulated as the plume of a hearse waves to
the wind & knew that that music which seems as mournfully
triumphant as the scriptural verse
        'Oh Grave where is thy sting;
        Oh Death where is thy victory'
was exciting him & quickening his ever rapid pulse 'Miss Bronte
what are you thinking about?' said a voice that dissipated all
the charm & Miss Lister thrust her little rough black head into
my face, 'Sic transit' &c.

                          C. Bronte, Dec^br 19^th
                                    Haworth 1835

MS: N
First Publication:  Wise Saul 1913 partial; SHB C and B
Text:  Line numbers in the text and in the left margin are Charlotte's


**107**        Come now, I am alone, the day's wild riot
               Self-lulled to slumber, I feel somewhat weary
               Can I not rest?  all looks serene & quiet

                                    [January 1836]

MS:  P
First Publication:  Winnifrith PCB


170

1.

Long since as I remember well
My childish eyes would weep
To read how calmly Stephen fell
    In Jesus' arms asleep
Oh! could I feel the holy glow                    5
    That brightened death for him
I'd cease to weep that all below
    Is grown so drear & dim

Could I but gain that lofty faith
    Which made him bless his foes            10
I'd fix my anchor, firm till death
    In hope's divine repose
And is it now a contrite heart
    That brings me Lord to thee
Or is it but the goading smart                    15
    Of inward agony?

And could my spirit heavenward spring
    And could I upward glance
With murderer's round me thickening
    To God, in holy trance                        20
And could my mangled relics cry
    O Lord their deed forgive
And Jesus Saviour graciously
    Thy martyr's soul receive!

A thousand early thoughts & dreams                25
    Of heaven & hope were mine
And musings sweet by placid streams
    In childhood's vision shine
In summer evening's mild & dim
    Oh it was sweet to me                         30
To sit & say some simple hymn
    Beneath a lonely tree

A tree that by the garden wall
    Drooped down its graceful head
And oft its golden flowers let fall              35
    On the green grass neath it spread
Not hid from sight & scarcely veiled
    Was my loved seat beneath
But still the wind around it wailed
    I thought with softer breath                  40

And still, the latest, lingering ray
Of sunset warmed me there
As all the ephemerals ceased their play
In the dimmed & dew chilled air
As night closed I might hear the moan                45
Of water murmuring low
As amid the stillness hushed & lone
Past on its viewless flow

It was a beck that far away
Washed many a bending tree                           50
Unnoticed through the busy day
At twilight sounding free
I knew the valley where it flowed
The weeds that edged its current
I could recall the shady road                        55
That wound beside the torrent
                              56 lines

Tranquil the sound & sweet the thought
Of woodland rest & shade
That low & sea-like murmur brought
In music from the glade                              60
Listening to that & feeling still
The charm of being alone
I never thought how damp & chill
The night was drawing on

The garden all involved in gloom                     65
Seemed vaster than by day
The house stood silent as a tomb
In outline huge & grey
The cheering shine of firelight beaming
Through the parlour window told                      70
That while I was out in the darkness dreaming
48      All within was bright as gold
56
---
104  I never since have known such bliss
As then came o'er my mind
And a trace of such pure happiness                   75
I ne'er again shall find
My heart was better then than now
Its hopes soared far more free
I felt a blind, but ardent glow
Of love for piety                                    80

172

How sweetly then the strain still fell
 To Bethlehem's sacred star
And how my heart of hearts would swell
 To those that shone afar
Not long so rapt in thoughts of heaven          85
 I was a child of clay
And soon by sinful terrors driven
 I almost feared to pray

The gloom increased, the church was nigh
 Its tower with awful frown                      90
As I glanced upward to the sky
 Looked like a giant down
I thought of God & heaven no more
 A sudden awe rushed on
I wished myself by the bolted door               95
 I shook as I sat alone

I had forgotten the gloomy night
 That brooded o'er every tomb
But now with a strange & thrilling might
 It struck me to my spirit home                 100
What if then from the grave were fleeting
 What the grave would again receive
To tell in the tone of a spectre's greeting
 That I had not long to live

Words cannot tell the ghastly power             105
 That such thoughts then had o'er me
I have wept when I woke at the midnight hour
104   At their grinding tyranny
Sometimes they would come in the sunny day
 And haunt me unceasingly                       110
And no tone of pleasure could charm away
 The nameless misery

The books that I read all caught the tone
 Of ghostly & spectral dread
And their tales would come o'er me again alone  115
 At night on my sleepless bed
I read of a wizard who suffering died
 In his hut on a desert moor
On a winter's night when the hollow wind sighed
 Through the chinks of the shuddering door      120


173

And none but a little lonely child
　To watch his release was there
And the sound of his ravings so strange & wild
　Were more than that child could bear
But it did not faint, it stood sick & pale          125
　Waiting the old man's death
And there sounded (so ran the awful tale)
　A tramp o'er the desolate heath

And the boy as he looked to the cottage door
　Saw it shaken & opened slow                        130
While a dark shade fell on the lamp-lit floor
　And he heard a sullen low
Something passed him, a bodiless shade
　Something stood by the bed
A sign to the starkened corpse was made             135
　And uprose the sheeted dead

They went, they past--like a waft of the wind
　Silent & viewless & sweeping
And dread o'er the watcher came dizzy & blind
　And <stretched> him in trance-like sleeping       140
There was more of the tale but even now
　A touch of the ancient feeling
Checks the tide of memory's flow
　With its influence cold & chilling

I read of a man who just at even                    145
　When the sun declined on high
Saw by the dying light of heaven
　His own wraith standing by
And before another sun had brightened
　The wood on the blue loch's verge                 150
With his cold cheek blanched, & his mute lip <whitened>
　He was sleeping beneath its surge

I read of an old man whose only daughter
　Was taken to fairy-land
And he used to wander alone by the water            155
　On the beach of silver sand
Through many an endless summer day
　Seeking her wind-bleached bones
In his dotage gathering pebbles & clay
　From the mossy & shattered stones                 160

Or the relics of lambs who years ago
　Had died in some April storm
Sunk in the curling drifts of snow
　That untimely tempests form

174

I read of a city smit by the plague
   Where thousands died day by day
And the horror I felt so strange & vague
164    It was vain to chase away

Such were my dreams in infancy
   I have other visions now        170
Which touch not the nerve so painfully
   But yet fever the blood in its flow

When no eye is on me & all is still
   I yet cannot feel alone
When no voice speaks, yet the ear will thrill    175
   To a sudden &            tone
When I sit in a quiet and cheerful room
   Watching the firelight play
My thoughts will wander far from home
   A thousand miles away      180

I see an ancient & stately hall
   I stand in the sun at its door
And feel the soft summer shadows fall
   From the foliage that veils it o'er

I step within & a vast saloon      185
   Lifts its proud dome for me
Showering from radiant sky-lights down
   The day's resplendency

And glorious flowers are flushing through
   Each sash, in crimson bloom    190
And winds as sweet as ever blew
   Play round the regal room

All mute & still in solitude
   Watched only by the skies
Where pours the sun his rosiest flood    195
   A youthful lady lies

And dreams she of Norwegian seas
   The dread the wild the dark,
And thinks she how this balmy breeze
   May speed the Pirate's bark    200

And dreads she lest the arctic wave
   Congealed & clear & green
Has given her Sire a glassy grave
   In its shrine of ice serene
200

But she lifts her eyes, & she sees around                205
    The painted & splendid Hall
For there flashes life though there breathes <no> sound
    From the forms that glow on that wall

Glorious heads from the golden frames
    Bend with a dream like smile                         210
Parting with snowy hand the gleams
    Of their lustrous hair the while

The teeth of pearl, through the lips of rose
    Archly but stilly shew
Nothing that coral mouth can close                       215
    Which has smiled through centuries so
Glimpses of English scenery
    Northumbrian hills & halls
And Glorious plains of Italy
    Shine on the magic walls                             220

And chevaliers of old English days
    Lords of the Percy race
With bold dark eyes of passion gaze
    On that youthful lady's face
Her thoughts are changed I see her start                 225
    Another feeling stirs
A longing for some kindred heart
    To blend its fire with hers

Now dreams she that the whispering trees
    Which wave that dome above                           230
Reveal her future destinies
    And tell her time of love
A hundred shadowy oracles
    Around the windows moan
Is bliss the theme of that prophesy                      235
    Which comes with so wild a tone
We'll leave her to her haunted dream
    I speak not what befel
How flowed with[in] her life's changeful stream
236     I may not dare not tell                          240
 56
 92 'Tis all delusion!--yet again
    The curtain falls & shews
Another scene as bright as vain
    That too must clearly close
Tis all delusion, still once more                        245
    The glancing lightning glows
And brighter than the flash before
    Its fitful glory throws

176

Succeeding fast & faster still
    Scenes that no words can give                          250
And gathering strength from every thrill
    They stir, the[y] breathe, they live
They live! they gather round in bands
    They speak, I hear the <tone>
The earnest look, the beckoning hands                      255
    And am I now alone

Alone! there passed a noble line
    Alone! there thronged a race
I saw a kindred likeness shine
    In every haughty face                                  260
I know their, deeds I know their fame
    The legends wild that grace
Each ancient house, around each name
    Their mystic <vigils> trace

I know their parks, their halls their towers              265
    The sweet lands where they shine
The track that leads through        bowers
    To each proud gate, is mine
I've seen the dark & silent aisles
    Where all their dead repose                            270
And the cold white memorial piles
    That tell their lofty woes

The saint in stone for them must mourn
    The marble angel pray
When their proud sons & sires return                       275
    To man's primeval clay
Return they must, no power can save
    Their noblest fairest, best
'Tis doomed, the chill & sunless grave
    At last must be their rest                             280

They come again, such glorious forms
    Such brows, & eyes divine
The heart exults, the life-blood warms
    To see, to feel their shine
Oh stay! Oh fix! Oh start to life                          285
    Flash out reality
Methinks a strange commencing strife
    Of dream & truth I see

177

A sound of breath, a wakening hum
    Stirs the great silent band                      290
Some vanish, then again they come
    And brighter, taller stand
Some in wide, waving, rich array
    Sweep through the sterner lines
And who are these? but Lo! away                       295
    They fade, the dream declines

292
 68
360 Dim the bright curls, bloodless the cheeks
    Rayless the radiant eyes
They fade like the last languid streaks
    Of day in twilight skies                          300
Even that head with awful brow
    Bare, cold & white as stone
Whose keen, blue eagle eye but now
    Flashed more than life, is gone

Even that Grecian bust, whose glance                  305
    From marble eye-lids shewed
Promethean fire had lit the trance
    Of sculpture's still repose
Even that pure ideal form
    Just smiled, then passed away                     310
No star, dissevering clouds of storm
    Ere shot so brief a ray

Even that face which turned aside
    And shewed its high profile
With all the lofty lines of pride                     315
    That western woods reveal

Even that full-length form which bowed
    Half backward in the throng
Yet rose from the receding crowd
    In light so clear & strong                        320
Held forth his hand which as it waved
    Shewed a gleamy shine of rings
A flash of crimson jewels graved
    With crest & crowns of Kings

Even he is gone, and all are gone                     325
    And wakening Reason cries
Thy dream is like a wild-bird flown
    To summer climes & skies
Twill fitfully return & then
    As fitfully will go                               330
Each joy has its attendant pain
    Each bliss its following woe

178

And if thou hast the solace felt
    Of Fancy's pictured play
Bewail not when her visions melt                    335
    Like morning mists away
Is it not well, that thou can'st call
    Her hallowing scenes to thee
When haply in thy spirit all
    Sinks chill and hopelessly                      340

Is it not well when severed far
    From those thou love'st to see
That she has hung her golden star
    O'er alien hill & tree
Remember those sweet evenings when                  345
    Behind the sun's farewell
A gentle light rose up again
    And round thee calmly fell

Remember how she sanctified
    The moon ascending slow                         350
And silvering pure & pale & wide
    The dewy field below
And if it chanced as oft has been
    That music wandered by
And from the grove of aspens green                  355
    Stole up & sought the sky

What hast thou felt? What soothing gush
    Of full unbroken thought
And by the breezless evening's hush
    What glorious spells were wrought               360
Seemed it not then that all the West
    Spread round thee in that night
Seemed not that moon boding pure & blest
    Her own, her holiest light

Remember those grey steps of stone                  365
    Beneath that bowery tree
With wild green, glittering ivy grown
    Around luxuriantly

Remember how reclining there
    One evening thou did'st see                     370
A little dark-haired child draw near
    And lie down silently
He laid his cheek on the clustering flowers
    That grew there sweet & soft
And he lifted his eyes to a pile of towers         375
    Whose dark heads frowned aloft

179

And he hearkened to the ceaseless moan
    Of a deep stream past him flowing
And as that child lay thus alone
    How his little heart was glowing                    380
Glowing with the thoughts he could not tell
    That the countless stars inspired
And the dim night & the river's swell
    With higher beauty fired

He rose up, through the wild brier sprays              385
    Of the coppice o'er him waving
His dark eyes looked with eager gaze
    On the stream Fort Adrian laving
A mighty stream, broad blue & deep
    Its waves in the clear sky melted                   390
Scarce through the gloom was seen the sweep
    Of walls where its flow they belted
Yet he thinks he sees the far-off shine
    Of lights from his father's dwelling
Where the terraced front of his halls recline          395
    On the river's azure swelling

And he longs for the wing of the bird to seek
    That home, o'er the rolling river
Fain would that child repose his cheek
    On the breast that shall greet him never            400
Doomed to die, erelong to feel the sleep
    Of a bloody death come o'er him
Far from the eye that shall darkly weep
200    When no tear can e'er restore him
Doomed on a cold & stormy heath                         405
    In the arms of a noble mourner
To breath[e] his last struggling breath
    On the heart of the gallant Warner

Born in a stormy midnight's gloom
    In a stormier midnight dying                        410
The flower that shewed too fair a bloom
    Trampled & crushed is lying
The marble slab that Warner laid
    Above his relics telling
Who lies beneath amid the shade                         415
    Of wild moors round him swelling
And the motto on the headstone gives
    That faith which will not perish
"I know that my Redeemer lives"
    A blessed hope to cherish!                          420

```
       Dreamer awake & close the strain
         A summons has been spoken
       "Thou must depart" so burst the chain
         And leave the bright links broken
       The morn is up then come away                    425
         Let dreams of night be banished
       The task the toil the hum of day
         Draw on, & rest is vanished
       Haste to the field & when the heat
         Of sultry noon is burning                      430
       Oh cheer thee with the prospect sweet
         Of eve again returning!
```

                    Finis

                [January 1836]

MS:  P
First Publication:  Twelve lines in facsimile in **Meditations of an**
                    **Autograph Collector**, Adrian H. Joline, New York:
                    Harper & Bros., 1902; Winnifrith PCB
Text:   l. 176:  blank space in the manuscript
        l. 267:  blank space in the manuscript
        Line numbers in left margin are Charlotte's


**109**            All is change! the night the day
                   Winter, summer; cloud & sun
                   Early flourish--late decay
                   So the years, the ages run.

                   Beats the heart with bliss awhile        5
                   Soon it throbs to agony
                   Where a moment beamed the smile
                   Soon the bitter tear shall be
                   This is Nature's great decree--
                   None can 'scape it for on all           10
                   Drops the sweet, distills the gall
                   All are fettered, all are free!

                        [January 1836]

MS:  P
First Publication:  Winnifrith PCB

**The Wounded Stag**

Passing amid the deepest shade
Of the wood's sombre heart
Last night I saw a wounded deer
Laid lonely and apart

Such light as pierced the crowded boughs                5
(Light scattered, scant and dim)
Passed through the fern that formed his couch,
And centred full on him

Pain trembled in his weary limbs
    Pain filled his patient eye                         10
Pain-crushed amid the shadowy fern
    His branchy crown did lie

Where were his comrades? where his mate?
    All from his death-bed gone
And he thus struck & desolate                           15
    Suffered and sobbed alone

Did he feel what a man might feel
    Friend-left & sore distrest
Did Pain's keen dart & Griefs sharp sting
    Strive in his mangled breast?                       20

Did longing for affection lost
Barb every deadly dart
Love unrepaid and faith betrayed
Did these torment his heart?

No leave to man his proper doom                         25
    These are the pangs that rise
Around the bed of state & gloom,
    Where Adam's offspring dies

[January 1836]

MS: P
First  Publication: **The Life of Charlotte Brontë**, E.C. Gaskell
              London: Smith, Elder & Co., 1857
Text:  1. 8: "centred full" written above "gently fell"; neither i
       canceled

Unloved, I love, unwept I weep
Grief I restrain hope I repress
Vain is this anguish fixed and deep
Vainer desires or dreams of bliss

My life is cold love's fire being dead                    5
That fire self-kindled--self-consumed
What living warmth erewhile it shed
Now to how drear extinction doomed!

Devoid of charm how could I dream
My unasked love would meet return?                        10
What fate what influence lit the flame
I still feel inly, deeply burn?

Alas there are who should not love
I to this dreary band belong
This knowing let me henceforth prove                      15
Too wise to list delusion's song

No Syren-Beauty is not mine
Affection's joys I ne'er shall know
Lonely will be my life's decline
Even as my youth is lonely now                            20

Come Reason--Science--Learning--Thought
To you my heart I dedicate
I have a faithful subject brought
Faithful because most desolate

Fear not a wandering feeble mind                          25
Stern Sovereign it is all your own
To crush--to cheer to loose to bind
Unclaimed--unshared it seeks your throne

I hear your thunders forcing seas
Beyond whose waves I left all love                        30

Soft may the breeze of summer blow
Sweetly its sun in vallies shine
All earth around with love may glow
No warmth shall reach this heart of mine

Vain boast & false even now the fire                      35
Though smothered slacked repelled is burning
At my life's source--and stronger higher
Waxes the spirits natural yearning

It waits to be crushed again
Faint I will not, nor yield to sorrow                           40
Conflict and force will quell the pain
Doubt not I shall be strong to-morrow

Have I not fled that I may conquer
Crost the dark sea in firmest faith
That I at last might plant my anchor                            45
Where love cannot prevail to death

[January 1836]

MS:  P
First Publication:  Wise Saul 1913
Text:  l. 38:  "trampled" written above "natural"; neither is canceled


**112**          But once again, but once again
                    I'll bid the strings awake
                 Just one more strain, just one more strain
                    For ancient friendship's sake

                 We must part, we must part                      5
                    But comrades drop no tear
                 There's a warm nook still in every heart
                    To keep each image dear

                 One talisman one magic spell
                    Is ours where 'ere we be                     10
                 And what shall hold the prize so well
                    As deathless memory?

                 Not far we go! not far we go!
                    And time fleets fast away
                 And none can stop a torrent's flow              15
                    For none its course can stay

                 Now hollow wind a moment cease
                    And let thy priboch die
                 The voice that should speak hope & peace
                    Will sadden to thy sigh                      20

                 Now flickering flame now dying fire
                    More <burning> more warmly glow
                 As embers quench as sparks expire
                    So sinks my song to woe


184

There trim the lamp there rouse the light          25
    Now high their red beams burn
But who can whisper to the night
    O veiled one cease to mourn

From the lone moor descends that strain
    From glen & heathery hill                       30
And as I hear its voice again
    I scarce can wish it still

The harp of heaven is tuned aright
    Now free its music flows
With what a wild & wondrous might                   35
    That sudden swell arose

That is the touch that is the tone
    The old the hallowed sound
O! sorrowing minstrel breathe alone
    Thy requiem sweet, profound                     40

40

When I'm away its memory
    My heart of hearts will thrill
'Tis the rush of sound that fills the sky
    Above my native hill

'Tis the wakener of a hundred dreams                45
    With joy with glory fraught
'Tis the loosener of a thousand streams
    Of poetry of thought

And oft when breathes the lonely night
    No other voice but thine                        50
My soul delivered to thy might
    Shall fleet to realms divine

When fitfully thy blasts are <telling>
    That stars their lustre veil
In clouds whose misty vapours swelling             55
    Below the bright worlds sail

Then on thy wings whose waft is thunder
    Then on thy wings I'll lean
And from the strange home torn asunder
    Wrapt in thy cloudy screen                      60
    I'll travel away, far away
Where the dream in the darkness lies shrouded & grey
    Time shall not chain me
    Place not restrain me
Mind is not matter & soul is not clay               65


185

And there I'll meet you comrades
　　And we'll shake hands again
Though twenty miles between us lie
　　Of night & wind & rain

62

But alas! alas! I cannot hope                    70
　　My anchor sinks away
And riven from its faithless prop
　　My ship drifts out to sea

'Tis bitterness to leave you all
　　My heart is bound to home               75
I cannot drink the cup of gall
　　I was not made to roam

I know I shall again return
　　But life meantime is failing
The lamp that may not always burn          80
　　Its transient light is paling

All the sweet time of spring will be
　　An hour of dreamless sleeping
A blank a vacancy to me
　　Dark with the mists of weeping          85

I will not hold those strangers dear
　　With whom I dwell unwilling
My thoughts all rest on those who hear
　　This farewell wild & thrilling

I have no outside, surface love             90
　　My hearts nor wide nor roomy
No stray affection forth may rove
　　Bound in exclusion gloomy

Just us & those we've formed in dreams
　　Our own divine creations                 95
These are my soul's unmingled themes
　　I scorn the alien nations
Shake hands dark Percy! breathe & live
　　Shalt thou in nothing perish?
No flesh & life & soul Ill give             100
And faithfully in thee believe
　　And still thy memory cherish

Shake hands Zenobia glorious form
    Art thou a vapour, lady?
A rainbow traced upon the storm            105
    Where the clouds lie black & shady
Is thy pirate husband but a name
    Is the bucaneer a vision
Is the red Rover's fearful fame
Are the deeps o'er which it went & came    110
    Food for the world's derision?

Are the great Houses of the West
    The high clans of the North
Nothing but thought in language dressed
    And breathed in bright words forth      115

Must their stern woods & all the glory
    Of their old & noble homes
Pass off in mystery dim & hoary
Like an old song or magic story
    Like the voice of their own domes      120
When the echo to the sound replies
Then all in utter silence dies

And the star I saw intensely burning
    Through the black but splendid night
Whose beams into its self returning      125
Decked the mi[l]d heaven's solemn mourning
    With self concentered light

Blinding in radiance as the sun
    But deepening only the blue gloom
In which a white clear orb it shone      130
    A gem upon the brow of doom

I mean Zamorna! do not say
    I speak in egotism now
This is our last our farewell day
    So here's my open unmasked brow      135

I owe him something, he has held
    A lofty, burning lamp to me
Whose rays surrounding darkness quelled
    And shewed me wonders, shadow free

And he has been a mental King      140
    That ruled my thoughts right regally
And he has given me a <steady> spring
    To what I had of poetry

I've heard his accents sweet & stern
　Speak words of kindled wrath to me　　　　　　145
When dead as dust in funeral urn
　Sank every note of melody
And I was forced to wake again
　The silent song the slumbering strain　　　　150
He's moved the principle of life
　Through all I've written or sung or said
The war-song rousing to the strife
　The life-wind wakening up the dead

He's not the temple but the god
　The idol in his marble shrine　　　　　　　155
Our grand dream is his wide abode
　And there for me he dwells divine

I can walk in the structure vast
　A while and never think of him
Only at times there wander's past　　　　　160
　A consciousness all strange & dim
That it was his shrined divinity
Which brought me there to bow the knee

Others as mighty rest around
　The great Pantheon has many a god　　　　165
But to his altar I am bound
　For him the consecrated ground
　My pilgrim steps have trod

At time's by Percy's pedestal
　More deeply awed I worship low　　　　　170
But grovelling in the dust I fall
　Where Adrian's shrine lamps dazzling glow

It is his light it is his star
　That leads me on resistlessly
Ascending high or wandering far　　　　　175
　Or diving deep in sullen sea

Now plunged amid the wild green waves
　Where storms & storm-lashed waters war
Now standing where <the> breaker raves
　In wrath against its rocky bar　　　　　180

Still the revolving beacon throws
　Its glory o'er the brightning sea
Whose dark floor far off burns & glows
While reddened billows part & close
　Upon its surface changefully　　　　　185
　Gleaming & flickering liquidly

146

164

And art thou nothing sea-light high
And thou sublime divinity?
Shake hands Zamorna! God or man
And though thou be'est incarnadined                    190
I vow by blessing swear by ban
Thy spirit is in bright flesh shrined

Somewhere--somewhere all the dream
Lives breathes in glory that I know
I feel its truth in sudden gleam                       195
Flashing around me Lord! & thou
Thou & thy consort! living pearl
Are not a wreath of morning mist
Not sparks that dart from reason's whirl
When vexed by the minds unrest                         200
Alnwick! & solemn Mornington!
And Grassmere Grange! & Percy hall!
Your lattices now feel that sun
Through their clear panes of crystal fall
Its pallid gold on many a wall                         205
Under your roofs rests placidly
These airs & breezes whispering call
Answers from ancient grove & tree
Where in far years, in times gone by
In summer evenings past away                           210
Your ancestors walked pensively
Watching the close of twilight grey
Where Duchess! thy fair mother strayed
Dying so long before the time
When, the last chord of music played                   215
Wood-church tolled out the passing chime
Often the glory of the sun
Burned on that land whose beauty none
In words may say unspeakable
And round the heath-couched lady fell                  220
And Alderwood the summer's heat
Is in thy woods, among the bowers
Languidly lingering soft & sweet
Scented by wild & hidden flowers
That silver moon shone long ago                        225
On the old porch with roses veiled
Where listening to the Wansbecks flow
That through the twilight, falling slow
    Mournfully wailed
Sat Victorine, the lily bright                         230
Of Sunart's sheet of stormy light
Her lonely beauty pale & still
    Pensive & saddening ever more
What thoughts, what dreams her bosom fill!

As she sits by the Norman door                                235
With flowers & ivy shadowing o'er
And golden stars & deep blue skies
Above, & stre[t]ching on before
Tall, stirless trees in alleys rise
    Deepening & deepening still                               240
A wood in June at even-tide
The plumy foliage all in pride
    While plants its green recesses fill
That scent each glade from side to side
    And summer eve that breathes no chill                     245
Is softly darkening far & wide
Victorine thou art not there
With thee the leaf of life is sere
    Though in its early spring
She thinks of academic groves                                 250
Far off & waving solemnly
Over the blue & quiet sea
    Where the young Southern roves
And watches haply now the gloom
Gathering in that vast marble tomb                            255
On whose bright surface shining lies
The mirrored moon & starry skies
Lighting the high & stately bowers
That soar above their classic towers
And in that distant island-home                               260
At midnight shed light o'er the ocean foam

Sadly the Highland Baroness
Looks on the scene of awful bliss
In kindling, vivid thought she sees
Lord Douro lean against the trees                             265
As he looks down on the mighty deep
Through all its green realms hushed in sleep
She sees his hand patrician white
Circling the bough o'er which <he> bends
Fain would she touch those fingers slight                     270
Flashing with many a gem of light
A torch remembrance lends
To show her how in other times
In distant lands in sterner climes
By the tall youthful strangers side                           275
She wandered oft at eventide
While that same hand would warmly press
His own fair northern Baroness
While poured his lips seductively
Their tones of foreign melody                                 280
And now the very agony
Of longing love thrills through her <heart>

Her eyes are gazing piercingly
Where those high elms in vista part
O heaven could she, might she see                                285
Through the leaf-checquered moonlight gliding
That form that in her memory
Is firmly even to pain abiding
The slender boy with soft dark eyes
And curls upon his neck descending                               290
Shading a face where mingled lies
Sweetness & untold passions blending
And marble beauty finely wrought
Like Artist's dream or Sculptor's thought

To hear his clear voice speak her name                           295
With that strange smile she knew so well
"Helen" e'ven the accent came
She started so distinct it fell
As she had heard it in the hall
When suddenly he stood beside her                                300
300      And when she trembled at the call
How gently would he feign to chide her

She rose, the ivy gently waving
Stirred to the rustling of her dress
And Wansbeck moaned it[s] green banks laving                     305
300      All else was utter voicelessness
Douro six hundred miles away
Was gazing on the moonlight main
And thinking as alone he lay
Of her he n'er should see again                                  310
Little he dreamt her lonely grave
Should greet him when he crossed the wave
That is enough, too much 'tis over
Helen is dead, still lies her lover
But no more of the wondrous dream                                315
My time of pleasant holiday
Jany     Is faded like a sunny beam
19       And I must here no longer stay
1836     May we all meet in joy again
And then I'll sing a lighter strain                              320
This evening hear the solemn knell
320      Farewell! & yet again farewell!!

                                            C Brontë

MS:  P
First Publication:   Joline 1902, partial; Winnifrith PCB
Text:  Line numbers in left margin are Charlotte's

191

113      I've a free hand and a merry heart
           I dwell in gay Madrid
         My hair is like a night-cloud when
           Its veil the moon has hid
         My blood is not the high Castile                    5
           The Moor has breathed his flame
         Through every blushing artery
           That leads the crimson stream
         And yet I am of noble birth
           My father's long ago                             10
         Were mighty lords e'er Granada
           Quailed to the Christian foe
         But what care I for noble birth
           I'm young & gay & free
         I've jet-black eyes & coal-black locks             15
           & brow of ivorie
         I've a quick hand & a sweet guitar
           And a light foot for the dance
         And many a mystic reel I know
           And many a blithe romance                        20
         When I see the clear blue skies of Spain
           And feel her glad warm sun
         I've nought to jar the harmony
           They breathe my soul upon
         I'm happy when the early light                     25
           Looks through my casement panes
         I'm happy when the suns farewell
           Their hue with amber stains
         I'm happy when the moon uplights
           The green vine's leafy veil                       30
         And smiles as I lie wakefully
           To watch her lustre pale
         And oh! when far beneath my bower
           A wild sweet air is played
         My soul leaps up to bless the hour                 35
           Of star & serenade

                              [April 1836]

MS:   F(2)
First Publication:   Shorter 1918

192

**114**       Lanes were sweet at summer midnight
Flower & moss were cool with dew
There was neither blast nor breeze to chill me
Silent shade of solemn hue
Stole o'er skies intensely blue             5
I looked & thought the stars were piercing
That gazed on me like eyes of light
So still & fixed they seemed to watch me
Ranked in myriads high & bright
Kindling, burning through the night       10
If the hazel waved above me
Or the wild-rose stretched its spray
O'er the green & dewy coppice
I have shuddered where I lay
At thoughts which never came by day     15

                                [April 1836]

MS:  F(2)
First Publication:  Shorter 1923

**115**       The chapelle stood & watched the way
    Its cross still mouldered there
But neither priest nor penitent
    Now bowed the Knee in prayer
The lamps around our Lady's shrine     5
    Were dimmed, were quenched for aye
But still upon her brow divine
    The moon-beams slumbering lay
That night Maria thought her fair
    And pure & meet to be          10
The offerer of a fervid prayer
    O! God in heaven to thee!
And for her fierce and faithless love
    Maria wildly prayed
St Mary did'st thou smile above     15
    Thine altar's solemn shade
As rose amid the eerie hush
    All through thy lone chapelle
Petitions breathed in agony
    For one beloved too well      20
Maria die before that shrine
    Thy lord will love thee then
When thou art gone in bitterness
    He'll wish the[e] back again!
Amid a life of woes & tears       25

193

O Brightest! cease to stay
Hark the wailing wind in the rifted arch
    Says "lady pass away"
The lake the chapel looks upon
    Is calm & still & deep                         30
Maria thinks how pleasantly
    She there might sink to sleep
The Chapelle & the holy cross
    Gaze calmly from the brae
On another shrine & crucifix                        35
    As fair & clear as they
It chanced upon that summer night
    Dark Henry home did ride
For ancient fondness fitfully
    Came o'er him for his bride                     40
Dark Henry sought his lady's bower
    But his lady's bower was lone
It was mirk midnight at that shadowy hour
    O! where could she be gone
Dark Henry hied to St Mary's lake                   45
    He hied to Madonna's shrine
Not a whispered word does the silence break
    That reigns where those wall-flowers twine
A ripple curls on the placid mere
    Though there is no wind to sigh                  50
And a single foam-bell bubbles clear
    Where the leaves of that lily lie
For Far under the fairy sea
    Slumbers Maria placidly!

                                   [April 1836]

MS:  F(2)
First Publication:  Shorter 1918


**116**   And when you left me what thoughts had I then
              Percy I would not tell you to your face
          But out of sight & thought of living men
              Wandering away on the lone ocean's face
          I may say what I think & how & when          5
          The mood comes on me I may give it space
          Confessing like a dying man to heaven
          Anxious alone to have his sins forgiven



194

Not caring what the world he leaves may say
Heedless of its forgotten hate & scorn                                    10
But giving full & free & fearless way
To secrets that the fear of death has torn
From his concealing bosom where they lay
Scorching the soul in which their sparks were born
Aye Alexander just so recklessly                                          15
I give my dreams to the wild wind & sea

You are a fiend, I've told you that before
I've told it half in earnest half in jest
I've sworn it when the very furnace roar
Of hell was rising fiercely in my breast                                  20
And calmly I confirm the oath once more
Adding however as becomes me best
That I'm no better & we two united
Each other's happiness have fiend-like blighted

Let us consider, let us just look back                                    25
     And trace the pleasant path we've trod together
The retrospect is dreary, cold & black
     And threatens rain our own grim Angrian weather
There are some slips of greensward on the track
Glorious with sunshine, but dark slopes of heather                        30
Copses of night-shade, thickets void of flowers
These are the chief types of those by-past hours

How oft we rung each other's callous hearts
Conscious none else could so effectively
Waken the pain or venom the keen darts                                    35
We shot so thickly so unsparingly
Into those sensitive & tender parts
That veiled from all besides ourselves could see
like eating cankers pains that heaven had dealt
On devotees to crime, sworn slaves of guilt                               40

And still our mutual doom accomplishing
Blind as the Damned our anti-types if one
Had in his treasures, some all priceless thing
Some jewel that he deeply doated on
Dearer to him than life, the fool would fling                             45
That rich gem to his friend, he could not shun
The influence of his star, though well he knew
His friend that treasure to the winds would strew

Percy your daughter was a lovely being
Truly you must have loved her, her sweet eyes                    50
Showed in their varied lustre changing fleeing
Such warm & intense passion, that which lies
In your own breast & save to the All-seeing
Not fully known to any could not rise
To stronger inspiration, than their ray                          55
Revealed when I had waked her nature's wildest play

When Mary was grown up an open rose
A western girl, just ripe for woman-hood
With those Milesian eyes whose lids disclose
Spirits that only glad the Gambia's flood                        60
Glowing like sunlight on the stream which flows
Hesperia through thy land of lake & wood
I tell thee Percy not one Nation's breast
Bears women like our own infernal West

But then they're mostly hasty soon excited                       65
To wrath with little reason, theres thy wife
She's just the clear dark skin, the glance uplighted
With thoughts that always fill the soul with strife
The gait the form the fervent mind benighted
Which might suit Italy, or else the knife                        70
That eastern ladies, crowned sultanas wear
A glittering sign to bid their lords beware!

However I'll return again to Mary
There's something sweet & soothing in that word
A dreamy charm as if some wandering fairy                        75
Had breathed it or some little spirit bird
Had warbled it unseen for soft & airy
And oft divinely holy it is heard
I know my dark speech does not need explaining
For Percy well thou knowest it hath a meaning                    80

Well sir when Mary on some pleasant even
Has sat beside you perhaps at Percy-Hall
And in the richest purest light of heaven
You've seen the curls around her temples fall
And when the coming gloom of Dusk has given                      85
A tone of such sad loveliness to all
Could you look on her sir & think that she
Must sometime be a prey to such as me

196

18
 8
144
 6

I well remember on our marriage-day
An hour or two after the bridal rite                    90
She & I somehow chanced to find our way
Into a large & empty hall whose light
Streaming through painted windows shed its ray
On nothing save our-selves, the floor of stone
And the pure fountain falling there alone               95

I gazed on her Ionian face, so fair
In all its lines so classically straight
Her marble forehead with the haloing hair
Sunnily cluster[ed] round it, whereon sate
A shade that soon might deepen into care               100
Even such dark care as has gloomed there of late
Though then t'was but the sadness said to lie
On the fair brows of those who early die

I asked her if she loved me and she said
That she would die for me with such a glance           105
Talk of the fiery arrowy lustre bred
By the hot southern suns of Spain & France
I say again as I before have said
Our western tenderness does so enhance
The ardour of our women's souls & spirits              110
That nought on earth such fire divine inherits

She said she'd die for me & now she's keeping
Her word far off at Alnwick, o'er the sea
The very wind around this vessel sweeping
Will steal unto her pillow whisperingly                115
And murmur o'er her form which shall be sleeping
Ere-long beneath some quiet pall-like tree
I would she were within my reach just now
Not long that shade should haunt her Grecian brow

She'd feel the stream of life run strong again         120
If I could only take her to my breast
She'd feel a balm poured on her aching pain
Her day-long weariness would know a rest
But then there's the profound wide, thundering main
Tossing between us its triumphant crest                125
Of snow-white foam, & then I've pledged my faith
To break her father's heart by Mary's death

A holy resolution and it will
Be visited upon me thirty-fold
For human-nature feels a shuddering chill                    130
To hear of life for bloody vengeance sold
An animal passion when unmoved & still
And vulture-like it fixes its stern hold
Deep, in the very vitals of its slave
Making his bosom but a hungry grave                          135

144   And so my lord if you have ruined me
 56   And ruined all the hopes I ever cherished
200   I've paid you back & that abundantly
      You'll feel it when that flower of yours has perished
      And dark & desolate that hour shall be                 140
      When the place where my dazzling lily flourished
      Shall know no more its past magnificence
      Death having gathered it & borne it hence

      I'm walking on the Deck & King is leaning
      O'er the ship's rails & communing with me              145
      Would you could hear the bloody tales he's gleaning
      From the dark harvest of his memory
      Would you could see his eye's ferocious meaning
      Bent gloatingly upon the surging sea
      He says that monarch of exhaustless founts             150
      Is the best balancer of men's accounts

      He say's if I'd been wise I should have taken
      My lady with me on this distant sail
      And kindly tenderly have striven to waken
      That bliss again which had begun to fail               155
      And that I should defyingly have shaken
      My fist in fortune's face & made her quail
      The old blind jade, & turned my hand like thee
      To blood & pillage on the rolling sea

      And some sweet night the hoary saint is saying         160
      Some heavenly, holy tropic summer night
      When dying gales upon the deep are straying
      As soft as if they came down with the light
      The moon diffuses while the stars decaying
      Before her beam imperial, still may yield              165
      A radiant tremor o'er that deep, blue field

Then says the Mentor when my Mary's sleeping
Wrapt blissfully in dreams of love & me
Quietly ghost-like to her cabin creeping
I should have brought her up all tenderly                    170
And while the lulling waves were past us sweeping
Have given her to the bosom of the sea
As she still slumbered, & no sob or moan
Was wakened to tell which way the bird had flown

It would look well says Sdeath to see her sinking           175
All in white raiment through the placid deep
From the pure limpid water never shrinking
Calmly subsiding to eternal sleep
Dreaming of him that's drowning her, not thinking
She's soon to be where sharks & sword-fish leap             180
And if she rose again a few days hence
Looking like death it would but stand to sense

To common sense, a corpse laid in the water
Must putrify whosever corpse it be
And neither Adrian's wife nor Percy's daughter              185
Can be left out in Nature's great decree
He'd seen stout men who'd fallen by pirate slaughter
A few days after float up buoyantly
And laughed to watch the light & fleet career
They held upon the water's surface clear                    190

He'd seen you stand upon the Rover's deck
As calm as if t'were sea-weed floating by
Order a weight to be tied round their neck
Cool as a cucumber, for proud & high
You'd too much sense to suffer such a speck                 195
To dim a moment your rejoicing sky
Your spirit was a sun which drove away
200  Such slight obscurers of the light of day.

                    *   *   *   *   *

Of late our ship along the coast of France
Was gliding in the gentle gales which blow                  200
Of from the storied hills of old Provence
We saw Marseilles frown on the waves below
It's pleasant when the sunny billows dance
All gladsomely around the vessel's prow
And when a town & shore before you lie                      205
The home of thousands neath their native sky

It's pleasant then to think that you are hasting
As fast as wind & flowing sail can fleet
To a black jail of rocks & keen & wasting
Are the strong impulses & pangs that eat                210
At that thought through the heart & were they lasting
They'd soon infold you in your winding sheet
But they pass off in sickness, sometimes tears
And then again the dim sky coldly clears

I stood upon the deck, the vessel's rails              215
I was convulsive grasping, for around
The life & gaiety of Proud Marseilles
Were poured upon its harbour, not a sound
Rung o'er the deep but glad as chiming bells
It spoke of life & made my bosom bound                 220
With a wild wish for freedom, worse than vain
My breast but struck the stronger 'gainst a chain

At that dark moment something spoke my name
My title rather which ought now to die
'Twas from a female that the soft sound came           225
She said in French "Zamorna will you buy?"
I turned it was like the kindling of a flame
To utter that word 'neath an alien sky
I saw a girl beside me dark & tall
Her face all shaded by her tresses' fall               230

The curls as black & bright as jet descended
From under the Provencal hat she wore
A basket full of grapes & vine leaves blended
With roses all in Gallic taste she bore
And as on her my silent gaze I bended                  235
She offered me her rich corbeille once more
Murmuring in the soft tone of sympathy
You shall not buy them, you shall have them free

I took a rosebud dropping in its stead
A coin of my own ruined kingdom graced                 240
With the wreathed impress of my own wise head
And then, you know my ways, however placed
Were it upon the scaffold flashing red
With noble blood & forms all death defaced
Or were it underneath the gallows tree                 245
I'd kiss the lovely lips that pitied me

My slaughtered, hunted Angrians, shall I ever
Your Ransomer, your Conquering King return
Your brutal Taskmasters will never never
Rule you as I have ruled you, they will burn                    250
The slave mark on your brows & they will sever
The last domestic ties & make you mourn
Wildly & hopelessly, while I am lying
Far in yon dreary Isle alone it may be dying

And what made me speak thus, why I recalled                     255
The times Bright East when I was King in thee
And when thy wildest mountains heather-palled
With all their iron vassalage knew me
And my land's daughters now with bondage galled
Were as the Gordon red deer chainless free                      260
And thousands of their ruby lips have known
The touch of Adrian's when he claimed his own

Well when I lifted up the fruit-girl's head
To give her that salute the black curls parted
And the revealed & flashing eye-balls shed                      265
A ray upon me not unknown, I started
And half indignantly I would have said
"This must not be," but then so broken-hearted
So full of dying hope was that dark eye
I could not put its mute petition bye                           270

And so I turned again towards the town
And looked down on its vast & busy quay
And meekly obstinate the Girl sat down
Beside me on the deck & murmuringly
She said, "Zamorna I have borne your frown                      275
Often before & now I dare not be
Delicate in my duties, those must dwell
In gloom habitual, who would serve you well

I stayed in Angria sire until the hour
Was past when I could serve my master their                     280
Until they had dug up the cherished flower
He gave unto my sleepless, deathless care
Until they'd broken his own domestic bower
Shivered his shrine & scattered in the air
The relics he loved well, & this task done                      285
I rose & followed where my lord was gone

I will be with you Sire you'll want me soon
In that lone, dreary Island where you go
You'll sicken of the melancholy tune
The waves will play around you in their flow          290
And wandering on its shore with ship-wrecks strewn
You'll feel its solitude full well & I know
Go to your heart & then a wretch like me
Might serve you still in that extremity

She spoke I made no answer we were now                295
Leaving the harbour of Marseilles behind
Sdeath had weighed anchor & the Rover's prow
Was flashing through the wave before the wind
The gleaming walls & towers began to grow
Dim in the distance, scarce the eye might find       300
More than the misty outlines of their forms
Shadowy as rocks obscured by coming storms

Our captain came & swore that she should stay
He'd have no boats sent off to land not he
She might have known the ship was under weigh        305
She saw it moving through the severed sea
And by his soul & by the light of day
He'd never stir a step to pleasure me
And Mina smiled to see her end was gained
Fortune had favoured her & she remained              310

Now for my Mary's sake I have not given
One smile or glance of love to that poor slave
And I have seen her woman's feelings riven
With pangs that made her look down on the wave
As if it were her home her hope her heaven           315
Because a semblance of repose it gave
She sees I do not want her, none can tell
What torments from that chill conviction swell

I cannot spurn her, though my wife is dying
Cheerless & desolate in solitude                     320
This moment like a faithful dog she's lying
Crouched at my feet, for with a sad subdued
Untiring constancy she's ever trying
To gain one word or even one look embued
With some slight touch of kindness, there then take  325
A brief caress, for all thy labour's sake

I did but grasp her little hand & press
The taper fingers as a brother might
And she looked upward in her meek distress
While such a glad adoring ray of light                                330
Shot from her large black eyes as if to bless
A God for mercies given & full & bright
The gathered tear ran over, then again
They bent their radiance on the solemn main

Last night she told me all the dreary tale                            335
Of what has happened Percy to my son
How all her watchful care could not avail
How she had struggled how her prize was won
And the departing blood left cold & pale
The cheek that lately it glowed so brightly on                        340
As she revealed what floating rumour said
That the young lord of Avon-dale was dead

That my brave Angrians to the rescue flew
Urged on by Warner, that the boy they found
Alive but as their noble leader true                                  345
A bloody bandage from his eyes unbound
Lo he was sightless! & a faintness grew
Over her as she told of many a wound
In his young frame & she fell down & prayed
That I would bear with what was still unsaid                          350

96   E're I could speak, the impetuous words came gushing
 99  Forth from her lips, It was by night she cried
195  The tryst was on a moor & there came rushing
The thousand serfs to Warner's house allied
He stood up in the midst, the red blood flushing                      355
His face & brow, his voice rung far & wide
As in that hour he bade them look upon
The mangled relics of their monarch's son

And out into the ghastly moonlight holding
A sheet all stained with blood he turned aside                        360
The drapery a gory corpse infolding
A corpse though still the blood in gentle tide
crept through its veins, but death the face was moulding
Rightly for that home which the earth shall hide
Oh sire dread was that midnight's staring gloom                       365
Which saw thy flower so blighted in its bloom

Men's hearts were toned to horror & their feelings
Were wound up to the highest pitch of dread
And Warner's voice & look shot forth revealings
Of a soul into whose wild depth was shed                      370
A kind of inspiration, not the sheilings
Of Highland seers who commune with the dead
'Ere gloomed in such a cloud of awe as then
Fell on that host of brave & desperate men

In Warner's arms & on his breast reposing                     375
Ernest died calmly on that awful night
Before a thousand men his brief life closing
Amid the wild wind & the wandering light
Of moon & stars his death a spirit rousing
Through all the land which saw it that in fight               380
Shall henceforth strong & terrible & dread
Burst forth & reap dark vengeance for the dead

                           394

Warner with knitted brow the struggle watched
Which parted flesh from spirit then he pressed
The little corpse whose limbs in death were stretched        385
Ardently strongly to his noble breast
And then his silent lifted eye beseeched
In prayer that though unheard might well be guessed
The Judgment of the Highest all was still
While thus he spoke with God on that wild hill               390

They buried Gordon on the moor that night
Warner with his own hands the body laid
Low in its narrow house, no funeral rite
No prayer no blessing o'er the grave was said
Only as all the host their lances bright                      395
Reversed in homage to the royal dead
Their chief cried solemnly "O Lord how long
"Shall thine elected people suffer wrong!"

How did I feel when Mina ceased her speaking
I stronger than an Indian in my love                          400
For that which now beyond the power of waking
Sleeps in its gory grave, Theres heaven above
And earth around me & beneath me shaking
With cries of the tormented! Hell may move
But neither from Hell nor Earth nor Righteous heaven          405
Can rest or comfort to my heart be given

                           204

Thou whom I nurtured in my bosom child
Thou whom I doated on & gently cherished
Thou to die thus! when I was far exiled
In Gloom in Grief in agony he perished                          410
Sundered from me by that storm dread & wild
Which was sent over Angria, all that flourished
Fairest upon her plains, died in the blast
Leaving her lorn & barren as it past

I've nothing but Revenge to think on now                       415
Nothing to lean upon my staff is broken

O if exerting more than human might
I could have burst my bonds in time to save
I should have thought that hour more blest & bright
Than all the triumphs I have known which gave                  420
My darling to my bre[a]st, my star of light
My first born son snatched [from] a fearful grave
Rescued from wild-beasts, from the demon stranger
"Clasped in my arms his home in every danger!"

Oft at Fort-Adrian in the nights of storm                      425
That used to rush all madly on the river
I've taken protectingly his sleeping form
To the paternal heart that beat for ever in
In love to him & while all calm & warm
My nestling lay what cared I for the shiver                    430
Of roof & casement & the deepening war
Of winds that vext the impetuous Calabar

So like his sainted mother looked he, sleeping
The wild eyes that reflected mine being closed
The lamps his soft & lovely features steeping                  435
With shaded light, the darkness that reposed
All day upon his brow, his bright dreams sweeping
With airy wing away then nothing roused
That spirit of the Gordons which when awaking
Oft crossed his face like sullen lightening breaking           440

The ringlets dark & silken waved away
From his young forehead left it calm & clear
And on his polished cheek the shadow lay
Of lashes black as ebon, not more fair
Helen has ever looked & not a ray of                           445
Of my fierce likeness, mingled with the dear
And hallowed impress that so sweetly moulded
The green bud to the blossom all unfolded

Yet he was like me, like me in his passion
And like me in his rapture when some sight                              450
Of glory sent a kindling inspiration
All through the quickened current red & bright
Of his high blood, he was my own creation
The offspring of my boyhood, the delight
Of my first fiery youth, my hope my pride                               455
A mightier branch of my own kingly tide

You would not save him Percy nor will I
Save yours from desolation, with wild pleasure
I'll now call down the doom from the most high
His curse upon my head in fullest measure                              460
I'll fit me for a passage to the sky
By heaving overboard my choicest treasure
Yea I'll leave all, take up my cross & follow
All Flesh is grass all joys are vain & hollow

King, Dog & Fiend you cannot tell me now                               465
The thing I would not do to make another
Feel the same horror that bedews my brow
With bloody sweat. Hot harried crime might smother
The choking suffocating thoughts that grow
Like fungi round my wasted heart & wither                              470
Its vital greenness, deeply deeply eating
Into my life pulse madly beating

Warner I thank you you're the only man
I would shake hands with at this passing hour
I thank you for you perilled all your clan                             475
To save my dead child from a demon's power
I bless you for you nobly led the van
To snatch from Hell my crushed uprooted flower
I'm bound to you for ever, for your breast
Was my departed Ernest's dying rest                                    480

Mina come hither weep no more I love you
As a hawk loves a lark I've cast away
Patrician ladies throned as high above you
As that large star serene above the ray
The glow-worm flings, let not this world's scorn move you             485
And waste not in my passion's fiery ray
I know that you can bear a fierce caress
My arm grows strong nerved by my heart's distress

You'll never fear nor tremble to draw nigh
When I am scarce myself with torment stinging                490
Into the principle of life, you'd die
To save my bosom from a moment's wringing
Faithful devoted martyr through her eye
Her soul its ray of fevered joy is flinging
Because I said she might the victim be                       495
Of a chained vulture, caged amid the sea

Beautiful creature once so innocent
With such a seriousness & strength of mind
Beaming upon her youthful brow & blent
With what seemed like religion, so refined                   500
So firm in principle, her soul ne'er bent
Nor wavered midst the soft voluptuous wind
A western palace round the wild rose blew
504    But shook not from it one pure drop of dew

What is she now look at her as the flashing                  505
Of her dark Asian eye shines full on me
Look at the little hand so proudly dashing
The gloomy rain that will stream fitfully
From the full sphere--her cheek of roses washing
Till even its bright bloom fades, & we may see              510
Traces of sorrow there, lit up the while
With that lost fated God-abandoned smile

She asks for work and now she'll labour on
From the first murmur of the morning breeze
To the descending of the evening sun                        515
With careful aspect vigilant to please
And now & then if she is all alone
The tear will drop no energy can freeze
As a remembrance comes of parted hours
Dimly discerned through years of mists & showers            520

I'll go & sit beside her & recline
My forehead on her shoulder, there all's calm
Her faithful heart was blest as it felt mine
Beating against it, now amid the balm
Blown o'er the summer sea by gales divine                   525
Singing as sweet as some old mournful psalm
I'll bow resigned a man of many woes
528    The sea shall soothe me saddening as it flows

July 19$^{th}$ 1836

Tormented! O tormented! Mina love
Thy neck is wet with tears they would come forth          530
I cannot one brief hour of respite prove
The sweetest sights & sounds that bless this earth
Only the fiend to busier madness move
That eats my life away, what is their worth
Nothing! Oh Mina love I cannot rest                      535
I could not if heaven's glories round me prest

And it is misery when all's so bright
In earth & sea & sky as they were wooing
My mind to sympathy & in their light
Their evening light I feel around me growing              540
Some thing no words can tell an inward night
Downward unceasingly & darkly flowing
In clouds--yes pity me & wildly strain
Thy master to thy breast 'tis all in vain

Wave thy soft ringlets round me press my brow            545
With that cool supple hand & point again
Unto that western sky.  I see its glow
I feel it, rosily upon the main
Pouring its flush, I hear the cooing flow
Of the hushed, waters lulling their deep strain          550
Answering the winds as those enkindled seas
Respond to the bright burning sunset's blaze

I seem to have lived for nothing, wandering
Through all my early youth, mong fields of flowers
Tracking the green-paths where the fairest spring        555
Culling the richest bloom of dells & bowers
When all at once the unrelenting wing
Of some cold blast swept by with sleety showers
Scattered the roses & buds & leaves away
Save one or two left shrivelled by decay                 560

That simile's absurd, all words are weak
Tongue cannot utter, what the victim feels
Who lies outstretched upon that burning lake
Whose flaming eddy now beneath me reels
All that breathes happiness seems to forsake             565
His blighted thoughts, a demon hand unseals
That little well so treasured in man's breast
Whose drop of hope so sweetens all the rest

And out it flows & slips unseen away
Trickling to nothingness & leaving gall                           570
Rank gall behind.  Such bitter briny spray
As might be brought up by a sulphurous squall
From the Dead Lake the Sodomitish Sea
But halt I've said enough & yonder wave
Shall give my words an unrevealing grave                          575

    576 lines                                    July 19<sup>th</sup> 1836

MS:  D(1)
First Publication:  Ratchford Legends
Text:  Line numbers in text and in left margin are Charlotte's


**117**    Look into thought & say what dost thou see
Dive, be not fearful how dark the waves flow
Sink through the surge & bring pearls up to me
Deeper ay deeper, the fairest lie low

I have dived I have sought them, but none have I found         5
In the gloom that closed o'er me no <form> flowed by
As I sunk through the void depths so black & profound
How dim died the sun & how far hung the sky

What had I given to hear the soft sweep
Of a breeze bearing life through that vast realm of death       10
Thoughts wear untroubled & dreams were asleep
The spirit lay dreadless & hopeless beneath

    [October 1836]

MS:  D(1)
First Publication:  Benson 1915


**118**    Well the day's toils are over, with success
I've laboured since the morning, hand in hand
With those I love, & now our foe's distress
Seems gathering to its height, my stalwart band
Desperate in purpose, cool & rock-like press                   5
Near to their aim before another day
We hope to smite our snared & stricken prey

All seems in train for triumph, calm & stern
We see our clouded sun look out again
Not like its summer dawn the white beams burn          10
But withering chilly, still subdued by rain
The rain of storms that part & still return
In a dim shower sometimes, & momently
Cloud as with tears the light on land & sea

Brief fits of weeping! they can ne'er subdue          15
The hidden yet glorious sense of victory nigh
I feel it, all whose hearts to me are true
Feel & yet veil the impulse, still no eye
That, deep & secret consciousness may view
Save, that which would flash fierce with sympathy     20
It is the Avenger's latest hope & he
Waits for its full fruition,--silently!

I've borne too much to boast, even now I know
While I advance to triumph, all my host
So sternly reckless to the conflict go                25
Because each charm & joy of life they've lost
Because on their invaded thresholds grow[s]
Grass from their children's graves, because the cost
Of their lands's red redemption, has been blood
From gallant hearts poured out in lavish flood        30

Yet Oh! there is a sure & steadfast glory
In knowing that the scale ascends again
And that when we with age are bent & hoary
And when our children's children spring to men
As we tell o'er this dark invasion's story            35
How fires of war ran wild through every glen
And crowned each blue hill-top with crimson crest
How then at last we found victorious rest

And did not bow to demons, though their goad
With teeth of iron, urged us to despair               40
And though men called us rebels as they trode
Upon our yoke-bowed necks, & though the air
The pure air of our mountains, felt the load
Of putrid plague & corpses every where
Lay livid in our lonely homes, & tombs                45
Ceased to unclose in the rank churchyards-glooms

For none had time to bury, if the rite
Were half-commenced the summons of dismay
The cry to arms, the strange appalling sight
Of squadrons charging, called each friend away                50
And often thus, even, at the dead of night
Corpses were left alone midst clods of clay
And the armed mourners hurried to repel
The whirlwind onslaught of the tribes of hell

But the bare ravaged land is swept & free                     55
Out of her shattered towns, & blighted fields
The wind has driven the locusts, gallantly
We chased the scum before us, Vengeance wields
A sword none can withstand, & as a tree
To the bleak autumn storm its foliage yields                  60
So scarce resisting, the oppressor flew
As our tornado coming nearer drew

Rising at once, the peasantry hemmed round
Arab & Scot retreating, hearths were quenched
& homes deserted, if some hut was found                       65
To yield a moment's shelter, to the drenched
And starved & ravenous fiends, on the cold ground
No glowing fire gleamed, & trodden bread
& scattered flour, to greet their eyes were spread

Their corpses fell like famished wolves before us            70
Along the winter-roads, spotting the waste
Of drifted snow, vindictive joy flashed o'er us
As the grim, belted skeletons we past
And were we wrong? and should remorse have tore us
As we beheld them in black ditches cast                       75
Laid under leafless hedges, pale & gaunt
Murdered with hardships, dead with grinding want

Should we have wept? shades of our fathers say
Spirits of our dead comrades rise & tell
Angels of those whose dying relics lay                        80
On beds of pestilence, Speak where ye dwell
Should we have wept?, some in your early day
The plague cut down, like shrunken flowers ye fell
And withered hopeless in a land of slaves
And knew the tyrants would tread o'er your graves            85

211

By the last sun you saw, by the wild weeping
That closed your earthly pilgrimage in gloom
By the unhallowed graves where darkly sleeping
You lie forgetful of the sorrowing home
That wails your long departure, vain the sweeping          90
Of the sweet native breezes o'er your tomb
Icy & mute, you never can return
But bow from heaven & hark what I have sworn

Oh by your memories martyr's, there shall be
Bloody reprisal for your fearful fate                      95
My arm is strung with giant energy
By the convulsing thought that all's too late
New strength, springs from that stinging agony
And firmer resolution, hotter hate
Weep for the pangs of fiends! by God by heaven             100
I'd kill the man who wept for that, unshriven!

I am alone, it is the dead of night
I am not gone to rest, because my mind
Is too much raised for sleep, the silent light
Of the dim taper streams in unseen wind                    105
And quite as voiceless, on the hearth burns bright
The ruddy ember, now no ear could find
A sound however faint to break the lull
Of which the shadowy realm of dreams is full

So then I've time to think of each event                   110
That hath befallen of late to all below
I've leisure to recall the sudden rent
That tore my heart, a few short weeks ago
T'was at an inn in Calais, & the faint
Cold, sense of death, brought by that deadly blow          115
Whitened my cheek, & glazed my eyes awhile
Darkness o'erswept the noon-day's sunny smile

In a far foreign land with stranger's round
Reading a journal of my native West
Rung from the black-edged funeral page the sound           120
Expected & yet dreaded, there the crest
The arms, the name were blazoned & the ground
Marked where the corpse should lie & all exprest
Even to the grim procession, hearse & pall
The grave, the monument to cover all!                      125

212

I went out sick & dizzy to the street
The air revived me, something inward said
Tis but thine own work finished, time is fleet
And early has the gloomy task been sped
Yet still, tis thy behest, now firmly meet                    130
Its prompt fulfillment, turn thee from the dead
And go on prospering thy way is free
And they are punished, crushed that thwarted thee

Amongst the multitudes of thoughts that came
Rolling upon me I remembered well                             135
My feelings some months since, before this aim
Of death was ripe when it began to swell
And form within my breast & like a dream
The keen & racking recollections fell
How I then watched my prey [and] slowly wrought              140
My mind to union with the awful thought

Nothing was bodied forth distinctly then
I was too frantic, but at this lone hour
The bitter recollection comes again
Of many a night I spent within her bower                     145
Of all the musings that came o'er me when
Gently asleep beside me lay my flower
Blushing in blissful dreams & pressing nigher
To the dark breast that filled with                fire

Watching her thus through many a sleepless night             150
I never utterly resolved to slay
I could not when--all young & soft & bright
Trusting adoring me in dreams she lay
Her fair cheeks pillowed on the locks of light
That Gleamed upon her delicate array                         155
Veiling with gold her neck & shoulders white
& varying with their rich & silken flow
Her forehead's smooth expanse of stainless snow

Sometime's in sleep she'd put her hand on mine
And fold it in her slight & fairy clasp                      160
As if my fatal thoughts she could divine
And as in terror she would faintly gasp
And nearer closer all around me twine
Holding me with an anxious, jealous grasp
And when I woke & cheered her she would say                  165
She dreamt I'd cast her scornfully away

213

Often at night after a long day spent
In hearing of her father's mad designs
In toilsomely reclaiming projects bent
By his perverseness, out of the set lines          170
I'd furrowed in the future, all I meant
With deepest thoughts to execute, the mines
I'd laid most carefully effaced & sprung
And all that loved me by his insults stung

Harrassed by his malignity so cold                 175
And unprovoked & bitter, I've come home
And full of stricken thoughts I never told
Bearing upon my brow my spirits gloom
Entered the atmosphere of aerial gold
Of light & fragrance in my Lady's room             180
And passing her, unable to reply
To the warm wish of her saluting eye

'Twas strange but Mary never seemed to dread
Or shun me in my ireful mood, she'd steal
Silently to my side & droop her head               185
And rest it on my knee & gently kneel
Down at my feet & then her raised glance said
Adrian I do not fear though I can feel
You'r gaze is stern & dark, but I can brook
Even ferocity in that fixed look                   190

Sometimes her lips as well as eyes would say
If you are here I'm happy, though in wrath
But when you keep through the long night away
Repose, existence, luxury I loathe
Your presence forms the bright the cheering ray    195
That makes life glorious, Adrian what can soothe
Your ruffled mind, tell me & I will try
To light the gloom of that denouncing eye

Trouble yourself no more with me I said
The last time she spoke thus, when I took you      200
Into my bosom Mary, though your head
Was haloed, with the lustre beauty threw
And mind & youth & glowing feeling shed
Yet then I swore that if your father drew
His hand from mine, I'd give him back his gift     205
Of happiness, & hope & fame bereft

214

Percy the demon! playing with the feeling
Of an enthusiast's heart, he shall be paid
For his deceit, for his cold treacherous dealing
In miseries keen as those himself has made                    210
Wounds festered deep beyond the power of healing
My part in the great game is also played
I've had his daughter loved her made her mine
And now the bright deposit I'll resign--

Fade love! before his sight, consume away                     215
Reproach him with your dying gaze my Mary
It is his fault, I love you each fresh day
Intenselier than the last, I never weary
Of gazing on that young, pale face whose ray
Of deep, warm, anxious ardour, dashed with dreary             220
Poetic melancholy--charms me more
Than all the bloom which other eyes adore

"You love me yet you'll kill me!" she said starting
While an electric thrill of passion woke
In all her veins & wild reproaches darting                    225
From her dark eyes, in native heat she broke
Fully upon me, all the calm departing
And classic grace, as if the sudden stroke
Had changed her nature, her most perfect form
Shaken dilated, trembling in the storm                        230

Anger & grief & most impassioned love
Gathered upon her cheek in burning blushes
One with the other, struggling, warring strove
And each by turns prevailed in whelming gushes
She flashed a frantic glance to heaven above                  235
She called me cruel as the fiend that crushes
Its victim after snaring it in toils
Baited with rosy flowers & golden spoils

Why have you chained me to you Adrian by
Such days of bliss, such hours of sweet carressing            240
Such looks of glory--words of melody
Glimpses of all on earth that's worth possessing
And now when I must live with you or die
Out of your sight distracted, every blessing
Your hand withdraws & all my anguish scorning                 245
You go & bid me hope for no returning!

Adrian don't leave me" then the gushing tears
Smothered her utterance, so I tried my power
To soothe her terrors & allay her fears
And feed her passion with a sunny shower                           250
Of my accustomed spells, as the sky clears
After a summer storm, in one brief hour
Happy & blest she'd given again her charms
Trembling but yet confiding to my arms

Did I think then she'd die & that for ever                         255
The grave would hide her from me, did I deem
That after parting I should never, never
Behold her save in some delusive dream
That she would cross death's cold & icy river
Alone, without one hope one cheering beam                          260
Of bliss to come, all dark, all spectral, dreary
Was this thy fate? my loved my sainted Mary!

Will no voice answer no? will no tongue say
That still she lives & longs & waits for me
That burning still though haply in decay                           265
The spark of life is lingering quenchlessly
And that again the bright awakening ray
Of passion in her pale face I may see
And watch the fervid, lightning thoughts whose shine
Kindled each feature with a beam divine                            270

Again o'er Hawkscliffes wide green wilderness
The harvest moon her boundless smile will fling
Again the savage woods will take their dress
Of dewy leaves from the refulgent spring
Darken in summer, & to autumn pass                                 275
In their wan robes of foliage withering
September's eves will close, with dreary light
Of moon & holy stars foretelling night

And shall I never wander in those shades
Where the trees sweep the earth o'ercharged with plumes            280
Mary! among those solemn moonlight glades
Are all our roamings over? will their glooms
Parting & bending as the breezes sway<sup>ed</sup>
Shadow our love no more, like natural tombs
Where sound breathed out of darkest hush, each grove               285
Of Giant oaks, buried & watched that love

Others I've met by night, in field & wood
Many a burnside has been my rendezvous
And anxiously impatiently I've stood
Under the sunless sky of sombre blue                        290
While the encroaching gloaming o'er the flood
Crept dark & still, & gathering drops of dew
Hung on the flowers & twilight breezes swung
Chilly & low, the whispering trees among

And some bright eyes are closed that once to me             295
Were stars of hope & heart's that loved me well
For years have stilled their beating neath some tree
Waving above the mounds where mortals dwell
After they've put on immortality
But long since I have learnt the pangs to quell             300
Their memories brought & now again, again
Torture is wakened by reviving pain

                                       c   304 lines

It cannot be, and has she cold & dying
Been stretched alone, on her forsaken bed
A stormy midnight's voice her requiem crying                305
And hasting, on the last dark hour of dread
With speed none could avert, and Mary lying
Conscious that death was near, her spirit led
While her soul waved its wings prepared to soar
Back to the days she never might see more                   310

The ghastly trance increasing and above
Her thorny pillow, bent her father's brow
In agony a clouded glance of love
The lady on her sire was seen to throw
Of love & strange reproach--how thought will rove          315
How scenes we think of suddenly will glow
Present before us, Oh I see him bending
Over his child, I watch her soul ascending

Out of her dying eyes--now is my time
All rushes on me, could I speak the feeling                 320
Now Percy whom in spite of blood & crime
I loved intensely--Dark thy doom is sealing
Am I not well avenged, struck in her prime
Dies thy fair daughter, her last look revealing
Her last word telling--to what hand she owes               325
Her grave beneath this avalanche of woes

To thine! she's gone aye shudder & stoop lower
Speak, call her back the winged spirit may hear
Paramount ruler, try thine utmost power
Revive thy faded hope, thy blossom sere                          330
Vainly the task of the last awful hour
Is finished, now the cloud the pang, the tear
Are thine for ever, brow & heart & eye
Shall keep till death thy daughter's legacy

Different it might have been, the actual doom                    335
Is such as I have said & Mary's gone
Floating away in light--Grief called her home
Her angel heard & answered, & the sun
Smiles over Alnwick Church & oer the tomb
Where couched in marble lies her corpse alone                    340
And balmy gales come murmuring from each glade
And pastoral walk; where long ago she strayed

I must forget her I must cease to pine
After the days the dreams the hopes I cherished
In truth I could have wished to see the shine                    345
Of her clear eyes before their lustre perished
Their sad soft beam like the subdued decline
Of twilight parting--could I but have nourished
Her languid wasted strength & faded bloom
And taken her to my breast again her home                        350

But that is not vouchsafed & so at last
I must shut out her image from my heart
And mingling that with other glories past
Look back on what I leave before I start
On a divided track, a winter's blast                             355
Howls o'er a desert, where our journeys part
And noon is past the shades of eve draw nigh
Dimly reflected from a stormy sky

Turning amid the driving sleet & rain
I look along the path way she has taken                          360
Now far away, a slip of emerald plain
With lingering sun &, freshened foliage shaken
By a sweet Eden breeze, and once again
I see her like an apparition beckon
In the bright distance, e'er a moment gone                       365
She'll ne'er return tis past & I'm alone

Victory the plumed the crowned, I hear her calling
Again my diadem, my land she flings
Redeemed before me, Glorious sunlight falling
On the vermilion banner, lights its wings                        370
With the true hue of conquest

And alone shall I be when the trumpet is sounding
To tell to the world that my kingdom is free
Alone while a thousand brave bosoms are bounding
The yoke & the fetter-bolt shivered to see          375

Alone in the hall where the last flash is shining
Of embers that wane in their mid night decay
How shall I feel as the wild gale's repining
Fitfully whispers & wanders away?

What will it tell me of days that will never          380
Smile on the life-weary mourner again
What will it murmur of hours that for ever
Are past like the spring shower's glitter of rain

Blown by the wind to the verge of the torrent
Cluster the last leaves that fell long ago          385
Some that are scattered by chance on its current
Withered & light, fleet away in its flow

Sooner shall these on the tree or the flower
Wave in their bloom as they waved ere they fell
Than I shall behold that return of the hour          390
Whose sorrowful parting the night-breezes tell

Then in the silence her picture will glimmer
Solemn & shadowy, high in the hall
Still as the embers wax dimmer & dimmer
Stirring her life, to their flicker & fall          395

How shall I feel as the soft eyes revealing
Sweetness, & sorrow gaze down through the gloom
How shall I feel when her image comes stealing
Over me such as she was in her bloom

Twining around, me crowding the tresses          400
Curled on her white forehead into my breast
Wooing the love that with passionate kisses
Wildly & warmly her beauty carest

Then shall I know that all mutely reposing
Lulled in the slumbering gloom of her shrine          405
With Death on her white face in shadow disclosing
The trace of his truest and awfullest sign

Then shall I know that her lip would not quiver
Though with the pressure of love it met mine
Then shall I know that no glance can dissever          410
The sealed lids that cover her eye's ghastly shine

219

All will be frozen, all cold & unfeeling
Passion forgotten & sympathy gone
Neither a motion, nor murmur revealing
Life, in that colourless image of stone                    415

I shall not see it, for Mary is buried
Far from the Calabar's war-trampled strand
And oh! her career to its dark close was hurried
Many a long league from her own native land

420   Could she have died with its woods waving round her   420
 16   Could she have slept with their moan in her ear
      Rapt in romance the last slumber found her
      Fleeting away on the tone singing near

Oh that the sun of the West had been beaming
Glorious & soft on the bed where she lay                   425
Then she had died not lamenting but dreaming
Borne on the haloes of sunset away!

Had she but known all the love that I bore her
Though I had left her in sorrow awhile
Then when the wing of the spectre swept o'er her           430
Her death-frozen features had fixed in a smile

But she perished in exile, she perished in mourning
Wild was the evening that closed her decline
She withered for ever, I hope no returning
And tears are so fruitless, I need not repine              435

God gave the summons, farewell then my Mary
Thou hast found haven, where no tears may swell
Hopeless & weary, and joyless & dreary
I must forget thee,--for ever farewell!

      436 lines                          Charlotte Brontë
                                       Jan^y 9^th 1837

MS:   D(1)
First Publication:  Ratchford Legends
Text:   l. 149:   blank space in manuscript
        line numbers in text and in left margin are Charlotte's

220

119     Charge on the enemy
        Victory leads
       Capture their battery
       Footmen or Cavalr'y
       He shall be conqueror      5
        Fastest who speeds

       Think not of danger now
        Enter the breach
       Dream not of cannon-ball
       Mount by the shattered wall    10
       Soon shall their banner-staff
        Bend to your reach

       War is an ecstasy
        Risk is wild
       What though their battlements   15
        Stand like a rock

        [January 1837]

MS: D(1)
First Publication: SHB C and B


120     Lady-bird!, lady-bird! fly away home
       Night is approaching & sunset is come
       The herons are flown to their trees by the Hall
       Felt but unseen the damp dew-drops fall
       This is the close of a still summer day   5
       Lady-bird! lady-bird haste fly away

        The grand old Hall is wrapped in shad[e]
       The woodland park around it spread
       Is gathering gloom in every glade
       This is the moment this the hour    10
       To feel Romance in all her power
       Is there not something in a name
       In noble blood & ancient fame
       Something in that ancestral pride
        Which brings the memory of the dead  15
       Sailing adown time's hoary tide
        With 'sacred' halos round it shed
       Halos Oh far too bright to shine
        Round ought whose home is still below
       The starlight thoughts the dreams divine  20
        From man's creative soul that flow

And stream upon the idols bright
    He forms through all his earthly way
As if weary of the light
That smiles upon his own dull clay                        25
That clay he feels will not for ever
Cumber the spirit that would soar
Even to that deep & swelling river
29  Which bears the life-tree on its shore
And he that hour would still forsee                       30
That sets his inward angel free

    This Hall & park might wake such dreams
They speak of pride of ancestry
Yes every fading ray which gleams
On antique roof & hoary tree                              35
Shows in knarled boughs & mossy slate
The grand remains of ancient state

And thinks he of Patrician pride
    He who sits lonely there
Where oaks & elms spread dark & wide                      40
    Their huge arms in the air

He wanders in the world of thought
    He's left this world behind
On that high brow are clearly wrought
    A thousand dreams of mind                             45

And ere they dream of bliss or bale
    Of Happiness or woe
Methinks that face is all too pale
    For pleasure's rosy glow

Methinks the mellowing haze of years                      50
    Is o'er that tall form spread
And Time has poured her smiles & tears
    Full freely round that head

He must have once been beautiful
    The relics still remain                               55
Though wasted sore with sorrow
    And darkened much with pain

At morn he sought this lone retreat
    When the sun first crowned the hill
And now the twilight calm & sweet                         60
62      Beholds him lingering still


222

Yet not to reveries of woe
Clings Percy's wounded spirit so
Scarce bound by its worn chains of clay
The soul has almost soared away                                65
Lightened & soothed insensibly
By the lone hum of wind & tree
Where now his mental broodings dwell
Vainly would man divine or tell
His upward look--his earnest eyes                              70
Seem gazing ev'n beyond the skies
Who calls him back to earth again
Will bring a wild revulse of pain
And so thought he who glided now
With step as light as falling snow                             75
Forth from the bowery arch of trees
That whispered in the gloaming breeze
That step he might have used before
When stealing on to lady's bower
Even at the same still twilight hour                           80
For The moon now beaming mild above
Shewed him a son of war & love
His eye was full of that sinful fire
Which oft' unhallowed passions light
It spoke of quickly kindled ire                                85
Of love too warm & wild & bright
Bright but yet sullied, love which could never
Bring good in arising, leave peace in decline
Woe to the gifted, crime to the Giver
Wherever reposed all the light of its shine                    90

Beauty had lavished her treasures upon him
Youth's early sunshine was poured on his brow
Alas that the magic of sin should have won him
But he is her slave & her chained victim now

How from his curled & shining hair                             95
Circling the brow of marble fair
His dark keen eyes on Percy gaze
With stern & yet repenting rays
Sometimes they shimer through the haze
Of sadly gushing tears                                        100
And then a sudden flash of flame
Speaking wild feelings none could tame
    The dim suffusion clears

Young savage! how he bends above
The object of his wrath & love                                         105
How tenderly his fingers press
The hand that shrinks from their caress
And from his lips in Percy's ear
Flow tones his blood congeals to hear
Those tones were softer than the moan                                  110
Of echo when the sound is flown
125   And sweeter than a flute's reply
To skylark's song or wild wind's sigh
Yet Percy heard them as they fell
Like the dull toll of a passing bell                                   115
Sternly they summoned him back again
To a dark world of woe & pain
The blood from his visage fell away
And left it as pallid as coffined clay
Like clouds the charmed visions broke                                  120
From his day-long dream at once he woke
He woke to feel & see at his side
The very man who dared to roll
Marahs unsounded briny tide
Over the Eden of his soul                                              125
Who dared to pluck his last fair flower
To quench his last star's cheering beam
The last sweet drop of bliss to sour
That mingled with his Being's stream

Up rose he & stretched forth his hand                                  130
In mingled menace & command
With voice subdued & steady look
Thus to the man of sin he spoke

What brought you here I called you not
Youv'e tracked me to a lonely spot                                     135
Are you a Hawk to follow the prey
When mangled it flutters feebly away
A sleuth-hound to track the deer by his blood
When wounded he wins to the darkest wood
There if he can to die alone                                           140
Unsought by the archer whose shaft has flown
So right & true to its living mark
That it quenches even now the vital spark

Zamorna is this nobly done
To triumph o'er your Consort's sire                            145
Gladly to see his gory sun
Quench in the sea of tears its fire
But haply you have news to tell
Tidings that yet may cheer me well
You've crushed at last my rose's bloom                         150
And scattered its leaves on her mother's tomb


   Or its faded buds all ready lie
To deck my coffin when I die.
Bring them here--'twill not be long
'Tis the last line of the wo[e]ful song                        155
And those final & dying words are sung
To the discord of lute-strings all unstrung
Oh Adrian do not harshly sweep
The chords that are quivering to voiceless sleep.

No but I'd string them once more to a sound                    160
That should startle the nations that rest around
I'd call forth the glorious chorous again
Which flooded the earth with a bloody main
Have I crushed you Percy?  I'd raise once more
The beacon-light on the rocky-shore                            165
Percy my love is so true & deep
That though kingdoms should wail & worlds should weep
I'd fling the brand in the hissing sea
The brand that must burn unquenchably
Your Rose is mine when the sweet leaves fade                   170
They must be chaplet to wreath my head
The blossoms to deck my home with the dead
I repent not--that which my hand has done
Is as fixed as the orb of the burning sun
But I swear by heaven & the mighty sea                         175
That wherever I wander my heart is with thee
Bitterly deeply I've drank of thy woe
When thy stream was troubled did mine calmly flow?
And yet I repent not I'd crush thee again
If our vessels sailed adverse of life's stormy main           180
But listen the earth is our campaign of war
Her children are rank & her kingdoms spread far
Who shall say Hah! to the mingling star
Is there not havock & carnage for thee
Unless thou castest thy lance at me                           185
The heart in my bosom beats high at the thought
Of the deeds which by blended strength may be wrought
Then might thy Mary bloom blissfully still
This hand should ne'er work her sorrow or ill
No fear of grief in her bright eyes should quiver             190

225

```
I'd love her & guard her forever forever
What! shall Zamorna go down to the dead
With blood on his hand that he wept to have shed
What! shall they carve on his tomb with the sword
The slayer of Percy, the scourge of the Lord!                195

Bright flashed the fire in the young Duke's eye
     As he spoke in the tones of the trumpet swelling
Then he stood still & watched earnestly
How those tones were on Percy's spirit telling
Nothing was heard but his quick short breath                 200
And his fiery heart aroused panting
The dark wood lay as hushed as death
     Nor hum nor murmur it's valleys haunting
Then the low voice of Percy woke
And thus in strange response he spoke                         205
```

204 lines

[January 1837]

MS:  H and D(1)
First Publication:  Dodd Mead 1902 partial; Shorter EJB 1910
Text:  l. 24:  originally read "As if grown weary . . ."; "grown" is
       canceled, but no alternative provided
       Line numbers in left margin are Charlotte's

**121(a)**

```
          I never sought my mother's face
               To tell my grief & make my moan
          But crept away to some lone place
               And sat until the cloud was gone

          But it would give so strange a tone             5
          Even to things inanimate
          Yes all that then I looked upon
          Took the dark boding hue of fate

          And if I turned some storied page
          So wild a glamour o'er it grew                  10
          That scarce in youth's increasing age
               Dared I the feeling to renew
          T'was like a foretaste from the tomb
          A warning voice to call me home
```

```
In that mood I have watched the sun                    15
Go down upon my Sire's domain
Its long day's course of glory done
    Its bower of roses spread again
And oh how solemn seemed the wane
    Solemn! that word can never tell          20
The deadly sense of mental pain
That wrung me as the evening-bell
Tolled out each castle sentinel
And I beheld them measure slow
Their walk upon the flags below             25
And heard them whistle clear & shrill
My own wild woodland's melodies
The soft, sweet plaintive airs that thrill
Through all the land of lakes &
And knew that they with                      30
Could gaze
```

**121(b)**        Charlotte Bronte    January 17
                        1837

```
On the bright scene around them spread
Lit tenderly with those mild rays
The last the dying sun had shed

The park with its broad slopes of green       35
Where now the mighty shadows lay
Of tower & turret kindling sheen
With amber lights on stone work grey
For the Ducal Castle like a screen
Stood against the farwell & level ray          40
Shot still from the refulgent west
O'er Lismore's town and Gambia's flood
Kindling the river's azure breast
Till it ran like a red stream of blood
All this was fair but not to me                45
And O my heart sank heavily
When from the casement arched & tall
That dimly lit that Norman Hall
I looked far down ------------------
```

                         129

MS:  D(1) & D(2)
First Publication:  Shorter 1923 partial; Winnifrith PCB
Text:  ll. 29-31:  the corner of the manuscript page is torn off

**122(a)**     & few have felt the avenging steel
Rankle as now its blade I feel

Ambition
Power & Glory where are ye
Kindle your watch-fires by this star                              5
Light them along its stormy steep
Your lamps are quenched your spirits sleep
& wake, wake each beacon Powers divine
I've knelt before your Moloch shrine
& even though tost on Sorrow's wave                             10
Yet still I kneel although the grave
Of Beauty's best & brightest daughters
Lies under this wild waste of waters

Am I like Saul? these times of gloom
Come to me as they came to him                                  15
Stealing from life its sunny bloom
& spreading shadows drear & dim
But music would not charm me now
Its lightest airs, its freest flow
Its wildest swell, its softest strain                           20
Would stir no life-pulse thrill no vein

I'll turn then to those happy hours
When childhood plucked its earliest flowers
Roaming the live-long summer day
Where bright they grew on bank & brae                           25
But vainly even in infancy
Life had its darkling spots for me
Times would come when sudden fell
        I knew not whence or how
        would all unbidden swell                                30
        sorrow cloud my brow

**122(b)**     I can speak no more of infancy
I am farther out on this sullen [sea]
& Darker waves of its waters come
Driving me faster from peace & home                             35
Never a beacon burns on the deep
The fires are out & the watchers sleep
And the wild rack of the swaying main
The foam wreaths bursting & foaming again
The scream of the sea-birds, the deep-toned blast              40
The billows that roll ceaseless past
Ay the thoughts of an evil heart

The croaks of a conscience not yet <scar[r]ed>
The visions that will not depart
Are worse than all that man has <feared>                45
On the most troubled sea that ever
Made the strongest vessel quiver

[January 17, 1837]

MS:  D(1) & D(2)
First Publication:  Shorter 1923 partial; Winnifrith PCB
Text:  ll. 29-31:  corner of the manuscript page torn away


**123**                 Dreams, dreams, are
                        Life fleets away
                        And that Spirit world all dim & grey
                        Shadows my brain, rapid they glide

[early 1837]

MS:  D(1)
Not previously published
Text:  l. 1:  the latter portion is obliterated by ink doodles
       l. 4:  the last three words seem to be canceled


**124**                 The Nurse believed the rich man slept
                        For motionless he lay
                        She rose & from the bed-side crept
                        With cautious step away

[early 1837]

MS:  D(1)
First Publication:  Winnifrith PCB


**125**     An early draft of ll. 7-12 of **Pilate's Wife's Dream** in the
            1846 volume of poems--see No. **189**

Look Wife the clouds are full of snow
A few large flakes already fall
The cold north wind begins to blow
White hills will soon be piled o'er all
Haste we before the drifts are deep                     5
To house the kine and fold the sheep

I come--the sheep are scattered wide
Ere all are safe the night will close
I led them up to Parret's side
Where green the winter grass still grows              10
Stranger beside the hearth remain
Keep guard till we return again

Take heed--unclose the door to none
A Dane might knock--a wolf might howl
For always after set of sun                           15
Things strange & fierce these forests prowl

The herdsman and his wife are gone
The passive guest remains alone
He draws his oaken tripod near
The wood-fire burning red and clear                   20

Docile he turns the barley-cake
Placed on the heated stone to bake
He brings more wood and seems with care
To tend the simple evening-fare
This done he folds his arms again                     25
And thoughts disturbed resume their train

"'Tis Christmas-eve--I mark the date
(Thus did he self-communing say)
Here lone I sit--before me Fate
Arrested, seems her course to stay                    30
And having done her worst, to stand
With blade depressed and weary hand

Her stony gaze is on my eyes
Her dark-bent brow confronts my own
She seems to ask--"Who yet defies                     35
Disaster that so deep has gone?
What heart beneath my blunted knife
Still quivers with the throb of life--
His efforts one by one defeated
His arms disgraced--his friends dismayed              40

His troops to mountain holds retreated
Vanquished or sold, refuse him aid
And he lives still and still he dares
To search for hope 'mongst myriad fears

[early 1837]

MS: D(1)
First Publication: SHB C and B
Text: l. 16: "fierce" written above "dangerous"; neither is canceled
      l. 17: "are gone" above "go forth"; neither is canceled
      l. 19: "tripod" above "buffet"; neither is canceled
      l. 38: Much amended with no cancelations:
                 retains the            throb of life
             Still the strong and glowing beats with life?
                 bounds with strength and glows
             Still quivers with the throb of life


**127**    The original draft of ll. 213-27 of **Frances** in the 1846
           volume of poems--see No. **190**


**128**         When thou sleepest, lulled in night
                    Art thou lost in vacancy?
                Does no silent inward light
                    Softly breaking fall on thee?
                Does no dream on quiet wing                    5
                    Float a moment mid that ray?
                Touch some answering mental string
                    Wake a note & pass away

                When thou watchest as the hours
                    Mute & blind are speeding on               10
                O'er that rayless path that lowers
                    Muffled midnight, black & lone
                Comes there nothing hovering near
                    Thought, or half reality
                Whispering marvels in thine ear               15
                    Every word a mystery

Chanting low an ancient lay
      Every plaintive note a spell
Clearing memory's clouds away
      Showing scenes thy heart loves well                     20
Songs forgot, in childhood sung
      Airs in youth, beloved & known
Whispered by that airy tongue
      Once again are made thine own

Oh how happy, how unbroken                                    25
      Seems that watchful hour to fly

Be it dream in haunted sleep
      Be it thought in vigil lone
Drink'st thou not a rapture deep
      From the feeling, tis thine own                          30
All thine own, thou need'st not tell
      What bright form thy slumber blest
All thine own, remember well
      Night & shade were round thy rest

Nothing looked upon thy bed                                   35
      Save the lonely watch-light's gleam
Not a whisper, not a tread
      Scared thy spirit's glorious dream
Sometimes when the midnight gale
      Breathed a moan & then was still                         40
Seemed the spell of thought to fail
      Checked by one ecstatic thrill
Felt as all external things
      Robed in moonlight smote thine eye

Then thy spirit's waiting wings                               45
      Quivered, trembled, spread to fly
Then th' aspirer wildly swelling
      Looked where mid transcendancy
Star to star was mutely telling
      Heaven's resolve & fate's decree                         50

Oh! it longed for holier fire
      Than this spark in earthly shrine
O! it soared & higher higher
      Sought to reach a home divine

Hopeless quest, soon weak & weary                             55
      Flagged the pinion, drooped the plume
And again in sadness dreary
      Came the baffled wanderer home

And again it turned for soothing
    To the half-finished broken dream                    60
While the ruffled current smoothing
    Thought rolled on her startled stream
I have felt this cherished feeling
    Sweet & known to none but me
Still I felt it nightly healing                           65
    Each dark day's despondency

                    [April-May 1837]

MS:  D(1)
First Publication:  **Cornhill Magazine,** August 1861




**129**  The trees by the casement are moistened with dew
         The first star has risen o'er that long ridge of heath
    And it smiles from the verge of that sky's boundless blue
         Through the green garden-bowers on the still walks beneath

    She stood by the casement & looked at the sky            5
         It was cloudless as summer & breezeless as June
    She thought as a bird to its nest fluttered by
         Of her home & she murmured a soft western tune

    There was no one to hear it, the Hall in repose
         Lay vacant & dark save where firelight was thrown    10
    Where broad mirror gleamed & where high pillar rose
         Round the lady still singing her vesper alone

             Sweetly died both words & air
                 It was over & her face
             Told by its soft shade of care                   15
                 Thought had stolen to music's place
             Canst thou tell by that dark eye
                 Lifted & that suffering brow
             Fair yet clouded what thoughts lie
                 In that lady's bosom now                     20

             Thou may'st feel but ne'er can words
                 Tell their rise their aim their flow
             Who the course of wandering birds
                 Through the trackless skies may know
             Lo she smiles, in solitude                       25
                 Twilight grief, she smiles again
             She has hope, some flowers are strewed
                 O'er her path though drenched in rain


                            233

Through a dim uncertain track
    Long her pilgrimage hath lain                        30
Fleeting sunshine, shadows black
    Transient pleasure, lingering pain
No keen grief, few floods of tears
    Distant hope to call her on
Still each day that hope appears                          35
    Fainter promised, farther flown

Sad existence! O she feels
    All its misery even now

                                        [April-May 1837]

MS:  D(1)
First Publication:  SHB C and B


**130**                 He could not sleep! the couch of war
                            Simple & rough beneath him spread
                        Scared sleep away & scattered far
                            The balm its influence might have shed

                        He could not sleep!, his temples prest        5
                            To the hard pillow throbbed with pain
                        The belt around his noble breast
                            His heart's wild pulse could scarce restrain

                        And stretched in feverish unrest
                            Awake the Great Commander lay              10
                        In vain the cooling night-wind kist
                            His brow with its reviving play

                        As through the open window streaming
                            All the fresh scents of night it shed
                        And mingled with the moonlight beaming         15
                            In broad clear lustre round his bed

                        Out in the night Cirhala's water
                            Lifted its voice of swollen floods
                        On its wild shores the bands of slaughter
                            Lay camped amid its savage woods           20

                        Beneath the lonely auberge's shelter
                            The Duke's rough couch that night was spread
                        The sods of batle round him welter
                            In noble blood that morning shed


                                 234

And gorged with prey & now declining          25
From all the fire of glory won
Watchful & fierce he lies repining
O'er what may never be undone

        The morn will bring him back his power
        His strength, his pride his energy

                                [April-May 1837]

MS:  D(1)
First Publication:  Benson 1915 partial; Shorter 1923


**131 and 132**  Early drafts of **The Teacher's Monologue,** dated May 12
             and 15, 1837, in the 1846 volume of poems--see No. **191**


**133**          This ring of gold, with the small curl
             Of chestnut hair beset with pearl
             This ring & ringlet bright reveal
             What time & tears would fain conceal
             Time might have touched with his decay          5
             And hid with his grey moss the scene
             And tears might long have washed away
             The traces of where that thought has been
             But this my mystic amulet
             Revives the picture when it fades          10
             Heightens the lights I would forget
             And deepens the declining shades

             Though quite alone & knowing well
             That none on earth now think of me
             How to the summons of that spell          15
             Answers the voice of memory
             And what delusive hopes it brings
             Fanning me with their rainbow wings
             I stood in that habitual mood
             Of anxious thought I feel all day          20
             Watching the starlight solitude
             That round my forest mansion lay
             I looked into the deep dark wood
             Down a dim path soon lost in gloom
             Then from, the window where I stood          25
             Glanced round upon my firelit room


                            235

I thought of phantoms for so still
Was all in the dim flushing glimer
There crept a kind of winter chill
Over my flesh to watch the shimmer                    30
Of shapeless shadows o'er the walls
And o'er the high & gilded ceiling
And o'er the draperies dark as palls
Festooned apart & now revealing
Through the clear panes gigantic trees                 35
Waving their plumes against a heaven
Glorious with stars, a summer breeze
That movement to their boughs had given
And then it swept the slips betwe[e]n
Of dewy lawn & stirred the flowers                     40
And down the alleys calm & green
Went singing to remoter bowers
Well as I stood a thousand dreams
Into my restless mind came thronging
With quick & strange & varying gleams                  45
With wild regret & wilder longing
I felt impatient that my life
Was so unmarked, unloved & fated
While on the world's turmoil & strife
I gazed with interest never sated                       50
While all day long my heart & eye
Traversed a hundred regions over
In city domes, neath open sky
Wandered & watched a viewless rover
Viewless yet anxious on the fate                        55
Of battles & of armies pondering
Resting at many a lordly gate
That oped not to relieve my wandering
And turning desolate away
Knowing that none would now remember                    60
The friend of one brief summer day
Forgotten in her life's November
This ring then, as I moved my hand
Flashed, suddenly a star uplighting
Its clear dark stone & like a wand                      65
The sounding chords of memory smiting
A full, soft, deep but fitful tone
By that mysterious harp was uttered
It sounded as I sat alone
As if a hidden spectre muttered                         70
It called back such a sweet remembrance
It placed so fair a scene before me
I longed to shake of[f] time's encumbrance
To check the years that had flowed o'er me
And roll them back and see again                        75

The moonlight on that glorious region
That broad unbounded green champaigne
With here and there a scattered legion
Of trees from the great pathless wood
Like plumy tropic headlands stretching                    80
Over the deep green quiet flood
Of verdure to th' horizon reaching
I stood in a low fretted door
One of the antique range of arches
Pierced in the Hall front towering o'er                   85
The noble fertile Western marches
And that was in my early youth
Before by sin & sorrow shaded
I gazed on Love & life & truth
Through mists all dim in hues all faded                   90
I lived in an heroic land
Heroic spirits round me moving
And thought took my humble stand
Beneath them I looked up with loving
A kind of loving though a sense                           95
Of vassal awe blent with the feeling
My sires had died in their defence
And I to tread their path was willing
Could I be otherwise when eyes
So dark so radiant smiled on me                          100
Smiled in their haughtiness like skies
Of midnight, starlit suddenly
Young noble Idol, I have given
My last at thy exacting shrine
And thou hast lavished an earthly heaven                 105
Upon me in thy love divine
True it is past & all is vanished
Into forgetfulness with thee

A softened look a kindly word
An epithet of gentleness                                 110
Would thrill me like a subtle sword
And urgently my heart would press
To show by answering gratitude
My deep devotedness of spirit
The fervour almost wild & rude                           115
My fathers gave me to inherit

237

That eve he by chance had found me
At the threshold of the door alone
Watching the wide expanse around me
Of park & wood beneath the moon                              120
He spoke and at his princely bidding
I sat down humbly at his feet
He asked me and his anger dreading
I sang a ballad wild & sweet

Wild sweet & full of Western fire                            125
I know not how the words flowed forth
But I felt the night my heart inspire
And the glory of the moonlit earth
And I felt though I dared not look & see
Who stood half bending over me                               130
And there was a vague strange sense of wrong
That he stood so near & gazed so long
And I would not that any beside had seen
His eagle eye & his smiling mien
And felt a kind of troubled joy                              135
That the shade was so deep in that solemn sky
That the close veil of ivy clustering near
Had shut out the moonbeam broad & clear
And yet there was terror in that delight
And a burning dread of the lonely night                      140
I would have given life to be away
And out in the pure & sunny day

                                        [May 1837]

MS:  D(1)
First Publication:  SHB C and B




**134**    An early draft of **Apostacy** in the 1846 volume of poems,
           dated May 29, 1837--see No. **192**




**135**              I scarce would let that restless eye
                     Which haunts my solitude behold
                     The secret which each smothered sigh
                     And every silent tear unfold




                                238

If it were near & if its beam                          5
Fell on me from a human brow
I would awake from that wild dream
Which spell-binds every talent now

The voice of Pride should sometimes speak
When softer feelings enervate                          10
And bid the heart; that bondsman break
Its self-locked chain ere yet too late

Passion has surged itself to rest
And calms from hope descending tell
How soft she comes, a golden guest                     15
To shine where tears of darkness fell!

But O! exult not hush thy joy
That sunshine still is blent with rain
And over that blue glimpse of sky
The storm's dim clouds may close again                 20

Kneel & look up & pierce with prayer
The far, clear hollow, arched above
And ask thine unseen Father's care
To fill the void of earthly love

Then safe in haven, o'er the sea                       25
And o'er its wild, white waves of foam
Look forth and cry triumphantly
What storm, what grief can vex my home!

                              May 30<sup>th</sup> -- 37

MS:  D(1)
First Publication:   SHB C and B partial



**136**          It is not at an hour like this
                 We would remember those we love
                 As the far hills commingling kiss
                 That grey & sunless heaven above
                 All dim & chill, a time of tears        5
                 And dying hopes, & gathering fears


                              239

But I am lone and so art thou
And leagues of land between us lie
And though we moaned expiring now
One could not watch the other die                                   10
And till corruption's work was done
Neither could gaze his idol on

And well I know this cloudy close
Sealing a long dark day of gloom
Will bring o'er that soft brow's repose                             15
A token of untimely doom
And it will droop in heart-felt pain
As though it ne'er might rise again

All pale that cheek, no fevered glow
Of longing watching waiting love                                    20
No swell of that white breast to show
How pants in hope my suffering dove
But one hand on the other laid
She sits & weeps in twilight shade

[May 1837]

MS:   D(1)
First Publication:   Benson 1915


**137**      Again I find myself alone, and ever
         The same voice like an oracle, begins
         Its, vague & mystic strain, forgetting never
         Reproaches for a hundred hidden sins
         And setting mournful penances in sight                     5
         Terrors & tears for many a watchful night

         Fast change the scenes upon me all the same
         In hue & drift the regions of a land
         Peopled with phantoms & how dark their aim
         As each dim guest lifts up its shadowy hand                10
         And parts its veil to shew one withering look
         That mortal eye may scarce unblighted brook

         I try to find a pleasant path to guide
         To fairer scenes--but still they end in gloom
         The wilderness will open dark & wide                       15
         As the sole vista to a vale of bloom
         Of rose & elm & verdure, as these fade
         Their sere leaves fall on yonder sandy shade


240

My dreams, the Gods of my religion linger
In foreign lands, each sundered from his own                          20
And theire has passed a cold destroying finger
O'er every image & each sacred tone
Sounds low & at a distance, sometimes dying
Like an uncertain sob, or smothered sighing

Sea-locked, & cliff-surrounded, or afar                               25
Asleep upon a fountain's marble brim
Asleep in heart, though yonder early star
The first that lit its taper soft & dim
By the great shrine of heaven, has fixed his eye
Unsmiling though unsealed on that blue sky                            30

Left by the sun, as he is left by hope
Bowed in dark, placid cloudlessness above
As silent as the Island's palmy slope
All beach untrodden, all unpeopled grove
A spot to catch each moon-beam as it smiled                           35
Towards that thankless deep so wide & wild

Thankless he too looks up, no grateful bliss
Stirs him to feel the twilight-breeze diffuse
Its balm that bears in every spicy kiss
The mingled breath of southern flowers & dews                        40
Cool & delicious as the fountain's spray
Showered on the shining pavement where he lay

[May 1837]

MS:   D(1)
First Publication:   SHB C and B

**138**        Dream of the West! the moor was wild
               Its glens the blue Guadima ploughed
               An August sunset rich & mild
               Over the heath in amber glowed

               Dream of the West! two thousand miles                  5
               Between me and the Gambia spread
               Land of the sun! transcendant smiles
               Like thine, his orb departing shed

               Birth-place of gods! thy forests proud
               Hung in the air their sea-green piles                  10
               Eden of earth!, the sunset cloud
               Pourtrayed thee, in its golden isles

241

Now what shall tell the scene the sound
I wrought from eye's voluptuous gale
Singing of bright & hallowed ground                    15
Where wild wood moans from wilder ground

Linked with the name of every land
Some thought will rise, some scene unfold
The bending wood, the barren sand
The Lake, the hill, the dreary wold                    20

Speak of the North a lonely moor
Silent & dark & trackless swells
The waves of some wild streamlet pour
Hurriedly through its ferny dells

Profoundly still, the twilight air                     25
Lifeless the landscape, so we deem
Till like a phantom gliding near
A stag bends down to drink the stream

And far away a mountain zone
A cold, white waste of snow-drifts lies                30
And one star large, & soft & lone
Silently lights th' unclouded skies

Speak of the South--a sun-bright sea
Washes a land of vines & flowers
Where lowly huts lie pleasantly                        35
In the green arms of guardian bowers

[May 1837]

MS: D(1)
First Publication: Benson 1915 partial; Shorter 1923


**139**     An earlier draft of **Stanzas** in the 1846 volume of poems,
            dated May 14, 1837--see No. **193**


**140**         Is this my tomb, this humble stone
                Above this narrow mound
                Is this my resting place, so lone
                So green so quiet round?

Not even a stately tree to shade                    5
    The sunbeam from my bed
Not even a flower in tribute laid
    As sacred to the dead

I look along those evening hills
    As mute as earth may be                         10
I hear not even the voice of rills
    Not even a cloud I see
How long is it since human tread
    Was heard on that dim track
Which through the shadowy valley's bed               15
    Winds far & farther back

And was I not a lady once
    My home a princely hall
And did not hundreds make response
    When e're I deigned to call                      20
Methinks as in a doubtful dream
    That dwelling proud I see
Where I caught first the early beam
    Of being's dayspring free

Methinks the flash is round me still                 25
    Of mirro[r]s broad & bright
Methinks I see the torches fill
    My chambers with their light
And o'er my limbs the draperies flow
    All gloss & silken shine                         30
On my cold brow the jewels glow
    As bright as festal wine

Who then disrobed that worshipped form
    Who wound this winding sheet
Who turned the blood that ran so warm                35
    To winter's frozen sleet
O can it be that many a sun
    Has set as that sets now
Since last its fervid lustre shone
    Upon my living brow                              40

Have all the wild dark clouds of night
    Each eve for years drawn on
While I interred so far from light
    Have slumbered thus alone
Has this green mound been wet with rain              45
    Such rain as storms distil
When, the wind's high & warning strain
    Swells loud on sunless hill

243

```
And I have slept where roughest hind
   Had shuddered to pass by                        50
And no dread did my spirit find
   In all that snow-racked sky
Though shook the iron rails around
   As swept by deepened breeze
They gave a strange & hollow sound               55
   That living veins might freeze

O was that music like my own
   Such as I used to play
When soft clear & holy shone
   The summer moon's first ray                     60
And saw me lingering to feel
   The influence of that sky
O words may not the peace reveal
   That filled its concave high

As rose & bower how far beneath                   65
   Hung down o'ercharged with dew
And sighed their too sweet & fragrant breath
   To every gale that blew,
The hour for music but in vain
   Each ancient stanza rose                         70
To lips that could not with their strain
   Break Earth's & heaven's repose

Yet first a note & then a line
   The fettered tongue would say
And then the whole rich song divine              75
   Found free & gushing way
Past, Past, forgotten I am here
   They dug my chamber deep
I know no hope I feel no fear
   I sleep--how calm I sleep!                       80
```

556<br> 46<br>602

June 4<sup>th</sup>
1837

MS:   D(1)
First Publication:   SHB C and B
Text:   Line numbers in the left margin are Charlotte's

**141**     An early draft of **The Letter** in the 1846 volume of poems,
            dated June 1837--see No. **194**

**142**     Two early drafts of **Mementoes** in the 1846 volume of
poems--see No. **195**


**143**          Why should we ever mourn as those
                 Whose star of hope has ceased to smile
                 How dark soe'r succeeding woes
                 Be still and wait and trust the while
                 A time will come, when future years                          5
                 Their veil of softening haze shall fling
                 Over that mournful vale of tears
                 Which saw thy weary wandering

                 From Beulah's bowers the pilgrim gazed
                 On Danger conquered dread defied                             10

                 Wild, rough, and desolate the way
                 To every pilgrim here below--
                 All rough the path, all dim and grey
                 The lonely wastes through which we go
                 But think of Beulah's bowers, the home                      15
                 That waits thee when this path is trod
                 Lying all free from clouds & gloom
                 Celestial in the smile of God

                 One stream to cross, one sable flood
                 Silent, unsounded, deep & dim                               20
                 It blights the flesh--it chills the blood
                 But deathless spirit, trust in him
                 Far on the shore of heaven that lies
                 So sweet, so fair so bathed in light
                 Angels are waiting--lift thine eyes                         25
                 Behold them where they walk in white

                 A little while, an hour of pain
                 One struggle more one gasp for breath
                 And it is over ne'er again
                 Shall sin or Sorrow Hell or Death                          30
                 Prevail o'er him he passed away
                 A shade, a flower, a cloud from earth
                 On glory looked, forgot decay
                 And knew in heaven an angel's birth

                                          [June-July 1837]

MS:  L
First Publication:  Shorter 1918

**144**

No harp on earth can breathe a tone
In unison with thoughts like mine
It is the night descending lone
It is the winds that wildly pine
Among the trees and seem to tell          5
Of all things sorrowful & drear
'Tis these that weave so strange a spell
Of causeless sorrow, aimless fear
I sat and played, in solitude
A hundred old, sweet         airs          10
Their spirit all my heart embued
Till it was even touched to tears
I turned to wipe the drops away
My glance unthinking met the sky
So drear it looked so cold so grey         15

[July 1837]

MS: D(1)
First Publication: SHB C and B
Text: 1. 10: blank space in manuscript


**145**

She was alone that evening--and alone
She had been all that heavenly summer day
She scarce had seen a face, or heard a tone
And quietly the hours had slipped away
Their passage through the silence hardly known    5
Save when the clock with silver chime did say
The number of the hour, and all in peace
Listened to hear its own vibration cease

Wearied with airy task, with tracing flowers
Of snow on lace, with singing hymn or song        10
With trying all her harp's symphonious powers
By striking full its quivering strings along
And drawing out deep chords & shaking showers
Of brilliant sound, from shell & wires among
Wearied with reading books, weary with weeping    15
Heart-sick of Life she sought for death in sleeping

She lay down on her couch--but could she sleep?
Could she forget existence in a dream
That blotting out reality might sweep
Over her weariness the healing stream             20

246

Of hope and hope's fruition--Lo the deep
And Amber glow of that departing beam
Shot from that blood-red sun--points to her brow
Straight like a silent index, mark it now

Kindling her perfect features, bringing bloom                    25
Into the living marble, smooth and bright
As sculptured effigy on hallowed tomb
Glimmering amid the dimmed and solemn light
Native to Gothic pile--so wan, so white
In shadow gleamed that face, in rosy flush                       30
Of setting sun, rich with a living blush

Up rose the lonely lady and her eyes
Instinctive raised their fringe, of raven shade
And fixed upon those vast and glorious skies
Their lustre that in Death alone might fade                      35
Skies fired with crimson clouds, burning with dies
Intense as blood--they arched above and rayed
The firmament with broad & vivid beams
That seemed to bend toward her all their gleams

It was the eve of battle, leagues away                           40
In the direction of that setting sun
An army saw that lurid summer day
Closing their serried ranks and squared upon
Saw it with awe, so deeply was the ray
The last ray tinged with blood--so wild it shone                 45
So strange the semblance gory, burning given
To pool & stream & sea by that red heaven

                                        [July 1837]

MS:    D(1)
First Publication:   SHB C and B


**146**      An early draft of **Presentiment** in the 1846 volume of poems,
             dated July 11, 1837--see No. **196**

**147**    I thought in my childhood how pleasant would be
The day when Life opened its portals for me
When I should leave home, and go wandering away
Out into sunshine and forth into day
Shut in from the world seemed Woods of the West          5
Silent and lonely & hidden from view

I would sit in a chamber for hours alone

    I remember the time when years to come
      Seemed brighter than those gone by
    When I longed from my native woods & home          10
      O'er the wide world to fly
    My native woods seemed a pleasant spot
      Sacred to calm and rest
    But all who lived there were soon forgot
      They never saw a guest          15

    Wild fruits & flowers & flocks of birds
      And green grass through all the year
    And deer in the park in graceful herds
      But nothing else came there

    Life and marriage I have known          20
      Things I dreamed of long ago

                   [July 1837]

MS:   D(1)
First Publication:   Winnifrith PCB

**148**    O! would I were the golden light
    That shines around thee now
As slumber shades the spotless white
    Of that unclouded brow
It watches through each changeful dream          5
    Thy features varied play
It meets thy waking eyes soft gleam
    By dawn by opening day.

O would I were the crimson veil
    Above the couch of snow          10
To dye that cheek so soft so pale
    With my reflected glow

O would I were the cord of gold
    Whose tassel set with pearls
Just meets the silken coverings fold                          15
    And rests upon thy curls.

Dishevelled in thy rosy sleep
    And shading soft thy dreams
Across their bright and raven sweep
    The golden tassel gleams                                  20
I would be anything for thee
    My love my radiant love
A flower a bird for sympathy
    A watchful star above.

                              [July 21, 1837]

MS: Unknown
First Publication: **Cornhill Magazine,** December 1860


**149**    An early draft of **Regret** in the 1846 volume of poems--see
           No. **197**


**150**         But a recollection now
                    But a dream is she
                Not of earth the rays that glow
                    Round her memory
                'Tis not now her youthful face                5
                    Nor her soft blue eye
                Wakes again the fading trace
                    Of fondness ere it die

                Those are dim and those are cold
                    Sealed & mute & hid                      10
                Open not the grave sheet's fold
                    Nor lift the coffin-lid
                If you wish to think again
                    Of her who loved & died
                O look upward to the plain                   15
                    Of heaven expanding wide

                Does it not by moonlight tell


                              249

When all calm the early moon
    But looks o'er bower & stream
And the unclouded heaven has grown        20
    O'er whelming in its beam
Then though thou an exile be
    Though far from hope & home
O seek her angel memory
    In that deep solemn dome              25

Not hers alone--for mingled dreams
    Will come if thou but gaze
Along dim hills & wandering streams
    To that pure source of rays
I have stood thus when not a sound        30
    Arose and none were by
And in the impending heaven I found
    A whole world's mystery

Many like her depart but still
    That glorious moon will rise          35
And in her radiant rising fill
    With hope divine the skies
And every tree at such an hour
    And every bud and leaf
So sweetly silvered take the power        40
    To staunch the wounds of grief

And each blue mount that sleeps in gold
    Is but a step to heaven
Whose glorious realms seem nearer rolled
    To meet the summer even               45
But now farewell to all awhile
    A lingering, fond adieu
To happy dreams to midnight's smile
    To skies of cloudless blue
Farewell farewell a pleasant isle         50
Cresting life's sea with sunlit pile
    I leave bright thoughts in you.

            C. Brontë.  July 21<sup>st</sup> 1837.

MS:  Unknown
First Publication:   Shorter 1918

151          **Stanzas**
       **On the Death of a Christian**


       Calm, on the bosom of thy God
            Fair spirit! rest thee now:
       Ev'n while with ours, thy footsteps trod
            His seal was on thy brow.

       Dust! to its narrow house beneath;                          5
            Soul! to its place on high;
       They that have seen thy look in death
            Will never fear to die

                         C Brontë
                         Haworth  July 27<sup>th</sup> 1837

MS:  D(2)
First Publication:  Winnifrith PCB

152          Turn not now for comfort here
             The lamps are quenched the guests are gone
             Cold and lonely, dim an[d] drear
             Void are now those halls of stone

             Sadly sighing Anvale woods                            5
             Whisper peace to my decay
             Fir-tree over pine-tree broods
             Dark & high and piled away

             Gone are all who saw my glory
             Fill on festal nights the trees                       10
             Distant lit now silver hoary
             Bowed they to the freshening breeze

             They are dead who heard at night
             Woods and winds and waters sound
             Where my casements cast their light                   15
             Red upon the snow-piled ground

             Some from afar in foreing regions
             Some from drear suffering--wild unrest
             All light on land and winged legions
             Fill the old woods and parent nest                    20

                    [October-November, 1837]

                         251

MS: D(1)
First Publication: SHB C and B

**153**         **My**

A single word--a magic spring
   That touched, revealed a world
A tone from one sweet trembling string
   That deepest feelings stirred

I cannot tell and none can tell                                   5
   How flashed the mighty stream
At once as on the vision fell
   Its silent, written name

The Calabar! The Calabar!
   The sacred land it laves                                       10
I little thought so lone so far
   To hear its rolling waves

To see and hear them in their course
   As clear, as they who stand
And watch the unbridled torrent force                             15
   Its way through Angria's land

As clear as they who oft at eve
   Here from the lattice dim
Looked forth where Adrian's towers receive

How many summer nights of balm                                    20
   Have given those walls their glow
And still their soft and golden calm
   Alas saw only woe
The eye with sleepless day-dreams dim
   The cheek with vigils pale                                     25

On the rolling water gaze
   As it sweeps beneath the sky
Where the sun's descending rays
   In the path of twilight die
All is warm, and dim and calm                                     30
   All in heaven is mellow blue
And there falls a sacred calm
   On the earth with summer's dew

252

Through the flowers and shining leaves
   From her lofty bower she bends         35
Where the rose a curtain weaves
   And the vine a shadow lends

How sadly her speaking eye
   Still looks down the castle slope
Though the moon be lifted high         40
   Like the golden lamp of hope
As she leans her long black curls
   On the glossy ivy lie
With the strings of lucid pearls
   That their splendid clusters tie         45

As she leans the moon's full beam
   Softly lights her cheek & brow
And though fair as angel's dream
   She is pale as marble now
Through checquering leave and flower         50
   That ray her chamber shows
And no dark Sultana's bower
   With such fairy splendour glows

In that mirror's mystic gleam
   With its massive mouldings round         55
There is shadowed like a dream
   Yonder hill's aerial bound
And soft green woods, and skies
   With a moon of milder light
And more shadowy stars that rise         60
   But to gem a dimmer night

Scarce imagined, e'er tis gone
   O bright dream a moment stay
Though so sweet, so calm, and lone
   It is fading fast away         65
I scarce saw thee by the light
   Of the moon that filled thy cell
E'er thy form was wrapt in night
   Thou lovely sentinel!

And thy vigil never more         70
   In that watch-tower came again
For the sands on Fancy's shore
   Lost the trace in stormy rain

Nov$^{br}$ 17$^{th}$ 1837

MS: D(1)
First Publication: SHB C and B
Text: l. 12: "its" written above "thy"; neither is canceled
l. 40: "be" written above "is"; neither is canceled

154
       Yet sleep my lord and know
         One true heart beats for thee
       That neither pain nor want nor woe
         Can taint with treachery

       If in this lonely wood           5
         A host now sought thy life
       How freely would I pour my blood
         To shield thee in the strife

       Whitened and cold thy brow
       And wasted thy young cheek      10

       [November 1837-January 1838]

MS: D(1)
First Publication: SHB C and B

155(a)
    Long, long ago--before the weight of pain
    Made life a weary burden--I would dream
    Of such a time as this--and now again
    Comes memory with that faint and doubtful gleam
    Her faded taper yields, and shews how vain    5
    Is Hope--Anticipation--Checked the stream
    I thought would flow forever----------.

155(b)
    I ask no more--for all that earth can give
    I see around me gathered--soft and bright
    Be[a]uty arises, wooing me to live      10
    And never quit these scenes of placid light
    Half shrouded--half revealing through the night

155(c)
    As midnight veils and hides in shade
       This vast and domed saloon
    As all those clouds in piles arrayed     15
       Have screened the unsullied moon

    So thou my Lord hast been to me
    A cloud that darkened life-----

254

O'er hill and wood--the evening bells
    Their holy tones diffuse                                    20
That sound of peaceful starlight tells
    And summer's falling dews

Silent, and golden--shines that star
    In blue unclouded space

                    [November 1837-January 1838]

MS: D(1)
First Publication:  SHB C and B


**156**
What does she dream of, lingering all alone
On the vast terrace o'er the stream impending
Through all the still dim night no life-like tone
With the soft rush of wind and wave is blending
Her fairy step upon the marble falls                            5
With startling echo through those silent halls

Chill is the night though glorious and she folds
Her robe upon her breast to meet that blast
Coming down from the barren Northern wolds
There how she shuddered as the breeze blew past            10
And died on yonder track of foam with shiver
Of giant reed & flag fringing the            river

Full, brilliant shines the moon--lifted on high
O'er noble land and nobler river flowing
Through parting hills that swell upon that sky              15
Still with the hue of dying daylight glowing
Swell with their plumy woods and dewy glade[s]
Opening to moonlight in the deepest shades

Turn lady to thy--halls, for singing shrill
Again the gust descends--again the river                    20
Frets into foam--I see thy dark eyes fill
With large bitter tears--thy sweet lips quiver

                    [November 1837-January 1838]

MS: D(1)
First Publication:  SHB C and B
Text: l. 12:  blank space in the manuscript


                            255

An early draft of **The Wife's Will** in the 1846 volume of
poems--see No. **198**

**158(a)**
                   Obscure and little seen my way
                      Through life has ever been
                   But winding from my earliest day
                      Through many a wondrous scene
                   None ever asked what feelings moved          5
                      My heart, or flushed my cheek
                   And if I hoped or feared or loved
                      No voice was heard to speak

                   I watched, I thought, I studied long
                   The crowds I moved unmarked among           10
                   I nought to them and they to me
                   But shapes of strange variety
                   The Great with all th' illusive shine
                   Of power--and wealth, and lofty line
                   I long have marked and well I know          15

**158(b)**
                   The voice of Lowood speaks subdued
                   In the deep shadowy solitude
                   Inured to loneliness--I know
                   No gloom in that communing low
                   Of tree with tree and gale with gale        20
                   Telling to each a plaintive tale

                   Unhonoured, little thought of now
                   I come to rest my weary head
                   Where leafy branch and ivied bough
                   Their canopy of calm will spread            25
                   And dreams will dawn like angel's bright
                   From the long vista's tender light

                   Have many lived as I have lived
                   Existence but a reverie
                   Born all for kindness yet b[e]reaved        30
                   Of human smiles and sympathy
                   Passing through scenes of grandeur high
                   And doomed with noble hearts to dwell
                   Burning with love yet forced to sigh
                   That none will mark that passion swell      35
                   Yes one, by fiery glimpses oft

The cloud enkindling changed to flame
Then sun and balm immingling soft
To melt the frozen winter came
And even I have tasted joy                                    40
Pure, bright from heaven without alloy

Yet strange it seems--that born to be
A being all unchained and free
With powers of bliss all self contained

[November 1837-January 1838]

MS:  D(1)
First Publication:  SHB C and B partial; Winnifrith PCB


**159**        And not alone seems she from pillared halls
               To look forth on the night--so to note the sky
               Bending above Fidena's moon-tipt walls
               And mirrored in the flood that wanders by
               And where beside her in the chamber falls                5
               The window's clear reflection broad & high
               She deems another stands, that half-checked breath
               Now tells of wakened thought that know[s] not death

[November 1837-January 1838]

MS:  D(1)
First Publication:  Winnifrith PCB


**160**        An early draft of **Winter Stores** in the 1846 volume of
               poems--see No. **199**


**161**        An early draft of **Evening Solace** in the 1846 volume of
               poems--see No. **200**

257

162            Holy St Cyprian! thy waters stray
                  With still and solemn tone
            And fast my bright hours pass away
            And somewhat throws a shadow grey
            Even as twilight closes day          5
                  Upon thy waters lone

            Farewell! if I might come again
                  Young as I was & free
            And feel once more in every vein
            The fire of that first passion reign        10
            Which sorrow could not quench nor pain
                  I'd soon return to thee
            But while thy billows seek the main
                  That never more may be!

                          [January 17, 1838]

MS:  G
First Publication:  Shorter 1918


163            "O! let me be alone" he said
                  And he was left alone
            None wished to stay--a sense of dread
                  Came with that hollow tone
            Upon his couch he rose to see        5
                  If through the chamber wide
            There shone an eye to watch how he
                  How Pain could quell his pride

            No all was void--before his bed
                  A lofty arch disclosed        10
            An iron sky with clouds o'er spread
                  With clouds where sullen storms reposed
            Unwilling still to break, but full
                  Of awful days to be
            When that high concave dense & dull     15
                  Should burst convulsively

            The light that touched the sufferer's brow
                  Was brassy faint & wan
            Yet shewed it well what sense of woe
                  Worked in that dying-man        20
            He looked forth on the dreary sky
                  And back he sank again
            But not to sleep or faint his eye
                  Shewed strength still strove with pain

He spoke for burning fever, wrought                    25
  So wildly in his brain
He knew not whether voice or thought
  Took up the 'phrenzied strain
He spoke aloud his vision wild
  Seemed something to pourtray                          30
He gazed on space then strangely smiled
  And bid the phantom stay

Be mine for evermore, I go
  Where none shall watch us rove
O heal this anguish, soothe this woe                    35
  And then my true heart prove
Shall I not by the cane-brake find
  Some home, some nest for thee
Where haply on thy breast reclined
  My future heaven shall be                             40

These are my father's halls but here
  I feel I may not stay
I grieve not so these arms may bear
  Mine Idol too away
And thou wilt go that heavenly smile                    45
  Forgives & grants me more
Than hours & months & years of toil
  And fondness can restore

O is it Fever brings that form
  So near my dying bed                                  50
And waves that hand so soft & warm
  Above my throbbing head
Is it delirium shews her now
  With pitying aspect nigh
I see the dark curls o'er her brow                      55
  With love in that deep eye?

Hollow & vapour-like it seems
  I see but cannot feel
Like glorious thoughts, like golden dreams
  Which youth & Hope reveal                             60
But I must wake I know she said
  She never loved but one
And all my adoration paid
  In fire she seemed to shun

Again if raised from this death-bed                     65
  I'll peril life to try
If she for whom I          and bled
  Will let me hopeless die


259

And if an Angels voice divine
   From God should bid me tell
In what bright heaven of glorious shine
   My spirit longed to dwell

I'd say let it be shadowy night
   On earth let stars look down
And let her lips in that dim light
   Confess her heart my own
Be it in black & frozen wild
   Be it in lonely wood
So she but loved & cheered & smiled
   I'll buy such bliss with blood

The white lips of the dying man
   Turned whiter still & he
With up-turned eyes & aspect wan
   Seemed stricken with agony
He felt himself alone, he knew
   All the cold lonely-room around

70

75

80

85

[January 1838]

MS:  D(1)
First Publication:  SHB C and B

Text:   l. 8:  penciled variant; the original line, uncanceled, reads:
"Could quail to pain his pride"; penciled in the margin opposite
is "Nor leech nor nurse still watched to see"
l. 11:  penciled variant; uncanceled original line reads:  "How
gloomily the sky was spread"
l. 24:  all in pencil
ll. 31-32:  penciled variant; uncanceled original lines read:
               And as the phantom waned, he smiled
               And beckoned it to stay
l. 67:  blank space in manuscript
l. 68:  "hopeless" canceled, but no alternative given


**164**     An early draft of **Parting** in the 1846 volume of poems,
dated January 29, 1838--see No. **201**

**165**  The rumour of invaders through all Zamorna ran
Then Turner Gray his watch-word gave
   "Ho! Ardsley to the Van!

Lord Hartford called his yeomen and Warner raised his clan
But first in fiercest gallop--rushed Ardsley to the van!     5
On came Medina's turbans, Sir Jehu hurled his ban
'Mid the thousand hearts who scorned it still Ardsley kept
   the van!

The freshening gales of battle, a hundred standards fan
And doubt not Ardsley's pennon floats foremost in the van
Cold on the field of carnage they have fallen man for man    10
And no more in march or onslaught will Ardsley lead the van

Loud wail lamenting trumpets--for all that gallant clan
And Angrians shout their signal
   Ho! Ardsley to the van!

Give them the grave of honour where their native river ran    15
Let them rest they died like heroes
   In the battle's fiery van!

And when their names are uttered this hope may cheer each man
That land shall never never perish
   Where such true hearts led the van    20

                        [June 1838]

MS:  D(1)
Not previously published


**166**          **The Town besieged**

        With moaning sound, a stream
        Sweeps past the Town's dark walls
        Within her streets a bugle's voice
        Her troops to slumber calls

        The sentinels are set.             5
        The wearied soldiers sleep,
        But some shall know to-morrow-night
        A slumber far more deep

A chill and hoary dew,
On tower, and bastion shines                                10
What dew shall fall when War arrays
Her fiery battle-lines?

Trump and triumphant drum,
    The conflict soon shall spread;
Who then will turn aside, and say                           15
    "We mourn the noble dead?"

Strong hands, heroic hearts
Shall homeward throng again,
Redeemed from battle's gory grasp.
Where will they leave the slain?                            20

Beneath a foreign sod,
Beside an alien wave;
Watched by the martyr's holy God
Shall sleep the martyred brave.

                                        June 1838

MS:  D(1) & F(1)
First Publication:  Winnifrith PCB


**167  Review at Gazemba--July 7<sup>th</sup> 1838**

All the summer plains of Angria were asleep in perfect peace
And the soldier as he rested deemed that foreign wars
    would cease
All the slain were calmly buried--the survivors home returned
Crossed again--the silent thresholds--where their faithful
    consorts mourned

Stained & soiled from Leyden's carnage--Dark & stern from
    Eveshams fall                                           5
Every chieftain of the army sought once more his ancient hall
And the proud commander slumbered on a couch's velvet swell
Yea beneath his lady's bower slept the Gallant Arundel

And the knight who never yielded in the battle to a foe
Now like Manoah's son is fettered with encircling arms of snow  10
The stalwart Thornton lingers by soft lawn & shady tree
All the ills of war forgotten in his Julia's sorcery


                        262

And why may not soldiers rest--when the fiery charge is sped
They may gather thornless flowers, who on bristled spears
      have bled
The[y] may lie without upbraiding in the mildest sunbeam's          15
      light
Who have watched through winter tempest and through cold
      December night

Wherefore then that sound of trumpets--sent at noonday
      through the land
Why that rustling waft of banners and that gathering band by
      band
Are there hosts upon the frontiers are there ships upon
      the sea
Are there chains in senates forging--for the children of the
      free                                                          20

No though every foe is conquered & though every field is won
Yet Zamorna thinks his labours--for the Kingdom but begun
And those trumpets are his summons--those deep bugles are his
      call
From bower, from couch & chamber he has roused his nobles all

The horse again is saddled--that from conflict scarce has
      breathed                                                      25
The sabre flashed in daylight--that the peace had hardly
      sheathed
And vaulting to their chargers--a hundred heroes spring
Yea ten thousand to Gazemba are gone to meet the King

The morning just awaking--lights the sky from pole to pole
Where the waters of a torrent--through the arid deserts roll        30
A banner from yon fortress--waves brightly in the sun
And from citadel & rampart--peals deep the matin gun

Heart-stirring soul-exalting whence bursts that warlike
      strain
Whose are the armed battallions that fill Gazemba's plain
On snow-white charger mounted--with snow-white plumes               35
      displayed
The herald of Arundel is at his horseman's head

To louder bursts of music--the desert thrills again
As onward spurs Lord Hartford to marshall all his men
And Eitrei's jungles quiver--when the blood-hounds send afar
To greet their own Fernando--the Bandit's wild Hourra!              40

Forth staff & plume & banner--forth crest & sword and lance
Amid the battery's thunder--the royal guards advance

A flash from every cannon--a shout from every man
For the king is dashing forward he is spurring to the van

Tall as a soldier should be and dark and quick of eye          45
He rises in his stirrups the pageant to descry
He cannot speak his answer to the sounds that hail him now
But he reins his fiery horse & he halts to bare his brow

There with eyes that meet the sun of the desert undismayed
He bends before his warriors that curled & helmless head       50
And then he signs for silence and he bids the charge begin
The cheer is drowned the shout is lost in the mimic battles din

They wheel they close they part--to the signal to the word
Every bosom every heart by that Kingly voice is stirred
The veterans of Benguela that voice before had known           55
It had cheered the midnight march with its deep arousing tone

By Cirhala's rapid water that very Leader spoke
Ere the day that closed in slaughter over Glorious Westwood
     broke--
And thus along the ranks had passed that haughty form
With bare white brow--& gallant smile on the night of
     Evesham's fall!                                            60

And a faithful noble few could remember years ago
How young Douro--led them through on a night of wail and woe
When by far Guadima's shore & by Angria's sieged town
With blast & volleying roar the mountain storm rushed down

Is there one in all that host 'neath Gazemba's rampart dread   65
But would deem life nobly lost if for Adrian's sake he bled
Is there one would shrink from death in the rudest rush of
     fight
If he gave his latest breath for his sake & in his sight?

You have followed me in dangers--says the monarch to his men
When we scarce had hope to cheer us--will you follow me again  70
While you keep my kingdom free--I will reign your sovereign
     true
While your hearts are staunch for me shall my hand be strong
     for you

To seal--his haughty vow--and his solemn league to bind
Once more he gave his brow--bare & glancing to the wind
The trumpets breathed a thrill and then paused then wild
     & high                                                    75
Pipe & horn & clarion shrill--burst in triumph on the sky

264

With hearts too rapt for words--stood the troops as still
     as death
Then arose a clash of swords--but there never stirred a breath

MS:   D(1)
First Publication:  BST 1934

**168**              'Tis the Siesta's languid hour
                        The sun burns fierce & strong
                     Softly the bird in Helen's bower
                        Soothes her light sleep with song
                     Of tropic isles & groves it sings                    5
                        She dreams of mountains grey
                     Where the lone heron folds its wings
                        By streams--how far away!

                     Fain would that weary bird return
                        Over the sea's white foam                        10
                     Gladly would Helen cease to mourn
                        Safe in her mountain home
                     <Serene> the damask buds of summer breathe
                        Their fragrance through her bower
                     In sleep she roams where summer heath             15
                        Waves in the winds its flower

                     Deeply the lowland river flows
                        Its rush sounds in her dreams
                     She thinks the fall of winter snows
                        Have swelled her native streams                 20
                     All in meridian light she lies
                        Faint in this burning noon
                     To her it seems that evening skies
                        Disclose a rising moon

                     No sound is in her garden heard                    25
                        Save the soft hum of bees
                     Scarcely a blossom's leafe is stirred
                        So softly swells the breeze
                     That silence sinks too on her sleep
                        But there the sleep of night                    30
                     Glides on with dews & shadows deep
                        Over a hill's dim height

                     The bird is flown--her dream is gone
                        Moon--hills--and shadows wane
                     And Helen lies awake, alone                        35

She fain would sleep again
No lady rise--the time of sleep
For thee has glided by
Wake now & watch the transient sweep
Of clouds across the sky                               40

Sit by the dial-piece--as oft
Thy weary wont has been
And mark the sunshine passing soft
Each shadowed hour between
And wait for night for sunset yearn                    45
Then long again for day
Thus shalt thou wait & watch & mourn
Till life is past away!

C. Brontë  July 7<sup>th</sup> 1838

MS:  D(1)
First Publication:  SHB C and B
Text:  l. 13:  first word of the pencil revision is undecipherable; un-
        canceled original line reads "Serene the summer roses breathe"
        l. 14:  "fragrance" written above "odours"; neither is canceled
        ll. 18-20:  Penciled in the right-hand margin:
                        Its rush sounds
                        As cataract hurled from mountain brows
                        Or rapid mountain stream


**169**            Beneath Fidena's Minster
                       A stranger made her grave.
                   She had longed in death to slumber
                       Where trees might o'er her wave.

                   An exile from her country                5
                       She died on mountain ground,
                   The Flower of Senegambia
                       A northern tomb has found.

                   Why did he cease to cherish
                       His Harriet when she fell?          10
                   Why did he let her perish
                       Who had loved him all too well?

                   She called on Alexander
                       As she sickened, as she died,
                   When fever made her wander              15
                       For him alone she cried.


266

But Percy would not listen,
Would not hear when Harriet wailed.
Where Europe's ice-bergs glisten,
Far, far away he sailed.                                    20

But memory shall discover
Her woes some future time.
Ere long that haughty Rover
Shall darkly mourn his crime.

[July 1838]

MS: Unlocated: last known to be in the possession of Sir Alfred Law
First Publication: Ratchford Legends partial; SHB Misc II


**170**     Why do you linger and why do you roam?
I'm feared o' the gude-wife: I dare not go home.
What will she do lad, and what will she say?
She'll send me to Hell man, the Devil to pay.

Just cut her a stick lad and give it her well,      5
Let her pay the Devil, let her go to Hell.
As I've settled my wife, go thee settle thy wife,
What bother 'twill save thee it is not to tell.

Down from the Barracks
Came four bold Dragoons.             10
Every man swore roundly
And shouted 'Blood and 'oons.'

Each had a red coat
And each had a helm.
These are the fellows                15
For holding the helm.

[July 1838]

MS: Unlocated: see No. **169**
First Publication: SHB Misc II


**171**     Your mama's in the dairy, your father's in the field,
The moon's rising slowly as round as a shield,
Come through the back door, there's no one to see,
'Tis a sweet summer evening for courtship with thee.

267

The dusk follows sunset with hush and with hum,
Now I'll tell you my secret to-night if you'll come.
Hidden and wondrous and dark though it be,
You shall know all if you'll hasten to me.

Wave me no signals and glance me no signs,
Evening is wasting and daylight declines.                    10
'Tis not in laughter or love that I crave,
Hasten, remember the promise you gave.

                                        [July 1838]

MS: Unlocated: see No. 169
First Publication: SHB Misc II


172    The ante-room is hushed and still,
           The lattice curtained close.
       The tempest sweeping round the hill
           Awakes not its repose.

       And there before him reclined his own Augusta--       5
       her beauty and splendour as mute as a dream--her large
       eyes are open but they never move--her cheek ne'er
       changes--her robes never wave.
           He calls upon her--

       AUGUSTA! but the silence round                        10
           Could give him no reply
       And straightway did that single word
           Without an echo die!

                                        [July 1838]

MS: Unlocated: see No. 169
First Publication: SHB Misc II


173    And with that thought came an impulse
           Which broke the dreamy spell
       For no longer on the picture
           Could her eye endure to dwell
       She vowed to leave her visions                        5
           And seek life's arousing stir
       For she knew Sir William's slumber
           Would not bring a thought of her

                       268

```
        How fruitless then to ponder
          O'er such dreams as chained her now          10
        Her heart should cease to wander
          And her tears no more should flow
        The trance was over--over
          The spell was scattered far
        Yet how blessed were she whose lover          15
          Would be Angria's young Hussar!

        Earth knew no hope more glorious
          Heaven gave no nobler boon
        Than to welcome him victorious
          To a heart he claimed his own            20
        How sweet to tell each feeling
          The kindled soul might prove!
        How sad to die concealing
          The anguish born of love!
```

Such were Miss Hastings musings--such were almost the          25
words that arranged themselves like a song in her mind--
words, however, neither spoken nor sung--She dared not
so far confess her phrenzy to herself--only once she
paused in her walk through the drawing-room by the
open piano--laid her fingers on the keys--& wakening          30
a note or two of plaintive melody--murmured the last
lines of the last stanza--

```
        How sad to die concealing
          The anguish born of love!
```

                                        [March 1839]

MS:  A
First Publication:  Gérin Five Novelettes


**174**     An early draft of **Life** in the 1846 volume of poems, dated
            March 26, 1839--see No. **202**
```
```

**175**   There's not always

An Angrian campaign--going on in the rain
Nor a Gentleman Squire lighting his fire
Up on the moors with his blackguards & boors
Nor a Duke & a lord drawing the Sword          5
Hectoring & lying the whole world defying
    Then sitting down crying

There's not always

A shopkeeper militant coming out iligant
With King Boy & King Jack both genteely in black    10
Forming Holy Alliance & breathing defiance
Nor a Prince finding brandy every day coming handy
While he's conquering of lands with his bold nigger bands
    Like a man of his hands

There's not always                             15

A Death & a marriage--a Hearse & a Carriage
A Bigamy cause--A King versus laws
Nor a short Transportation for the good of the nation
Nor a speedy returning mid national mourning
While him & his father refuse to foregather     20
    'Cause the earl hadn't rather

                  [July-December 1839]

MS:  A
First Publication:  Gérin Five Novelettes


**176**   A better lot is thine fair maid
    A happier lot is thine
And who would weep in dungeon shade
    Whom fate had marked for Mine
    Come do not pine                    5
But fly to arms that open to receive
    Thy youthful form divine
Clasped to this heart of fire thoul't never grieve
    No thou shalt shine
Happy as houris fair--that braid their hair    10
    Glorious in Eden's bowers

Where noxious flowers
With fragrant reptiles twine
But thou my blooming gem wilt far out-flourish them
My radiant Caroline!

[July-December 1839]

MS: A
First Publication: Gérin Five Novelettes


**177**

A Rowland for your Oliver
    We think you've justly earned;
You sent us each a valentine,
    Your gift is now returned.

We cannot write or talk like you;                     5
    We're plain folks every one;
You've played a clever jest on us,
    We thank you for your fun.

Believe us when we frankly say
    (Our words, though blunt are true),          10
At home, abroad, by night or day,
    We all wish well to you.

And never may a cloud come o'er
    The sunshine of your mind;
Kind friends, warm hearts, and happy hours,     15
    Through life we trust you'll find.

Where'er you go, however far
    In future years you stray,
There shall not want our earnest prayer
    To speed you on your way.                         20

A stranger and a pilgrim here,
    We know you sojourn now;
But brighter hopes, with brighter wreaths,
    Are doomed to bind your brow.

Not always in these lonely hills                       25
    Your humble lot shall lie;
The oracle of fate foretells
    A worthier destiny.

And though her words are veiled in gloom,
   Though clouded her decree,                                 30
Yet doubt not that a juster doom
   She keeps in store for thee.

Then cast hope's anchor near the shore,
   'Twill hold your vessel fast,
And fear not for the tide's deep roar,                        35
   And dread not for the blast.

For though this station now seems drear
   'Mid land-locked creeks to be,
The helmsman soon his ship shall steer,
   Out to the wide blue sea.                                  40

Well officered and staunchly manned,
   Well built to meet the blast;
With favouring winds the bark must land
   On glorious shores at last.

   February, 1840.            Charlotte Bronte.

MS: Unknown
First Publication: **Whitehaven News**, February 17, 1876


**178**   An early draft of **Passion** in the 1846 volume of poems,
          dated December 12, 1841--see No. **203**


**179**   On its bending stalk a bonny flower
             In a yeoman's home-close grew
          It had gathered beauty from sunshine & shower
             From moonlight & silent dew
          Till the tufted leaves of the garden bower          5
             Like a star it sparkled through

          It was a little budding rose
          Round like a fairy globe
          And shyly did its leaves unclose
          Hid in their mossy robe                             10
          But sweet was the slight & spicy smell
          It breathed from its heart invisible


                              272

Keenly his flower the yeoman guarded
  He watched it by day & by night
From the frost from the wind from the storm he warded          15
  That flush of roseate light
And ever it glistened bonnilie
Under the shade of the old roof-tree

The morning sunshine had called him forth
His garden was full of dew                                     20
And green light slept on the happy earth
And the sky was calm & blue
The yeoman looked for his lovely flower
There were leaves, but no buds in the sheltring bower

The rose was borne to another land                            25
  & grew in another bed
It was cultured by another hand
  And it sprung & flourished
And fairer it budded day by day
Beneath a new sun's cheering ray                              30

But long lies the dew on its crimson leaves
It almost looks like tears
The flower for the yeoman's home-close grieves
Amid a King's parterres
Little moss-rose cease to weep                                35
Let regret & sorrow sleep

The rose is blasted withered blighted
  Its root has felt a worm
And like a heart, beloved & slighted
  Failed, faded, shrunk its form                             40
Bud of beauty bonnie flower
I stole thee from thy natal bower
I was the worm that withered thee
Thy tears of dew all fell for me
Leaf & stalk & rose are gone                                 45
Exile earth they died upon
Yes that last breath of thy faint balmy scent
God with alien breezes sadly blent

                                        [October 1842]

MS:  H
First Publication:  Shorter EJB 1910
Text:  l. 47:  "breath of thy" faintly canceled in pencil
       l. 48:  "God" seems to be faintly canceled in pencil and "sadly"
       added in pencil

At first I did attention give
Observance--deep esteem
His frown I failed not to forgive
His smile--a boon to deem

Attention rose to interest soon                    5
Respect to homage changed
The smile became a returned boon
The frown like grief estranged

The interest ceased not with his voice
    The homage tracked him near                    10
Obedience was my heart's free choice
    Whatere his word severe

His praise unfrequent--favour rare
    Unduly <dream's> grew
And too much power--a haunting fear                15
    Around his anger threw--

His coming was my hope each day
    His parting was my pain!
The chance that did his steps delay
    Was ice in every vein                          20

I gave entire affection now
    I gave devotion sure
And strong took root and fast did grow
    One mighty feeling more

The truest love that ever heart                    25
    Felt at its kindled core
Through my veins with quickened start
    A tide of life did pour

[A] halo played about the brows
    Of life as seen by me                          30
And <bribing> bliss within me rose
    And anxious ecstacy

I dreamed it would be nameless bliss
    As I loved--loved to be
And to this object did I press                     35
    As blind as eagerly

But wide as pathless was the space
That lay our lives between
    And dangerous as the foamy race
    Of ocean's surges green                        40

And haunted as a robber path
    Through wilderness or wood
For might & right woe & wrath
    Between our spirits stood

I dangers dared--I hindrance scorned          45
    I omens did defy
Whatever menaced--harassed warned
    I passed impetuous by

On sped my rainbow fast as light
    I flew as in a dream                      50
For glorious rose upon my sight
    That child of shower & gleam

And bright on clouds of suffering dim
    Shone that soft-solemn joy
I care not then how dense & grim              55
    Disaster's gather nigh

I care not in this moment sweet
    Though all I have rushed o'er
Should come on pinions strong and fleet
    Proclaiming vengeance sore                60

Hate struck me in his presence down
    Love barred approach to me
My rival's joy with jealous frown
    Declared hostility

Wrath leagued with calumny transfused         65
    Strong poison in his veins
And I stood at his feet accused
    Of false          stains

Cold as a statue's grew his eye
    Hard as a rock his brow                   70
Cold--hard to me but tenderly
    He kissed my rival now

She seemed my rainbow to have seized
    Around her form it closed
And soft its <iris> splendour blazed          75
    Where love & she reposed

                [January 1845]

MS:  H
First Publication:  **Jane Eyre,** ed., Margaret Smith, Oxford:  Oxford
                    University Press, 1975

Text:  1. 28:  The original version of the line reads "And life a glory bore"--uncanceled

1. 29:  "halo" written above "It played"; neither is canceled

1. 56:  "gather nigh" written above "bring nigh"; neither is canceled

1. 57:  originally the line read "The hate the love the joy the sweet"--uncanceled

1. 58:  originally the line read "the wrath I had passed o'er"--uncanceled

1. 59:  "Should come" written above "There came"; neither is canceled

1. 68:  blank space in the manuscript


**181**    An early draft of parts II and III of **Gilbert** in the 1846 volume of poems--see No. **185**


**182**    An early draft of "I gave, at first, attention close" from **The Professor**--see No. **205**


**183(a)**    A week ago September dead October's moon set in
For some days heavy mists were shed upon her crescent horn
A night of rain the fog remained, then sunrise fresh and
    clear
With gentle smile the doubt reproved which mourned the
    failing year
The Autum day its course has run--the Autum evening falls    5
Already ris'n, the Autum moon gleams quiet on these walls
A frost her light upon the fields--to silver bleaches pale
The untrodden road a lustre yields as white as hoary hail
But dark the line of woodland farms where heavy boughs
    embrowned
Still wait November's sleety storms to shed their honour
    round    10
Sable and pale the scene appears and but for Heaven's deep
    blue
And Luna's gold this landscape wears a wan and phantom hue
        No blush, no flush no amber brightness
        A neutral shade--a tintless whiteness
Chaste night and tranquil! not too chill    15
No wintry frostiness breathes from the hill

Bent from my lattice I feel no breeze
Sweep o'er those pale fields--stir dusk trees
Lone flows the water--my ear receives
Its sound like the murmur of light airs in leaves          20
Even from the road not a whisper comes
Nor traveler nor wanderer its white track roams
And my house is silent--in every room
There is but moonlight--and vacant gloom
How 'mid this marble--this darkness, this snow             25
Can my heart beat and my warm blood flow?
How where there is but shade and gleam
Can my mind vary its tinted dream
I see only woods as black as clouds
I trace only meadows blanched as shrouds                   30
In the starlight and moonlight darkly clear
Hollow silence is in my ear
Yet I think

**183(b)**    My parents to the distant town this morning early went
To meet them on the mountain road the servant I have sent  35
The autum day its course has run--the autumn evening falls
Already ris'n the autum moon gleams quiet on these walls
And Twilight to our lonely house a silent guest is come
In mask of gloom through every room she passes dusk and dumb
I've followed her--through every door--I've cautious
    glanced to see                                         40
That only shade and moonbeams filled each chamber's vacancy

**183(c)**    The Autumn day its course has run--the Autumn evening falls
Already risen the autumn moon gleams quiet on these walls
And Twilight to my lonely house a silent guest is come
In mask of gloom through every room she passes dusk & dumb  45
Her veil is spread, her shadow shed o'er stair and chamber
    void
And now I feel her presence steal even to my lone fireside
Sit, silent Nun--sit there and be
Comrade and Confidant to me

[Spring 1845]

MS: D(1)
First Publication: BST 1924 partial; Winnifrith PCB
Text:    l. 1:   "set" written above "came"; neither is canceled
        l. 12:  "a wan and phantom" written above "too wan & weird a";
        neither is canceled
        l. 20:  "light" written above "soft"; neither is canceled
        l. 30:  "meadows" canceled, but no alternative offered
        l. 46:  "void" written over "still"; neither is canceled

277

**184**
                         Early wrapt in slumber deep
                           Rest the serving-me[n]
                         Master, dame, and handmaids sleep
                           Sound at Bonny-glen

                         Time's dark stream in yonder vales          5
                           Glides with shadowed flow
                         O'er each latticed window falls
                           A drapery sweeping low

                         While within the house is spread
                           Shade o'er weary eyes                     10
                         Screenless in his out-door shed
                           A little herd-boy lies

                         Splendid light from summer moon
                           Falls on each green tree
                         Soft as twilight--clear as noon             15
                           Smiles each dewy lea

                         Water in the clear brook flows
                           Fast with trembling brightness
                         By its side the causeway shews
                           A track of silver whiteness               20

                              [Spring 1845]

MS: D(1)
First Publication: BST 1931
Text: l. 12: "herd-boy" written above "shepherd"; neither is canceled


        Nos. 185-203 comprise the nineteen poems Charlotte included in the
**Poems** by Currer, Ellis, and Acton Bell, published in May 1846. The
manuscript for the volume was retained by the publisher, Aylott and
Jones, and has long ago disappeared. In 1848 Smith Elder & Co. purchased
the remaining stock from Aylott and Jones, and reissued the **Poems**
with exactly the same text including the errata slip contained in the
1846 issue. The text given here is that of the 1846 volume, but with the
corrections indicated on the errata slip. However, because I have been
unable to discover any rationale, chronological or thematic, for the
order in which Charlotte arranged her poems, I have changed the order to
reflect something of the chronology of their composition. For all but
four of the poems--**Gilbert**, **Preference**, **The Missionary**, and
**The Wood**--there is manuscript material predating Charlotte's time in
Brussels. **Gilbert** and **The Missionary** were almost certainly composed in 1845; **Preference** is quite possibly a reworking of an earlier

Angrian poem and **The Wood** definitely is. Because of the lack of any evidence for date of composition, I have grouped **Preference** with **Gilbert** and **The Missionary**, the two 1845 poems, at the beginning of this section. The other sixteen poems, which are all revisions and recastings of earlier manuscript materials, are arranged according to the dates of their earliest drafts (although there is no manuscript extant for **The Wood**, it would seem to date from December 1836 or January 1837--see comment for No. **188**--and is therefore placed at the beginning of this group). In what order these revisions and recastings were actually carried out during 1845 it is impossible to tell.


**185**        **GILBERT.**

        I.

        THE GARDEN.

        ABOVE the city hung the moon,
            Right o'er a plot of ground
        Where flowers and orchard-trees were fenced
            With lofty walls around:
        'Twas Gilbert's garden--there, to-night                    5
            Awhile he walked alone;
        And, tired with sedentary toil,
            Mused where the moonlight shone.

        This garden, in a city-heart,
            Lay still as houseless wild,                           10
        Though many-windowed mansion fronts
            Were round it closely piled;
        But thick their walls, and those within
            Lived lives by noise unstirred;
        Like wafting of an angel's wing,                          15
            Time's flight by them was heard.

        Some soft piano-notes alone
            Were sweet as faintly given,
        Where ladies, doubtless, cheered the hearth
            With song, that winter-even.                          20
        The city's many-mingled sounds
            Rose like the hum of ocean;
        They rather lulled the heart than roused
            Its pulse to faster motion.

Gilbert has paced the single walk 25
    An hour, yet is not weary;
And, though it be a winter night,
    He feels nor cold nor dreary.
The prime of life is in his veins,
    And sends his blood fast flowing, 30
And Fancy's fervour warms the thoughts
    Now in his bosom glowing.

Those thoughts recur to early love,
    Or what he love would name,
Though haply Gilbert's secret deeds 35
    Might other title claim.
Such theme not oft his mind absorbs,
    He to the world clings fast,
And too much for the present lives,
    To linger o'er the past. 40

But now the evening's deep repose
    Has glided to his soul;
That moonlight falls on Memory,
    And shows her fading scroll.
One name appears in every line 45
    The gentle rays shine o'er,
And still he smiles and still repeats
    That one name--Elinor.

There is no sorrow in his smile,
    No kindness in his tone; 50
The triumph of a selfish heart
    Speaks coldly there alone;
He says:  "She loved me more than life;
    And truly it was sweet
To see so fair a woman kneel, 55
    In bondage, at my feet.

There was a sort of quiet bliss
    To be so deeply loved,
To gaze on trembling eagerness
    And sit myself unmoved. 60
And when it pleased my pride to grant,
    At last some rare caress,
To feel the fever of that hand
    My fingers deigned to press.

'Twas sweet to see her strive to hide                    65
    What every glance revealed;
Endowed, the while, with despot-might
    Her destiny to wield.
I knew myself no perfect man,
    Nor, as she deemed, divine;                          70
I knew that I was glorious--but
    By her reflected shine;

Her youth, her native energy,
    Her powers new-born and fresh,
'Twas these with Godhead sanctified                      75
    My sensual frame of flesh.
Yet, like a god did I descend
    At last, to meet her love;
And, like a god, I then withdrew
    To my own heaven above.                              80

And never more could she invoke
    My presence to her sphere;
No prayer, no plaint, no cry of hers
    Could win my awful ear.
I knew her blinded constancy                             85
    Would ne'er my deeds betray,
And, calm in conscience, whole in heart,
    I went my tranquil way.

Yet, sometimes, I still feel a wish,
    The fond and flattering pain                         90
Of passion's anguish to create,
    In her young breast again.
Bright was the lustre of her eyes,
    When they caught fire from mine;
If I had power--this very hour,                          95
    Again I'd light their shine.

But where she is, or how she lives,
    I have no clue to know;
I've heard she long my absence pined,
    And left her home in woe.                           100
But busied, then, in gathering gold,
    As I am busied now,
I could not turn from such pursuit,
    To weep a broken vow.

Nor could I give to fatal risk                           105
    The fame I ever prized;
Even now, I fear, that precious fame
    Is too much compromised."
An inward trouble dims his eye,
    Some riddle he would solve;                          110
Some method to unloose a knot,
    His anxious thoughts revolve.


He, pensive, leans against a tree,
    A leafy evergreen,
The boughs, the moonlight, intercept,                    115
    And hide him like a screen;
He starts--the tree shakes with his tremor,
    Yet nothing near him pass'd,
He hurries up the garden alley,
    In strangely sudden haste.                           120


With shaking hand, he lifts the latchet,
    Steps o'er the threshold stone;
The heavy door slips from his fingers,
    It shuts, and he is gone.
What touched, transfixed, appalled, his soul?           125
    A nervous thought, no more;
'Twill sink like stone in placid pool,
    And calm close smoothly o'er.



II.

THE PARLOUR.

WARM is the parlour atmosphere,
    Serene the lamp's soft light;                        130
The vivid embers, red and clear,
    Proclaim a frosty night.
Books, varied, on the table lie,
    Three children o'er them bend,
And all, with curious, eager eye,                        135
    The turning leaf attend.


Picture and tale alternately
    Their simple hearts delight,
And interest deep, and tempered glee,
    Illume their aspects bright;                         140
The parents, from their fireside place,
    Behold that pleasant scene,
And joy is on the mother's face,
    Pride, in the father's mien.


282

As Gilbert sees his blooming wife,                    145
    Beholds his children fair,
No thought has he of transient strife,
    Or past, though piercing fear.
The voice of happy infancy
    Lisps sweetly in his ear,                         150
His wife, with pleased and peaceful eye,
    Sits, kindly smiling, near.

The fire glows on her silken dress,
    And shows its ample grace,
And warmly tints each hazel tress,                    155
    Curled soft around her face.
The beauty that in youth he wooed,
    Is beauty still, unfaded,
The brow of ever placid mood
    No churlish grief has shaded.                      160

Prosperity, in Gilbert's home,
    Abides, the guest of years;
There Want or Discord never come,
    And seldom Toil or Tears.
The carpets bear the peaceful print                   165
    Of comfort's velvet tread,
And golden gleams from plenty sent,
    In every nook are shed.

The very silken spaniel seems
    Of quiet ease to tell,                            170
As near its mistress' feet it dreams,
    Sunk in a cushion's swell;
And smiles seem native to the eyes
    Of those sweet children, three;
They have but looked on tranquil skies,               175
    And know not misery.

Alas! that misery should come
    In such an hour as this;
Why could she not so calm a home
    A little longer miss?                             180
But she is now within the door,
    Her steps advancing glide;
Her sullen shade has crossed the floor,
    She stands at Gilbert's side.

She lays her hand upon his heart,
   It bounds with agony;
His fireside chair shakes with the start
   That shook the garden tree.
His wife towards the children looks,
   She does not mark his mien;       190
The children, bending o'er their books,
   His terror have not seen.

In his own home, by his own hearth,
   He sits in solitude,
And circled round with light and mirth,    195
   Cold horror chills his blood.
His mind would hold with desperate clutch
   The scene that round him lies;
No--changed, as by some wizard's touch,
   The present prospect flies.      200

A tumult vague--a viewless strife
   His futile struggles crush;
'Twixt him and his, an unknown life
   And unknown feelings rush.
He sees--but scarce can language paint   205
   The tissue Fancy weaves;
For words oft give but echo faint
   Of thoughts the mind conceives.

Noise, tumult strange, and darkness dim,
   Efface both light and quiet;    210
No shape is in those shadows grim,
   No voice in that wild riot.
Sustained and strong, a wondrous blast
   Above and round him blows;
A greenish gloom, dense overcast,    215
   Each moment denser grows.

He nothing knows--nor clearly sees,
   Resistance checks his breath,
The high, impetuous, ceaseless breeze
   Blows on him, cold as death.    220
And still the undulating gloom
   Mocks sight with formless motion;
Was such sensation Jonah's doom,
   Gulphed in the depths of ocean?

Streaking the air, the nameless vision,                           225
    Fast-driven, deep-sounding, flows;
Oh! whence its source, and what its mission?
    How will its terrors close?
Long-sweeping, rushing, vast and void,
    The Universe it swallows;                                     230
And still the dark, devouring tide,
    A Typhoon tempest follows.


More slow it rolls; its furious race
    Sinks to a solemn gliding;
The stunning roar, the wind's wild chase,                         235
    To stillness are subsiding.
And, slowly borne along, a form
    The shapeless chaos varies;
Poised in the eddy of the storm,
    Before the eye it tarries.                                    240


A woman drowned--sunk in the deep,
    On a long wave reclining;
The circling waters' crystal sweep,
    Like glass, her shape enshrining;
Her pale dead face, to Gilbert turned,                            245
    Seems as in sleep reposing;
A feeble light, now first discerned,
    The features well disclosing.


No effort from the haunted air
    The ghastly scene could banish;                               250
That hovering wave, arrested there,
    Rolled--throbbed--but did not vanish.
If Gilbert upward turned his gaze,
    He saw the ocean-shadow;
If he looked down, the endless seas                               255
    Lay green as summer meadow.


And straight before, the pale corpse lay,
    Upborne by air or billow,
So near, he could have touched the spray
    That churned around its pillow.                               260
The hollow anguish of the face
    Had moved a fiend to sorrow;
Not Death's fixed calm could rase the trace
    Of suffering's deep-worn furrow.


285

All moved; a strong returning blast,    265
    The mass of waters raising,
Bore wave and passive carcase past,
    While Gilbert yet was gazing.
Deep in her isle-conceiving womb,    270
    It seemed the Ocean thundered,
And soon, by realms of rushing gloom,
    Were seer and phantom sundered.

Then swept some timbers from a wreck,
    On following surges riding;
Then sea-weed, in the turbid rack    275
    Uptorn, went slowly gliding.
The horrid shade, by slow degrees,
    A beam of light defeated,
And then the roar of raving seas,    280
    Fast, far, and faint, retreated.

And all was gone--gone like a mist,
    Corse, billows, tempest, wreck;
Three children close to Gilbert prest
    And clung around his neck.
Good night! good night! the prattlers said    285
    And kissed their father's cheek;
'Twas now the hour their quiet bed
    And placid rest to seek.

The mother with her offspring goes
    To hear their evening prayer;    290
She nought of Gilbert's vision knows,
    And nought of his despair.
Yet, pitying God, abridge the time
    Of anguish, now his fate!
Though, haply, great has been his crime,    295
    Thy mercy, too, is great.

Gilbert, at length, uplifts his head,
    Bent for some moments low,
And there is neither grief nor dread
    Upon his subtle brow.    300
For well can he his feelings task,
    And well his looks command;
His features well his heart can mask,
    With smiles and smoothness bland.

Gilbert has reasoned with his mind--               305
    He says 'twas all a dream;
He strives his inward sight to blind
    Against truth's inward beam.
He pitied not that shadowy thing,
    When it was flesh and blood;                    310
Nor now can pity's balmy spring
    Refresh his arid mood.


"And if that dream has spoken truth,"
    Thus musingly he says;
"If Elinor be dead, in sooth,                       315
    Such chance the shock repays:
A net was woven round my feet,
    I scarce could further go,
Ere Shame had forced a fast retreat,
    Dishonour brought me low."                      320


"Conceal her, then, deep, silent Sea,
    Give her a secret grave!
She sleeps in peace, and I am free,
    No longer Terror's slave:
And homage still, from all the world,               325
    Shall greet my spotless name,
Since surges break and waves are curled
    Above its threatened shame."


III.

THE WELCOME HOME.

ABOVE the city hangs the moon,
    Some clouds are boding rain,                     330
Gilbert, erewhile on journey gone,
    To-night comes home again.
Ten years have passed above his head,
    Each year has brought him gain;
His prosperous life has smoothly sped,              335
    Without or tear or stain.


'Tis somewhat late--the city clocks
    Twelve deep vibrations toll,
As Gilbert at the portal knocks,
    Which is his journey's goal.                     340
The street is still and desolate,
    The moon hid by a cloud;
Gilbert, impatient, will not wait,--
    His second knock peals loud.


287

The clocks are hushed; there's not a light      345
    In any window nigh,
And not a single planet bright
    Looks from the clouded sky;
The air is raw, the rain descends,
    A bitter north-wind blows;                   350
His cloak the traveller scarce defends--
    Will not the door unclose?

He knocks the third time, and the last;
    His summons now they hear,
Within, a footstep, hurrying fast,              355
    Is heard approaching near.
The bolt is drawn, the clanking chain
    Falls to the floor of stone;
And Gilbert to his heart will strain
    His wife and children soon.                  360

The hand that lifts the latchet, holds
    A candle to his sight,
And Gilbert, on the step, beholds
    A woman, clad in white.
Lo! water from her dripping dress               365
    Runs on the streaming floor;
From every dark and clinging tress,
    The drops incessant pour.

There's none but her to welcome him;
    She holds the candle high,                   370
And, motionless in form and limb,
    Stands cold and silent nigh;
There's sand and sea-weed on her robe,
    Her hollow eyes are blind;
No pulse in such a frame can throb,             375
    No life is there defined.

Gilbert turned ashy-white, but still
    His lips vouchsafed no cry;
He spurred his strength and master-will
    To pass the figure by,--                     380
But, moving slow, it faced him straight,
    It would not flinch nor quail:
Then first did Gilbert's strength abate,
    His stony firmness fail.

He sank upon his knees and prayed;                    385
    The shape stood rigid there;
He called aloud for human aid,
    No human aid was near.
An accent strange did thus repeat
    Heaven's stern but just decree:                   390
"The measure thou to her didst mete,
    To thee shall measured be!"


Gilbert sprang from his bended knees,
    By the pale spectre pushed,
And, wild as one whom demons seize,                   395
    Up the hall-staircase rushed;
Entered his chamber--near the bed
    Sheathed steel and fire-arms hung--
Impelled by maniac purpose dread,
    He chose those stores among.                      400


Across his throat, a keen-edged knife
    With vigorous hand he drew;
The wound was wide--his outraged life
    Rushed rash and redly through.
And thus he died, by a shameful death,                405
    A wise and worldly man,
Who never drew but selfish breath
    Since first his life began.


                                        CURRER.

MS:  D(1)
First Publication:  Poems 1846
Text:  Line 239 - errata sheet changes "to" to "of"
       Line 384 - errata sheet changes "quail" to "fail"


**186**            **PREFERENCE.**


        NOT in scorn do I reprove thee,
        Not in pride thy vows I waive,
        But, believe, I could not love thee,
        Wert thou prince, and I a slave.
        These, then, are thine oaths of passion?        5
        This, thy tenderness for me?
        Judged, even, by thine own confession,
        Thou art steeped in perfidy.
        Having vanquished, thou wouldst leave me!

Thus I read thee long ago;                                    10
Therefore, dared I not deceive thee,
Even with friendship's gentle show.
Therefore, with impassive coldness
Have I ever met thy gaze;
Though, full oft, with daring boldness,                       15
Thou thine eyes to mine didst raise.
Why that smile? Thou now art deeming
This my coldness all untrue,--
But a mask of frozen seeming,
Hiding secret fires from view.                                20
Touch my hand, thou self-deceiver;
Nay--be calm, for I am so:
Does it burn? Does my lip quiver?
Has mine eye a troubled glow?
Canst thou call a moment's colour                             25
To my forehead--to my cheek?
Canst thou tinge their tranquil pallor
With one flattering, feverish streak?
Am I marble? What! no woman
Could so calm before thee stand?                              30
Nothing living, sentient, human,
Could so coldly take thy hand?
Yes--a sister might, a mother:
My good-will is sisterly:
Dream not, then, I strive to smother                          35
Fires that inly burn for thee.
Rave not, rage not, wrath is fruitless,
Fury cannot change my mind;
I but deem the feeling rootless
Which so whirls in passion's wind.                            40
Can I love? Oh, deeply--truly--
Warmly--fondly--but not thee;
And my love is answered duly,
With an equal energy.
Wouldst thou see thy rival? Hasten,                           45
Draw that curtain soft aside,
Look where yon thick branches chasten
Noon, with shades of eventide.
In that glade, where foliage blending
Forms a green arch overhead,                                  50
Sits thy rival thoughtful bending
O'er a stand with papers spread--
Motionless, his fingers plying
That untired, unresting pen,
Time and tide unnoticed flying,                               55
There he sits--the first of men!
Man of conscience--man of reason;
Stern, perchance, but ever just;

290

Foe to falsehood, wrong, and treason,
Honour's shield, and virtue's trust!                    60
Worker, thinker, firm defender
Of Heaven's truth--man's liberty;
Soul of iron--proof to slander,
Rock where founders tyranny.
Fame he seeks not--but full surely                      65
She will seek him, in his home;
This I know, and wait securely
For the atoning hour to come.
To that man my faith is given,
Therefore, soldier, cease to sue;                       70
While God reigns in earth and heaven,
I to him will still be true!

                                        CURRER.

MS: Unknown
First Publication:  Poems 1846


187       **THE MISSIONARY.**


PLOUGH, vessel, plough the British main,
Seek the free ocean's wider plain;
Leave English scenes and English skies,
Unbind, dissever English ties;
Bear me to climes remote and strange,                    5
Where altered life, fast-following change,
Hot action, never-ceasing toil,
Shall stir, turn, dig, the spirit's soil;
Fresh roots shall plant, fresh seeds shall sow,
Till a new garden there shall grow,                     10
Cleared of the weeds that fill it now,--
Mere human love, mere selfish yearning,
Which, cherished, would arrest me yet.
I grasp the plough, there's no returning,
Let me, then, struggle to forget.                       15

But England's shores are yet in view,
And England's skies of tender blue
Are arched above her guardian sea.
I cannot yet Remembrance flee;
I must again, then, firmly face                         20
That task of anguish, to retrace.
Wedded to home--I home forsake,

Fearful of change--I changes make;
Too fond of ease--I plunge in toil;
Lover of calm--I seek turmoil:                          25
Nature and hostile Destiny
Stir in my heart a conflict wild;
And long and fierce the war will be
Ere duty both has reconciled.

What other tie yet holds me fast                        30
To the divorced, abandoned past?
Smouldering, on my heart's altar lies
The fire of some great sacrifice,
Not yet half quenched.  The sacred steel
But lately struck my carnal will,                       35
My life-long hope, first joy and last,
What I loved well, and clung to fast;
What I wished wildly to retain,
What I renounced with soul-felt pain;
What--when I saw it, axe-struck, perish--               40
Left me no joy on earth to cherish;
A man bereft--yet sternly now
I do confirm that Jephtha vow:
Shall I retract, or fear, or flee?
Did Christ, when rose the fatal tree                    45
Before him, on Mount Calvary?
'Twas a long fight, hard fought, but won,
And what I did was justly done.

Yet, Helen! from thy love I turned,
When my heart most for thy heart burned;                50
I dared thy tears, I dared thy scorn--
Easier the death-pang had been borne.
Helen! thou mightst not go with me,
I could not--dared not stay for thee!
I heard, afar, in bonds complain                        55
The savage from beyond the main;
And that wild sound rose o'er the cry
Wrung out by passion's agony;
And even when, with the bitterest tear
I ever shed, mine eyes were dim,                        60
Still, with the spirit's vision clear,
I saw Hell's empire, vast and grim,
Spread on each Indian river's shore,
Each realm of Asia covering o'er.
There, the weak, trampled by the strong,                65
Live but to suffer--hopeless die;
There pagan-priests, whose creed is Wrong,
Extortion, Lust, and Cruelty,
Crush our lost race--and brimming fill

The bitter cup of human ill;                                70
And I--who have the healing creed,
The faith benign of Mary's Son;
Shall I behold my brother's need
And, selfishly, to aid him shun?
I--who upon my mother's knees,                              75
In childhood, read Christ's written word,
Received his legacy of peace,
His holy rule of action heard;
I--in whose heart the sacred sense
Of Jesus' love was early felt;                             80
Of his pure full benevolence,
His pitying tenderness for guilt;
His shepherd-care for wandering sheep,
For all weak, sorrowing, trembling things,
His mercy vast, his passion deep                           85
Of anguish for man's sufferings;
I--schooled from childhood in such lore--
Dared I draw back or hesitate,
When called to heal the sickness sore
Of those far off and desolate?                             90
Dark, in the realm and shades of Death,
Nations and tribes and empires lie,
But even to them the light of Faith
Is breaking on their sombre sky:
And be it mine to bid them raise                           95
Their drooped heads to the kindling scene,
And know and hail the sunrise blaze
Which heralds Christ the Nazarene.
I know how Hell the veil will spread
Over their brows and filmy eyes,                          100
And earthward crush the lifted head
That would look up and seek the skies;
I know what war the fiend will wage
Against that soldier of the cross,
Who comes to dare his demon-rage,                         105
And work his kingdom shame and loss.
Yes, hard and terrible the toil
Of him who steps on foreign soil,
Resolved to plant the gospel vine,
Where tyrants rule and slaves repine;                     110
Eager to lift Religion's light
Where thickest shades of mental night
Screen the false god and fiendish rite;
Reckless that missionary blood,
Shed in wild wilderness and wood,                         115
Has left, upon the unblest air,
The man's deep moan--the martyr's prayer.
I know my lot--I only ask

293

Power to fulfil the glorious task;
Willing the spirit, may the flesh                                    120
Strength for the day receive afresh.
May burning sun or deadly wind
Prevail not o'er an earnest mind;
May torments strange or direst death
Nor trample truth, nor baffle faith.                                 125
Though such blood-drops should fall from me
As fell in old Gethsemane,
Welcome the anguish, so it gave
More strength to work--more skill to save.
And, oh! if brief must be my time,                                   130
If hostile hand or fatal clime
Cut short my course--still o'er my grave,
Lord, may thy harvest whitening wave.
So I the culture may begin,
Let others thrust the sickle in;                                     135
If but the seed will faster grow,
May my blood water what I sow!

What! have I ever trembling stood,
And feared to give to God that blood?
What! has the coward love of life                                    140
Made me shrink from the righteous strife?
Have human passions, human fears
Severed me from those Pioneers,
Whose task is to march first, and trace
Paths for the progress of our race?                                  145
It has been so; but grant me, Lord,
Now to stand steadfast by thy word!
Protected by salvation's helm,
Shielded by faith--with truth begirt,
To smile when trials seek to whelm                                   150
And stand 'mid testing fires unhurt!
Hurling hell's strongest bulwarks down,
Even when the last pang thrills my breast,
When Death bestows the Martyr's crown,
And calls me into Jesus' rest.                                       155
Then for my ultimate reward--
Then for the world-rejoicing word--
The voice from Father--Spirit--Son:
"Servant of God, well hast thou done!"

                                                        CURRER.

MS:  Unknown
First Publication:  Poems 1846

BUT two miles more, and then we rest!
Well, there is still an hour of day,
And long the brightness of the West
Will light us on our devious way;
Sit then, awhile, here in this wood--            5
So total is the solitude,
     We safely may delay.

These massive roots afford a seat,
Which seems for weary travellers made.
There rest.  The air is soft and sweet        10
In this sequestered forest glade,
And there are scents of flowers around,
The evening dew draws from the ground;
     How soothingly they spread!

Yes; I was tired, but not at heart;             15
No--that beats full of sweet content,
For now I have my natural part
Of action with adventure blent;
Cast forth on the wide world with thee,
And all my once waste energy                   20
     To weighty purpose bent.

Yet--say'st thou, spies around us roam,
Our aims are termed conspiracy?
Haply, no more our English home
An anchorage for us may be?                    25
That there is risk our mutual blood
May redden in some lonely wood
     The knife of treachery?

Say'st thou--that where we lodge each night,
In each lone farm, or lonelier hall            30
Of Norman Peer--ere morning light
Suspicion must as duly fall,
As day returns--such vigilance
Presides and watches over France,
     Such rigour governs all?                  35

I fear not, William; dost thou fear?
So that the knife does not divide,
It may be ever hovering near:
I could not tremble at thy side,
And strenuous love--like mine for thee--       40
Is buckler strong, 'gainst treachery,
     And turns its stab aside.

I am resolved that thou shalt learn
To trust my strength as I trust thine;
I am resolved our souls shall burn,
With equal, steady, mingling shine;
Part of the field is conquered now,
Our lives in the same channel flow,
    Along the self-same line;

And while no groaning storm is heard,
Thou seem'st content it should be so,
But soon as comes a warning word
Of danger--straight thine anxious brow
Bends over me a mournful shade,
As doubting if my powers are made
    To ford the floods of woe.

Know, then it is my spirit swells,
And drinks, with eager joy, the air
Of freedom--where at last it dwells,
Chartered, a common task to share
With thee, and then it stirs alert,
And pants to learn what menaced hurt
    Demands for thee its care.

Remember, I have crossed the deep,
And stood with thee on deck, to gaze
On waves that rose in threatening heap,
While stagnant lay a heavy haze,
Dimly confusing sea with sky,
And baffling, even, the pilot's eye,
    Intent to thread the maze--

Of rocks, on Bretagne's dangerous coast,
And find a way to steer our band
To the one point obscure, which lost,
Flung us, as victims, on the strand;--
All, elsewhere, gleamed the Gallic sword,
And not a wherry could be moored
    Along the guarded land.

I feared not then--I fear not now;
The interest of each stirring scene
Wakes a new sense, a welcome glow,
In every nerve and bounding vein;
Alike on turbid Channel sea,
Or in still wood of Normandy,
    I feel as born again.

45

50

55

60

65

70

75

80

The rain descended that wild morn                    85
When, anchoring in the cove at last,
Our band, all weary and forlorn,
Ashore, like wave-worn sailors, cast--
Sought for a sheltering roof in vain,
And scarce could scanty food obtain                  90
    To break their morning fast.

Thou didst thy crust with me divide,
Thou didst thy cloak around me fold;
And, sitting silent by thy side,
I ate the bread in peace untold:                     95
Given kindly from thy hand, 'twas sweet
As costly fare or princely treat
    On royal plate of gold.

Sharp blew the sleet upon my face,
And, rising wild, the gusty wind                    100
Drove on those thundering waves apace,
Our crew so late had left behind;
But, spite of frozen shower and storm,
So close to thee, my heart beat warm,
    And tranquil slept my mind.                     105

So now--nor foot-sore nor opprest
With walking all this August day,
I taste a heaven in this brief rest,
This gipsy-halt beside the way.
England's wild flowers are fair to view,            110
Like balm is England's summer dew,
    Like gold her sunset ray.

But the white violets, growing here,
Are sweeter than I yet have seen,
And ne'er did dew so pure and clear                 115
Distil on forest mosses green,
As now, called forth by summer heat,
Perfumes our cool and fresh retreat--
    These fragrant limes between.

That sunset! Look beneath the boughs,               120
Over the copse--beyond the hills;
How soft, yet deep and warm it glows,
And heaven with rich suffusion fills;
With hues where still the opal's tint,
Its gleam of prisoned fire is blent,                125
    Where flame through azure thrills!

Depart we now--for fast will fade
That solemn splendour of decline,
And deep must be the after-shade
As stars alone to-night will shine;                    130
No moon is destined--pale--to gaze
On such a day's vast Phoenix blaze,
    A day in fires decayed!

There--hand-in-hand we tread again
The mazes of this varying wood,                        135
And soon, amid a cultured plain,
Girt in with fertile solitude,
We shall our resting-place descry,
Marked by one roof-tree, towering high
    Above a farm-stead rude.                           140

Refreshed, erelong, with rustic fare,
We'll seek a couch of dreamless ease;
Courage will guard thy heart from fear,
And Love give mine divinest peace:
To-morrow brings more dangerous toil,                  145
And through its conflict and turmoil
    We'll pass, as God shall please.

                                        CURRER.

(The preceding composition refers, doubtless, to the scenes acted in
France during the last year of the Consulate.)

MS:  Unknown
First Publication:  Poems 1846


**189    PILATE'S WIFE'S DREAM.**

        I'VE quenched my lamp, I struck it in that start
        Which every limb convulsed, I heard it fall--
        The crash blent with my sleep, I saw depart
        Its light, even as I woke, on yonder wall;
        Over against my bed, there shone a gleam            5
        Strange, faint, and mingling also with my dream.

                        298

It sunk, and I am wrapt in utter gloom;
How far is night advanced, and when will day
Retinge the dusk and livid air with bloom,
And fill this void with warm, creative ray?                    10
Would I could sleep again till, clear and red,
Morning shall on the mountain-tops be spread!

I'd call my women, but to break their sleep,
Because my own is broken, were unjust;
They've wrought all day, and well-earned slumbers steep        15
Their labours in forgetfulness, I trust;
Let me my feverish watch with patience bear,
Thankful that none with me its sufferings share.

Yet, Oh, for light! one ray would tranquilise
My nerves, my pulses, more than effort can;                    20
I'll draw my curtain and consult the skies:
These trembling stars at dead of night look wan,
Wild, restless, strange, yet cannot be more drear
Than this my couch, shared by a nameless fear.

All black--one great cloud, drawn from east to west,           25
Conceals the heavens, but there are lights below;
Torches burn in Jerusalem, and cast
On yonder stony mount a lurid glow.
I see men stationed there, and gleaming spears;
A sound, too, from afar, invades my ears.                      30

Dull, measured, strokes of axe and hammer ring
From street to street, not loud, but through the night
Distinctly heard--and some strange spectral thing
Is now upreared--and, fixed against the light
Of the pale lamps; defined upon that sky,                      35
It stands up like a column, straight and high.

I see it all--I know the dusky sign--
A cross on Calvary, which Jews uprear
While Romans watch; and when the dawn shall shine
Pilate, to judge the victim will appear,                       40
Pass sentence--yield him up to crucify;
And on that cross the spotless Christ must die.

Dreams, then, are true--for thus my vision ran;
Surely some oracle has been with me,
The gods have chosen me to reveal their plan,                  45
To warn an unjust judge of destiny:
I, slumbering, heard and saw; awake I know,
Christ's coming death, and Pilate's life of woe.

I do not weep for Pilate--who could prove
Regret for him whose cold and crushing sway
No prayer can soften, no appeal can move;
Who tramples hearts as others trample clay,
Yet with a faltering, an uncertain tread,
That might stir up reprisal in the dead.

Forced to sit by his side and see his deeds;
Forced to behold that visage, hour by hour,
In whose gaunt lines, the abhorrent gazer reads
A triple lust of gold, and blood, and power;
A soul whom motives, fierce, yet abject, urge
Rome's servile slave, and Judah's tyrant scourge.

How can I love, or mourn, or pity him?
I, who so long my fettered hands have wrung;
I, who for grief have wept my eye-sight dim;
Because, while life for me was bright and young,
He robbed my youth--he quenched my life's fair ray--
He crushed my mind, and did my freedom slay.

And at this hour--although I be his wife--
He has no more of tenderness from me
Than any other wretch of guilty life;
Less, for I know his household privacy--
I see him as he is--without a screen;
And, by the gods, my soul abhors his mien!

Has he not sought my presence, dyed in blood--
Innocent, righteous blood, shed shamelessly?
And have I not his red salute withstood?
Aye,--when, as erst, he plunged all Galilee
In dark bereavement--in affliction sore,
Mingling their very offerings with their gore.

Then came he--in his eyes a serpent-smile
Upon his lips some false, endearing word,
And, through the streets of Salem, clanged the while,
His slaughtering, hacking, sacrilegious sword--
And I, to see a man cause men such woe,
Trembled with ire--I did not fear to show.

And now, the envious Jewish priests have brought
Jesus--whom they in mockery call their king--
To have, by this grim power, their vengeance wrought;
By this mean reptile, innocence to sting.
Oh! could I but the purposed doom avert,
And shield the blameless head from cruel hurt!

50

55

60

65

70

75

80

85

90

300

Accessible is Pilate's heart to fear,
Omens will shake his soul, like autumn leaf;
Could he this night's appalling vision hear,
This just man's bonds were loosed, his life were safe,
Unless that bitter priesthood should prevail,                    95
And make even terror to their malice quail.

Yet if I tell the dream--but let me pause.
What dream? Erewhile the characters were clear,
Graved on my brain--at once some unknown cause
Has dimmed and rased the thoughts, which now appear,            100
Like a vague remnant of some by-past scene;--
Not what will be, but what, long since, has been.

I suffered many things, I heard foretold
A dreadful doom for Pilate,--lingering woes,
In far, barbarian climes, where mountains cold                  105
Built up a solitude of trackless snows,
There, he and grisly wolves prowled side by side,
There he lived famished--there methought he died;

But not of hunger, nor by malady;
I saw the snow around him, stained with gore;                   110
I said I had no tears for such as he,
And, lo! my cheek is wet--mine eyes run o'er;
I weep for mortal suffering, mortal guilt,
I weep the impious deed--the blood self-spilt.

More I recall not, yet the vision spread                        115
Into a world remote, an age to come--
And still the illumined name of Jesus shed
A light, a clearness, through the unfolding gloom--
And still I saw that sign, which now I see,
That cross on yonder brow of Calvary.                           120

What is this Hebrew Christ? To me unknown,
His lineage--doctrine--mission--yet how clear,
Is God-like goodness, in his actions shewn!
How straight and stainless is his life's career!
The ray of Deity that rests on him,                             125
In my eyes makes Olympian glory dim.

The world advances, Greek, or Roman rite
Suffices not the inquiring mind to stay;
The searching soul demands a purer light
To guide it on its upward, onward way;                          130
Ashamed of sculptured gods--Religion turns
To where the unseen Jehovah's altar burns.

301

Our faith is rotten--all our rites defiled,
Our temples sullied, and methinks, this man,
With his new ordinance, so wise and mild,                   135
Is come, even as he says, the chaff to fan
And sever from the wheat; but will his faith
Survive the terrors of to-morrow's death?

   *    *    *    *    *    *    *

I feel a firmer trust--a higher hope
Rise in my soul--it dawns with dawning day;                 140
Lo! on the Temple's roof--on Moriah's slope
Appears at length that clear, and crimson ray,
Which I so wished for when shut in by night;
Oh, opening skies, I hail, I bless your light!

Part, clouds and shadows! glorious Sun appear!             145
Part, mental gloom! Come insight from on high!
Dusk dawn in heaven still strives with daylight clear,
The longing soul, doth still uncertain sigh.
Oh! to behold the truth--that sun divine,
How doth my bosom pant, my spirit pine!                    150

This day, time travails with a mighty birth,
This day, Truth stoops from heaven and visits earth,
Ere night descends, I shall more surely know
What guide to follow, in what path to go;
I wait in hope--I wait in solemn fear,                     155
The oracle of God--the sole--true God--to hear.

                                    CURRER.

MS:  D(1)
First Publication:  Poems 1846

**190**       **FRANCES.**

SHE will not sleep, for fear of dreams,
But, rising, quits her restless bed,
And walks where some beclouded beams
Of moonlight through the hall are shed.

Obedient to the goad of grief,                              5
Her steps, now fast, now lingering slow,
In varying motion seek relief
From the Eumenides of woe.

302

Wringing her hands, at intervals--
But long as mute as phantom dim--                          10
She glides along the dusky walls,
Under the black oak rafters, grim.

The close air of the grated tower
Stifles a heart that scarce can beat,
And, though so late and lone the hour,                     15
Forth pass her wandering, faltering feet;

And on the pavement, spread before
The long front of the mansion grey,
Her steps imprint the night-frost hoar,
Which pale on grass and granite lay.                       20

Not long she stayed where misty moon
And shimmering stars could on her look,
But through the garden arch-way, soon
Her strange and gloomy path she took.

Some firs, coeval with the tower,                          25
Their straight black boughs stretched o'er her head,
Unseen, beneath this sable bower,
Rustled her dress and rapid tread.

There was an alcove in that shade,
Screening a rustic-seat and stand;                         30
Weary she sat her down and laid
Her hot brow on her burning hand.

To solitude and to the night,
Some words she now, in murmurs, said;
And, trickling through her fingers white,                  35
Some tears of misery she shed.

"God help me, in my grievous need,
God help me, in my inward pain;
Which cannot ask for pity's meed,
Which has no license to complain;                          40

Which must be borne, yet who can bear,
Hours long, days long, a constant weight--
The yoke of absolute despair,
A suffering wholly desolate?

Who can for ever crush the heart,                          45
Restrain its throbbing, curb its life?
Dissemble truth with ceaseless art,
With outward calm, mask inward strife?"

303

She waited--as for some reply;
The still and cloudy night gave none;                    50
Erelong, with deep-drawn, trembling sigh,
Her heavy plaint again begun.

"Unloved--I love; unwept--I weep;
Grief I restrain--hope I repress:
Vain is this anguish--fixed and deep;                    55
Vainer, desires and dreams of bliss.

My love awakes no love again,
My tears collect, and fall unfelt;
My sorrow touches none with pain,
My humble hopes to nothing melt.                         60

For me the universe is dumb,
Stone-deaf, and blank, and wholly blind;
Life I must bound, existence sum
In the strait limits of one mind;

That mind my own. Oh! narrow cell;                       65
Dark--imageless--a living tomb!
There must I sleep, there wake and dwell
Content, with palsy, pain, and gloom."

Again she paused; a moan of pain,
A stifled sob, alone was heard;                          70
Long silence followed--then again,
Her voice the stagnant midnight stirred.

"Must it be so? Is this my fate?
Can I nor struggle, nor contend?
And am I doomed for years to wait,                       75
Watching death's lingering axe descend?

And when it falls, and when I die,
What follows? Vacant nothingness?
The blank of lost identity?
Erasure both of pain and bliss?                          80

I've heard of heaven--I would believe;
For if this earth indeed be all,
Who longest lives may deepest grieve,
Most blest, whom sorrows soonest call.

Oh! leaving disappointment here,                         85
Will man find hope on yonder coast?
Hope, which, on earth, shines never clear,
And oft in clouds is wholly lost.

Will he hope's source of light behold,
Fruition's spring, where doubts expire,
And drink, in waves of living gold,
Contentment, full, for long desire?

90

Will he find bliss, which here he dreamed?
Rest, which was weariness on earth?
Knowledge, which, if o'er life it beamed,
Served but to prove it void of worth?

95

Will he find love without lust's leaven,
Love fearless, tearless, perfect, pure,
To all with equal bounty given,
In all, unfeigned, unfailing, sure?

100

Will he, from penal sufferings free,
Released from shroud and wormy clod,
All calm and glorious, rise and see
Creation's Sire--Existence' God?

Then, glancing back on Time's brief woes,
Will he behold them, fading, fly;
Swept from Eternity's repose,
Like sullying cloud, from pure blue sky?

105

If so--endure, my weary frame;
And when thy anguish strikes too deep,
And when all troubled burns life's flame,
Think of the quiet, final sleep;

110

Think of the glorious waking-hour,
Which will not dawn on grief and tears,
But on a ransomed spirit's power,
Certain, and free from mortal fears.

115

Seek now thy couch, and lie till morn,
Then from thy chamber, calm, descend,
With mind nor tossed, nor anguish-torn,
But tranquil, fixed, to wait the end.

120

And when thy opening eyes shall see
Mementos, on the chamber wall,
Of one who has forgotten thee,
Shed not the tear of acrid gall.

The tear which, welling from the heart,
Burns where its drop corrosive falls,
And makes each nerve, in torture, start,
At feelings it too well recalls:

125

305

When the sweet hope of being loved,
Threw Eden sunshine on life's way;                    130
When every sense and feeling proved
Expectancy of brightest day.

When the hand trembled to receive
A thrilling clasp, which seemed so near,
And the heart ventured to believe,                    135
Another heart esteemed it dear.

When words, half love, all tenderness,
Were hourly heard, as hourly spoken,
When the long, sunny days of bliss,
Only by moonlight nights were broken.                 140

Till drop by drop, the cup of joy
Filled full, with purple light, was glowing,
And Faith, which watched it, sparkling high,
Still never dreamt the overflowing.

It fell not with a sudden crashing,                   145
It poured not out like open sluice;
No, sparkling still, and redly flashing,
Drained, drop by drop, the generous juice.

I saw it sink, and strove to taste it,
My eager lips approached the brim;                    150
The movement only seemed to waste it,
It sank to dregs, all harsh and dim.

These I have drunk, and they for ever
Have poisoned life and love for me;
A draught from Sodom's lake could never              155
More fiery, salt, and bitter, be.

Oh! Love was all a thin illusion;
Joy, but the desert's flying stream;
And, glancing back on long delusion,
My memory grasps a hollow dream.                     160

Yet, whence that wondrous change of feeling,
I never knew, and cannot learn,
Nor why my lover's eye, congealing,
Grew cold, and clouded, proud, and stern.

Nor wherefore, friendship's forms forgetting,        165
He careless left, and cool withdrew;
Nor spoke of grief, nor fond regretting,
Nor even one glance of comfort threw.

And neither word nor token sending,
Of kindness, since the parting day,                    170
His course, for distant regions bending,
Went, self-contained and calm, away.

Oh, bitter, blighting, keen sensation,
Which will not weaken, cannot die,
Hasten thy work of desolation,                         175
And let my tortured spirit fly!

Vain as the passing gale, my crying;
Though lightning-struck, I must live on;
I know, at heart, there is no dying
Of love, and ruined hope, alone.                       180

Still strong, and young, and warm with vigour,
Though scathed, I long shall greenly grow,
And many a storm of wildest rigour
Shall yet break o'er my shivered bough.

Rebellious now to blank inertion,                      185
My unused strength demands a task;
Travel, and toil, and full exertion,
Are the last, only boon I ask.

Whence, then, this vain and barren dreaming
Of death, and dubious life to come?                    190
I see a nearer beacon gleaming
Over dejection's sea of gloom.

The very wildness of my sorrow
Tells me I yet have innate force;
My track of life has been too narrow,                  195
Effort shall trace a broader course.

The world is not in yonder tower,
Earth is not prisoned in that room,
'Mid whose dark pannels, hour by hour,
I've sat, the slave and prey of gloom.                 200

One feeling--turned to utter anguish,
Is not my being's only aim;
When, lorn and loveless, life will languish,
But courage can revive the flame.

He, when he left me, went a roving                     205
To sunny climes, beyond the sea;
And I, the weight of woe removing,
Am free and fetterless as he.

307

New scenes, new language, skies less clouded,
May once more wake the wish to live;                    210
Strange, foreign towns, astir, and crowded,
New pictures to the mind may give.

New forms and faces, passing ever,
May hide the one I still retain,
Defined, and fixed, and fading never,                   215
Stamped deep on vision, heart, and brain.

And we might meet--time may have changed him;
Chance may reveal the mystery,
The secret influence which estranged him;
Love may restore him yet to me.                         220

False thought--false hope--in scorn be banished!
I am not loved--nor loved have been;
Recall not, then, the dreams scarce vanished,
Traitors! mislead me not again!

To words like yours I bid defiance,                     225
'Tis such my mental wreck have made;
Of God alone, and self-reliance,
I ask for solace--hope for aid.

Morn comes--and ere meridian glory
O'er these, my natal woods, shall smile,                230
Both lonely wood and mansion hoary
I'll leave behind, full many a mile.

                                        CURRER.

MS:  D(1)
First Publication:  Poems 1846
Text:  Line 153 - errata sheet changes "drank" to "drunk"

**191**          **THE TEACHER'S MONOLOGUE.**

THE room is quiet, thoughts alone
People its mute tranquillity;
The yoke put off, the long task done,--
I am, as it is bliss to be,
Still and untroubled.  Now, I see,                      5
For the first time, how soft the day
O'er waveless water, stirless tree,

Silent and sunny, wings its way.
Now, as I watch that distant hill,
So faint, so blue, so far removed,                    10
Sweet dreams of home my heart may fill,
That home where I am known and loved:
It lies beyond; yon azure brow
Parts me from all Earth holds for me;
And, morn and eve, my yearnings flow                  15
Thitherward tending, changelessly.
My happiest hours, aye! all the time,
I love to keep in memory,
Lapsed among moors, ere life's first prime
Decayed to dark anxiety.                              20

Sometimes, I think a narrow heart
Makes me thus mourn those far away,
And keeps my love so far apart
From friends and friendships of to-day;
Sometimes, I think 'tis but a dream                   25
I treasure up so jealously,
All the sweet thoughts I live on seem
To vanish into vacancy:
And then, this strange, coarse world around
Seems all that's palpable and true;                   30
And every sight, and every sound,
Combines my spirit to subdue
To aching grief, so void and lone
Is Life and Earth--so worse than vain,
The hopes that, in my own heart sown,                 35
And cherished by such sun and rain
As Joy and transient Sorrow shed,
Have ripened to a harvest there:
Alas! methinks I hear it said,
"Thy golden sheaves are empty air."                   40

All fades away; my very home
I think will soon be desolate;
I hear, at times, a warning come
Of bitter partings at its gate;
And, if I should return and see                       45
The hearth-fire quenched, the vacant chair;
And hear it whispered mournfully,
That farewells have been spoken there,
What shall I do, and whither turn?
Where look for peace? When cease to mourn?            50

———————

309

'Tis not the air I wished to play,
    The strain I wished to sing;
My wilful spirit slipped away
    And struck another string.
I neither wanted smile nor tear,                    55
    Bright joy nor bitter woe,
But just a song that sweet and clear,
    Though haply sad, might flow.

A quiet song, to solace me
    When sleep refused to come;                     60
A strain to chase despondency,
    When sorrowful for home.
In vain I try; I cannot sing;
    All feels so cold and dead;
No wild distress, no gushing spring                 65
    Of tears in anguish shed;

But all the impatient gloom of one
    Who waits a distant day,
When, some great task of suffering done,
    Repose shall toil repay.                        70
For youth departs, and pleasure flies,
    And life consumes away,
And youth's rejoicing ardour dies
    Beneath this drear delay;

And Patience, weary with her yoke,                  75
    Is yielding to despair,
And Health's elastic spring is broke
    Beneath the strain of care.
Life will be gone ere I have lived;
    Where now is Life's first prime?                80
I've worked and studied, longed and grieved,
    Through all that rosy time.

To toil, to think, to long, to grieve,--
    Is such my future fate?
The morn was dreary, must the eve                   85
    Be also desolate?
Well, such a life at least makes Death
    A welcome, wished-for friend;
Then, aid me, Reason, Patience, Faith,
    To suffer to the end!                           90

                                        CURRER.

MS:  D(1)
First Publication:  Poems 1846

                    310

THIS last denial of my faith,
   Thou, solemn Priest, hast heard;
And, though upon my bed of death,
   I call not back a word.
Point not to thy Madonna, Priest,--          5
   Thy sightless saint of stone;
She cannot, from this burning breast,
   Wring one repentant moan.

Thou say'st, that when a sinless child,
   I duly bent the knee,          10
And prayed to what in marble smiled
   Cold, lifeless, mute, on me.
I did. But listen! Children spring
   Full soon to riper youth;
And, for Love's vow and Wedlock's ring,      15
   I sold my early truth.

'Twas not a grey, bare head, like thine,
   Bent o'er me, when I said,
"That land and God and Faith are mine,
   For which thy fathers bled."      20
I see thee not, my eyes are dim;
   But, well I hear thee say,
"O daughter, cease to think of him
   Who led thy soul astray.

Between you lies both space and time;      25
   Let leagues and years prevail
To turn thee from the path of crime,
   Back to the Church's pale."
And, did I need that thou shouldst tell
   What mighty barriers rise      30
To part me from that dungeon-cell,
   Where my loved Walter lies?

And, did I need that thou shouldst taunt
   My dying hour at last,
By bidding this worn spirit pant      35
   No more for what is past?
Priest--must I cease to think of him?
   How hollow rings that word!
Can time, can tears, can distance dim
   The memory of my lord?      40

311

I said before, I saw not thee,
    Because, an hour agone,
Over my eye-balls, heavily,
    The lids fell down like stone.
But still my spirit's inward sight                           45
    Beholds his image beam
As fixed, as clear, as burning bright,
    As some red planet's gleam.

Talk not of thy Last Sacrament,
    Tell not thy beads for me;                               50
Both rite and prayer are vainly spent,
    As dews upon the sea.
Speak not one word of Heaven above,
    Rave not of Hell's alarms;
Give me but back my Walter's love,                          55
    Restore me to his arms!

Then will the bliss of Heaven be won;
    Then will Hell shrink away,
As I have seen night's terrors shun
    The conquering steps of day.                            60
'Tis my religion thus to love,
    My creed thus fixed to be;
Not Death shall shake, nor Priestcraft break
    My rock-like constancy!

Now go; for at the door there waits                         65
    Another stranger guest:
He calls--I come--my pulse scarce beats,
    My heart fails in my breast.
Again that voice--how far away,
    How dreary sounds that tone!                            70
And I, methinks, am gone astray
    In trackless wastes and lone.

I fain would rest a little while:
    Where can I find a stay,
Till dawn upon the hills shall smile,                       75
    And show some trodden way?
"I come! I come!" in haste she said,
    "'Twas Walter's voice I heard!"
Then up she sprang--but fell back, dead,
    His name her latest word.                               80

                                        CURRER.

MS:  D(1) & F(1)
First Publication:  Poems 1846

IF thou be in a lonely place,
    If one hour's calm be thine,
As Evening bends her placid face
    O'er this sweet day's decline;
If all the earth and all the heaven                5
    Now look serene to thee,
As o'er them shuts the summer even,
    One moment--think of me!

Pause, in the lane, returning home;
    'Tis dusk, it will be still:                   10
Pause near the elm, a sacred gloom
    Its breezeless boughs will fill.
Look at that soft and golden light,
    High in the unclouded sky;
Watch the last bird's belated flight,             15
    As it flits silent by.

Hark! for a sound upon the wind,
    A step, a voice, a sigh;
If all be still, then yield thy mind,
    Unchecked, to memory.                          20
If thy love were like mine, how blest
    That twilight hour would seem,
When, back from the regretted Past,
    Returned our early dream!

If thy love were like mine, how wild              25
    Thy longings, even to pain,
For sunset soft, and moonlight mild,
    To bring that hour again!
But oft, when in thine arms I lay,
    I've seen thy dark eyes shine,                 30
And deeply felt, their changeful ray
    Spoke other love than mine.

My love is almost anguish now,
    It beats so strong and true;
'Twere rapture, could I deem that thou            35
    Such anguish ever knew.
I have been but thy transient flower,
    Thou wert my god divine;
Till, checked by death's congealing power,
    This heart must throb for thine.              40

And well my dying hour were blest,
    If life's expiring breath
Should pass, as thy lips gently prest
    My forehead, cold in death;
And sound my sleep would be, and sweet,          45
    Beneath the churchyard tree,
If sometimes in thy heart should beat
    One pulse, still true to me.

                                    CURRER.

MS:   D(1) & F(1)
First Publication:   Poems 1846


**194**          **THE LETTER.**

WHAT is she writing? Watch her now,
    How fast her fingers move!
How eagerly her youthful brow
    Is bent in thought above!
Her long curls, drooping, shade the light,        5
    She puts them quick aside,
Nor knows, that band of crystals bright,
    Her hasty touch untied.
It slips adown her silken dress,
    Falls glittering at her feet;                  10
Unmarked it falls, for she no less
    Pursues her labour sweet.

The very loveliest hour that shines,
    Is in that deep blue sky;
The golden sun of June declines,                  15
    It has not caught her eye.
The cheerful lawn, and unclosed gate,
    The white road, far away,
In vain for her light footsteps wait,
    She comes not forth to-day.                    20
There is an open door of glass
    Close by that lady's chair,
From thence, to slopes of mossy grass,
    Descends a marble stair.

Tall plants of bright and spicy bloom                    25
    Around the threshold grow;
Their leaves and blossoms shade the room,
    From that sun's deepening glow.
Why does she not a moment glance
    Between the clustering flowers,                      30
And mark in heaven the radiant dance
    Of evening's rosy hours?
O look again! Still fixed her eye,
    Unsmiling, earnest, still,
And fast her pen and fingers fly,                        35
    Urged by her eager will.

Her soul is in th' absorbing task;
    To whom, then, doth she write?
Nay, watch her still more closely, ask
    Her own eyes' serious light;                         40
Where do they turn, as now her pen
    Hangs o'er th' unfinished line?
Whence fell the tearful gleam that then
    Did in their dark spheres shine?
The summer-parlour looks so dark,                        45
    When from that sky you turn,
And from th' expanse of that green park,
    You scarce may aught discern.

Yet o'er the piles of porcelain rare,
    O'er flower-stand, couch, and vase,                  50
Sloped, as if leaning on the air,
    One picture meets the gaze.
'Tis there she turns; you may not see
    Distinct, what form defines
The clouded mass of mystery                              55
    Yon broad gold frame confines.
But look again; inured to shade
    Your eyes now faintly trace
A stalwart form, a massive head,
    A firm, determined face.                             60

Black Spanish locks, a sunburnt cheek,
    A brow high, broad, and white,
Where every furrow seems to speak
    Of mind and moral might.
Is that her god? I cannot tell;                          65
    Her eye a moment met
Th' impending picture, then it fell
    Darkened and dimmed and wet.
A moment more, her task is done,
    And sealed the letter lies;                          70
And now, towards the setting sun
    She turns her tearful eyes.

315

Those tears flow over, wonder not,
    For by the inscription, see
In what a strange and distant spot                      75
    Her heart of hearts must be!
Three seas and many a league of land
    That letter must pass o'er,
E'er read by him to whose loved hand
    'Tis sent from England's shore.                      80
Remote colonial wilds detain
    Her husband, loved though stern;
She, 'mid that smiling English scene,
    Weeps for his wished return.

                                    CURRER.

MS:  D(1)
First Publication:   Poems 1846


**195**          **MEMENTOS.**


ARRANGING long-locked drawers and shelves
Of cabinets, shut up for years,
What a strange task we've set ourselves!
How still the lonely room appears!
How strange this mass of ancient treasures,            5
Mementos of past pains and pleasures;
These volumes, clasped with costly stone,
With print all faded, gilding gone;
These fans of leaves, from Indian trees--
These crimson shells, from Indian seas--               10
These tiny portraits, set in rings--
Once, doubtless, deemed such precious things;
Keepsakes bestowed by Love on Faith,
And worn till the receiver's death,
Now stored with cameos, china, shells,                 15
In this old closet's dusty cells.

I scarcely think, for ten long years,
A hand has touched these relics old;
And, coating each, slow-formed, appears,
The growth of green and antique mould.                 20

All in this house is mossing over;
All is unused, and dim, and damp;
Nor light, nor warmth, the rooms discover--
Bereft for years of fire and lamp.

The sun, sometimes in summer, enters                        25
The casements, with reviving ray;
But the long rains of many winters
Moulder the very walls away.

And outside all is ivy, clinging
To chimney, lattice, gable grey;                            30
Scarcely one little red rose springing
Through the green moss can force its way.

Unscared, the daw, and starling nestle,
Where the tall turret rises high,
And winds alone come near to rustle                         35
The thick leaves where their cradles lie.

I sometimes think, when late at even
I climb the stair reluctantly,
Some shape that should be well in heaven,
Or ill elsewhere, will pass by me.                          40

I fear to see the very faces,
Familiar thirty years ago,
Even in the old accustomed places
Which look so cold and gloomy now.

I've come, to close the window, hither,                     45
At twilight, when the sun was down,
And Fear, my very soul would wither,
Lest something should be dimly shown.

Too much the buried form resembling,
Of her who once was mistress here;                          50
Lest doubtful shade, or moonbeam trembling,
Might take her aspect, once so dear.

Hers was this chamber; in her time
It seemed to me a pleasant room,
For then no cloud of grief or crime                         55
Had cursed it with a settled gloom;

I had not seen death's image laid
In shroud and sheet, on yonder bed.
Before she married, she was blest--
Blest in her youth, blest in her worth;                     60
Her mind was calm, its sunny rest
Shone in her eyes more clear than mirth.

And when attired in rich array,
Light, lustrous hair about her brow,
She yonder sat--a kind of day                               65
Lit up--what seems so gloomy now.
These grim oak walls, even then were grim;
That old carved chair, was then antique;
But what around looked dusk and dim
Served as a foil to her fresh cheek;                        70
Her neck, and arms, of hue so fair,
Eyes of unclouded, smiling, light;
Her soft, and curled, and floating hair,
Gems and attire, as rainbow bright.

Reclined in yonder deep recess,                             75
Ofttimes she would, at evening, lie
Watching the sun; she seemed to bless
With happy glance the glorious sky.
She loved such scenes, and as she gazed,
Her face evinced her spirit's mood;                         80
Beauty or grandeur ever raised
In her, a deep-felt gratitude.

But of all lovely things, she loved
A cloudless moon, on summer night;
Full oft have I impatience proved                           85
To see how long, her still delight
Would find a theme in reverie.
Out on the lawn, or where the trees
Let in the lustre fitfully,
As their boughs parted momently,                            90
To the soft, languid, summer breeze.
Alas! that she should e'er have flung
Those pure, though lonely joys away--
Deceived by false and guileful tongue,
She gave her hand, then suffered wrong;                     95
Oppressed, ill-used, she faded young,
And died of grief by slow decay.

Open that casket--look how bright
Those jewels flash upon the sight;
The brilliants have not lost a ray                          100
Of lustre, since her wedding day.
But see--upon that pearly chain--
How dim lies time's discolouring stain!
I've seen that by her daughter worn:
For, e'er she died, a child was born;                       105
A child that ne'er its mother knew,
That lone, and almost friendless grew;
For, ever, when its step drew nigh,

Averted was the father's eye;
And then, a life impure and wild                    110
Made him a stranger to his child;
Absorbed in vice, he little cared
On what she did, or how she fared.
The love withheld, she never sought,
She grew uncherished--learnt untaught;              115
To her the inward life of thought
    Full soon was open laid.
I know not if her friendlessness
Did sometimes on her spirit press,
    But plaint she never made.                      120
The book-shelves were her darling treasure,
She rarely seemed the time to measure
    While she could read alone.
And she too loved the twilight wood,
And often, in her mother's mood,                    125
Away to yonder hill would hie,
Like her, to watch the setting sun,
Or see the stars born, one by one,
    Out of the darkening sky.
Nor would she leave that hill till night            130
Trembled from pole to pole with light;
Even then, upon her homeward way,
Long--long her wandering steps delayed
To quit the sombre forest shade,
Through which her eerie pathway lay.                135
You ask if she had beauty's grace?
I know not--but a nobler face
    My eyes have seldom seen;
A keen and fine intelligence,
And, better still, the truest sense                 140
    Were in her speaking mien.
But bloom or lustre was there none,
Only at moments, fitful shone
    An ardour in her eye,
That kindled on her cheek a flush,                  145
Warm as a red sky's passing blush
    And quick with energy.
Her speech, too, was not common speech,
No wish to shine, or aim to teach,
    Was in her words displayed:                     150
She still began with quiet sense,
But oft the force of eloquence
    Came to her lips in aid;
Language and voice unconscious changed,
And thoughts, in other words arranged,             155
    Her fervid soul transfused
Into the hearts of those who heard,

And transient strength and ardour stirred,
    In minds to strength unused.
Yet in gay crowd or festal glare,
Grave and retiring was her air;
'Twas seldom, save with me alone,
That fire of feeling freely shone;
She loved not awe's nor wonder's gaze,
Nor even exaggerated praise,
Nor even notice, if too keen
The curious gazer searched her mien.
Nature's own green expanse revealed
The world, the pleasures, she could prize;
On free hill-side, in sunny field,
In quiet spots by woods concealed,
Grew wild and fresh her chosen joys,
Yet Nature's feelings deeply lay
In that endowed and youthful frame;
Shrined in her heart and hid from day,
They burned unseen with silent flame;
In youth's first search for mental light,
She lived but to reflect and learn,
But soon her mind's maturer might
For stronger task did pant and yearn;
And stronger task did fate assign,
Task that a giant's strength might strain;
To suffer long and ne'er repine,
Be calm in frenzy, smile at pain.

Pale with the secret war of feeling,
Sustained with courage, mute, yet high;
The wounds at which she bled, revealing
Only by altered cheek and eye;

She bore in silence--but when passion
Surged in her soul with ceaseless foam,
The storm at last brought desolation,
And drove her exiled from her home.

And silent still, she straight assembled
The wrecks of strength her soul retained;
For though the wasted body trembled,
The unconquered mind, to quail, disdained.

She crossed the sea--now lone she wanders
By Seine's, or Rhine's, or Arno's flow;
Fain would I know if distance renders
Relief or comfort to her woe.

160

165

170

175

180

185

190

195

200

Fain would I know if, henceforth, ever,
These eyes shall read in hers again,
That light of love which faded never,
Though dimmed so long with secret pain.

She will return, but cold and altered,                              205
Like all whose hopes too soon depart;
Like all on whom have beat, unsheltered,
The bitter blasts that blight the heart.

No more shall I behold her lying
Calm on a pillow, smoothed by me;                                   210
No more that spirit, worn with sighing,
Will know the rest of infancy.

If still the paths of lore she follow,
'Twill be with tired and goaded will;
She'll only toil, the aching hollow,                                215
The joyless blank of life to fill.

And oh! full oft, quite spent and weary,
Her hand will pause, her head decline;
That labour seems so hard and dreary,
On which no ray of hope may shine.                                  220

Thus the pale blight of time and sorrow
Will shade with grey her soft, dark hair;
Then comes the day that knows no morrow,
And death succeeds to long despair.

So speaks experience, sage and hoary;                               225
I see it plainly, know it well,
Like one who, having read a story,
Each incident therein can tell.

Touch not that ring, 'twas his, the sire
    Of that forsaken child;                                         230
And nought his relics can inspire
    Save memories, sin-defiled.

I, who sat by his wife's death-bed,
    I, who his daughter loved,
Could almost curse the guilty dead,                                 235
    For woes, the guiltless proved.

And heaven did curse--they found him laid,
    When crime for wrath was rife,
Cold--with the suicidal blade
    Clutched in his desperate gripe.                                240

321

'Twas near that long deserted hut,
    Which in the wood decays,
Death's axe, self-wielded, struck his root,
    And lopped his desperate days.

You know the spot, where three black trees,          245
    Lift up their branches fell,
And moaning, ceaseless as the seas,
Still seem, in every passing breeze,
    The deed of blood to tell.

They named him mad, and laid his bones               250
    Where holier ashes lie;
Yet doubt not that his spirit groans,
    In hell's eternity.

But, lo! night, closing o'er the earth,
    Infects our thoughts with gloom;                 255
Come, let us strive to rally mirth,
Where glows a clear and tranquil hearth
    In some more cheerful room.

                                        CURRER.

MS:  D(1)
First Publication:  Poems 1846


**196**          **PRESENTIMENT.**


"SISTER, you've sat there all the day,
    Come to the hearth awhile;
The wind so wildly sweeps away,
    The clouds so darkly pile.
That open book has lain, unread,                     5
    For hours upon your knee;
You've never smiled nor turned you head;
    What can you, sister, see?"

"Come hither, Jane, look down the field;
    How dense a mist creeps on!                      10
The path, the hedge, are both concealed,
    Ev'n the white gate is gone;
No landscape through the fog I trace,
    No hill with pastures green;
All featureless is nature's face,                    15
    All masked in clouds her mien.

                    322

"Scarce is the rustle of a leaf
    Heard in our garden now;
The year grows old, its days wax brief,
    The tresses leave its brow.                          20
The rain drives fast before the wind,
    The sky is blank and grey;
O Jane, what sadness fills the mind
    On such a dreary day!"

"You think too much, my sister dear;                     25
    You sit too long alone;
What though November days be drear?
    Full soon will they be gone.
I've swept the hearth, and placed your chair,
    Come, Emma, sit by me;                               30
Our own fireside is never drear,
Though late and wintry wane the year,
    Though rough the night may be."

"The peaceful glow of our fireside
    Imparts no peace to me:                              35
My thoughts would rather wander wide
    Than rest, dear Jane, with thee.
I'm on a distant journey bound,
    And if, about my heart,
Too closely kindred ties were wound,                     40
    'T would break when forced to part.

"'Soon will November days be o'er:'
    Well have you spoken, Jane:
My own forebodings tell me more,
For me, I know by presage sure,                          45
    They'll ne'er return again.
Ere long, nor sun nor storm to me
    Will bring or joy or gloom;
They reach not that Eternity
    Which soon will be my home."                         50

Eight months are gone, the summer sun
    Sets in a glorious sky;
A quiet field, all green and lone,
    Receives its rosy dye.
Jane sits upon a shaded stile,                           55
    Alone she sits there now;
Her head rests on her hand the while,
    And thought o'ercasts her brow.

323

She's thinking of one winter's day,
   A few short months ago,               60
When Emma's bier was borne away
   O'er wastes of frozen snow.
She's thinking how that drifted snow
   Dissolved in spring's first gleam,
And how her sister's memory now           65
   Fades, even as fades a dream.

The snow will whiten earth again,
   But Emma comes no more;
She left, 'mid winter's sleet and rain,
   This world for Heaven's far shore.      70
On Beulah's hills she wanders now,
   On Eden's tranquil plain;
To her shall Jane hereafter go,
   She ne'er shall come to Jane!

                              CURRER.

MS:   D(1) & F(1)
First Publication:  Poems 1846
Text:  Line 40 - errata sheet changes "bound" to "wound"

**197**       **REGRET.**

LONG ago I wished to leave
"The house where I was born;"
Long ago I used to grieve,
My home seemed so forlorn.
In other years, its silent rooms         5
Were filled with haunting fears;
Now, their very memory comes
O'ercharged with tender tears.

Life and marriage I have known,
Things once deemed so bright;       10
Now, how utterly is flown
Every ray of light!
'Mid the unknown sea of life
I no blest isle have found;
At last, through all its wild wave's strife,   15
My bark is homeward bound.

Farewell, dark and rolling deep!
Farewell, foreign shore!
Open, in unclouded sweep,
Thou glorious realm before!                                    20
Yet, though I had safely pass'd
That weary, vexed main,
One loved voice, through surge and blast,
Could call me back again.

Though the soul's bright morning rose                          25
O'er Paradise for me,
William! even from Heaven's repose
I'd turn, invoked by thee!
Storm nor surge should e'er arrest
My soul, exulting then:                                        30
All my heaven was once thy breast,
Would it were mine again!

                                        CURRER.

MS:  D(1) & F(1)
First Publication:  Poems 1846


**198**          **THE WIFE'S WILL.**

SIT still--a word--a breath may break
(As light airs stir a sleeping lake,)
The glassy calm that soothes my woes,
The sweet, the deep, the full repose.
O leave me not! for ever be                                     5
Thus, more than life itself to me!

Yes, close beside thee, let me kneel--
Give me thy hand that I may feel
The friend so true--so tried--so dear,
My heart's own chosen--indeed is near;                         10
And check me not--this hour divine
Belongs to me--is fully mine.

'Tis thy own hearth thou sitt'st beside,
After long absence--wandering wide;
'Tis thy own wife reads in thine eyes,                         15
A promise clear of stormless skies,
For faith and true love light the rays,
Which shine responsive to her gaze.


                         325

Aye,--well that single tear may fall;
Ten thousand might mine eyes recall,                          20
Which from their lids, ran blinding fast,
In hours of grief, yet scarcely past,
Well may'st thou speak of love to me;
For, oh! most truly--I love thee!

Yet smile--for we are happy now.                             25
Whence, then, that sadness on thy brow?
What say'st thou? "We must once again,
Ere long, be severed by the main?"
I knew not this--I deemed no more,
Thy step would err from Britain's shore.                     30

"Duty commands?" 'Tis true--'tis just;
Thy slightest word I wholly trust,
Nor by request, nor faintest sigh
Would I, to turn thy purpose, try;
But, William--hear my solemn vow--                           35
Hear and confirm!--with thee I go.

"Distance and suffering," did'st thou say?
"Danger by night, and toil by day?"
Oh, idle words, and vain are these;
Hear me! I cross with thee the seas.                         40
Such risk as thou must meet and dare,
I--thy true wife--will duly share.

Passive, at home, I will not pine;
Thy toils--thy perils, shall be mine;
Grant this--and be hereafter paid                            45
By a warm heart's devoted aid:
'Tis granted--with that yielding kiss,
Entered my soul unmingled bliss.

Thanks, William--thanks! thy love has joy,
Pure--undefiled with base alloy;                             50
'Tis not a passion, false and blind,
Inspires, enchains, absorbs my mind;
Worthy, I feel, art thou to be
Loved with my perfect energy.

This evening, now, shall sweetly flow,                       55
Lit by our clear fire's happy glow;
And parting's peace-embittering fear,
Is warned, our hearts to come not near;
For fate admits my soul's decree,
In bliss or bale--to go with thee!                           60

                                        CURRER.

                        326

MS:   D(1)
First Publication:   Poems 1846

**199**          **WINTER STORES.**

WE take from life one little share,
  And say that this shall be
A space, redeemed from toil and care,
  From tears and sadness free.

And, haply, Death unstrings his bow          5
  And Sorrow stands apart,
And, for a little while, we know
  The sunshine of the heart.

Existence seems a summer eve,
  Warm, soft, and full of peace;          10
Our free, unfettered feelings give
  The soul its full release.

A moment, then, it takes the power,
  To call up thoughts that throw
Around that charmed and hallowed hour,          15
  This life's divinest glow.

But Time, though viewlessly it flies,
  And slowly, will not stay;
Alike, through clear and clouded skies,
  It cleaves its silent way.          20

Alike the bitter cup of grief,
  Alike the draught of bliss,
Its progress leaves but moment brief
  For baffled lips to kiss.

The sparkling draught is dried away,          25
  The hour of rest is gone,
And urgent voices, round us, say,
  "Ho, lingerer, hasten on!"

And has the soul, then, only gained,
  From this brief time of ease,          30
A moment's rest, when overstrained,
  One hurried glimpse of peace?

327

No; while the sun shone kindly o'er us,
  And flowers bloomed round our feet,--                    35
While many a bud of joy before us
  Unclosed its petals sweet,--

An unseen work within was plying;
  Like honey-seeking bee,
From flower to flower, unwearied, flying,
  Laboured one faculty,--                                   40

Thoughtful for Winter's future sorrow,
  Its gloom and scarcity;
Prescient to-day, of want to-morrow,
  Toiled quiet Memory.

'Tis she that from each transient pleasure                 45
  Extracts a lasting good;
'Tis she that finds, in summer, treasure
  To serve for winter's food.

And when Youth's summer day is vanished,
  And Age brings Winter's stress,                           50
Her stores, with hoarded sweets replenished,
  Life's evening hours will bless.

                                        CURRER.

MS:  D(1) & F(1)
First Publication:  Poems 1846


**200**       **EVENING SOLACE.**

THE human heart has hidden treasures,
In secret kept, in silence sealed;--
The thoughts, the hopes, the dreams, the pleasures,
Whose charms were broken if revealed.
And days may pass in gay confusion,                        5
And nights in rosy riot fly,
While, lost in Fame's or Wealth's illusion,
The memory of the Past may die.

But, there are hours of lonely musing,
Such as in evening silence come,                                10
When, soft as birds their pinions closing,
The heart's best feelings gather home.
Then in our souls there seems to languish
A tender grief that is not woe;
And thoughts that once wrung groans of anguish,                 15
Now cause but some mild tears to flow.

And feelings, once as strong as passions,
Float softly back--a faded dream;
Our own sharp griefs and wild sensations,
The tale of others' sufferings seem.                           20
Oh! when the heart is freshly bleeding,
How longs it for that time to be,
When, through the mist of years receding,
Its woes but live in reverie!

And it can dwell on moonlight glimmer,                          25
On evening shade and loneliness;
And, while the sky grows dim and dimmer,
Feel no untold and strange distress--
Only a deeper impulse given
By lonely hour and darkened room,                               30
To solemn thoughts that soar to heaven,
Seeking a life and world to come.

                                        CURRER.

MS:  F(1)
First Publication:  Poems 1846


**201**          **PARTING.**

          THERE'S no use in weeping,
          Though we are condemned to part:
          There's such a thing as keeping
          A remembrance in one's heart:

          There's such a thing as dwelling                      5
          On the thought ourselves have nurs'd,
          And with scorn and courage telling
          The world to do its worst.

329

We'll not let its follies grieve us,
We'll just take them as they come;                    10
And then every day will leave us
A merry laugh for home.

When we've left each friend and brother,
When we're parted wide and far,
We will think of one another,                         15
As even better than we are.

Every glorious sight above us,
Every pleasant sight beneath,
We'll connect with those that love us,
Whom we truly love till death!                        20

In the evening, when we're sitting
By the fire perchance alone,
Then shall heart with warm heart meeting,
Give responsive tone for tone.

We can burst the bonds which chain us,                25
Which cold human hands have wrought,
And where none shall dare restrain us
We can meet again, in thought.

So there's no use in weeping,
Bear a cheerful spirit still;                         30
Never doubt that Fate is keeping
Future good for present ill!

                                    CURRER.

MS:  D(1) & F(1)
First Publication:  Poems 1846


**202**        **LIFE.**


LIFE, believe, is not a dream
     So dark as sages say;
Oft a little morning rain
     Foretells a pleasant day.
Sometimes there are clouds of gloom,                  5
     But these are transient all;
If the shower will make the roses bloom,

O why lament its fall?
    Rapidly, merrily,
Life's sunny hours flit by,                          10
    Gratefully, cheerily,
Enjoy them as they fly!

What though Death at times steps in,
    And calls our Best away?
What though sorrow seems to win,                     15
    O'er hope, a heavy sway?
Yet hope again elastic springs,
    Unconquered, though she fell;
Still buoyant are her golden wings,
    Still strong to bear us well.                     20
        Manfully, fearlessly,
    The day of trial bear,
        For gloriously, victoriously,
    Can courage quell despair!

                                    CURRER.

M:  A; F(1)
First Publication:  Poems 1846


**203**          **PASSION.**


SOME have won a wild delight,
    By daring wilder sorrow;
Could I gain thy love to-night,
    I'd hazard death to-morrow.

Could the battle-struggle earn                       5
    One kind glance from thine eye,
How this withering heart would burn,
    The heady fight to try!

Welcome nights of broken sleep,
    And days of carnage cold,                         10
Could I deem that thou wouldst weep
    To hear my perils told.

Tell me, if with wandering bands
    I roam full far away,
Wilt thou, to those distant lands,                   15
    In spirit ever stray?

                    331

Wild, long, a trumpet sounds afar;
    Bid me--bid me go
Where Seik and Briton meet in war,
    On Indian Sutlej's flow.                      20

Blood has dyed the Sutlej's waves
    With scarlet stain, I know;
Indus' borders yawn with graves,
    Yet, command me go!

Though rank and high the holocaust          25
    Of nations, steams to heaven,
Glad I'd join the death-doomed host,
    Were but the mandate given.

Passion's strength should nerve my arm,
    Its ardour stir my life,                       30
Till human force to that dread charm
Should yield and sink in wild alarm,
    Like trees to tempest-strife.

If, hot from war, I seek thy love,
    Darest thou turn aside?                        35
Darest thou, then, my fire reprove,
    By scorn, and maddening pride?

No--my will shall yet control
    Thy will, so high and free,
And love shall tame that haughty soul--         40
    Yes--tenderest love for me.

I'll read my triumph in thine eyes,
    Behold, and prove the change;
Then leave, perchance, my noble prize,
    Once more in arms to range.                    45

I'd die when all the foam is up,
    The bright wine sparkling high;
Nor wait till in the exhausted cup
    Life's dull dregs only lie.

Then Love thus crowned with sweet reward,        50
    Hope blest with fulness large,
I'd mount the saddle, draw the sword,
    And perish in the charge!

                                CURRER.

MS:  F(1)
First Publication:  Poems 1846

204      **Haworth:**

**Christmas Day**
‾‾‾‾‾‾

This is Thy Natal Day, O Saviour dear,
    The Day of Joy--to Christians full of bliss:
When nearer comes, with each revolving year,
    The hour to spring to brighter worlds than this.

                                ‾‾‾‾‾   Charlotte Bronte
                                ‾‾‾‾‾     [1845]

MS:   R
Not previously published


205          I gave, at first, Attention close;
                Then interest warm ensued;
            From interest, as improvement rose,
                Succeeded gratitude.

            Obedience was no effort soon,                    5
                And labour was no pain;
            If tired, a word, a glance alone
                Would give me strength again.

            From others of the studious band,
                Erelong he singled me;                       10
            But only by more close demand,
                And sterner urgency.

            The task he from another took,
                From me, he did reject;
            He would no slight omission brook,              15
                And suffer no defect.

            If my companions went astray,
                He scarce their wanderings blamed;
            If I but falter'd in the way,
                His anger fiercely flamed.                   20

            When sickness stayed awhile my course,
                He seemed impatient still,
            Because his pupil's flagging force
                Could not obey his will.


333

One day when summoned to the bed                                25
    Where Pain and I did strive,
I heard him, as he bent his head,
    Say "God--she <u>must</u> revive!"

I felt his hand, with gentle stress
    A moment laid on mine,                                      30
And wished to mark my consciousness
    By some responsive sign.

But powerless then to speak or move,
    I only felt within,
The sense of Hope, the strength of Love                         35
    Their healing work begin.

And as he from the room withdrew
    My heart his steps pursued,
I longed to prove by efforts new
    My speechless gratitude.                                    40

When once again I took my place,
    Long vacant, in the class,
Th' unfrequent smile across his face
    Did for one moment pass.

The lessons done; the signal made                               45
    Of glad release and play,
He, as he passed, an instant stayed
    One kindly word to say.

"Jane, till to-morrow you are free
    From tedious task and rule;                                 50
This afternoon I must not see
    That yet pale face in school.

Seek in the garden-shades a seat
    Far from the play-ground din;
The sun is warm, the air is sweet;                              55
    Stay till I call you in."

A long and pleasant afternoon
    I passed in those green bowers;
All silent, tranquil and alone
    With birds and bees and flowers.                            60

Yet when my Master's voice I heard
    Call from the window "Jane!"
I entered, joyful, at the word,
    The busy house again.

334

He, in the hall, paced up and down;                    65
  He paused as I passed by;
His forehead stern relaxed its frown;
  He raised his deep-set eye.

"Not quite so pale," he murmured low:
  "Now, Jane, go rest awhile."                         70
And as I smiled, his smoothened brow
  Returned as glad a smile.

My perfect health restored, he took
  His mien austere again,
And as before, he would not brook                      75
  The slightest fault from Jane.

The longest task, the hardest theme
  Fell to my share as erst,
And still I toiled to place my name
  In every study first.                                80

He yet begrudged and stinted praise,
  But I had learned to read
The secret meaning of his face,
  And that was my best meed.

Even when his hasty temper spoke                       85
  In tones that sorrow stirred,
My grief was lulled as soon as woke
  By some relenting word.

And when he lent some precious book,
  Or gave some fragrant flower,                        90
I did not quail to Envy's look,
  Upheld by Pleasure's power.

At last our school ranks took their ground;
  The hard-fought field, I won;
The prize, a laurel wreath, was bound                  95
  My throbbing forehead on.

Low at my master's knee I bent,
  The offered crown to meet;
Its green leaves through my temples sent
  A thrill as wild as sweet.                           100

The strong pulse of Ambition struck
  In every vein I owned;
At the same instant, bleeding broke
  A secret, inward wound.

335

The hour of triumph was to me                   105
    The hour of sorrow sore;
A day hence I must cross the sea,
    Ne'er to recross it more.

An hour hence, in my Master's room
    I, with him sat alone,                       110
And told him what a dreary gloom
    O'er joy, had parting thrown.

He little said; the time was brief,
    The ship was soon to sail,
And while I sobbed in bitter grief,             115
    My master but looked pale.

They called in haste; he bade me go,
    Then snatched me back again;
He held me fast and murmured low,
    "Why will they part us, Jane?"               120

"Were you not happy in my care?
    Did I not faithful prove?
Will others to my darling bear
    As true, as deep a love?

"O God, watch o'er my foster child!             125
    O guard her gentle head!
When winds are high and tempests wild
    Protection round her spread!

"They call again; leave then my breast;
    Quit thy true shelter, Jane,                 130
But when deceived, repulsed, opprest,
    Come home to me again!"

                        [June 27, 1846]

MS:  D(1) & F(2)
First Publication:  **The Professor** 1857


**206**         I now had only to retrace
                    The long and lonely road
                So lately in the rainbow chase
                    With fearless ardour trod



                        336

Behind I left the sunshine now                          5
    The evening setting sun
Before, a storm rolled dark & low
    Some gloomy hills upon

It came with rain--it came with wind
    With swollen stream it howled               10
And night advancing black and blind
    In ebon horror scowled

Lost in the hills--all painfully
    I climbed a heathy peak
I sought I longed afar to see                   15
    My life's light's parting streak

The West was black as if no day
    Had ever lingered there
As if no red, expiring ray
    Had tinged the enkindled air                20

And morning's portals could not lie
    Where yon dark orient spread
The funeral North--the black dark sky
    Alike mourned for the dead

                [late 1846-early 1847]

MS:  D(1)
First Publication:  SHB C and B


**207**            The house was still--the room was still
                       'Twas eventide in June
                   A caged canary to the sun
                       Then setting--trilled a tune

                   A free bird on that lilac bush          5
                       Outside the lattice heard
                   He listened long--there came a hush
                       He dropped an answering word--

                   The prisoner to the free replied

                           [late 1846-early 1847]

MS:  D(1)
First Publication:  Benson 1915


                        337

**208**     "My feet they are sore, and my limbs they are weary;
            Long is the way, and the mountains are wild;
            Soon will the twilight close moonless and dreary
            Over the path of the poor orphan child.

            "Why did they send me so far and so lonely,                        5
            Up where the moors spread and grey rocks are piled?
            Men are hard-hearted, and kind angels only
            Watch o'er the steps of a poor orphan child.

            "Yet distant and soft the night-breeze is blowing,
            Clouds there are none, and clear stars beam mild;                  10
            God, in His mercy, protection is showing,
            Comfort and hope to the poor orphan child.

            "Ev'n should I fall, o'er the broken bridge passing,
            Or stray in the marshes, by false lights beguiled,
            Still will my Father, with promise and blessing,                   15
            Take to His bosom the poor orphan child.

            "There is a thought that for strength should avail me,
            Though both of shelter and kindred despoiled:
            Heaven is a home, and a rest will not fail me;
            God is a friend to the poor orphan child."                        20

                                        [late 1846]

MS:  B(2)
First Publication:  **Jane Eyre** 1847


**209**            The truest love that ever heart
                     Felt at its kindled core
                   Did through each vein, in quickened start,
                     The tide of being pour.

                   Her coming was my hope each day,                           5
                     Her parting was my pain;
                   The chance that did her steps delay,
                     Was ice in every vein.

                   I dreamed it would be nameless bliss,
                     As I loved, loved to be;                                 10
                   And to this object did I press
                     As blind as eagerly.

338

But wide as pathless was the space
   That lay, our lives, between,
And dangerous as the foamy race               15
   Of ocean-surges green.

And haunted as a robber-path
   Through wilderness or wood;
For Might and Right, and Woe and Wrath,
   Between our spirits stood.               20

I dangers dared; I hindrance scorned;
   I omens did defy:
Whatever menaced, harassed, warned,
   I passed impetuous by.

On sped my rainbow, fast as light;            25
   I flew as in a dream;
For glorious rose upon my sight
   That child of Shower and Gleam.

Still bright on clouds of suffering dim
   Shines that soft, solemn joy;          30
Nor care I now, how dense and grim
   Disasters gather nigh:

I care not in this moment sweet,
   Though all I have rushed o'er
Should come on pinion, strong and fleet,     35
   Proclaiming vengeance sore:

Though haughty Hate should strike me down,
   Right, bar approach to me,
And grinding Might, with furious frown,
   Swear endless enmity.             40

My Love has placed her little hand
   With noble faith in mine,
And vowed that wedlock's sacred band
   Our natures shall entwine.

My Love has sworn, with sealing kiss,       45
   With me to live--to die;
I have at last my nameless bliss:
   As I love--loved am I!

               [early 1847]

MS: D(1) & B(2)
First Publication: **Jane Eyre** 1847

**210**    He saw my heart's woe discovered my soul's anguish
How in fever--in thirst, in atrophy it pined
Knew he could heal yet looked and let it languish
To its moans spirit-deaf, to its pangs spirit-blind

But once a year he heard a whisper low and dreary          5
Appealing for aid, entreating some reply
Only when sick soul-worn, and torture weary
Breathed I that prayer--heaved I that sigh

He was mute as is the grave--he stood stirless as a tower
At last I looked up and saw I prayed to stone              10
I asked help of that which to help had no power
I sought love where love was utterly unknown

Idolater I kneeled to an idol cut in rock
I might have slashed my flesh and drawn my heart's best blood,
The granite God had felt no tenderness no shock            15
My Baal had nor seen nor heard nor understood

In dark remorse I rose--I rose in darker shame
Self-condemned I withdrew to an exile from my kind
A solitude I sought where mortal never came
Hoping in its wilds forgetfulness to find                  20

Now Heaven heal the wound which I still deeply feel
Thy glorious hosts look not in scorn on our poor race
Thy King eternal doth no iron judgment deal
On suffering worms who seek forgiveness comfort, grace

He gave our hearts to love, he will not love despise       25
E'en if the gift be lost as mine was long ago
He will forgive the fault--will bid the offender rise
Wash out with dews of bliss the fiery brand of woe

And give a sheltered place beneath the unsullied throne
Whence the soul redeemed may mark Time's fleeting course
   round earth                                             30
And know its trial past--its sufferings are gone
And feel the peril past of Death's immortal birth

[December 1847]

MS:  H
First Publication:  Benson 1915
Text:  1. 4:  "moans" written above "moaning"; "pangs" written above
       "travail"; no cancelations

340

Not many years but long enough to see
No fo[e] can deal such deadly misery
As the dear friend untimely called away
And still the more beloved, the greater still
Must be the aching void the withering chill          5
Of each dark night & dim beclouded day

[December 23, 1848]

MS:  H
First Publication:  Shorter EJB 1910


212          **Dec 24 [1848]**

My darling thou wilt never know
Such grinding agony of wo[e]
     As we have felt for thee.
Thus may we consolation tear
E'en from the depth of our despair          5
     & wasting misery.

The nightly anguish thou art spared
When all the crushing truth is bared
     To the awakening mind.
And the galled heart is pierced with grief          10
Till wildly it implores relief--
     But small relief can find.

Nor knewst thou what it is to lie
Beholding forth with tear dimmed eye
     Life's lone wilderness.          15
'Weary weary dark & drear
How shall I the journey bear,
     The burden & distress?'

Then since thou art spared such pain
We will not wish thee here again          20
     He that lives must mourn
God relieve us through our misery
And give us rest & joy with thee
     When we reach our bourne!

MS:  N
First Publication:  **The Woman at Home,** December 1896
Text:   l. 2:   "Such" written above "He"; neither is canceled
        l. 3:   "As" written above "That"; neither is canceled
        l. 3:   "felt" written above "known" and "borne"; no cancelations
        l. 10:  "And" written above "When"; neither is canceled
        l. 14:  Uncanceled earlier versions read:
                "Exploring with tear dimmed eye"
                "Looking with streaming eye"
        l. 15:  Uncanceled earlier version:  "On life's wilderness"
        l. 19:  "Then" written above "O"; neither is canceled
        l. 22:  "relieve" written above "help"; neither is canceled


**213      June 21 1849**


  There's little joy in life for me
  & little terror in the grave
  I've lived the lingering death to see
  Of one I would have died to save.

  Calmly to watch the failing breath      5
  Wishing each sigh might be the last
  Longing to see the shade of death oe'r those beloved
    features cast.

  The shade the stillness that must part
  The darling of my life from me,
  And then to thank God from my heart    10
  To thank him well & fervently!
  Although I knew that we had lost
  The hope & glory of our life,
  And now benighted tempest tossed
  Must meet alone the weary strife.     15

MS:  N
First Publication:  **The Woman at Home,** December 1896
Text:   l. 3:   "lingering death" written above "parting hour"; neither i
        canceled
        l. 5:   "the failing" written above "struggling for" and "each gas
        of"; no cancelations
        l. 6:   "Wishing" written above "Still hoping"; "might" writte
        above "would"; no cancelations
        l. 7:   "shade" written above "cloud"; neither is canceled
        l. 15:  "meet" written above "bear"; neither is canceled


342

Verse Translations

214     FIRST BOOK OF VOLTAIRES HENRIADE, translated
           from the French

```
        I sing that hero over France who reigned
        Whose right by conquest & by birth was gained
        Who by long miseries severe was taught
        To rule his subjects as a father ought
        Who knew to vanquish & to pardon all                         5
        To calm dread factions loud incessant brawl
        Who overcame Mayenne the 'federate league
        Iberia and stopped the horrid plague
        Of civil war, then King of France became;
        Adding the father's, to the victors' name.                  10

        Come awful Truth descending from on high
        Shed power and splendor on this history;
        That Kings may hear thee, it is for thee to shew
        What dread effects from their divisions grow
        Tell how fierce Discord troubled all our land               15
        Holding fair France chained in her iron band
        Tell the misfortunes that her people bore
        The wrongs done by the princes of her shore
        Come, & if Fiction did in olden time
        Join to thy voice her own sweet silver chime                20
        If her fair hand adorned thy lofty head
        If her dark shade enhanced thy glory shed
        Let her with me walk in thy steps of light
        And show thy wond'rous charms in their attraction bright.

        Valois reigned still, of energy bereft                      25
        His weak hands lose the reins of power left
        To float in air:  the shaken state unbound
        Had forceless laws & rights which all confound:
        Or rather, Great Valois now reigned no more;
        It was not now that prince whom glory bore                  30
        To fields of battle, e'ven in infancy,
        Ever instructed by proud victory.
        Whose progress Europe saw & trembling shook
        And who his countrys' sorrows with him took
        When all the admiring nations of the north                  35
        Full of his virtues called the warrior forth
        Low at his feet each laid a sparkling crown
        And Each awe-struck its head bowed humbly down
```

Then from a soldier free intrepid brave
Valois became a King, & softness' slave                          40
He slept effeminate on the imperial throne
His weakness bent beneath the o'er burd'ning crown.
Quelus, Saint Megrim, Joyeux Epernons
(All famed alone in festal banquet song:)
Ruled for him; while soft sunk in pleasure wave                  45
He there in languid lethargy did lave.
Now was the Guise's hour by fortune crowned
They in his downfall all their greatness found
In Paris they the league confederate formed
Whose rival might his pow'rless weakness stormed                 50
The mob unchained; vile vassals of the great
Served tyrants & with persecuting hate
Followed their prince, whom now his friends forsook
Trembling like dastards by pale terror shook
The people chased him from the Louvres wall                      55
And through the streets he fled unknown of all
Till Bourbon came to work each rebels fall

    The virtuous Bourbon full of warlike might
To his blind prince restored again the light
Gave back his pow'r, & led his wand'ring feet                    60
From shame to where bright Glory held her seat
From sports & pleasures to the battle plain
He took his King to honnour once again
Rome shook, the Spaniards trembled, Europe all
Now fixed their eyes on that unhappy wall                        65
For each felt inter'st in those miseries famed
And th' worlds attention Now Fair Paris claimed

    They saw inhuman Discord standing high
On tow'rs whose lofty summits threat the sky
In accents loud, the banded league excite                        70
With stately Mayenne to the bloody fight
And churchment Spanish succors to invite
That monster feirce inflexible bloodstained
On her own subjects is her vengeance rained
With the warm life-blood of her party dyed                       75
Of mortal ills she swells the o'erflowing tid[e]
Reign like a tyrant in her votaries breasts
And for the crimes she tempts a certain forfeit--wrests

    Near those Green borders of the Occident
Where Seine in silver foldings ever went                         80
Flying from Paris, in the present day
A still & fair retreat for Natures play
Then 'twas a sanguine Theatre of blood
Where armies for the dreadful combat stood

344

Th' unhappy King arrayed his warlike band                        85
And there the[y] saw each stately hero stand
The fierce supporter of his native land
Vengeance unites those, whom their sects divide
To Bourbo[n] each his fortune doth confide:
The noble Bourbon, in all bosoms reigns                          90
And binds in unity the hearts he gains
It seemed that all, one creed & cheiftain owned
For he in every breast thus pow'rful was--throned
The Bourbons ancestor Saint Louis held
His place 'mid angels & from thence beheld                       95
His son, & watched him with a fathers eyes
For from his radiant palace of the skies
He saw in him the splendor of his race
Which he through the futures mists could dimly trace
He wept his errors' & his brav'ry loved                          100
Which when it had by coming wars been proved
He willed to honour with a royal crown
And as from heavens high thrones he gazed adown
On this low earth a mightier purpose filled
His mind celestial & his spirit willed                           105
T' illuminate his soul with anger tight
To show religion clothed in glory bright
But towards this happiness great & supreme
Henry advanced by paths unknown, unseen
Saint Louis formed his strong unerring stay                      110
As still he travelled in that secret way
But yet concealing the extended arm
Which sheilded off all hostile force or harm
Lest that the hero of his conquest sure
Might with less danger less reward secure                        115


    And now already at the ramparts feet
Had the two parties oft' in battle met
And through our desert feilds the feind of war
Had borne his rage even to the seas afar
When Valois held with Bourbon sad discourse                      120
Of which his frequent sighs stopt oft the course
"See how the warring fates have humbled me
"My shame is yours, yours is my injury
"And lo! the hostile league which rears its brow
"Seditious against its prince hates also you                     125
"It threats us both; confounds us in its rage
"And war inveterate war doth now pursuing wage
"Paris as master, loves not to sustain
Nor I who rule, nor you who ought to reign
"They know when death has taken me to his                        130
"Realm that law high blood & merit to the helm
Will call you, but your greatness guessing now


                              345

"They from the crown which trembles on my brow
"Think to exclude you, & religion dread
"Her fatal curse has launched against your--head                    135
"Tremendous Rome of soldiers unpossessed,
"Yet bearing war in e'very field & breast
Has placed her thunder in the Spaniards hand
"To roll it forth o'er ocean shore & land.
Me, subjects, freinds & relatives, forsake                          140
All shun me, hate me, arms to oppose me take
And greedy Spain by my sad losses rich
Her utmost power her utmost might doth
Stretch, she sends her hosts my fields to overwhelm
To desolate thy much-loved fruitful realm                           145
Against these enemies destroying all
Then let us also foreign succors call
Of England let us gain the illustrious queen
Yes let her armies mixed with ours be seen
I know a hatred, everlasting, strong                                150
Hath reigned between us centuries past long
I know that London Paris emulates
And ardently her wished destruction waits
But since my glory, hath been touched with blight
After those insults offered to my might                            155
My subjects kingdom, country I resign
I hate this people, punishment condign
Shall be their portion, he who swiftest hurls
Vengeance upon them & who first unfurls
The bloody banner, shall be to my eyes                              160
The truest Frenchman, Bourbon now arise
I will not on this embassy employ
My secret agents their advance is slow
But Henry you, you Bourbon I implore
Go with your fame & seek fair Albions shore                        165
For Kings will only listen to your voice
'Tis you alone can make my heart rejoice
Your warrior help to unhappy Valois lend
For nought but that will peace or vic'try send

        He said, the hero jealous of his might                     170
Willed not to part the glory of the fight
He felt in listning greif & anger lower
For those past times when vigorous was his power
Strong in his virtue; & without intrigue,
Or help himself & Conde shook the league                           175
But forced his masters projects to fulfil
To leave his gathered laurels against his will
He held the stern strokes parting from his hand
And sorrowing left his sunlit native land
The astonished bands unknowing his design                          180
For his return with heartfelt wishes pine

And now already on the journey gone
Of all his favourites and freinds alone
Mornay went with him faithful confidante
Unflattering counsel in the day of want                          185
Too virtuous support of errors side
By love of Church & country equal tied
Hater of courtiers, but by courts beloved
Detesting Rome yet her esteem he proved

     Near two tall rocks where waves with sullen noise        190
Dash whitened waters to the o'er arching skies
Dieppes port appeared before the heros eyes
The sailors press on board in eager bands
While the ships guided by their skilful hands
Fly o'er the sea by hundred wings sustained                      195
Impetuous Boreas 'mid the loud winds chained
To Zephyrs breath those plains pellucid gave
With ev'ry glassy scarcely rippling wave
They raise the anchor far they fly the shore
Now dark & distant England rose before                           200
When instant vanished day-lights brilliant star
The dimmed air whistled bellowed from afar
The solemn sea & with old oceans moan
Was heard to mingle heavens cloud rending groan
Now thunder kindled splendor in the sky                          205
Now the blue lightning flashing from on high
With dread abysses gulphed in seas beneath
Showed ev'ry where to shudd'ring sailors death
The hero by a furious sea beseiged
All horribly around black billows raged                          210
With shroud like sheets of foam by tempests wrought
Still only of his countrys sorrows thought
He turned towards her in his greiving mind
Seemed to accuse the ship-arresting wind

     So but less gen'rous Ceasar to the wave                      215
His own & Romes almighty destinies gave
When for earths empire he with Pompey fought
And thus in stormswept seas his safety bravely sought

     And now the eternal Ruler of the skies
Who swells the waves & on the whirlwind flies                    220
That God whose will ineffable profound
Appoints each Kingdom its determined bound
From where the heavens are lighted by his throne
On the French hero looked in mercy down
He guided him th' unquiet seas along                             225
To Jersey who uprose the waves among
The howling world of waters round her cast
Tranquil she lay on ancient Oceans breast
There led by heaven the hero sought for rest

347

```
         Near to the banks a frowning forest grew                    230
Whose giant boughs a midnight darkness threw
Around a peaceful cavern, natures work
And lo amid the obscurity & mirk
An old man in the woodland silence lay
Who there wore out the remnant of his day                           235
Far from the hum of cities & the strife
Of gorgeous palaces; a courtiers life
Disdaining, here of bustling men unknown
He lived content, unenvying even a throne
Himself his study; from all sorrow free                             240
He thought of bygone days & pensively
Recalled his former follies unopressed
By riotous passions he abode at rest
Stre[t]ched on the enamelled border of a fount
While his aspiring thoughts to heaven would mount                   245
Beneath his feet he trod all human joys
And listened only to the still small voice,
Whispering within him, & the Eternals praise
He to the firmament for aye did raise
The God whom thus he served the Ever-Good                           250
Wisdom divine sent to his solitude
She showed him Gods uncomprehended ways
And in the book of fates instructed him to gaze

         This ancient hermit knew by wisdom taught
The might warrior destiny had brought                               255
To his secluded isle the warr[i]or here
Oft in the peasants Cabin did appear
Flying the noise of courts he sought t' oerthrow
The diadems pride which glittered on his brow
That tumult which disturbed the Christian State                     260
Formed their discourse as neath some tree they sate
Mornay who in his sect was still unshook
In Calvins faith a strong assurance took
Bourbon yet doubted: Yet he prayed to heaven
That some bright ray of splendor might be given                     265
To peirce the thick gloom that enwrapped his eyes
T'illume the righteous pathway to the skies
The holy truth said he, too often lost
In human errors on that wide sea tost
Must I who look for light to God alone                              270
Sorrowing in ignorance forever groan
Alas! that God so good, who holds the sway
O'er men I would have served if he had--taught the way
The ancient man replied Adore thy God
Weak mortal fear eternals iron rod                                  275
In former times I saw with saddend eyes
The faith of Calvin e'ven in France arise
```

Feeble in birth low walking in the shad[e]
She unsupported slow advances made
Still onward marching in obscurity                    280
She forced her foes at her advance to flee
At last I saw her seated on a throne--
Before her hundreds kneeling slave-like down
Insultingly I saw her raise her brow
& with disdainful foot our altars overthrow           285
Then fled I courts & to this grotto went
My loved religions downfall to lament
There on a lingering hope myself I cast
That this new doctrine would not always last

    To mens caprice, she her existence owes           290
They soon shall see her die as now she grows
The works of men are weak & fragile still
They dissipate & vanish at the will
Of that omnipotent who ever stands
Above the ruin of a hundred lands                     295
'Mid warring Kings & sectaries unmoved
Reposes at [h]is feet his best beloved
Meek truth who seldom shows her glorious light
To mortal man proud of his worthless--might
To those who ask sincerely from the heart            300
In happy hour she deigns herself to impart
You if you pray shall still in light rejoice
Amid the music of her welcome voice
The Lord of heaven his arms has round--you thrown
& leads you towards your natal countrys crown         305
Praise him weak mortal hark his dread command
Hath gone in thunder forth o'er sea & land
Victory! Victory! is thy portion now
A sunlike crown shall sparkle on thy brow
The ways of glory ope before thine eye                310
But until truth has visited from on hight
Thy inward sight think not the wall to mount
Of Paris till thou hast bathed in the fount
Of heavenly knowledge, but all things above
Fly the sweet poison of enchanting love               315
Resist the pleasures, 'gainst thy passions fight
With manly courage let them not affright
Thy yet undaunted soul, & know one day
When thou in triumph o'er the league dost sway
After a horrid seige which busy Fame will             320
Give to future ages with thy name
All the glad people shall in plenty live
On that which thy benevolence shall give
Then raise their spirits to their fathers God
Point to the ignorant the righteous road              325

349

Those who are humble may to him resort
And know the lowly have a sure support
He said each word seemed as a flaming dart
Peircing the troubled depths of Henrys heart
And as he heard the venerable sage                          330
He seemed transported to that happy age
When God conversing with the human kind
Taught e'en the wise & lightened e'en the blind
When simple virtue saw his wondrous might
And awed e'en Kings by their superior light                 335
He left the hermit with fast-bursting sighs
& tears in streams flowed sadly from his eyes
And as he left he saw the first born ray
Of that fair morning which a glorious day
Should soon before his longing soul arise                   340
Mornay beheld him with untouched surprise
God still from him the precious truth concealed
And but to Henry left her unrevealed
Thus though on earth he had the name of sage
Remained unoped to him to holy page.                        345
While the recluse comanded by the Lord
Showed Bourbon his imperishable word
The winds were hushed the cloud-veiled heavens cleared
The radiant sun in splendor reappeared
The glad prince now his stately vessel gains               350
& o'er the waters flew to Albions verdant plains

    Now when he reached at last the English shores
Round which eternally old Ocean roars
In secret he admired the happy fate
Of those who flourished in that powerful state             355
For now no more existed the abuse
Of those wise laws whose horrible misuse
Caused blood in streams to flow throug[h] plain & field
Of mighty heros the sad destiny sealed
Now on that throne whence hundred Kings                    360
Descend, a woman princess of her people reigned
Lo! at her feet the fates lie fast enchained
The splendours of her name all men surprise
With far renown far ring the lofty skies
It was Elizabeth whose wisdom great                        365
Made Europe chuse her to decide its fate
The people neath her reign forget their greif
As in the fields the sea the harvest sheaf
Their fruitful flocks oerspread the verdant plain
And their tall thundring ships the azure main             370
Feared on the earth o'er every sea they reign
Their fleet imperious Neptune condescends
Humbly to serve, from all the earths far ends

350

It summons fortune to their happy shores
Who swift obeying lavish riches pours                          375
London once barberous, now the bright day-star
Of arts & temple to the God of war
The worlds great granary renowned afar
Each year assemble in the ancient walls
Of Westminster, three powers whom wisdom calls                 380
With whose renown the universe doth ring
The peoples deputies the nobles & the King
These join'd form one strong formidable band
Spreading their terrors to the farthest land
Happy the nations who respect their Kings                      385
Happiest the sovereign that around him flings
Joy peace & plenty worships liberty
From dark suspicions of his subjects free

    Bourbon exclaimed when this fair scene he saw
Oh! when shall France like you obey the law                    390
Ye monarchs of the earth come from afar
Behold a woman close the doors of war
While discord reigns in all the earth around
England alone true happiness has found
And now he reached that city fair & vast                       395
Where as around his wandring eyes he cast
Freedom & peace appeared on e'vry side
Daughters of heaven & bold Britannias pride
He saw the conquerors tower appeared on high
& the proud palace threat the lofty sky                        400
Elizabeths abode & there he went
All unattended for his heart was bent
Not on parade & pomp & empty show
The heros thoughts in other channels flow
How best his masters interests to speed                        405
& with Elizabeth to intercede
He spoke; his speech was manly breif & free
No phrase unworthy his high dignity
Superfluous encumbered style or part
The eloquence welled freshly from his heart                    410
He told the need of France his masters need
& for her help nobly submissive prayed
Lowly in greatness humble nevver mean
You serve Valois exclaimed the astonished queen
For his sake have you crossed the dangerous sea                415
Doth Henri for Valois petition me
Your difference from the western shores--hath rung
To where the mornings gates are open flung
You for him armed incredulous I see!
You whose dread sword hath forced him oft to flee              420
Free from revenge or malice he replied

351

The miseries of Valois have quelled his--prid[e]
Chained like a slave by worthless pleasures power
They came to loose him in auspicious hour
Happier if resting on my firm support                    425
He had foregone the counsels of his court
And now great queen join in this needful war
Let the high name of England spread afar
T'crown your virtues now defend our laws
Revenge with me my masters righteous cause              430
Eliza heard & ardent longed to know
The source whence all these mighty troubles flow
She said impatient; Fame who swiftly flies
Around the globe of earth & arch of skies
Hath told me much, but mingled truth with lies         435
You were a witness of those quarrels long
You lived & fought those dreadful scenes among
Relate the cause, unfold the mystery,
Of that which joined you with you[r] enemy
None saving Bourbon know the heart to reach            440
Your warlike deeds all future Kings shall teach
Alas! cried Bourbon must my memory
Of those curst times recall the history
Rather that heaven high witness of my grief
Should in oblivion give my mind releif                  445
Why ask you of this slow reluctant tongue
That narrative which through the world hath rung
Of th' princes of my blood the shame to tell
& how my King in shameful pleasures fell
I feel my trembling heart refuse the task              450
O Queen some tale less darkly shaded ask
But you have ordered 'tis for me to obey
Though but unvarnished truths I know to say
I cannot hide the faults disguise the crimes
Or veil the horrors of those blood-stained times       455
Not armed with Sophistry or cunning vain
My words are sober unadorned & plain

Charlotte Bronte   August the 11th
1830 Ano Domino

MS:  A
First Publication:   **Voltaire's "Henriade," Book I Translated From the
                     French by Charlotte Brontë,** London:    Privately
                     printed by Clement Shorter, 1917

I.

'Twas New-Year's night; the joyous throng
    Of guests from banquet rose,
And lightly took their homeward path
    Across the drifted snows.
That night, e'en to the peasant's shed,          5
Some little gleam of gladness spread.

II.

That night, beside a chapel door,
    Two lonely children stood;
In timid tone, with utterance faint,
    They asked a little food:                     10
Careless, the laughing guests passed by,--
Too gay to mark the Orphans' cry.

III.

A lamp that lit the sacred shrine
    The Children's pale cheeks shewed;
The elder stretched his trembling hand           15
    For what was not bestowed;
The younger sung a plaintive strain,
Oft dropped, then feebly raised again:--

IV.

"Two friendless, helpless children, we,--
    "Our mother's death we weep;                  20
"Together, in one narrow grave,
    "She and our father sleep!
"We, too, of cold and want must die,
"If none will help or hear our cry!"

V.

This voice was lost; the winter-wind             25
    Bore off its tones subdued,
And soon the merry Feasters gone,
    Left all in solitude;
And none had looked towards the church,
Or marked the Orphans in its porch.              30

## VI.

Then turned they to the chapel door;--
   Their mother oft had said
That God will shield the friendless poor,
   When other aid is fled.
They knocked--an echo mocked the ear;     35
They waited--Death alone drew near!

## VII.

Time speeds; the lamp shines feebly still,
   The chimes of midnight sound;
Heard now from far, a chariot's wheels
   Ring o'er the frozen ground.     40
Rise, Orphans! Call! No!--hushed their cry;
Unchecked, the chariot thunders by.

## VIII.

A Priest his matins came to say,
   When dawn first lit the skies;
He found them on the threshold laid;     45
   He called--they would not rise!
The icy steps of stone, their bed;--
The white snow for their covering spread.

## IX.

Clasped closely in each other's arms,
   As if for warmth, they lay;     50
But perished is the fire of Life,
   And stilled the pulses' play;
Mute, motionless, and ashen pale,
They slept, no more to wake or wail!

## X.

The elder pressed the younger's lips,     55
   As if to check a prayer;--
As if to say, "'Tis vain to ask!--
   "Compassion dwells not here!"
And half he screened his brother's form,
To hide him from the frozen storm.     60

354

Lulled thus in everlasting sleep,
   The Orphan Babes are laid;
Now those their piteous fate may weep
   Who would not give them aid:
Crowds thronged the church by morning light,       65
   But none came near, that winter-night!

                   [February 1843]

MS: F(1)
First Publication: **Manchester Athenaeum Album,** 1850


**216**        **Napoleon**


O Corsican! thou of the stern contour
   Thy France, how fair was she,
When the broad, ardent sun of Messidor
   At length beheld her free!
Like a young mare, unbroke to servitude       5
   Bridle she scorned, and rein;
Still on her hot flanks smoked the recent blood
   Of kings on scaffolds Slain.

Proudly her free hoof struck the ancient soil;
   Insult by word or deed       10
She knew not; never hand of outrage vile
   Had passed on that wild steed.
Never had her deep flanks the saddle borne
   As harness, of the foe;
All virgin she; her heavy mane unshorn       15
   Wantonned in vagrant flow.

The eye of fire, set in her slender head
   Shot forth a tameless ray;
Reared up erect, the whole world she dismayed
   With her shrill, savage neigh.       20
Napoleon came; he marked her noble strain,
   Her blood, her mettle bold;
Grasping the thick locks of her gypsy mane,
   The centaur fixed his hold

Booted he mounted; since he knew full well                  25
    She loved the voice of war;
Musket and beating drum and trumpet's swell
    And cannon's roar
He gave the wide world for her hunting-ground
    His sport was war and toil.                              30
Nor rest, nor night, nor sleep his charger found
    Ever the <cries> and toil;

O'er flesh like clay, gallopped the goaded horse,
    Breast-deep in blood and tears;
She trampled generations in her course                      35
    For fifteen bloody years.
For fifteen years of carnage, woe and wrath,
    O'er prostrate lands she rode,
And still she wore not out the endless path
    Her hoof of iron trode                                   40

Weary at last, of ever onward hasting,
    Finding no resting-place;
Weary of grinding earth, of widely wasting
    Like dust, the human race;
With limbs unnerved, staggering at every pace,              45
    Weak as if Death were near,
She prayed the Corsican a moment's grace,
    Tyrant! he would not hear.

Closer he pressed her with his vigorous thigh,
    In rage her teeth he broke,                              50
Hard drew the bit, stifled the piercing cry
    That quickened torture woke.

Once more she rose; at length one battle-day
    Prone on the field she fell;
Unhorsed and unhelmed, her haughty rider lay               55
    Crushed on a heap of shell.

                    Auguste Barbier Mars 1843

MS:  D(1) & F(1)
First Publication: **Napoleon and the Spectre:  A Ghost Story, By**
              **Charlotte Brontë,** London:   Privately printed  by
              Clement Shorter, 1919 partial; Shorter 1923
Text:  l. 5:  "mare" penciled above "horse"; neither is canceled
       l. 10:  "by" penciled above "in"; neither is canceled.  The line
       originally read "Insult or wrong or force"
       l. 24:  Written above an uncanceled line:  "His hand took stedfast
       hold"
       l. 40:  "hoof or iron" penciled above "iron sabot"; neither is
       canceled
       l. 55:  "unhelmed" penciled above "unhorsed"; neither is canceled

                            356

Who ventures, knight or knave
To dive in this Gulph?
A golden goblet I throw therein
The black mouth hath already swallowed it;
He who can bring me back the goblet                                    5
May keep it, it is his own

The king spoke and flung from the summit
Of the cliff, that rugged and steep,
Hung over the boundless sea,
The goblet, into the howling whirl of Charybdis.                     10
"Who is the champion, I ask again
"To plunge in these depths?"

And the knights and vassals round him
Listen in silence
They look forth over the wild sea                                     15
And none desires to win the goblet
The king asks for the third time
Is there none who will venture below?

But all remained mute as before,
And a page, gentle and brave                                          20
Steps forth from the terrified band of vassals;
He throws aside belt and mantle
All the men and women around
Look on the noble youth with astonishment

And as he steps to the brow of the rock                               25
And looks into the gulph below
The water which whirled twisted in torment below
Which Charybdis roaring returned
And as with the roar of distant thunder
Flung itself foaming into the dark abyss                              30

And it bubbles and boils and roars and hisses
As when water with fire is blent,
The steaming vapour spouts to heaven
And flood presses endlessly on flood
And will never exhaust or empty itself                                35
As if the sea would bring forth another sea

At length the wild violence reposed itself
And black out of the white foam
Gapes beneath a yawning chasm
Bottomless as if it descended into the depths of hell                 40
And tearing the bursting waves are seen
Drawn down into the boiling cauldron-crater

357

Now quick ere the breakers return,
The youth commends his soul to God,
And--a cry from the beholders is heard around          45
Already has the vortex drawn him in
And mysteriously over the bold swimmer
Shuts the maw--it opens no more

All grows calm on the surface of the wave-abyss
In the depths only it roars hollow                      50
And faltering is heard from mouth to mouth
"Brave youth, farewell!
Hollower and more hollow it is heard to howl
And it lingers with fearful with hideous delay

"Wert thou to fling the crown itself therein,           55
"Wert thou to say, 'he who brings me the crown
Shall wear it and be king
I should not desire the costly recompense,
What the howling depths conceal below
No fortunate living being shall relate                  60

Full many a bark caught in the whirlpool
Descends sheer into the depths
Only keel and mast writhe shattered
Outside the devouring grave of all
Distincter and more distinct like the roar of the storm 65
It is heard growling, ever nearer and more near

And it bubbles and boils and roars and hisses
As when water is blent with fire
The vaporous cataract spouts to heaven
And wave presses endlessly on wave                      70
And as with the roll of distant thunder
Tumbles roaring into the dark gulph--

And lo! out of the dark, troubled gulph
There rises swan-white
An arm, and a gleaming neck becomes bare                75
And it rows with vigour & with indefatigable labour
It is he, and high in his right-hand
He waves the goblet with joyous signals

And he breathes long and he breathes deep.
And hails the heavenly light.                           80
With transport one cries to another
He lives! he is there! it retains him not
From the grave from the boiling water-cave
Has the brave youth saved the living soul.

And he comes, and the exulting band surround him                85
He falls at the king's feet
He presents him the goblet kneeling there,
And the king signs to his lovely daughter
Who fills it with sparkling wine to the brim
And the Youth thus addressed the king                          90

"Long live the king! and let all rejoice.
Who breathe in the rosy light!
Beneath all is fearful
And let not men tempt the Gods
And let them not desire to behold                              95
What they graciously conceal with night & darkness

It snatched me down with the speed of lightning
I was hurled into the rocky torrent
Wildly chafing at the meeting of the bursting flood,
The raging violence of the twofold flood seized me            100
And like a top, with giddy whirl
Turned me round, I could not resist

There shewed me, that God to whom I cried
Out of extreme and awful distress,
Rising out of the deep a ledge of rock                        105
That I seized quickly and escaped Death
And there also hung the goblet on a branch of coral
Else had it fallen into the bottomless abyss

For beneath me it lay still deep as mountains are high
    In purple gloom                                           110
And if here all sleeps eternally to the ear,
The eye with horror looked down
As amongst lizards and Sea-snakes and dragons
It wandered in the murky throat of Hell.

Black swarmed there, in frightful confusion,                  115
In hideous masses rolled,
The thorny ray, the-rock-fish
The terrific form of the Hammer-fish.
And threatening me with horrid teeth
The terrible shark, the Sea hyena.                            120

There I hung, and I remembered with horror
That I was so far from human aid
Amongst all misshapen things the only reasoning Being
Alone in the grisly solitude
Far from the sound of human speech,                           125
In the dreary haunt of monsters.

Shuddering I thought, what crawls towards me,
Moving a hundred arms together,
Will seize me: in the sense of terror
I let go the branch of coral,                                    130
The whirlpool seized me with impetuous force
It was the means of saving me, for it bore me to the surface

The king was astonished
He spoke--the cup is thine,
And this ring also I destine for thee                            135
Adorned with costly gems,
If thou wilt venture once more and bring me tidings
Of what thou seest in the profoundest depths of the sea

The Daughter heard this with tender emotion,
And with caressing voice she implored                            140
Cease Father! enough of this cruel game
He has achieved for you, what none ever achieved before
And if you cannot restrain the wish of your heart
At least let the knights now shame the vassals.

Thereupon the king seized the cup,                               145
And hurled it into the whirlpool;
"If thou canst bring the cup again to this place
"Thou shalt be my best knight
And this day thou shalt embrace as a bridegroom
Her who now pleads thy cause with tender pity                    150

The inspiration of Heaven seized his soul
And it flashed boldly out of his eyes
He sees that lovely face blush;
He sees her turn pale and sink away,
Then longs he the precious prize to win,                         155
He springs down for life and Death.

The torrent is duly heard, duly it returns
The sound of thunder announces its coming
She stoops to gaze with the eye of love,
It comes!, the whole flood of water comes!                       160
It roars above, it roars beneath--
But it brings not the young page with it.

----------

[April 1843]

MS:   D(1)
Not previously published


360

Text:   l. 43:   "no more" written above "never"; neither is canceled
        l. 52:   "brave" written above "valiant"; neither is canceled
        l. 85:   "exulting band" written above "joyous troop"; neither is
        canceled
        l. 92:   "breathe" written above "dwell"; neither is canceled
        l. 157:  "duly" written above "indeed"; neither is canceled


**218**        **The Count of Hapsburg**


In Aix-la-Chappelle, in his imperial pomp,
    In an ancient hall,
Sat the sacred power of King Rudolph
At the festal coronation-banquet.
The count-palatine of the Rhine bore the dishes,              5
The King of Bohemia poured out the pearly wine,
    And all the seven electors,
As the choir of stars encircles the Sun
Surround assiduously the Lord of the World
    To discharge the dignity of their office                  10

And around filled the lofty gallery
    The people in joyous throng
Loud, mingled the sound of the trumpet
With the exulting shouts of the multitude
For after long and ruinous contest                            15
The fearful time when there was no emperor
Was ended, and there was again a judge on Earth
No longer blindly ruled the iron spear
The weak, the peaceful dreaded no longer
    To become the prey of the Strong.                         20

The emperor took the golden cup
And said with a pleased regard:
"Well shines the feast, well seems the banquet
    My royal heart to ravish,
But I miss the minstrel, the Bringer of joy,                  25
Who with sweet sounds stirred my breast,
    And with divine and lofty lore
I have been used to him from my youth up
And what has been my wont and habit as knight
I will not forego as emperor.                                 30

And lo! into the circle surrounding the prince
  Enters the minstrel, clad in long robes;
His hair shines silver-white
  Bleached by the plenitude of years.
"Sweet harmony sleeps in the golden strings,                    35
The minstrel sings for the minstrel's hire,
  He esteems the highest, the best,
What the heart wishes, what the sense desires;
Yet say, what is worthy of the emperor
  At his magnificent feast?"                                    40


"I will not dictate to the Minstrel, said
  The Master with a smile
He stands in the obligation of great lords
  He obeys the commanding hour
As in the air the storm-wind moans                             45
  We know not from whence it comes and roars,
  As the spring in secret depths;
So the song of the minstrel sounds from within
And stirs the might of those hidden feelings
  That so marvellously sleep in the heart.                     50
And sudden the Minstrel struck the chords
  With power he swept the strings
"Forth to the chase rode a noble knight
  To the chase of the rapid roe-buck,
Him followed his vassal with quiver & lance                    55
  And on stately charger mounted
He entered a wide plain
He heard a little bell tinkle afar
'Twas a priest, who the body of Jesus bore
  Before came the Sacristan.                                   60


And the noble earl bowed himself to the earth
  Uncovering his head with humility
To honour in the believing spirit of Christianity
  That which ransomed all mankind.
But a rivulet murmured through the field                       65
  Swelled by the rapid flood of the Giesbach
  Which checked the wanderer's step,
He laid aside the sacred blood
He drew quickly the shoes from his feet,
  In order to pass through the brook.                          70


"What doest thou?" asked the Earl
  Who watches him with astonishment:
"My lord I go to a dying man,
  Who hungers after the bread of heaven                        75
And as I approach the bridge of the brook


362

I find that the swift-flowing Giesbach
   Has torn it away by the whirl of its waves,
And because Salvation may reach the dying man
   I will now hastily
   Wade barefoot through the streamlet                    80

The earl placed him on his knightly steed
   And placed in his hand the splendid reins
That he might console the sick man who longed for him
   And not delay the holy office
He himself mounting his vassal's horse                    85
Proceeded to gratify the passion of the chase
   The priest went on his way
The next morning with grateful look
He brought back to the earl his charger
   Modestly leading it by the bridle                      90

God forbid cried the earl with humility
   That again for chase or battle
I should mount the charger
   That has born my Creator.
And if thou wilt not have it for thine own profit         95
Let it rest dedicated to the service of God.
   For I have given it to him
From whom I hold in tenure
Honour, earthly wealth, flesh, blood,
   Soul, breath and life.                                 100

"May God the almighty protector
   Who hears the prayer of the feeble-one
Bring thee to honour in this world and the next
According as thou now honourest him--
Thou art a mighty Earl--famed                             105
For knightly deeds in Switzerland,
   Around the[e] bloom six lovely daughters
May they--" cried he as if inspired
Bring six crowns into thy house
And may thy children be illustrious to                    110
   The farthest generation.

With head declined sat the emperor,
   As though he thought on bygone days,
Now when he looked into the eyes of the minstrel
   The true meaning of his words struck him.              115
He immediately recognized the priest's features,
And hid the starting stream of tears

In the purple folds of his mantle
All looked at the emperor
And recognized the Earl who had done this                    120
And honoured the godlike deed.

[April 1843]

MS:  D(1)
Not previously published
Text:  l. 41:  "dictate to" written above "command"; neither is
       canceled
       l. 54:  "roe buck" written above "chamois"; neither is canceled
       l. 88:  "look" written above "air"; neither is canceled

219    **Coronach**
       **pour un montagnard écossais**

On ne le voit plus sur la montagne
On ne le voit plus dans la forêt;
Il s'est évanoui comme la source tarie,
Comme la fontaine déssechée par les chaleurs de l'été

La pluie peut faire renaître la source,                        5
Demain la fontaine peut reparaître,
Mais pour Duncan il n'y a plus de lendemain,
Pour nous--plus de joie.

La main du moissoneur
L'empare des épis dorés                                        10
Mais la voix de celles qui pleurent maintenant
Lamente un hero mort dans la fleur de son age

Les vents sombres d'Automne
Ne détachent que des feuilles jaunes et séches
Mais notre fleur venait de s'épanouir                         15
Quand le souffle de la Mort l'abattit.

O toi! dont le pied était le plus leger dans la chasse
Dont les conseils étaient les plus sages en temps de danger
Toi-qui avais toujours les mains rouges, en revenant du
    champ de bataille,
Que tu dors maintenant d'un sommeil lourd et muet            20

Comme la rosée de la montagne,
Comme l'écume de la rivière,
Comme l'onde de la fontaine
Tu t'es évanoui! tu ne reviendras jamais!

[1842-1843]

MS: K
Not previously published

## 220    La Plainte de la jeune fille

Le vent mugit dans le bois de chênes,
Les nuages voilent le ciel;
La jeune fille est assise seule
Sur le rivage vert de l'océan
Les vagues se brisent avec violence,                    5
Entourée des ombres de la nuit elle soupire en solitude
Les yeux s'obscurcissent de larmes.

Mon coeur est mort; pour moi la terre est deserte
Elle n'offre rien de plus à mes souhaits
Sainte Vierge! reprends ton enfant                      10
J'ai joui du bonheur terrestre
J'ai vecu et j'ai aimé!

[Spring 1843]

MS: B(1)
Not previously published

## 221    Le Chasseur des Alpes

"Ne veux-tu pas garder l'agneau?
"L'agneau est si doux, si paisible
"Il branle les fleurs de l'herbe
"En bondissant sur les bords du ruisseau
Ma mère, ma mère laisser moi partir                     5
Pour la chasse sur les montagnes

"Ne veux tu pas appeler les troupeaux
"Avec le son joyeux du cor?
"Les accords doux des cloches
"Se mêlent avec les chants de la forêt                    10
Ma mère, ma mère laissez moi partir
Pour traverser les montagnes sauvages

Ne veux tu pas cultiver les fleurs
"Qui naissent amicalement dans les parterres du jardin
"La-haut nul jardin t'invite                              15
"Tout est desert sur les montagnes solitaire
Laissez les fleurs, laissez les fleurir;
Ma mère, ma mère laissez-moi partir!

Et le jeune montagnard est parti;
L'ardeur de la chasse le pousse, l'entraine;             20
Il ne s'arrête pas un instant, aveuglé de son zèle
Il s'elance dans les solitudes sombres des montagnes
La, légère comme la brise,
S'enfuit devant lui la craintive gazelle.

Elle grimpe sur les rochers herisés;                     25
Elle bondit à travers les abimes profonds;
En arrière le chasseur la suit
Avec l'arc de la mort

Maintenant elle atteint à la cime du rocher
Elle s'arrête sur la rude crête                          30
Ou la descente roide et soudaine du précipice
Fait disparaître le sentier.
Au-dessous d'elle est le gouffre béant
Derrière elle est l'ennemi

Avec un regard muet de desespoir                         35
Elle supplie l'homme cruel
Elle le supplie en vain, déjà la corde de l'arc est tendue
Lorsque s'elevant du vaste abîme
Apparaît le spectre, le genie des montagnes

Et avec sa main divine                                   40
Il protége l'animal tourmenté
"Faut-il" s'ecrie-t-il, "que tu apportes la mort et
    la souffrance
Jusqu'ici dans mon empire?
Il y a place pour tous dans la terre;
Pourquoi persecutes-tu mon troupeau?"                    45

[Spring 1843]

MS:  B(1)
Not previously published

366

Chevalier! mon coeur te consacre
L'affection fidèle d'une soeur
Ne cherche pas un autre amour
Car cela me fait de la peine
Je voudrais te voir toujours tranquille                    5
Lorsque tu viens, lorsque tu pars
Les larmes silencieux dans tes yeux
Je ne sais pas supporter.

Il l'écoute avec un douleur muette
À ses paroles le coeur lui saigne                          10
Il la serre vivement dans ses bras
Il s'élance sur son cheval de bataille
Il a envoyé chercher tous ses vassaux, dans la Suisse
Ils partent pour la Terre sainte
Chacun porte sur sa poitrine la Croix.                     15

Des grandes actions sont accomplies
Par le bras du héros
Les plumes de son casque flottent
Dans les rangs de l'ennemi
Et le nom de Toggenburg                                    20
Devient terrible à l'infidèle
Cependant son coeur de sa blessure
Ne peut pas se guérir

Pendant tout un an il s'est resigné à son chagrin
Il ne péut plus s'y résigner                               25
Le Repos il n'a jamais trouvé
Il abandonne l'armée
Il voit un vaisseau sur le rivage de Joppa
Dont les voiles sont enflées
Il retourne dans cette chère patrie                        30
Ou respire sa bien-aimée.

Le pelerin frappe à la porte de son chateau
Hélas elle s'ouvre avec un mot foudroyant
"Celle que tu cherches est la fiancée de Jesus;
"Hier était la fête du jour                                35
"Où elle epousa Dieu"

Alors il quitte à jamais
Le chateau de ses ancetres
Il ne voit plus ses armes
Ni son fidéle cheval de bataille                           40
Il se batît une cabane

Ou le couvent s'élevait
Au mileu de tilleuls sombres
Là il attendait de l'aube jusqu'au crépuscule
Il attendait seul, le calme de l'espérance sur front          45

Pendant des heures entières
Il regardait vers le couvent
Vers la fenêtre de son amante
Jusqu'à ce qu'elle s'y montra
Douce, sereine comme un ange.                                 50
Et alors il s'endormit paisiblement
Cherissant toujours un nouvel espoir pour le lendemain
Ainsi s'ecoulèrent plusieurs jours plusieurs années même
Il attendait toujours la sans plaintes sans larmes
Jusqu'à ce que là fenêtre s'ouvrit                           55

Jusqu'à ce que son amante se montra
    Se pencha vers la vallée
Douce, sereine comme un ange.

Un matin on le trouva mort
Sa figure pâle et calme                                      60
Etait encore tourné vers la fenetre de sa bien-aimée

[Spring 1843]

MS:   B(1)
Not previously published


223   **Chant funèbre pour l'Indien mort**


Il est assis là sur la natte;
Tout droit il est assis
Il conserve le maintien qu'il avait
Lorsqu'il vivait encore.
Mais où est la vigueur de sa main?                            5
Où est le souffle de son haleine
Où est la clarté de ses yeux?
Brillants, perçants comme ceux d'un faucon
Ses yeux qui autrefois savaient suivre
Les traces du renne                                          10
Sur les vagues de l'herbe longue et ondoyante;
Sur la rosée des savanes.

368

Ces membres agiles qui autrefois
Traversaient la neige,
Legers comme le cerf;                                                    15
Rapides comme le chevreuil.
Ces bras qui fléchissaient
L'arc fort et raide
Hélas! la vie est partie éteint
Il se relâchent, ils pendent sans mouvement                             20

Pour lui, il est bien-heureux
Il est allé dans un pays où il n'y a plus de neige, plus de
   faim, plus de travail
Où les champs sont couverts de blé
Qui naît spontanément.
Où les arbres sont peuplés d'oiseaux,                                    25
Les forêts d'animaux
Les fleuves de poissons dorés.

Il s'est enfui, au monde de fantômes,
Il nous a laissés ici seul
Il nous a laissé chanter son hymne funébre,                             30
Louer ses actions vaillantes,
Enterrer son cadavre frais

Apportez les derniers cadeaux;
Faites resonner la lamentation
Que tout soit enterré avec lui                                          35
Qui lui plaisait lorsqu'il vivait
Mettez sous sa tête la hâche
Qu'il maniail si vaillamment
Aussi une hanche d'ours
Car le voyage est long.                                                 40

Aussi son couteau tranchant et poli
Avec lequel de la tête de son ennemi
Vîte avec trois coups adroits
Il pêlait la peau et la chevelure

Mettez aussi dans sa main                                               45
Du fard pour peindre son corps,
Afin qu'il puisse paraître tout éclatant,
   Dans le monde d'esprits.

[Spring 1843]

MS:   B(1)
Not previously published

Je vois devant moi le Gladiateur, il repose sur l'arène;
Sa tête s'abaisse, il consent à la mort mais il dompte l'agonie.
Les dernières gouttes de son sang coulent de son flanc;
Elles tombent lourdes et lentement
Comme la pluiè qui prédit l'orage.                                    5
L'arène, la foule disparaissent à ses yeux éteints,
Il meurt en entendant les cris féroces
Qui signalent le triomphe de son antagoniste

Il les entendit avec indifference
Son âme errait sur les rives du Danube                               10
Elle planait sur le toit de cette rude chaumière
Où jouaient ses jeunes fils, où pleurait leur mère!
Lui! père, époux! il expire pour l'amusement d'un Romain!
Ces pensée allumaient les dernières étincelles
Dans ses veines epuisées;                                            15
Et faut-il qu'il meure sans trouver un vengeur!
Levez vous barbares, altérés de sang!
Levez-vous! étanchez votre soif!

[Spring 1843]

MS:  B(1)
Not previously published

## Appendix B

## Missing Poems

From information supplied by Charlotte, it is possible to establish the existence of at least ten poems for which the manuscripts have disappeared and which seem never to have been transcribed.

**(a)** **A Book of Rhymes**, dated December 17, 1829. The title-page was inscribed "Rhymes, Sold by Nobody. And Printed by Herself, &c, &c. Haworth, Dec 17, 1829. Anno Domini." It was part of Sotheby's sale of Mrs. Nicholls' property in 1914 (lot 193) and was again sold by Walpole Galleries in November, 1916. According to Charlotte's **Catalogue of my Books with the periods of their completion up to August 3 1830**--F(1), the volume contained nine poems:
1) the beauty of nature
2) a short poem
3) meditations while journeying in a Canadian forest
4) Song of an Exile
5) on seeing the ruins of the tower of Babel
6) A thing of 14 lines
7) lines written on the bank of a river one fine sumer evening
8) Spring a song
9) Autumn a song

**(b)** The September 1830 issue of **Blackwoods Young Mens Magazine** contained, according to Charlotte's General Index in the December number, one poem:
1) **The Midnight Song by the Marquis of Douro**

In addition, Sotheby's 1907 sale of Nicholls' property listed as lot 14 some verses by Charlotte in a Book of Common Prayer. Finally, Mildred Christian's Census notes "Twenty-two lines written in pencil, sold by Anderson Auction Co. on April 11, 1905." It is not clear, however, if these are lines of poetry or prose.

Appendix C

## Items of Disputed Authorship

All the items in this edition either carry Charlotte's signature or are in her hand. However from the available biographical information we know that she and Branwell often collaborated. It is likely therefore that Branwell contributed to some of the poems in this volume, but to what extent will probably never be known. Because of the activities of Wise and Shorter, some of the poems now definitely established as Branwell's were earlier ascribed to Charlotte. These include:

**(a)** How fast that Horse rushed thundering by
With Arching neck and flashing eye
So black the Night so loud the Storm
I scarce could know its fleeting form
And yet the those flanks all dashed with mire
Those Nostrils wide which seem to expire
The hot short breath of agony

The lines appear in Charlotte's manuscript **The Scrap Book** in the British Library, on the verso of the last page of a "Letter to the right honourable Arthur Marquis of Ardrah," dated December 6, 1834, and signed "Zamorna C Brontë." The lines are, however, in Branwell's hand, trial lines for the opening section of his poem **Misery**.

**(b)** It seems as to the bleeding Heart
    With dying torments riven
A quickened Life in every part
    By Fancys force was given
And all those dim disjointed dreams
Wherewith the railing memory teams
    Are but the bright reflection
Flashed upward from the scattered glass
Of Mirror broken on the grass
Which shapeless figures in each piece
    Reveals without connection

And is her Mirror broke at last
    Who motionless is laid


    As lifelike as before

She thought when that confusion crossed
    Upon her dying mind
Twas sense and soul and memory lost
    Though feeling burned behind
And that bright Heaven has touched a chord
And that Wide West has waked a word
    Can still the spirits storm
Tell all the griefs that brought her here
Each gushing with a bitterer tear
Round her returning sight appear
    In more tremendous form

These two fragments on a scrap of paper at the University of Texas
Library are undated and unsigned. Though first published as Emily's,
both are in Branwell's hand, and form part of his poem "Well! I will lift
my eyes once more," signed and dated "P.B. B___të, Feb. 7, 1838" (Feb.
9, 1837 in SHB C and B).


There remain, however, five poems and fragments attributed to
Charlotte, which I do not believe to be hers:

**(a)** "Highminded Frenchman love not the Ghost." Alexander (item
229) attributes the poem to Charlotte, but see the commentary for
Poem 1 in this volume.

**(b)** "What is more glorious in nature or art." Alexander (item
414) attributes the poem to Charlotte, but see the commentary for
Poem 1 in this volume.

**(c) I never can forget**

-----------

Tho' time may pass & years may flie
And every hope decay and die
Tho' distant thou yet still my heart
From love and thee can ne'er depart
I'll bless the hour when first we met
For thee I never can forget

These lines, at the BPM, unsigned and undated, are written on a square of
ink paper which has been glued to cream colored paper, folded to make an
envelope. They were found in Charlotte's desk, but are not in her hand.
In all likelihood they were presented to her.

**(d) Stanzas**

Often rebuked, yet always back returning
    To those first feelings that were born with me,
And leaving busy chase of wealth and learning
    For idle dreams of things which cannot be:

373

To-day, I will seek not the shadowy region;
    Its unsustaining vastness waxes drear;
And visions rising, legion after legion,
    Bring the unreal world too strangely near.

I'll walk, but not in old heroic traces,
    And not in paths of high morality,
And not among the half-distinguished faces,
    The clouded forms of long-past history.

I'll walk where my own nature would be leading:
    It vexes me to choose another guide:
Where the gray flocks in ferny glens are feeding;
    Where the wild wind blows on the mountain side

What have those lonely mountains worth revealing?
    More glory and more grief than I can tell:
The earth that wakes one human heart to feeling
    Can centre both the worlds of Heaven and Hell.

There is no known manuscript for this poem, published in 1850 by
Charlotte as Emily's. In his 1941 edition of Emily's poems (pp. 255-56)
Hatfield is inclined to attribute the poem to Charlotte. Yet, it seems
to me that the language and content are characteristically Emily's,
especially in the last two stanzas. Undoubtedly Charlotte "edited" the
poem, as she did others, in preparation for the 1850 edition, but it is
unlikely that she made up a whole poem and attributed it to her sister,
an opinion shared by Professor Edward Chitham, who is preparing a new
edition of Emily's poems.

### (e) To the horse black Eagle which I Rode at the battle of Zamorna

Swart steed of night, thou hast charged thy last
O'er the red war-trampled plain
Now fallen asleep is the battle blast
It is stilled above the slain

Now hushed is the clang of armour bright
Thou willt never bear me more
To the deadliest press of the gathering fight
Through seas of noble gore

And the cold eyes of midnight skies
Shall not pour their light on thee
When the wearied host of the conqueror lies
On a field of victory

Rest now in thy glory noble steed
Rest all thy wars are done
True is the love & high the meed
Thou from thy lord hast won

In daisied lawns sleep peacefully
Dwell by the quiet wave
Till death shall sound his signal cry
And call thee to thy grave.

These lines, on an undated and unsigned scrap in the Berg Collection (NYPL), have been attributed to Emily, Charlotte, and Branwell. Though first published as Emily's (Shorter EJB 1910), there is no evidence that Emily was ever involved with Angria. The content and language would seem to be Branwell's rather than Charlotte's.

Finally, a number of Charlotte's juvenile prose manuscripts contain bits of verse; many of these I have been able to identify as quotations (sometimes accurate, sometimes loosely quoted) from such authors as Shakespeare, Goldsmith, Thomas Campbell, Burns, Scott, Coleridge, and Byron, and from her own poems. There remain seven such bits for which I have not been able to find a source, but which I strongly suspect are also quotations:

**(a)** Whose long-long groves
Eternal murmer made

From "Liffey Castle," by Charles Wellesley, dated August 12, 1830, in **The Young Mens Magazine** for August 1830.

**(b)** The solemn hush of twilight lay
On every tongue around

From "A Day at Parry's Palace," by Lord Charles Wellesley, in **The Young Mens Magazine** for October 1830.

**(c)** when a human step suddenly broke the delicious
calm reigning around & (unromantic incident) the
apparition not of,
        "A lady fair and bright
        With a crown of flowers and a robe of light"
but of a smart footman in a blue coat with silver
epaulettes appeared stealing down from the brow
of one of the nearest hills.

From Chapter III of **The Green Dwarf,** dated July 10-September 2, 1833.

**(d)** "the vision for ever, ever vanished"

**(e)** I see the lake the mountain rill
    Before me darkly flowing
In the passes of the low great hill
    I hear the night wind blowing

Chapter epigraphs from **High Life in Verdopolis,** March 20, 1834.

**(f)** Of course she'll bring under her wing
    The unfledged dove that shares all our love

From a prose narrative dated July 21, 1838, these lines occur in a letter from George Vernon.

**(g)** His form would fill her eye by night
    His voice her ear by day
The touch that pressed her fingers slight
    Would never pass away

From a prose narrative dated March 26, 1839, these words are spoken by Sir William Percy about Elizabeth Hastings.

**Appendix D**

**Glossary of Glass Town/Angria Person and Placenames**

I wish to acknowledge my indebtedness in the preparation of this glossary to notes and glossaries in the following publications: Ratchford Legends; Gérin Five Novelettes; SHB Misc II; **Everyman's Companion to the Brontës**, ed. Barbara and Gareth Lloyd Evans, London: J.M. Dent & Sons Ltd., 1982; and Alexander, EW.

As many readers will not be fully familiar with Charlotte's juvenilia, I include a brief summary of the Glass Town/Angria narrative. In 1826 the Brontë children began the creation of a series of plays using a set of toy soldiers purchased by the Rev. Mr. Brontë for Branwell. Inspired by their reading of such adventurers as Mungo Park and using Goldsmith's **A Grammar of General Geography**, the children sent their twelve adventurers off in 1829 to found a new colony on the east coast of Africa, initially consisting of Wellingtonsland (Charlotte), Parrysland (Emily), Ross'sland (Anne), and Sneachiesland (Branwell), with Twelve Town as the capital of the Confederacy. Before the adventurers can begin construction of Twelve Town they have to defeat the local inhabitants, the Ashantee, who continue to attack the settlers periodically thereafter. Presiding over the activities of the Twelves as guardians and protectors are four Genii--Talli, Emmi, Anni and Branni--who have magical and divine powers, including instant healing and resurrection from the dead. At first the Confederacy is ruled by the Duke of York (Frederick Guelph), but Arthur Wellesley, after going back to England with news of the colony, returns as the famous Duke of Wellington, conqueror of Napoleon, and is chosen to be King of what has now become the Glass Town Confederacy with Great Glass Town as the capital, renamed by the end of 1830 as Verreopolis, then Verdopolis. Wellington has two sons: Arthur, Marquis of Douro, and Lord Charles Wellesley. Arthur falls in love with Marian Hume, the daughter of his father's physician, but is also the object of Lady Zenobia Ellrington's affections. After Arthur marries Marian in 1831, Charlotte reveals that both have had previous loves: Marian was betrothed to Henry Percy, who was murdered in the South Seas; Arthur had a child, Ernest Edward Gordon, by Lady Helen Victorine, who died in giving birth.

Arthur and Marian also have a child (Arthur Julius), but Arthur, who has by now become the Duke of Zamorna for his exploits in wars against the French and the Ashantee, falls in love with Mary, the daughter of Alexander Percy, Lord Ellrington and Earl of Northangerland. Marian steps aside, dies of a broken heart and consumption (as does her son), and Zamorna marries Mary. His son Ernest is given into the care of Mina Laury, Wellington's forester's daughter, who once nursed Douro/Zamorna and has subsequently become his devoted mistress. In 1834 Zamorna requests and is granted his own Kingdom of Angria within the Confederacy

377

by the legislature in Verdopolis as a reward for his courageous defense of the country. He appoints Northangerland, his father-in-law, as Prime Minister. The latter soon turns against Zamorna, however, and after much political conflict between the two, mounts a rebellion with the support of the government and its forces in Verdopolis. Zamorna's forces are defeated in a series of battles; Zamorna is eventually captured and sentenced to death, but is allowed by Northangerland to sail into exile on Ascension Island. During the civil war, Zamorna's eldest son, Ernest, is horribly murdered by Quashia, the son of the Ashantee King Sai Tootoo, defeated by Wellington. Wellington had adopted Quashia, but the latter has turned against his protectors. At the beginning of the conflict Zamorna decides to revenge himself on his father-in-law by abandoning his wife Mary, knowing that banishing her will kill her and cause her father terrible grief. With the help of Mina Laury and Warner Howard Warner, Zamorna is eventually able to return from exile and recapture his kingdom. Initially Mary dies while Zamorna is in exile, but Charlotte, unable to abandon her heroine, revises the history of events and has Mary survive to become Queen again. Northangerland, allowed by Zamorna to live as a private individual provided he stays out of politics, passes his time restlessly and querulously at Alnwick, the Percy residence. Zamorna, while continuing to rule Angria with his wife, also continues to keep his mistresses, Mina Laury and Caroline Vernon, who is his ward and the illegitimate daughter of his father-in-law.

**Adrian, Emperor:**  See Wellesley, Arthur Augustus Adrian

**Adrianopolis:**  Emperor Adrian's city on the banks of the Calabar; capital of Angria; 150 miles from Verdopolis; destroyed by Zamorna himself to prevent it falling into Northangerland's hands during the Revolution.

**African Queen:**  Quashia's mother.

**Agars, the:**  W.H. Warner's clan; Zamorna's supporters.

**Albion:**  Name given to Arthur Wellesley, the Marquis of Douro, in "Albion and Marina."

**Alnwick House:**  The Percy family home in Sneachiesland on the banks of the Derwent, where Mary is sent by Zamorna, becomes ill, and dies; later Charlotte changes her mind about Mary's death.

**Angria:**  Kingdom created in 1834 for Zamorna from African territories he conquered; capital Adrianopolis; has seven provinces--Zamorna, Angria, Douro, Calabar, Northangerland, Arundel, Etrei.  Province of Angria; capital, Angria; Lord Lieutenant, W.H. Warner.

**Angrian Wars:** (1) Against the local natives, the Ashantees, on landing in Africa; (2) against the Ashantee prince, Quashia, stirred up by Rogue and helped by the French; (3) an insurrection raised by Rogue in 1831 and a rebellion in 1832; (4) the Great Revolution raised by Northangerland against Zamorna, June 1836.

**Angus, Marina:** Name given to Marian Hume in **Albion and Marina**; d. June 18, 1815.

**Aornus:** Mountain; abode of the chief Genii.

**Aragua:** River in the Caucasus near Elborous Mountain.

**Arbor, Captain:** Literary figure and singer in Angria.

**Ardrah, Marquis of:** Arthur Parry, Prince of Parrysland; ally of Northangerland; defeated by W.H. Warner.

**Arundel:** Province of Angria; capital--Seaton; Lord Lieutenant--the Earl of Arundel, a gallant courteous chevalier.

**Ashantees:** Natives of Ashantee (Ashanti on the African Gold Coast) against whom the Twelves fight.

**Badey, Dr. Alexander Hume:** One of the Twelves; physician to the Duke of Wellington, and father of Marian Hume.

**Boulsworth:** Hill near Haworth.

**Bravey, Sir William:** One of the Twelves, co-founder of Glass Town.

**Bravey's Inn:** Inn in Glass Town where Wellington and his sons and friends meet to gossip and discuss war, politics, and literature.

**Bud, Captain John:** Author of **The History of the Young Men** and other works, the greatest prose writer of early Glass Town; a pseudonym of Branwell.

**Calabar:** Province in Angria; capital Gazemba; a river in Angria on which Adrianopolis is situated.

**Camalia:** Scene of a battle with the Ashantees.

**Caversham, Baron:** Joins with Percy against Zamorna.

**Charlesworth, Lady Emily:** Bravey's niece; abducted by Percy on eve of her marriage to Lord St Clair.

**Cirhala:** River on which Evesham is situated.

**Coomassie:** Ashantee capital at the foot of Mt. Aornus destroyed by the Twelves.

**De Lisle, Frederick:** Highly regarded and sought-after portrait painter and engraver in Verdopolis.

**Dongola:** Capital of Etrei, scene of a massacre.

**Douro:** Province; capital--Douro; Lord Lieutenant--Earl of Jordan; a river in Angria.

**Douro, Marquis of:** See Wellesley, Arthur Augustus Adrian.

**Edwardston:** The chief manufacturing town in Angria; Zamorna defeated there by Northangerland.

**Elborous:** Mountain in the Caucasus, and near the Great Lake of the Genii. The Genii hold court in the snows of Elborous and Kasibeck.

**Ellrington, Lady Zelzia:** Name given to Zenobia in **Albion and Marina.**

**Ellrington, Lady Zenobia:** Rival to Marian Hume for the love of the Marquis of Douro; m. Alexander Rogue (later Percy, Earl of Northanger-land) after being abducted to his ship, and became Countess of North-angerland; "the most learned woman of the age"; "the modern Cleopatra"; "the Verdopolitan de Staël."

**Enara, Henri Fernando di:** Baron and Lord Lieutenant of Etrei; un-defeated supporter of Zamorna in the Revolution; Commander-in-Chief of Angrian forces.

**Etrei:** Province; capital Dongola, Lord Lieutenant, Henri Fernando Di Enara.

**Etty, Sir William:** Angrian artist; supposed son of Northangerland by his first wife, Maria di Segovia; daughter--Zorayda.

**Evesham:** City on the Cirhala; fortified by Revolutionary troops; taken by General Thornton in the last major battle in Zamorna's return to power.

**Fidena, Prince of:** See Sneaky, John Augustus.

**Fidena:** Large city in Sneachiesland; 300 miles from Verdopolis.

**Flower, Sir John:** Becomes Baron Flower and Viscount Richton; eminent scholar in Verdopolis and Branwell's pseudonym from 1831-34.

**Gambia:**  River on which Glass Town is situated.

**Gazemba:**  Town and plain on the banks of the Calabar where Zamorna reviews his troops before the battle of Evesham.

**Genii:**  Chief Genii:  Talli--C; Branni--B; Emmi--E; Anni--A; guardians and protectors of the Twelves.

**Gifford, Sir John:**  Chief Judge in Glass Town; President of the Antiquarian Society; a caricature of Branwell.

**Glass Town:**  Town built when Twelves Town destroyed; area in West Africa where the Young Men settle after their voyage from England; divided into four countries--Wellingtonsland, Sneachiesland, Parrysland, Rossland.  Great Glass Town is a separate area with the same name for its capital, afterwards Verdopolis.

**Gravey's Inn:**  Named after Emily's soldier who was one of the Twelves, King of Parrysland, and Arch Primate of Verdopolis.

**Grey, George Turner:**  Owner of Ardsley Hall; throat cut after the battle of Edwardston.

**Guadima:**  River on which Verdopolis is built.

**Hart, Lily:**  Plays the harp and sings; nurses, then marries John Sneaky; becomes Marchioness of Fidena; son--John Augustus Sneaky.

**Hartford, Lord Edward:**  General in the Angrian army; fights with Zamorna over Mina Laury, courts Jane Moore.

**Hastings, Elizabeth:**  Henry's sister; companion to Jane Moore; rejects Sir William Percy's plea to become his mistress.

**Hastings, Captain Henry:**  Son of a farmer; captain in the Angrian Infantry; cashiered March 1839 for shooting his superior officer and involved in a plot against Zamorna; pseudonym for Branwell.

**Hawkescliffe Forest:**  Location of the Lodge of the Cross of Rivaulx, Zamorna's country residence, where he courts Mary Percy and keeps Caroline Vernon and Mina Laury.

**Hume, Florence Marian:**  Badey's daughter; wife of Douro/Zamorna; mother of Arthur Julius, Marquis of Almeida; as a child betrothed to Henry Percy; repudiated by Zamorna for Mary Percy; dies of consumption, as does her son.

**Hyla (Hyle, Hylle):**  Vast, stormy lake.

**Ierne:** Daughter of Zamorna and Mary.

**Indirce:** River on the banks of which Wellington's palace is situated.

**Justine:** Wife of Ned Laury and mother of Mina; Zamorna's nurse and foster mother.

**Kashna Quamina:** Old king of the Ashantees; dies 1779.

**Kashna, Quashia:** Sai Tootoo's son; adopted by Wellington and brought up with his children; becomes leader of the Ashantees, Zamorna's enemy and murders his son, Ernest.

**Kashna, Sai Tootoo:** Quamina's son; killed at the Battle of Coomassie.

**Kasibeck:** Mountain in the Caucasus; snowy region where Genii hold court.

**Laury, Edward (Ned):** Father of Mina; forester on Wellington's estates; Glass Town villain and body-snatcher.

**Laury, Mina:** Ned's raven-haired daughter; born on same day as, and brought up with Zamorna; companion to his wife Marian; nurse to his children; Zamorna's loyal mistress, established by him, first at Fort Adrian then at the Lodge of Rivaulx, Hawkescliffe; meets the exiled Zamorna at Marseilles; helps to restore him to his kingdom; Hartford and Zamorna duel over her.

**Manfred the Magician:** Brother to Crashey; President of the university on the Philosopher's Island, where the children of noblemen are educated.

**Marina:** See Angus, Marina.

**Moray:** Another name for Murry.

**Moore, Jane:** The "Rose of Zamorna"; a "handsome easy-conditioned creature," known for her beauty.

**Mornington:** Wellington's residence in the hills of Ellisbank.

**Murry (Murray):** A member of Wellington's military staff.

**Naughty, Richard (Young Man):** Cold, brutal follower of Northangerland with a cottage on the Great Glass Town Moors; Glass Town villain and body-snatcher.

**Northangerland:** Province of Angria; capital--Pequena; Lord Lieutenant--Earl of Northangerland--Alexander Percy.

**Olympia:** Angrian river on which Zamorna is situated.

**Parry, Sir William Edward:** Father of Arthur, Marquis of Ardrah; one of the Twelves; King of Parrysland.

**Percy, Alexander Augustus:** First wife, Maria de Segovia--son William Etty. In 1814 m. Lady Maria Henrietta Wharton; three sons--Henry, Edward, William, whom he orders S'Death to dispose of, but S'Death saves Edward and William; also one daughter--Mary Henrietta; wife dies of consumption; heartbroken, he leads dissipated life, gambling, drinking, cheating at cards; involved in the March 1831 and 1832 rebellions; after the battle of Haslingden, is captured, executed by a firing squad, but brought back to life again; returns as the handsome Colonel Alexander Augustus Percy; abducts Lady Emily Charlesworth, trying, unsuccessfully, to get rid of her fiance, Lord St Clair, by getting him arraigned for treason; is imprisoned for treachery; released, he elopes with Harriet Montmorency, later forsaking her; spends many years wandering the world in his boat "The Rover," as bandit, pirate, etc.; seizes Lady Zenobia Ellrington and her father from their ship, abruptly woos and marries her; returns to Verdopolis, entering politics as Leader of the Movement against the establishment and upper classes; produces bill to abolish the two Houses of Government and make the four kingdoms into one nation with a president; sets up his own provisional Government dissolving the House of Commons; becomes great friends with Arthur Wellesley (Zamorna), the Marquis of Douro; helps him to become King of Angria (1834); becomes his Prime Minister--an alliance sealed by the marriage of his daughter, Mary Henrietta, to Zamorna; leads a Revolution (1836) against Zamorna; defeats him in battle at Edwardston, but saves his life by sending him safely into exile in "The Rover"; on Zamorna's successful attempt to regain his country, Percy is allowed to live, provided he lives quietly as a private individual; grows more abrasive and irritable the older he gets. Variously known as Rogue, Percy, Ellrington, Northangerland; his mistresses include--Harriet O'Connor, Lady Georgina Greville, Lady St James, Louisa Dance (Vernon), Miss Delph, Madame Lalande.

**Percy, Edward:** Unpleasant, rejected eldest son of Northangerland; given at birth to S'Death to be destroyed but saved by him; a destitute and wicked childhood; later sets up his brother in the wool trade; saves the Marquis of Fidena's life; founds Edwardston, where owns a new mill; becomes MP, Lord Viscount Percy, rising to post of Secretary of Trade in Angria; duels with the Marquis of Ardrah; m. Maria Sneaky in June 1834; haughty, handsome, cruel, dishonest, with a coarse mind.

**Percy, Henry:** Northangerland's son; drowned at his father's command off Otaheite in the South Seas; as a child married to Marian Hume.

**Percy, Lady Mary**: Northangerland's first wife; mother of Henry, Edward, William and Mary Henrietta.

**Percy, Mary Henrietta**: Northangerland's daughter; Zamorna's second wife; Marchioness of Douro, Duchess of Zamorna, Queen of Angria; rejected by Zamorna when Northangerland begins his revolution; sent to Alnwick where Branwell allows her to die; Charlotte also at first, then lets her linger on in decline.

**Percy, William**: Captain; rejected younger son of Northangerland; m. Cecilia, daughter of the Earl of Seymour; purchases Elm Grove; becomes Sir William, Lieutenant General who tracks down Henry Hastings, and unsuccessfully woos Hastings' sister, Elizabeth, to be his mistress; grows to hate his elder brother Edward who dominates him; plays flute; "thin, pallid and taciturn."

**Rhymer, Henry**: Poet in a play, **The Poetaster**, in which Young Soult is satirized; caricature of Branwell.

**Rogue, Alexander**: See Percy, Alexander.

**Roslyn**: Supporter of Zamorna; son of Lord St Clair.

**Rover, The**: Northangerland's boat.

**S'Death, Robert Patrick**: Alias King; Rogue's partner and servant; saves William and Edward Percy as babies from death; captain of The Rover.

**Segovia, Maria di (later Augusta di Segovia)**: Alexander Percy's first wife.

**Selby, Lady**: Wife of Major-General Selby; member of Verdopolis society.

**Seymour, Charles**: Emperor Adrian's son.

**Seymours, the**: Seymour girls--Eliza, Georgiana (Northangerland's mistress), Cecilia, Agnes, Catherine, Helen.

**Sneaky, John**: 1$^{st}$ Duke of Fidena; m. Lily Hart.

**Sneaky, John Augustus**: 2$^{nd}$ Duke of Fidena, Marquis of Rossendale; m. Ierne.

**Soult**: Alexander, Duke of Dalmatia; Young Soult, "The Rhymer," "poet" of Glass Town (i.e. Branwell); his "apparel torn; his shoes often slipshod and his stockings full of holes"; his expression "wild and haggard, and generally he is eternally twisting his mouth to one side or another"; "devilish but humane and good hearted"; possessed of "true genius"; Charlotte recognizes his "beginnings are small" but believes "his end will be great." (Soult fought the Duke of Wellington; later ambassador at Queen Victoria's coronation.)

**Sunart, Lake**: The home of Lady Victorine.

**Sydney, Edward G.**: Hero of **The Foundling**; goes to Eton and Oxford; friend of Douro, marries and divorces Lady Julia Wellesley, Douro's cousin; story of his background as the unknown son of Guelph (Duke of York) later denied.

**Thornton, Lady Julia**: See Wellesley, Julia.

**Thornton, Sir William**: Guardian of Charles Wellesley; m. Lady Julia Wellesley.

**Tower of All Nations**: Landmark in Glass Town; modeled on the Tower of Babel.

**Townshend, Charles**: Lord Charles Wellesley renounces his family, becomes C. T., author of **Julia**, **Mina Laury**; selfish, arrogant, but always curious, wry cynical sense of humour; friend of Sir William Percy.

**Tree, Sergeant**: Publisher, printer and book-seller of Glass Town; one of Charlotte's pseudonyms.

**Twelves, The**: Originally B.'s toy soldiers; become the discoverers, explorers, and settlers of Ashantee, forming the Glass Town Confederacy; the original Twelves chosen were: C.'s--Marcus O'Donell, Ferdinand Cortez (Corky), Felix de Rothesay, Eugene Cameron, Harold FitzGeorge, Henry Clinton, Francis Stewart, Ronald Traquair, Ernest Fortescue, Gustavus Donaley, Frederic Brunswick, Arthur Wellesley; B's--Butter Crashey, age 140; Alexander Cheeky, surgeon, age 20; Arthur Wellesley, trumpeter, age 12; William Edward Parry, trumpeter, age 15; Alexander Sneaky, sailor, age 17; John Ross, lieutenant, age 16; William Bravey, sailor, age 27; Edward Gravey, sailor, age 17; Frederic Guelph, sailor, age 27; Stumps (died May 18, 1770) age 12; Monkey, age 11; Tracky, age 10; Crackey, age 5--these last four were middies. The First Twelves later became the House of Lords of Glass Town; a Second Twelves became the House of Commons; four of them--Arthur Wellesley, Sneaky, Parry and Ross became kings of their countries--Wellingtonsland, Sneachiesland, Parrysland and Ross(es)land.

**Verdopolis**: Capital of the Glass Town Confederacy--first called Glass Town, then Verreopolis, then Verdopolis; on the river Guadima; center for government, "high life," and commerce; "a splendid city rising with such graceful haughtiness from the green realm of Neptune" with walls, battlements, a cathedral, the domed Bravey's hotel, the Great Tower, and many fine streets with fine shops. (See also Glass Town)

**Vernon, Caroline:** Daughter of Northangerland and Louise Vernon (Dance); later Zamorna's ward, then his mistress.

**Victorine, Lady Helen:** Zamorna's first wife; dies giving birth to Ernest Edward Gordon Wellesley.

**Warner, Warner Howard:** Barrister; head of Clan Agars, Howards and Warners; Chancellor of the Exchequer and Home Secretary for Zamorna; Lord Lieutenant of Angria; Fellow of St Michael's; MP for the Philosophers' Isle; succeeds Northangerland as Zamorna's prime minister; m. Ellen Grenville; residences--Warner Hall, Warner Hotel (Verdopolis), Howard House (Adrianopolis), Woodhouse Cliffe (near Freetown); an honest man whose advice is often rejected by Zamorna; credited with the gift of second sight.

**Wellesley:** 16 noble ladies around Zamorna--Julia, Amelia, Sophia, Arabella, Harriet, Emily, Marcia, Madeleine, Zouey, Jessica, Olivia, Margaret, Geraldine, Augusta, Rosamund, Adela.

**Wellesley, Arthur:** Duke of Wellington; father of Arthur Augustus Adrian and Charles Albert Florian; adoptive father of Quashia; protector of Edward Sydney.

**Wellesley, Arthur Augustus Adrian:** b. 1812/13; Wellington's eldest son; Marquis of Douro and Alderwood; Earl of Evesham and Baron Leyden; becomes Duke of Zamorna; King of Angria; eventually Emperor Adrian; m. (1) Lady Helen Victorine, one son, Ernest Edward; (2) Marian Hume, one son, Arthur Julius, Marquis of Almeida; (3) Lady Mary Henrietta (Northangerland's daughter), 6 sons--Archduke Frederic Julius and Alexander (twins), Augustus Stanley, Charles Seymour, Edward Mornington and little Arthur, and a daughter, Ierne; mistresses include Rosamund Wellesley, Mina Laury, Caroline Vernon. Loved by Lady Zenobia Ellrington who tries to prevent his marriage to Marian Hume by trickery and magic. Awarded territory, Angria--taken from parts of the other provinces of the Confederacy--for his fighting on behalf of the Glass Town Confederacy against the Ashantee, Napoleon and the French; there builds his capital, Adrianopolis, which he later destroys to prevent it falling into the hands of Northangerland's Revolutionaries; goes into exile; returns, helped by Warner Howard Warner and Mina Laury; retakes his kingdom, demoting Northangerland to the status of private individual (see Percy, Alexander). As Douro is "tall and slender," with a slightly "Roman nose," "dark auburn hair" and of "mild and human disposition"; as Zamorna becomes more flamboyant--"impetuous and stormy pride, diving and soaring enthusiasm, war and poetry, are kindling their fires in his veins and his wild blood boils from his heart"; he suffers paroxysms and fits; his relationship with Northangerland the pivot of the many juvenile stories.

**Wellesley, Charles Albert Florian:** Twin brother to Arthur; when presented to the public he leans too far out of the window and falls, seemingly to his death; at first an ugly meddling imp called Charlie (with a drink named after him); later a "lively elegant" man with a "strong and handsome" countenance; as Charles Townshend, the author of several works including **The Green Dwarf, Corner Dishes, The Spell, My Angria and the Angrians.**

**Wellesley, Ernest Edward Gordon:** Baron Gordon; Lord of Avondale; son of Zamorna and Lady Helen Victorine; murdered by Quashia while in the care of Mina Laury.

**Wellesley, Ierne:** Daughter of Zamorna and Mary.

**Wellesley, Julia:** Zamorna's cousin; "a foolish petted little girl"; m. (1) Edward Sydney; (2) General Thornton.

**Wellesley, Rosamund:** Committed suicide for love of her cousin, Zamorna.

**Wiggins Family:** Patrick Benjamin, Charlotte, Emily and Anne; C's caricatures of the Brontë family--Patrick is a "slightly built man attired in a black coat and raven grey trousers, his hat placed neatly at the back of his head revealing a bush of carroty hair so arranged that at the side it projects like two spread hands, a pair of spectacles placed across a prominent Roman nose, black neckerchief adjusted with no great attention to detail"; the others--described by Patrick Wiggins (B.)--are "miserable creatures not worth talking about"; Charlotte "a broad dumpy thing whose head does not come higher than my elbow"; Emily "lean and scant with a face almost the size of a penny"; Anne "nothing, absolutely nothing."

**Zamorna:** Province of Angria; capital Zamorna, on the Olympia River; Lord Lieutenant--Viscount Castlereagh.

**Zamorna, Duchess of:** See Percy, Mary Henrietta.

**Zamorna, Duke of:** See Wellesley, Arthur Augustus Adrian.

**Zenobia:** See Ellrington, Zenobia.

**Zorayda:** Spanish lady who married the Duke of York; (1) mother of Edward Sydney; (2) daughter of Sir William Etty and Julia; Maid of Honour to Princess Ierne.

Commentary On The Poems

1

The poem constitutes the "Poetry" section in **Blackwoods Young Mens Magazine** for August 1829, the first of the miniature magazines edited by Charlotte and in her hand.  In the magazine's table of contents it is entitled "a song."  The signature "UT" (Us Two) would seem to indicate collaboration with Branwell who had begun the magazine in January 1829, although Alexander (EW, p. 38) suggests that the initials may refer to the Marquis of Douro and Lord Charles Wellesley, making the poem Charlotte's alone.  Whatever the case, this is the first poem we definitely know Charlotte had a hand in, although she had contributed prose material during Branwell's editorship (see Alexander, item 60 and EW, p. 36), and in Branwell's July issue a drama, **The Nights,** begun in the June issue, is headed PBB, but signed C. Brontë at the end.

The effect of her involvement becomes clearer when one compares this poem with one by Branwell in the same magazine.  His song is sung by Badey in the presence of the Duke of Wellington, who orders that Badey be taken to the triangle after his performance (for a glossary of Glass Town/Angrian names, see **Appendix D**):

what is more glorious in nature or art
than a bottle of Brandy clear
there's nothing I like so well for my part
it rids you of evry fear

it raises your spirits on stilly night
it carries you lightly along
it wings you away from this pitiful sight
& disposes your min[d] for a song

for a song like mine it makes you wish
& it keeps your eyes from a doze
unless you are dull as a kettle of fish
then't sends you of[f] to repose

I hope high Duke that you like my song
which for your pleasure I chant
as it is beautiful & not long
your approbation grant *

*Alexander attributes both this poem and one on Napoleon, dated July 17, 1829 and signed "Young Soult," to Charlotte (see Alexander, items 229 and 414).  However the fact that both are in Branwell's hand, the subject matter, and the signature "Young Soult" suggest that they are Branwell's. The signature "C. Bronte" appears below the poem on Napoleon, but much lower on the page, separate from the poem's signature.

2

From chapter IV of **The Search after Hapiness**, this is the earliest
known poem definitely composed solely by Charlotte.  Although the poem is
undated and unsigned, the manuscript has Charlotte's signature at four
places, and is dated July 28, 1829 at the beginning of chapter I and
August 17 on the cover and in three other places.  The manuscript of 16
pages is stitched in brown paper covers, has a title-page and a Preface,
and is "Printed by Herself and Sold by Nobody"; in short, it marks the
first time she poses as a "published" author.   For a complete
transcription of **The Search after Hapiness** see the edition by T.A.J.
Burnett, London:   Harvill Press, 1969.  The song, sung by fairies and
genii in a vision of a fabulous oriental palace, reflects the influence
of Sir Charles Morell's **Tales of the Genii** and **The Arabian Nights'
Entertainments** which Charlotte had read by April of 1829 (see Alexander
EW, pp. 18 and 30).


3

From the September 1829 issue of **Blackwoods Young Mens Magazine**, the
poem is part of a story entitled **A True Story by C:B**, signed C.
Bronte and dated August 20, 1829.  The song is sung by slaves as the
Chief Genii approach in a magical cave Charles and Arthur Wellesley have
entered.


4

Also from the September 1829 issue, the poem's signature, subject matter
and style all suggest it is by Branwell.  However, in the magazine's
table of contents the poem is listed as "The Pothouse by U T," and
Charlotte includes it in her December "General index" as by "U T."


5

The final major item in the September 1829 issue, it is listed as "A Poem
by U T" in the magazine's table of contents.


6

From the October 1829 issue of **Blackwoods Young Mens Magazine**, the
poem is listed as "the statue & goblet in the desert" in the magazine's
table of contents.

**7 and 8**

Both poems are from the November 1829 issue of **Blackwoods Young Mens Magazine.** Between stanzas four and five of No. **8** are two canceled stanzas, followed by the date September 7, 1829, which were taken directly from the first poem--stanzas seven and eight. There is also a canceled undecipherable final stanza, with the alternate version added at the bottom of the page.

**9 and 10**

The manuscript text of these poems, bound in green morocco by Sangorski and Sutcliffe, varies considerably from the published versions, yet they have the same dates as the manuscripts. The SHB C and B notes for No. **9** an earlier draft "dated September 18, 1829," but there is no evidence to corroborate the existence of such a draft; rather the existing manuscript version seems to be an earlier draft of the SHB version, yet has the same date. Although in all published versions the title reads "belonging to E," the manuscript reads "belonging to you." No. **10** appears in the BST version with the extra title "THE WALK," deleted in the SHB. In the manuscript the title "THE WALK" and two undecipherable lines of verse are part of a third poem (possibly an early draft of **The Evening Walk?**) and are canceled. The SHB version of No. **10,** except for the deletion of the extra title, follows the BST version. One can only conclude that the two poems were either carelessly mistranscribed or, given the difficulty of reading the microscopic script, liberally "edited." The size and nature of the manuscripts suggest that both poems were intended for the **Young Mens Magazine,** but for reasons unknown never included.

**11 and 12**

The two poems are on the same side of a leaf originally quite separate and folded in quarters, but bound by T.J. Wise with eleven other un- related items of poetry and prose in random order ranging in date from March 12, 1829 to July 17, 1834. It is a good example of how Wise's activities have made the editing of Brontë manuscripts so difficult. In the lower right-hand quarter (following **Sunrise**) appear a number of pen and ink sketches, mainly of heads, labelled "Young Soult," "The Book of Nature," "Us Two," "Me," "Y Mirot," "Y Lucian," "Y Nap," "Eugene." The verso of the leaf is blank except for the name "Charlotte" (three times) and the word "genius." The regular capitalization in the two poems, in contrast to the other 1829 poems, suggests they may be fair copies made later, perhaps at the time of the 1830 volume (see comment for No. **19**), with the original dates of composition retained. A fac- simile of the manuscript appears in Dodd Mead 1902. For a possible source, see **Paradise Lost,** Book IV.

**13, 14** and **15**

All three poems appear in the first number of **Blackwoods Young Mens Magazine** for December 1829 (the quantity of material necessitated two numbers for December). The signature W T at the end of No. **14** signifies "We Two" (Charlotte's table of contents lists No. **14** as "On the Transfer of this Magazine by U T"). Poems **14** and **15**, though presumably both written in collaboration, point to the differences of interest and emphasis that had arisen between Charlotte and Branwell, and mark the end of Branwell's involvement with the magazine. In 1830, Charlotte launched a new series of the magazine (see comment for No. **39**).

**16**

From the second number of **Blackwoods Young Mens Magazine** for December 1829. The separation between Charlotte and Branwell is indicated by the fact that Charlotte first signed the poem in her own name, then changed it to the customary "U T." The change from the quatrain to blank verse quite possibly reflects Charlotte's reading of Milton (see Gérin CB, p. 24).

**17**

Also from the second number for December 1829, the poem, undated, is part of a section entitled "Conversations." It is sung by Douro and Charles Wellesley, and marks the first time Charlotte uses either signature for her poems.

**18**

Hatfield published the poem as Emily's in 1941 and dated it 1839 because he had not seen the manuscript and had to rely on Shorter's transcription. However, the date and signature on the manuscript are quite clear, again pointing up the carelessness of some of the early transcriptions of these materials. To the left of the date and signature appear the words "from the Young Mens Intelligencer," which according to various entries in the **Young Mens Magazine** is one of the many newspapers/magazines in Glass Town. Branwell turned the editorship of the magazine over to Charlotte in July 1829 to devote his time and attention fully to a newspaper he was conducting. "The Young Mens Intelligencer" may, therefore, have been an early version of his later newspaper, **The Monthly Intelligencer,** of which there is a manuscript at the BPM for March 27-April 26, 1833.

**19**

This is the first poem in a hand-sewn volume, with coarse brown wrapping-paper covers, labelled **Miscellaneous Poems By C. Brontë May 31 1830,** containing fair copies of six poems and one prose piece. The sixteen lines published in Benson 1915 vary considerably; they begin with lines 47-54 of the present version (with minor variations), then continue:

> My sister, may it ever be
> That from thy home on high
> A hymn of peace may check in me
> Each dark rebellious sigh.
>
> Then, sister, shall I truly know
> That mansions of the blest
> Wait, till from weariness below
> My spirit enters rest!

According to the SHB C and B, these lines, also dated December 24, 1829, were taken from another manuscript, but there is no evidence to corroborate the existence of such a manuscript, and the last eight lines seem uncharacteristic of the fourteen-year-old Charlotte. This volume represents her second attempt to gather some of her poems. She had put together a volume of poems entitled **A Book of Rhymes** containing nine poems, dated December 17, 1829, just seven days before this poem was written. The manuscript of **A Book of Rhymes** seems never to have been transcribed and has disappeared since it was sold in the U.S.A. in November 1916 (see **Appendix B**).


**20**

The date in the manuscript is a little unclear; it seems to read January 8, 1829, with 1829 blotted out. The 1830 is virtually undecipherable, but all previous editions give the poem the same date. The poem, which is item 5 in the miscellaneous collection bound together by Wise (see comment for Nos. **11** and **12**), emphasizes the importance given to literature in Glass Town society.


**21**

This poem is the fifth item in **Miscellaneous Poems** (see comment for No. **19**). To the right of the title appears a "2," suggesting that Charlotte intended the poem to occupy second place in her manuscript, a suggestion reinforced by the fact that the second item in the booklet is a canceled version of the poem, dated January 12, 1830, which reads:

**Written on the sumit of A High Mountain
In the North of England----------------**

1   How lonely is this spot, deep silence reigns
    The silence of all human stir and sound
    But nature's voice is heard in gentle strains
    Which with a stilly noise float softly round

2   Each leaf which quivers in yon blasted oak         5
    Falls audibly upon the listning ear
    As if solemn language it had spoke
    A warning of some death or danger near

3   And now strange thoughts and mournful slowly rise
    Each after other in a gloomy train         10
    Each quickly born, And each as quickly dies
    Drunk by the whirlpool of oblivions main

4   But sudden Bursting from a thick dark cloud
    Lo! the Bright sun illumines all the earth
    Tinting with amber light his wat'ry shroud         15
    Spread for his pavement As he now walks forth

5   Behold the valley glows with life and light
    Each raindrop bears a glory in its cell
    Of Saphire ruby or fair Em'rald bright
    Rejoicing in its palace clear to dwell         20

6   A wilderness of sweets yon wood appears
    Before a forest full of darksome, gloom
    But now a smilling face of joy it wears
    Not such as would befit the churchyard tomb

7   But all unseemly mid the gladness, stands         25
    That ancient castle mossed and grey with time
    Once the resort of warlike, feudal bands
    Where oft was heard the trumpets clanging chime

8   Now an unbroken stillness reigns around
    No warrior's step rings through the arched halls         30
    No hunting horns sweet thrilling mellow sound
    Or blood-hounds yell reverberates 'mid those walls

9   The gladsome sunshine suits not with this place
    The golden light seems but to mock the grey
    And sorrowing aspect of its furrowed face         35
    Too time-worn to be joyous with the day

    10    But when black night o'ershadows with her wing
          The prospect, and the solemn nightingale
          Sings while the moon her silver light doth fling
          In tremulous lustre o'er the sleeping vale                   40

    11    Then awfully that ancient castle towers
          From out its grove of venerable trees
          Amid whose scathed and withered leafless bowers
          Howls mournfully the peircing winter breeze

    12    Or on some day when dark and sombre clouds                    45
          Veil dismally the blue ethereal sky
          When the deep grandeur of their blackness shrouds
          The sun with all its majesty on high

    13    When fitful shadows hurry o'er the plain
          And curtain round this mountains hoary brow                  50
          Rolling voluminous in misty train
          Or curled in floating vapours even as now
          Those light soft clouds piled in the ambient air
          Of gentle lustre and of pearly hue
          Calm in the summer twilight mild and fair                    55
          Distilling from their pureness crystal dew

                    January 12 1830   CHARLOTTE BRONTE

**22**

The poem was originally dated 1829, with the "29" canceled and followed
by "30." The title is written over top of the words: "On the ninth of
December <undecipherable> I dreamt the following dream." Murry is a
member of Arthur Wellesley's staff when the latter returns to Glass Town
from Britain as Duke of Wellington. The poem is item 7 in the miscellaneous collection bound together by Wise.

**23**

The speaker "C W" is Charles Wellesley, second son of the Duke of
Wellington, and narrator of many of Charlotte's Angrian tales. He is
described in a short prose narrative by Charlotte, dated January 16,
1830, as "reclining under the shadow of an immense chestnut tree, playing
upon a small Spanish guitar, with a nightingale perched upon his
shoulder. A beautiful grey monkey, a small silky spaniel, and a young
kitten bounded and danced before him in the bright light of the uprisen
moon" ("Description of Duke of W's small palace situated on the Banks of
the Indirce"--BST 1978). The poem appears on the verso of **A wretch in
prison,** dated February 1. Because Charlotte's next poem is dated
February 3, February 2 would seem a likely date for this poem.

                               394

**24 and 25**

Although No. **24** is the sixth item in **Miscellaneous Poems**, a "3" appears to the right of the title, and the canceled title "Winter" precedes No. **25**, the third poem in the volume, indicating the placement Charlotte intended for No. **24**. Both poems reflect Charlotte's reading of James Thomson.

**26**

Written on one side of a single leaf 4" x 2 3/4", the other side of which is part of a letter. Opposite stanzas 3-5 is a crude sketch of part of a human figure.

**27**

The poem is from chapter one of **THE ADVENTURE'S OF MON EDOUARD de CRACK**, one of Charlotte's miniature booklets. The manuscript, dated February 22, 1830, is ascribed to Lord Charles Wellesley. In a preface Charlotte writes: "I began this Book on the 22 of February 1830 and finished it on the 23 of February 1830 doing 5 pages on the first day & 11 on the second. On the first day I wrote an hour and a half in the morning and an hour & a half in the evening. On the third [sic] day I wrote a quarter of an hour in the morning 2 hours in the afternoon and a quarter of an hour in the evening making in the whole 5 hours & a half." The song is sung by Eugene Beauchamp, dressed in "a green mantle his head crowned with a garland of wild laurel & blue everlasting flowers & a shepherds pipe in his hand."

**28**

Item 8 in **Miscellaneous Poems**. Alexander (item 408) reads the signature as "April the 13 1829 [canceled] April 13 1830."

**29**

From volume three, chapter one of **Tales of the Islanders**. The end of the chapter is signed "CB" and dated May 5, 1830. The words are sung by Charles Wellesley, who is searching for his missing brother Arthur just prior to the arrival of their father, the Duke of Wellington.

## 30

From volume three, chapter two of **Tales of the Islanders.**  The begin-
ning of the chapter is dated May 6, 1830, the end of the manuscript May
8.  At the end of volume three appear the words:  "I began this volume
May the third 1830 I finished it on Saturday May the 8 1830/ C Brontë."
During a visit by the Duke of Wellington to the Horse Guards, an officer,
Lord Rosslyn, makes a fawning, highly bombastic speech in praise of
Wellington.  The Duke rebukes Rosslyn, describing his language as "the
watery scum of a weak whining poet," unbecoming to an "officer of sense
and spirit," and threatens the officer with various degrading punishments
if he carries on in this way again.  Rosslyn rushes out in tears and is
heard singing the lines above.


**31**

From **The Adventures of Ernest Alembert   A Tale,** signed by Charlotte
and dated May 25, 1830 on the title-page and at the end of the
manuscript.  Ernest, on his way home from the land of the fairies, meets
an old man, who sings this song accompanying himself on the harp.  The
old man relates his adventures in the realm of supernatural beings when
he journeyed into the Caucasus to Mount Elborous and the valley of the
Aragua River (see also No. **39**).  Charlotte's fascination with the
Caucasus at this time reflects her reading of Goldsmith's **Grammar of
General Geography** (see Alexander EW, pp. 19, 52).  For ll. 33-34, see
**Paradise Lost,** VI, 3-4.


**32 and 33**

The seventh and ninth items in **Miscellaneous Poems.**


**34**

The poem is bound as a miniature booklet of eight leaves in blue paper
wrappers.  The full title-page reads:

THE!!!
EVENING WALK
A POEM
BY THE MARQUIS of
DOURO
IN PINDARIC METRE
PUBLISHED
AND SOLD
BY
CAPTAIN
TREE

AND ALL OTHER BOOKSELLERS in The Cheif Glass Town,
Wellingtons G T PARIS Parrys G T Ross's G T &c &c &c &c

PREFACE

The following pages are the production of my pen. not according to
a much-used scrap, of cut-and-dried-phraesology. the emanations of
leisure hours. But the fruit of some days labour I shall not introduce
them to my readers by a servile appeal to their indulgence & compassion.
But having cast them unprotected on the world I leave them entirely at
the public's mercy to praise or condemn them as she pleases
                                              DOURO June 28 1830

     This book contains 71 ordinary verses of four lines each, which is
284 lines
                                              Charlotte Brontë

June 28<sup>th</sup> 1830

Actually it contains only 276 lines and is not divided into four-line
stanzas. The reference to Pindar reflects Charlotte's "sharing" in Branwell's classical studies at this time (see also No. **51** and Alexander
EW, p. 22), and her reading of Thomas Gray.
l. 21: the city is Verreopolis or Verdopolis
l. 24: the Tower is the Tower of all Nations (see No. **10**)


**35**

The poem appears on two leaves bound in blue morocco; whether it was
originally part of a larger manuscript one cannot tell. Following the
signature appear the words:  "I wrote this in half an hour C Bronte."
The prototype of Marianne was Elizabeth Hume, daughter of the Duke of
Wellington's surgeon, Dr. John Robert Hume (Alexander EW, pp. 25, 46,
71). Her dream seems to be a premonition of the separation Charlotte
develops later in the year (see, for example, Nos. **49, 52, 54, 55,
59**).


**36** and **37**

From volume one, scene one, of **The Poetaster/ A Drama/ In/ Two Volumes
by Lord Charles/ Wellesley.** The manuscript of volume one is dated July
6, 1830 at the end, July 8 inside the front cover, and is signed "C B."
Volume two contains no verse. The words are spoken by Henry Rhymer,
described at the beginning of the scene as "alone in a garret with a sky-
light at the top surrounded by shreds of paper & a few old books time--
half past-11--at night." The whole first scene consists of a ridiculous
soliloquy in the most affected, sentimental and sublime strain on poetic

sensibility and artistic creation. Rhymer was one of Branwell's pseudonyms, and the whole play is a satirical depiction of his affected and
extravagant poses, part of a literary "war" between Charlotte and
Branwell (Alexander EW, pp. 64-66; see also Nos. **41** and **60**). No.
**37**, also spoken by Rhymer, ends the first scene. The play reflects
Charlotte's reading of Jonson's **Poetaster or His Arraignment.**


**38**

With these lines Charlotte closed the final volume of **Tales of the
Islanders.** The manuscript is signed and dated at the end "July the 30
1830  C Bronte." These lines Alexander suggests (EW, p. 63) mark the
beginning of the divergence between Charlotte and Branwell on the one
hand and Emily and Anne on the other that would lead to the separate
development of Gondal and Angria.


**39**

The poem is the second item in **The Young Mens Magazine,** second
series, for August 1830, now edited by Charlotte without Branwell's
participation. Paralleling the first series, the second series appeared
in six monthly numbers, August to December, 1830, with two numbers for
December. In fact, Charlotte wrote all the material contained in the six
numbers in the three weeks between August 12 and September 4 (see commentary for No. **47**).


**40**

Item two in the October 1830 issue of **The Young Mens Magazine.** The
September number seems to have been lost. For the poems it contained see
**Appendix B.** The version in Wise RCK 1917 has a number of minor
differences in wording which Alexander (item 297) attributes to Wise
having used a variant draft. I suspect rather that the differences are
the result of careless transcription.


**41**

Part of "Conversations" in the October issue of **Young Mens Magazine,**
signed "C Bronte Charlotte," and dated August 23, 1830. The poem is
spoken by Young Soult (Branwell) and concludes "sinks down in a fainting
fit but the Marquis of Douro who is sitting by catches him in his arms &
reinstates him in a chair." There follows a discussion between Wellesley
and Soult in which Wellesley lectures the latter on the need to bring his
feelings and poetic imagination under control (cf. Nos. **37** and

**60)**. For a discussion of Charlotte's views on the excesses of the Romantic imagination, see Alexander EW, p. 66.

### 42 and 43

No. **42** is item two in the November 1830 number of **Young Mens Magazine**; No. **43** is part of "A FRENCHMAN'S JOURNAL CONTINUED by Tree," dated August 28, 1830, in the same number.

### 44

From the first number of the **Young Mens Magazine** for December 1830. In Charlotte's "GENERAL INDEX TO THE CONTENTS" of the second series the title is given as "On seeing an ancient Dirk in the armoury of the tower of Babylon &c." The text used here is by Davidson Cook, who transcribed a number of the Brontë manuscripts in Sir Alfred Law's collection in 1925 and 1926 (see p.xxiii above). According to Charlotte's General Index, this was the only poem in the first December number. The equation of the Tower of Babylon and the Tower of All Nations suggests something of the Biblical influence in the creation of Glass Town.

### 45 and 46

No. **45** is the second item in the second number of the **Young Mens Magazine** for December 1830. No. **46** is part of "A Frenchman's Journal Concluded" by Tree, dated September 4, 1830, in the same number.

### 47

With these lines Charlotte concludes the **Young Mens Magazine**. The lines are followed by a General Index to the whole of the second series, concluding with the words: "the second series of the young mens magazine was begun August 12 1830 & finished September the 4 1830."

### 48 and 49

Both poems are part of **Albion and Marina: A Tale by Lord Charles Wellesley**, dated October 12, 1830. The Preface is signed "C. Wellesley," the end of the manuscript, "C. B." At the end of the preface Charlotte has noted "I wrote this in four hours C B." For the first complete transcription of **Albion and Marina**, Charlotte's first love story, see BST 1920. The first song, based on a poem composed by Albion for Marina (Douro and Marian), is sung by Lady Zelzia Ellrington (later Zenobia), "the most learned and noted woman in Glass Town," and Marian's rival (see No. **59**).   Alexander (EW, pp. 23-24) very plausibly suggests Gibbon as Charlotte's source for the character of Zenobia.   The second song is sung by the ghost of Marina when Albion returns, hoping still to find his wife alive.


**50**


The text is based on a transcription in the Hatfield papers at the BPM. There are, in fact, two transcriptions by Hatfield; the second does not contain the fourth stanza.   However both the Shorter and the SHB C and B versions do, suggesting that Hatfield may inadvertently have omitted it.


**51**


Poems **51-57** comprise a little hand-stitched booklet of poems, with blue paper covers, 16 pages, 3 3/4" x 2 1/4", entitled **THE VIOLET &** **etc.   A POEM BY THE/ MARQUIS/ OF DOURO,** dated November 14, 1830.   The title-page reads:


THE VIOLET

A POEM
WITH SEVERAL SMALLER PEICES
BY THE
MARQUESS OF
DOURO

MEMBER OF THE SOCIETY OF ANTIQ-
UARIANS:   PRESIDENT FOR 1830 OF
THE LITERARY CLUB:   HONORARY
MEMBER OF THE ACADEMY OF ARTISTS
& TREASURER TO THE SOCIETY FOR
THE SPREAD OF CLASSICAL KNOW-
LEDGE:   CHEIF SECRETARY OF THE
CONFEDERATE HUNDRED FOR PRO-
MOTING GYMNASTIC EXERCISES
&C. &C. &C.

PUBLISHED
BY

SEAGEANT TREE
AND SOLD
BY

ALL OTHER BOOKSELLERS IN THE CHEIF GLASS TOWN.
THE DUKE OF WELLINGTONS GLASS TOWN.   PARIS PARRYS
GLASS TOWN.   ROSS'S GLASS TOWN &C. &C. &C.
November the 14 1830

The title page reflects Douro's emergence as patron of the arts and intellectual leader in Glass Town society. Page two consists of a Preface, which reads: "I trust the Public will be as indulgent to my present work as the old lady - was to those formerly submitted to her supreme inspection MARQUIS OF DOURO"; a table of contents; and the comment "A Book of Rhymes by/ Charlotte Brontë--/ Alias the Marquess of Douro/ Begun November the 7$^{th}$/ 1830 finished November/ the 14$^{th}$ 1830." Unfortunately two leaves have been removed from the center of the booklet; one is at the BPM, the other in the Ashley Library of T.J. Wise at the British Library, suggesting that Wise was responsible for the dismemberment. Thus the first 40 stanzas of **The Violet** are in the Taylor Library, the last 10 at the BPM. Despite the Glass Town context, No. **51** is very much a personal poem reflecting Charlotte's poetic ambitions at age fourteen (see Introduction, pp.xxxiii-xxxiv). For a possible source, see Gray's "The Progress of Poesy."

**52**

The name left blank in the title is that of Marian Hume (Marina) betrothed to the Marquis of Douro. Edward DeLisle was one of the most accomplished and sought-after painters in Glass Town.

**53 and 54**

The single leaf from the booklet in the Ashley Library contains **Vesper** on the recto, and the first 8 stanzas of **Matin** on the verso. Because of the differences in wording in four lines of **Vesper**, Alexander suggests that the Shorter 1923 version is based on a variant manuscript, now lost (see item 405). In the absence of any evidence to corroborate the existence of such a manuscript, I suspect the differences arise from errors in transcription. Both poems are dedicated to Marian Hume.

**55 and 56**

In No. **55**, Z. E. stands for Zenobia Ellrington, Marian Hume's rival for the affections of Douro (see Nos. **48, 49** and **59**). Although the words of No. **56** are spoken by Douro, they reflect Charlotte's sense of herself as poet and artist, and are closely linked to No. **51**.

**57**

The poem is addressed to Marian Hume.

58-60

All three items are from volume one of **VISITS IN VERREOPOLIS** by Lord Charles Wellesley. A note on the title-page reads: "I began this volume on the 7$^{th}$ of December--1830 & finished it on the 11$^{th}$ of December 1830/ CHARLOTTE BRONTË." The text used here is by Davidson Cook who transcribed the manuscript in Sir Alfred Law's library in Aril 1926 for C.W. Hatfield; the transcription is now in the Hatfield papers at the BPM. No. **58** is sung by the Marquis of Douro to Marian Hume. No. **59** represents Charlotte's first serious attempt at verse drama, reflecting her reading of Shakespeare and Milton. From **A Visit to Young Soult**, No. **60** is an "extemporaneous effusion" by the poet of Angria when Lord Charles Wellesley makes the mistake of asking him if he has seen the rainbow. At the end of the poem the narrator continues: "When Young Soult had concluded this extempore effusion, which was uttered in a strange variety of tones,--first speaking which gradually changed to recitative, then chanting, and last to regular singing, he sat down and said: 'Pray Lord Charles, forgive my enthusiasm, but really my feelings do sometimes carry me utterly beyond the control of reason and politeness, more especially now as I have not the benefit of your noble brother's admonitions. I hope, by the by, that he is in good health?'" (cf. Nos. **36** and **41**).


61

From volume II, chapter 2 of **Visits in Verreopolis**, dated December 18, 1830, and also transcribed by Cook for Hatfield in April 1926. The title-page reads: "Visits in Weropolis" by "The Honorable Charles Albert Florian Lord Wellesley, aged 10 years."


62

The manuscript has been separated and is listed as two separate manuscripts at the BPM (see Alexander items 279 and 280). Lines 1-64 are on a single sheet folded in half with all four pages filled. In contrast to the rest of the text, the title is in script, suggesting it may have been added later. The first page of the second portion of the manuscript is numbered "2." The poem is followed by a brief prose passage: "Here the disconsolate maiden rose and quickly vanished over the eminence I could see by the rising light that she was young & very beautiful & I thought her features were familiar to me who she was I shall leave the reader to determine & merely observe that about 5 years since. when a certain Marquis of D was married to the fair lady Julia <I> Marian H- disappeared & no tidings of her fate have ever been received save a vague rumour that overcome by despair she had left Africa for ever & had returned to her native highlands of Scotland.
Lord Charles Albert Florian Wellesley
July 11$^{th}$<br>1831"

From this passage it is clear that the singer is Marian Hume, whom the Marquis of Douro (now Duke of Zamorna) has abandoned for Mary Percy. However, the source of much of the descriptive background is volume one of the **Tales of the Genii.**

**63**

In January of 1831 Charlotte set out for Roe Head School, temporarily interrupting her partnership with Branwell in the development of the Glass Town saga. During her absence Emily and Anne branched out on their own and began the development of their Gondal saga. When Charlotte returned home for the Christmas vacation, the four children decided formally to dissolve the imaginary kingdom they had created, a dissolution recorded in this poem. The influence of Byron's "The Destruction of Sennacherib" is readily apparent. Lines 64-65 may also refer to the final plague inflicted on the Egyptians in Exodus 12.

**64**

The poem seems to express Charlotte's regret over the destruction fourteen days earlier of their imaginary world. The poem is item 6 in the miscellaneous collection bound together by Wise.

**65** and **66**

Poem **65** opens a narrative consisting of poetry and prose relating to the marriage of the Marquis of Douro and Marian Hume. The manuscript has been divided and the prose narrative, which includes poem **66,** is in the Bonnell Collection at the BPM. It is dated August 20, 1832. Wise dates the poem July 1831, and Alexander (item 225) postulates a variant manuscript. However, because Wise's version is identical to the manuscript in every other respect, I suspect an error in transcription. Poem **66** is sung by Marian for the Marquis: "With a smiling blush she took a little ivory lyre & in a voice of the most touching melody sung the following stanzas."

**67**

The text is based on a transcription by the Rev. A.B. Nicholls in the Brotherton Collection at the University of Leeds. Below the signature at the end of the manuscript containing the previous poem appear the canceled words "St. John in the Isle of Palmis." Lines 21-24 are canceled in pencil in the transcription, presumably by Nicholls. For the poem's source, see The Revelation of John I:9-11.

68

The text is based on a photograph of the manuscript at the BPM. Bewick died in 1828, four years before Charlotte wrote this poem. She recommends Bewick to Ellen Nussey for natural history in a letter dated July 4, 1834, and, of course, it is Bewick that Jane Eyre reads in the opening chapter of the novel. Line 29 is adapted from Byron's "The Dream," l. 75. According to Gérin, Charlotte was reading Byron at age 10 (Five Novelettes, p. 13).


69

Part of a prose and verse narrative entitled **The African Queen's Lament**, dated February 12, 1833. Lord Charles Wellesley records his father's description of how he came to adopt Quashia, the son of Sai Tootoo, King of the Ashantees, after the Ashantees had been conquered by the Twelves, and Sai Tootoo killed. Wellington heard an African woman singing a requiem for the dead, and found the dying queen by the river, with her little son asleep beside her, singing these words. For a possible source, see Psalm 137. The real Duke of Wellington had adopted an Indian orphan during his Indian Campaign.


70

**The African Queen's Lament** occupies pp. 1-3 and the top portion of p. 4 of the four-page manuscript. This poem, undated, is on the same half of p. 4 as the end of **The African Queen's Lament** and in the same ink, but in minute print and with the page upside down. It is also sung by the dying African Queen. Mid-February would therefore seem to be the likely date of composition. The rather incongruous Hebraic references reflect Charlotte's reading of Byron's "Hebrew Melodies."


71

The poem, undated, follows the previous poem on the bottom half of the manuscript page, but is in pencil, with two ink corrections in stanza one. It does not seem to be linked thematically with the two previous poems. The speaker is Arthur Wellesley, Marquis of Douro; the daughter in l. 25 is Mina Laury. Late February-early March would seem to be the likely date of composition.

72

The poem occupies one side of a manuscript leaf. On the back appear the
words: "when Arthur Wellesley had finished and his audience had yielded
the tribute of applause Marian Hume exclaimed in her lively way 'I think
my Lord I know who you mean by Lord Rowan'": presumably Percy. It is
the fourth item in the miscellaneous collection bound by Wise (see Nos.
**11** and **12**). Alexander reads the date as "May" (item 209), but I
believe it reads "Mar."

**73** and **74**

Both poems are from chapter V of **Something About Arthur**; the manuscript is dated May 1, 1833 and signed both "Charlotte Bronte" and
"Charles Albert Florian Wellesley." The first song is sung for Arthur
Wellesley (Lord Douro) by Mina Laury, who is nursing him while he con-
valesces from wounds in a peasant cottage. She entitles her song "the
fallen soldiers hymn." Although this is their first meeting and Mina
does not know who her patient is, **Something About Arthur** marks the
beginning of their life-long affair; from here on Douro becomes the focus
of Charlotte's writing. The second is sung by a group (guards, over-
seers, free-labourers) partying at Lord Caversham's mill.

**75**

From chapter II of **The Foundling**. The manuscript is signed by
Charlotte in several places, and on the title-page she writes: "this
book was begun May 31$^{st}$ 1833 and finished June the 27$^{th}$ 1833."
It is Charlotte's earliest attempt to imitate Yorkshire dialect. **The
Foundling** relates the adventures of Edward Sydney, who came to
Verdopolis from England in search of his ancestors. Sydney provides a
detailed description of life in Glass Town, including this song by street
vendors.

**76** and **77**

From chapter V of **The Foundling**, both poems are songs, the first sung
by Captain Arbor at Lady Selby's request, the second by Lady Julia
Wellesley, with whom Edward Sydney thinks himself in love, at a dinner
and ball given by the Selbys.

405

**78**

From chapter VII of **The Foundling,** the song is sung by Lady Julia, now romantically intrigued by Sydney because her father is adamantly opposed to the match.

**79**

From chapter IX of **The Foundling,** the song is sung by Manfred, a magician, President of the university located on the Philosopher's Island. He is lamenting the death of the Marquis of Douro, which he has seen in a vision. Douro is, however, revived by the Genii. One can see the influence of Byron's "Manfred."

**80**

The poem occurs in chapter IV of **The Green Dwarf.** The manuscript is signed "Charlotte Bronte" and dated September 2, 1833 at the end, but the preface is signed "C Wellesley" and dated July 10, 1833, and at the bottom of the page Charlotte has written, "I began this book July 10$^{th}$ 1833." It is the last story in which the Duke of Wellington plays a major role. The plot is adapted from **Ivanhoe** and **Kenilworth** (see Alexander's edition of "Something About Arthur," pp. 19-20). The "petit chanson" above is sung by Lady Emily Charlesworth to express a secret grief; her meditations, says the narrator, "belonged rather to 'Il Penseroso' than 'L'Allegro.'"

**81**

From chapter II of a short story "Brushwood Hall" in **Arthuriana, or Odds and Ends Being A Miscellaneous Collection of pieces in Prose and Verse** by Lord Charles A. F. Wellesley. The manuscript was begun September 27, 1833 and finished November 20. "Brushwood Hall" is dated October 1, 1833 and signed "Charlotte Brontë."

**82**

From **Arthuriana, or Odds and Ends,** the poem, a satire on the Glass Town antiquarian, John Gifford, is preceded by the following words: "One day when the Rotunda of Gravey's Inn was more than usually crowded with rank & fashion, Worthy Mr John Gifford entered, having a large cross marked on the back of his cape in brilliant red chalk. This distinguishing symbol which doubtless he owed to the hands of some mischievous wight, was immediately observed by the noblemen & Gentlemen into whose company he had introduced himself. A general titter ran round the

ircle, several excellent jokes were coined at his expense & the waxen
neeks of the old lawyer who was wholly ignorant of the cause of this
ctually began to exhibit symptoms of a blush.  In the midst of the mirth
he Marquis of Douro took out his pocket-book scribbled a few minutes &
hen requesting the attention of the assembly which was instantaneously
ielded, read aloud the following poetic effusion."

## 3

rom **Arthuriana, or Odds and Ends,** the poem is preceded by the words:
Once when I was rummaging over a vast heap of papers in my brother
rthur's desk--I found the following bit of poetry signed E:S. & on the
ack was written in Arthur's hand 'stolen from Sydney it's a peice of
ursed cant.'"

## 4

rom chapter II of a tale entitled **The Secret,** combined with **Lily
art.**  The title-page of the manuscript reads "THE SECRET/ AND/ LILY
ART TWO TALES/ by Lord/ Charles/ Wellesley."   Only **Lily Hart** is
ated (see No. **85**).  The song is sung by Douro's wife, Marian.

## 5

rom a prose tale entitled **Lily Hart,** dated November 7, 1833, and
igned both "Charlotte Brontë" and "Lord Charles Wellesley."  The speaker
s Lily Hart at the grave of her mother.

## 6

rom **Arthuriana, or Odds and Ends,** the poem is introduced by the
ords: "Here I was 18 years since, standing by the new covered grave the
ourners being all departed, it was a glorious evening the sky & scene
ust as they are now
     Captain Flower's last <undecipherable word*>"

hese words are quoted from **The Politics of Verdopolis,** a tale by
aptain John Flower M. P., written by Branwell (November 15, 1833).  The
oem refers to the visit of Alexander Percy (Northangerland) to the grave
f his wife, Mary.

Alexander suggests "Novel" (item 188).

At the top of the first page, above the title, appear the words: "183. All that is written in this book, must be in a good, plain and legible hand. PB." This poem and four others--**Darius Codomanus** (No. **94**), **Saul** (No. **99**), **Memory** (No. **104**), and **Morning** (No. **105**)--are all written on the same distinctive lined paper and in a regular script rather than the usual miniscule print, suggesting that they were originally all part of the same notebook, a "public" volume of poems (see pp. xxxvi-xxxvii above). The notebook was dismembered probably by Wise, and all but the last of the poems bound individually in morocco by Rivière. The fortress in l. 19 is Dürrenstein in lower Austria, where Richard II was imprisoned in 1193.


**88** and **89**

From **A Leaf From an Unopened Volume Or the Manuscript of An Unfortunate Author**, edited by Lord Charles Albert Florian Wellesley. No. **88** is sung by Zorayda, mother of Edward Sydney and Maid of Honor to Princess Ierne, daughter of Zamorna and Mary Henrietta. The manuscript is signed and dated Charlotte Brontë, January 17, 1834 at the end, but at the bottom of page one appear the words, "Begun January 5 1834." A four-page (one leaf folded) undated manuscript also at the BPM contains various trial passages in pencil, affording some insight into the way in which Charlotte composed and revised:

> I see beneath me spreading
> Dark visions of the slain
> For my orb its light is shedding
> O'er many a battle plain
> Where heros famed in story                5
> There deeds of war have done
>     And gained a crown of glory
>     For mighty conflicts won
>
> Sound of the palm tree shaken
>     Sounds of the lonely well             10
> Whose fairy murmurs waken
>     To the zephyrs lightest swell
> The waving of a pinion
> The desert wild deers tread
> Is heard in that dominion                 15
> Of silence deep & dead

The moon dawns slow in the dusky gloaming
Dim beside it shines a star
Broken it glints on the waters foaming
    Of the rapid Calabar                                              20
The night was hushed the winds were still
And peace came down plain <& hill>*

        [*obscured by an ink-blot]

The lustrous moon the wailing river
Awoke in my breast the voice of thought
In that calm hour I blessed the Giver                                25
The source whence ray and moan were brought
And while they gleamed and while they sung
I gave them life & soul & tongue
I asked the river whence its stream
    Came in its thunderous pride                                     30
And a voice from the wave like some sound in a dream
    Thus solemnly replied

[p. 2]

Slow dawns the moon on the brow of the gloaming
Dimly beside it there shimers a star
All broken it glints on the waves wildly foaming                     35
Which rush in the course of the swift Calabar
The night is all hushed & the winds are all still
And a heaven-like repose rests on valley & hill

The light of the moon & the wail of the river
Woke the sweet voice of peace & the still voice of thought           40
I looked in that hour of repose <to the giver>
The source whence the ray and the murmur were brought
I looked where they murmured & looked were they sung
I gave them a spirit, a life & a <source>

I asked of the river, whence <        > its stream                   45
& wither it sped in its dark <       > pride
And a voice from the wave <whispered> sounding a dream
Thus solemn & brief to the question replied*

    [*lines 41-48 partially obscured by an ink-blot]

        From the caverned earth I rose
        Mortal like to thee                                          50
        On my tribute streamlet flows
        To the <monarch> sea
        Even as thy career will close
        Dark in eternity

```
And the[n] I asked the crescent moon                          55
O'er what her bow was bent
And thus the sweet response came down
From heaven earthward sent

        Beneath my midnight wandering
        All widely <lies> the earth                           60
        I view the streams meandering
        To the ocean from its birth
        I see the proud hill swelling
        Where foot has never trod
        The snow's eternal dwelling                           65
       _Beheld alone by God
        Alike my rays are glancing
        On cities filled with life
        Where sounds of mirth & dancing
        & harp & song are rife                                70
2       And on the ruined tower
        T[he] rifted arch & dome
        The fallen & trampled bower
        The desert hearth & home

        Where fitful winds are sighing                        75
        Through temple arch & hall
        & slowly calmly dying
        With many a wild faint fall

3       Sweet murmurs sad decaying
        Fill all the air with moans                           80
        Sounds through the desert straying
        Blent, mingled, nameless tones

[p. 3 has sketches of female faces and figures]

[p. 4]

        Where sunless clouds are sweeping
        Shades of eternal gloom
        Yet in peace my beams are sleeping                    85
        Above the warrior's tomb
6       My gentlest mildest splendor
        Is poured above the dust
        If mid the desert dreary
        Far, far, from war & strife                           90
        There rests the heroic weary
        Rests from the toil of life
7       Though no shade be o'er him given
        Though the pale sand is his shroud
        Yet above him bright in heaven                        95
        My silver arch is bowed
```

8    If to the wilds denying
     That high & holy trust
     The warrior's corpse is lying
     Amid ancestral dust                              100

     Still lov[e]lier is the lustre
     That lingers in his tomb
     & lights the trees that cluster
     Around his last dark home

7    From whence the earth shall render               105
     The brave, the good, the just

**90**

The dating of this poem is admittedly conjectural, but it seems to have
been written in response to something published by Thomas Aird, a
Scottish essayist and poet, friend of Carlyle, Hogg, De Quincey and
Lockhart, born 1802, died 1876.  Aird began to contribute to **Blackwoods** in 1827 and in June 1827 Professor Wilson reviewed his
**Religious Characteristics.**  Between 1827 and 1835 Aird contributed
one short story, one essay and five poems; after 1835 he does not re-
appear in **Blackwoods** until 1841.  In addition, he published a long
narrative poem, **The Captive of Fez**, in 1830, and **Othuriel and Other
Poems** in 1840.  Of his contributions to **Blackwoods** (which the
Brontes read regularly), the most likely to have triggered this satirical
response by Charlotte is the poem "Nebuchadnezzar," in the March 1834
issue.  In addition to similarities of subject matter, Aird's poem has
the same strident, bombastic tone, and is also in rhyming couplets.  The
manuscript of the poem was bound by Wise in a manuscript volume of fifteen leaves attributed to Emily.  Two of the items were, in fact,
Charlotte's (see also No. **120**) and one was Branwell's.

Adramelech:  one of the manifestations of the Babylonian sun god to whom
             children were sacrificed; see II Kings 17:31; **Paradise
             Lost** VI: 365
Nergal:  Babylonian god of the underworld and the dead; see II Kings
         17:30
sons of Anakim:  giants in the land of Canaan; see Numbers 13:33; Deuter-
                 onomy 9:2; Joshua 11:21-22
Argob:  a district of the Moabite Kingdom, in which the Israelites
        triumphed over the gigantic Ammonites; see Deut. 3:4-14; II Kings
        15:25; **Paradise Lost** I:398
Baal of Chaldee:  Baal was the chief god of the Phoenician and Canaanite
                  nations; hence of Chaldea in this case; Baal is men-
                  tioned repeatedly in the Old Testament; see also
                  **Paradise Lost** I:404-422

Media:    the ancient kingdom of the Medes, now part of Iran; see II Kings
          17:6; 18:11
Assyria:  an ancient empire centered in the upper valley of the Tigris;
          took Israel captive; see II Kings 15:19; 17:3
Ashtaroth:  the ancient Syrian and Phoenician goddess of sexual love and
          fertility; also Astarte; mentioned at various times in the
          Old Testament; see also **Paradise Lost** I:422, 438-39
Ammonites:  a Semitic tribe descended from Lot's son and Israel's enemy,
          conquered by David; see Deut. 2:19-20; II Samuel 12:26-27;
          **Paradise Lost** I:396
Semele:   the mother of Zeus' son Dionysus: when she desired to see Zeus
          as he appeared to the gods, she was destroyed by his lightning
Moloch:   an Ammonite deity worshipped with human sacrifice; see Amos
          5:26; **Paradise Lost** I:392; II:43; VI:357
Dagon:    the chief god of the Philistines, half fish, half man; see Judges
          16:23; I Samuel 5:2-7; **Paradise Lost** I:457-66
Belial:   in the Old Testament, the personification of wickedness; see
          Judges 19:22; **Paradise Lost** I:490ff; II:109ff
Mammon:   the worship of riches; see Matthew 6:24; Luke 16:9; **Paradise
          Lost** I:678ff; II:228ff


**91**

From chapter I of **High Life in Verdopolis, or the difficulties of
annexing a suitable title to our Work practically illustrated in Six
Chapters**, by Lord C A F Wellesley. The manuscript is dated March 20,
1834, but, at the foot of page one Charlotte wrote, "Begun February
20$^{th}$ 1834." Mary Percy, Zamorna's bride of three months is miserable
because of his deliberate flirting. Zamorna, moved to tenderness by the
sight of her misery, enquires in verse as to the reason for her sadness.
This is one of the manuscripts found in Brussels in 1892 by Professor
Ernest Nys, and therefore presumably one of the manuscripts Charlotte
took to Brussels to show to Heger.


**92**

From chapter III of **High Life in Verdopolis.** In the first two lines
Maria, fanning a recumbent Zamorna as he lounges in the garden on a hot
summer's day, gives her impression of the west wind, and evokes his
reply.


**93**

This poem in Charlotte's hand is unsigned and undated. Lines 1-104 constitute the first two pages of a four-page manuscript; page 3 contains 56
trial lines for **Darius Codomanus,** signed Charlotte Brontë and

dated May 1, 1834; page 4 contains the final 16 lines. Lines 89-120 are in pencil rather than ink, but the page of **Darius Codomanus** between lines 104-05 is in ink. The poem refers to the death of Alexander Percy. "Maria" in l. 93 is his wife who died of consumption, mother of Mary Henrietta who marries Zamorna.


**94**

The second poem in Charlotte's volume of "public" poems; see the comment for No. **87.** An earlier version of the last 56 lines in the Bonnell Collection at the Pierpont Morgan is dated May 1 (see previous comment).

<pre>
          For the green wood & lonely glen
          He views a throng of steel-armed men
          The hum & clash swell stern & loud
          And o'er him many a form is bowed
         _And many an eye of eagle light              5
          Meets piercingly his fading sight
          Tall warriors on their lances leaning
          Plume-shadowed brows of darkest-meaning
              Surround the dying King
         _Their shapes before his vision swim         10
          Ghost-like & wandering, faint & dim
          Their voice sounds like a sacred hymn
              Low, solemn murmuring
          One kneels beside & props his head
         _And from the rivers crystal bed             15
              Sprinkles his ghastly brow
          The cool clear water as it falls
          A moment, sight & speech recalls
              Darius knew his foe
         _He clasped his hands & raised his eyes       20
          Bright with forgiveness to the skies
          He blessed his conqueror in that hour
   204    He prayed for added might & power
     2    To walk by his resistless swoord
     1_To follow Asia's Alien lord                     25
          Statira's shade is near him now
          She lightens thus his kingly brow
          She sheds around him placid smiles
          Her lord & captor reconciles
         _But soon that gentle shade is gone           30
          & vengeance lingers there alone
          A sudden gloom falls round the King
          Stern thoughts within his bosom spring
          The traitor Satrap, & his band
         _Men of unhallowed heart & hand               35
          Before their slaughtered monarch rise
</pre>

413

```
                His curse falls on them 'ere he dies
                "Soldiers of Greece & Macedon
                For the black deed by Bessus done
               _I leave revenge to Ammon's son                    40
                He before whom all Persia fell
                The Glorious the Invincible
                The lord of Cyrus Solemn Throne
                The crowned in haughty Babylon
               _I charge him by his power & pride                 45
                To think how Iran's monarch died
                To turn the traitors, blood-stained sword
                Back to the bosom of its lord
                A bitter draught they gave their King
               _Their lips shall drain the same dark spring       50
                Warriors I may not longer stray
                For Mithra calls my soul away
                He said his pale lip ceased to quiver
          240   His soul soared to its awful Giver
               _The host stood round all hushed & still           55
                While dirge-like murmured breeze & rill

                                    Charlotte Brontë
                                    May 1st - 1834
```

The numbers in the left-hand margin are Charlotte's. For a possible source, see J. Lempriere, **Bibliotheca Classica; or A Classical Dictionary, containing A Full account of All the Proper Names mentioned in Ancient Authors,** London, 1797, owned by the Rev. Mr. Brontë.

Darius Codomanus (Darius III): King of Persia from 336 B.C. to 331 B.C.

Iran:   Persia occupied the western part of the plateau of Iran which stretched from the Caucasus and the Caspian Sea to the Persian Gulf, the Arabian Sea, and the Indus

Mithras:  the ancient Persian god of light and truth, supposed to be the sun or Venus Urania

Issus:  an ancient city in Cilicia, near which Darius was defeated by Alexander in 333 B.C.; his mother, wife and children were taken prisoner by Alexander

Granicus:  a river in Asia Minor, where Alexander defeated the Persians in 334 B.C.

Arbela:  a city in Assyria, Darius' headquarters before his final defeat by Alexander in 331 B.C.

Susa:  the capital of the ancient Persian Empire, and site of the royal palace

Ishmael's sons:  the Arabs, who claim to be descended from Ishmael, the son of Abraham and Hagar

Palmyra:  an ancient city in Syria, the seat of the celebrated Zenobia

Tyre:  an important seaport in ancient Phoenicia, now in Lebanon

Macedon:    an ancient kingdom north of Greece; now part of Greece,
            Bulgaria and Yugoslavia, founded in B.C. 814
Ammon's son:  when Alexander the Great conquered Egypt in 332 B.C., he
            was crowned King. The Pharaohs were held to be the sons of
            the god Ammon
Statira:  the wife of Darius, captured by Alexander after the battle of
            Issus, 331 B.C.
Bessus:  a satrap of Bactriana under Darius. He seized Darius after the
            battle of Arbela, 331 B.C., and pursued by Alexander, murdered
            Darius. Alexander had him executed in 328 B.C.
Cyrus the Great:  founder of the Persian Empire


**95**

From **Corner Dishes, Being A small Collection of Mixed and Unsubstantial
Trifles in Prose and Verse** by Lord Charles Wellesley, begun May 28 and
finished June 16, 1834. The poem reveals that previous to meeting
Zamorna, Marian Hume had been married to Henry Percy, son of Alexander
Percy, Earl of Northangerland. The father, disapproving of the marriage,
sends Henry on a voyage to the South Seas and has him drowned. The "one"
in l. 118 is Zamorna.


**96**

The poem, in pencil, is undated and unsigned, but in Charlotte's hand.
It is on the back of a letter from Charlotte to Branwell dated May 17,
1832, but the poem was most likely written about June-July 1834. It
marks Charlotte's fullest use of the Alexandrine, a form she used on only
two    previous    occasions--**Darius    Codomanus**    (December    1833)    and
**Stanzas On the Fate of Henry Percy** (June 1834). The content is
clearly Angrian, but the identity of the speaker is not clear.


**97**

The manuscript was originally a single sheet, folded in four; it is now
the first item (but latest in date) in Wise's miscellaneous volume (see
Nos. **11** and **12**).


**98**

From chapter two of **The Spell, An Extravaganza** by Lord Charles
Wellesley, signed by Charlotte and dated June 27, 1834 on the title-page,
July 21, 1834 at the end. A shorter version is recalled by Zamorna in
chapter one as he prepares to bury his son, Arthur Julius, who has died
of consumption.

When the wave of death's river
        Hides the rose in its bloom
When the gift & the Giver
        Lie low in the tomb
When the fresh fruit is shaken
        The bright blossom blown
When the flower falls forsaken
        And witherd and lone
Then upwards to heaven
        The dim cloud shall swell
The veil shall be riven
        And broken the spell

He feels that with his son's death "the mystery contained in those lines
I have so often heard in my infancy, and once since manhood's sun shone
fervidly on my path seems unfolding." The fuller version is recited by
the Verger at the end of the funeral service. This is another of the
manuscripts found by Nys in Brussels.


**99**

The third poem in Charlotte's volume of "public" poems (see the comment
for **Richard Cœur de Lion**--No. 87). For the background to the
poem, see I Samuel, chapter 17.


**100**

From **My Angria and the Angrians** by Lord Charles Wellesley. This text
is based on a transcription in the Symington papers made by Davidson Cook
in December 1925 and January 1926 in the library of Sir Alfred Law.
There are a number of pencil alterations to Cook's transcription,
probably made by Symington when he was preparing the poem for the SHB:

> l. 14: "lie" inserted
> l. 15: "Hush" capitalized
> l. 23: period changed to comma
> l. 84: "twilight"--'s added

Symington also changed the title-page of Cook's transcription from
"Transcribed by Davidson Cook" to "by Davidson Cook & J. A. Symington."
The poem does not describe Percy's actual burial; rather it is part of a
fantasy found among Zamorna's papers about Zenobia fulfilling her promise
to Percy on his deathbed "to visit the vault and unclose the coffin"
twenty years after his death. For ll. 124-25, see Ecclesiastes 12:6.

## 101

Also from **My Angria and the Angrians** as transcribed by Cook. The song is ascribed to Henry Hastings, the poet of Angria, and celebrates the birth of twin sons to Mary and Zamorna. Both Charlotte and Branwell wrote patriotic songs using this pseudonym.

**102**

This untitled poem is item 5 in **The Scrapbook**, another of the manuscripts found in Brussels by Nys. Both Shorter 1923 and the SHB C and B reprinted the Cornhill version which ends at l. 49. To my knowledge, the final 21 lines are printed here for the first time. In terms of content they seem to be tacked on, yet the manuscript is clearly one continuous piece. Because the poem does not appear in a prose context, it is difficult to say who the speaker is.

**103**

From "A Late Occurrence," item 7 in **A Scrapbook**. The piece is undated and unsigned, but from its placement among the dated items in **A Scrapbook** it would seem to have been written in November or December 1834. Zamorna recites these lines in ridiculing Lady Julia Wellesley after her recent divorce from Edward Sydney because she cannot resist Zamorna's fatal attraction.

**104**

There are earlier versions of the poem at the BPM, dated February 13, 1835 (published in **Scribners,** May 1871), and in the Berg Collection, NYPL, dated August 2, 1835. However, the 1833 date in the SHB C and B is incorrect, as is their note about the Berg version being the latest. In the SHB Misc I, an 1833 version of the 28 lines is listed as item 4 in the manuscript of **Arthuriana or Odds and Ends** (at the Pierpont Morgan Library); there is no such poem in the manuscript. The earliest version differs from the other two mainly in that it does not have stanzas 5 and 7. The August version, bound with **Saul** by Wise and published by him in Wise Saul 1917, was part of Charlotte's "public" volume of poems (see No. **87**). She seems, however, to have been dissatisfied with the final stanza (which does sound like a tacked on moral) and revised the poem again after she arrived at Roe Head to begin teaching; Wise also had this version bound separately. The August version reads:

## Memory

When the dead in their cold graves are lying
Asleep, to wake; never again
When, past are their smiles, and their sighing,
Oh! why should their memories remain?

Though sunshine, and spring may have lightened                    5
The wild-flowers which blow on their graves
Though summer their tombstones have brightened
And Autumn have pall'd them with leaves

Though Winter have wildly bewail'd them
With her dirge-wind as sad as a knell                             10
Though the shroud of her snow-wreath have veiled them,
Still--how deep in our bosoms they dwell!

The shadow, and sun-sparkle vanish,
The cloud, and the light fleet away
But man from his heart may not banish                             15
Ev'n thoughts that are torment to stay

The reflection departs from the river,
When the tree that hung o'er is cut down,
But on Memory's still current for ever
The shade without substance is thrown                            20

When quenched is the glow of the ember,
When the life-fire ceases to burn,
Oh! why should the Spirit remember?
Oh! why should the Parted return?

Because that the fire is yet shining,                             25
Because still the ember is bright
While the flesh is in darkness reclining
The soul wakes to glory and light

Aug$^{st}$ 2 -- 35

**105**

The poem is undated and unsigned but in Charlotte's hand.  Although in
pencil, it is in script and on the same paper as **Richard Cour de
Lion**, **Darius Codomanus**, **Saul**, and **Memory**.  Clearly visible
thread holes at the margin indicate that it was part of a larger manuscript, suggesting that it followed **Memory** in the "public" volume.
If this is the case, the poem reflects something of Charlotte's sense of
despair at leaving home at the end of July 1835 to teach at Roe

Head School (see her letter in SHB LL I. 129), a despair and loneliness intensified by Emily's departure for home in mid-October, and Branwell's failure in London. A plausible date of composition, then, would be late October or November. At the beginning of the last stanza are two canceled lines:

> If ever smiling eye met mine
> Or kind face turned to me

## 106

The significance of this poem has been pointed out by Ratchford, **The Brontës' Web of Childhood**. At the end of her first term of teaching at Roe Head, Charlotte embarked on a review and assessment of her previous work and achievements. At several points she numbered her own lines in the left-hand margin. The first two numberings are correct, but opposite l. 112 she wrote "122"; thus she wrote "195" rather than 185 at the end. For the Biblical lines quoted in the prose passage see I Corinthians 15:55; for the "mustard seed," Matthew 13:31; for the "almond rod" and "Aaron's sceptre," Numbers 17. The last sentence of the prose passage emphasizes again the debilitating division between the life of her imagination and the demands of her teaching duties.

## 107

The first of six poems and fragments, bound in full red morocco by Rivière for T. J. Wise. Only the last poem is signed and dated--"C. Brontè, Jan$^y$ 19, 1836." Of the twenty manuscript pages, sixteen, in terms of hand, ink and paper, clearly belong together; the other four are in pencil script and on different paper. All of the items seem to be related to a continuation of the review and assessment begun in No. **106**, but see the comment for Nos. **110** and **111**.

## 108

The poem is clearly related to No. **106**; it not only continues Charlotte's review of how her imaginative world has come to function for her, but also suggests her awareness of the religious conflict her involvement in the world of Angria has produced. In the margin opposite stanza two appear the words: "This hope's divine." Cf. ll. 399-408 with No. **116**, ll. 335 ff. For l. 419 see Job 19:25.

## 109

These lines would seem to be a separate fragment. They are written upside down on the bottom half of p. 4 of the manuscript, following l. 168 of No. **108**, but not related to that poem. However, Charlotte's unhappy state of mind is evident in all of the pieces in the manuscript volume.


**110** and **111**

These two poems appear on two leaves that may or may not belong with the rest of the manuscript. Although they are related to the rest thematically, they are on different paper, the two sheets tipped in, and in contrast to the miniature print in black ink of the rest, are in a pencil script that is similar to the pencil script in some of Charlotte's post-Brussels manuscripts. Mrs. Gaskell erroneously dated No. **110** "written before 1833"; both Shorter 1923 and SHB C and B date it 1836. Wise dated No. **111** "1834" in Wise Saul 1913, yet both Shorter 1923 and SHB C and B list it as "undated." For want of evidence to the contrary, therefore, both poems have been included here with the other poems in the manuscript volume.


**112**

The final poem in the manuscript, written just before Charlotte's departure for another term at Roe Head, suggests an increasing sense of panic and desperation as Charlotte concludes that she must give up the world of her imagination to pursue her teaching career, yet acknowledges what Zamorna, her "mental king," means to her.


**113**

Part of **Passing Events**, by Charles Townshend (formerly Lord Charles Wellesley). The first part of the manuscript, containing this poem, is signed "C. Brontë" and dated April 21, 1836. The song is sung by Lady Julia, formerly the wife of Edward Sydney, now the wife of General Thornton, as she tries to cheer herself in her husband's absence.


**114**

This song, from the second part of **Passing Events**, dated April 29, 1836, is sung by Major William Percy--an old ditty of Cacilla, he says--as he recalls much finer star-gazing when he was "a gipsy in the West" than is possible now. Townshend has just expressed his rapture over the night-sky above Adrianopolis.

**115**

Also from the second part of **Passing Events;** Townshend recalls this song as "snatches of old long forgotten songs came gushing back, songs that I used to read from my mother's cahier of romances."

**116**

The manuscript was sold to H. H. Bonnell in 1907 as three separate manuscripts. Fortunately Hatfield realized that the pieces belonged together, but the manuscript is still divided into two items in the Bonnell Collection at the BPM, with ll. 104-294 bound in blue morocco by Rivière and labeled "E.J.B." Although neither manuscript is signed, the hand and content are clearly Charlotte's. Her total of 576 lines is based on 72 stanzas of eight lines, but three of the stanzas have only seven, and there are two uncanceled trial lines following l. 414. As a result her line count in the left-hand margin is not always correct. Initially Charlotte intended to end the poem at l. 528, but the many revisions in the stanza indicate her dissatisfaction with the ending, so she added the last six stanzas to intensify the sense of Byronic anguish and despair. Reminiscent of **Childe Harold,** but in the Don Juan stanza, this is perhaps the most Byronic of all Charlotte's poems. It depicts Zamorna being sent into exile after his defeat by rebellious forces led by his father-in-law, Percy. In revenge, he has sent his wife back to her father's castle, knowing that the separation will kill her. Enroute he hears from Mina Laury, his faithful mistress, how his son Edward was tortured and killed.

**117**

The manuscript is unsigned and undated, but Arthur Bell Nicholls' transcription at the Pierpont Morgan is signed "C. Brontë" and dated 1836, a date supported by Hatfield in his transcription at the BPM. In terms of the hand, the paper and the ink used, the manuscript of the poem belongs with two prose passages in a group of manuscripts in the Bonnell Collection (No. 80) at the BPM. The ink and paper of these three items is quite different from that of the rest of the manuscripts in this group and the same as that of No. 116, dated July 19, 1836. The first of the two prose passages is dated August 11-October 14, 1836; the second, a half-sheet with prose on the recto and the top part of the verso, followed by the poem on the bottom half, though undated, follows the first passage. Therefore late October or early November would seem the likely date of composition (see also Alexander EW, p. 143). For the first of these prose passages, see Gérin CB, pp. 103-7; the second is reproduced here to provide the context for the poem.

I'm just going to write because I cannot help it. Wiggins might indeed talk of scriblomania if he were to see me just now encompassed by the bulls (query calves of Bashen) [see Deuteronomy 3] all wondering why I write with my eyes shut--staring, gaping hang their astonishments--A Crook on one side of me E. L----r on the other and Miss W----r in the back-ground, Stupidity the atmosphere, schoolbooks the employment, asses the society, what in all this is there to remind me of the divine, silent, unseen land of thought, dim now & indefinite as the dream of a dream the shadow of a shade. There is a voice, there is an impulse that wakens me up that dormant power which is in its torpidity I sometimes think dead. That wind pouring in impetuous current the air, sounding wildly unremittingly from hour, to hour, deepening its tone as the night advances, coming not in gusts, but with a rapid gathering stormy swell, that wind I know is heard at this moment far away on the moors at Haworth, Branwell & Emily hear it as it sweeps over our house down to the church-yard & round the old church, they think perhaps of me & Anne-- Glorious! that blast was mighty it reminded me of Northangerland, there was something so merciless in the heavier rush, that made the very house groan as if it could scarce bear this acceleration of impetus. O it has wakened a feeling that I cannot satisfy--a thousand wishes rose at its call which must die with me for they will never be fulfilled. Now I should be agonized if I had not the dream to repose on . . . its existences, its forms its scenes do fill a little of the craving vacancy Hohen linden! [Thomas Campbell] Childe Harold! [Byron] Flodden Field! [Scott, "Marmion"] the burial of Moore! [Charles Wolfe] Why cannot the blood rouse the heart the heart wake the head the head prompt the head to do things like these? Stuff!!--Pho! I wonder if Branwell has really killed the Duchess*--is she dead, is she buried is she alone in the cold earth on this dreary night with the ponderous gold coffin plate on her breast under the black pavement of a church in a vault closed up with lime mortar. Nobody near where she lies--she who was watched through months of suffering--as she lay on her bed of state, now quite forsaken because her eyes are closed, her lips are sealed and her limbs cold & rigid the stars as they are fitfully revealed through severed clouds looking--in through the church-windows on her monument. A set of wretched thoughts are rising in my mind, I hope she's alive still, partly because I cannot abide to think how hopelessly & cheerlessly she must have died and partly because her removal if it has taken place must have been to North----like the quenching of the last spark that averted utter darkness. What are Zenobia's thoughts among the stately solitudes of Ennerdale? She's by herself now in a large lofty room, that thirty years ago used nightly to look bright & gay as it now looks lone & dreary. Her mother was one of the beauties of the West, she's sleeping in the dust of a past generation--and there is her portrait a fine woman at her toilette--Vanity dictated that attitude, Pauline was noted for her profuse raven tresses, and the artist has shewn her combing them all out, the heavy locks uncurled & loose falling over her white arms as she lifts them to arrange the dishevelled masses. There for nine and twenty years has that lovely Spaniard sat looking down on the saloon that used

to be her drawing-room--Can she see her descendant a nobler edition of
her self--the Woman of a haughty & violent spirit--seated at that table
meditating how to save her pride & crush her feelings--Zenobia is not
easily warped by imagination--Yet she feels unconsciously the power of--

*Branwell had her die September 19, 1836 (Alexander EW, p. 153).


**118**

The poem is a continuation in both content and stanza form of No.
**116.** In a soliloquy Zamorna begins by recalling his return to power,
but the bulk of his reminiscence is concerned with the price he has had
to pay in the death of his wife, Mary.


**119**

The poem is undated and unsigned, but follows immediately after the
signature and date of the previous poem on the bottom half of the last
manuscript page. It would seem to be an unfinished rallying cry during
one of the battles in Zamorna's return to power.


**120**

The manuscript of this unfinished poem, printed in pencil, unsigned and
undated, but in Charlotte's hand, has been divided; ll. 1-151 are in the
Berg Collection, NYPL; ll. 152-205 in the BPM. The BPM portion, a single
leaf covered on both sides, was bound by Wise in a manuscript volume of
fifteen leaves, attributed to Emily. In fact two of the items in the
volume are Charlotte's (see No. **90**) and one is Branwell's. In the
chronology of Angrian events this poem clearly follows on from No.
**118;** Mary is dead, Percy has been destroyed and Zamorna restored to
power. Thus the probable date of composition is mid-January 1837. There
is no apparent reason for the discrepancies in Charlotte's line numbers.
For "Marah" (l. 124), see Exodus 15:23.


**121**

These two fragments seem to have been intended as parts of a single poem.
The first fragment in pencil in Charlotte's hand is on one side of a
scrap of paper with the bottom right-hand corner torn away. It is
unsigned and undated, and has not been previously published. The second
fragment is the first of two pencilled inside the front cover of
**Grammatical Exercises, French and English,** by Mr. Porney, 12th
ed., London, 1810. Above the two fragments in Porney appears "Charlotte

Bronte January 17 1837." The "129" at the end of the Porney fragment
would seem to be a line number. If so, a large portion of the poem has
been lost.

## 122

Again these two fragments seem to have been intended as parts of a single
poem. The first, in pencil, is on the other side of the scrap of paper
noted for No. **121.** The last three lines are again incomplete because
of the torn away corner. The second fragment is the second of the two
pencilled inside the front cover of **Grammatical Exercises.** Penciled
inside the cover of another of Charlotte's text-books at the BPM--**A New
and Easy Guide to Pronunciation and Spelling of the French Language,** by
Mr. Tocquot, London, 1806--are the following words:

> Like a vision came those sunny hours to me
> Where are they now? They have long since joined
> the past eternity
> Charlotte Bronte    Jan 17    1837

For "Moloch" (l. 9), see comment for No. **90**; for "Saul" (l. 24), see
I Samuel 16.

## 123

These lines are faintly pencilled on the rear fly-leaf of **Grammatical
Exercises.**

## 124

One of six fragments of verse on three fragments of a distinctive
grayish-blue paper Charlotte used only in 1837 and early 1838. The six
fragments (see Nos. **124-27, 135**) form a group in that they are in
pencil script, while all other verse on this type of paper is in the
usual print-writing in black ink. Since one of the fragments is an early
draft of a poem dated May 30, 1837 (see No. **135**), these fragments
would all seem to have been composed in early 1837. Nos. **124** and
**125** are on the recto of the first of these manuscript fragments, half
of a half-sheet. The top edge of the sheet is a torn edge, suggesting
that the beginning of No. **124** may be missing.

## 125

See the comment for No. **189.**

**126**

This unfinished poem covers both sides of the second scrap of the blue-gray paper--a half leaf. Two canceled lines at the end of stanza three read:

> Stay thou within and watch the bread
> And keep the hearth with fuel fed

On the verso of the first scrap containing the lines for Nos. **124** and **125** are eleven trial lines:

> Like wolf--black bull or goblin hound
> Or come in guise of spirit fair
> With wings and long, wet-wavy hair
> And at the fire its locks will dry
>    Which will be certain sign
> That one beneath this roof must die
>    Before the year's decline
> Forget not now what I have said
>    Sit close till we return
> The hearth is hot--watch well the bread
>    Lest haply it should burn

The top edge of the sheet is a torn edge, suggesting that the first part of these trial lines may be missing. Nos. **125-27** and the first draft of **135** may well belong to late March and April 1837, when Charlotte decided (not for long) to follow Southey's advice to abandon her Angrian world (see Gérin CB, p. 111). The poem is at least partially inspired by the legend of King Alfred and the burnt cakes.

**127**

See comment for No. **190**.

**128**

The first of a group of four poems (Nos. **128-31**) and one prose passage on three sheets of paper folded one inside the other; from the arrangement of the leaves they belong together in the order in which they appear here. All are unsigned but in Charlotte's hand and only the fourth poem is dated--May 12, 1837. A transcription of this poem by Nicholls in the Brotherton Collection at Leeds is dated 1837. The poem would seem to be at least partially autobiographical and linked to her comments on the relief she found in her imaginary world (see the prose passage in the comment for No. **117**).

The next three items in the manuscript described for No. **128**. The Bonnell Catalogue at the BPM lists No. **129** as two separate items of 12 and 26 lines, but they are clearly a single unit in the manuscript, and seem to describe Queen Mary (the Duchess of Zamorna). During the Christmas holidays of 1836, Charlotte had rejected Branwell's destruction of her heroine; instead Mary is now wasting away at Alnwick (see Alexander EW, pp. 156-57). There is an undated transcription of No. **130** by Nicholls at the Pierpont Morgan; the poem describes Zamorna during his campaign to retake his kingdom. For No. **131**, see the comment for No. **191**.


**132 and 133**

These are the first two items in a group of seven poems and fragments (Nos. **132-33**; **135-39**) on two folded sheets bound together with thread by Charlotte, with the same paper and ink as Nos. **128-31**. No. **132** is dated May 15 (not May 5 as in the BPM Bonnell Catalogue and in some previous editions of the poem); No. **135** is dated May 30; and No. **139** May 14. All these poems and fragments seem, therefore, to have been composed in May 1837. At the top of No. **133** but separated from it appears the line: "If I should die & leave thee." For No. **132** see comment for No. **191**.


**134 and 135**

No. **134** (see also the comment for No. **192**) occupies the recto and top half of the verso of a half-sheet. The first sixteen lines of No. **135** occupy the bottom half of the verso and have traditionally been published as a complete poem. But the paper and ink are the same as that of Nos. **132-33**, suggesting that this half-sheet may at one time have been part of the manuscript group described in the previous comment. Lines 17-28 are listed in the BPM Bonnell Catalogue as part of "Long ago I wished to leave" (see comment for No. **197**), but the first two stanzas of "Long ago" are quite different in theme, stanza form, and paper; also they are separated from these lines by an intervening stanza from another poem (see comment for No. **196**). That stanza completes a leaf; these lines begin another. In terms of theme, stanza form, paper, and ink, ll. 17-28 belong with 1-16. An earlier version of ll. 1-16 which appears on the recto of the manuscript fragment containing No. **124** reads:

> I scarce would let that restless eye
> Which haunts my solitude behold
> The secret which each smothered sigh
> And every silent tear unfold

If it were near and if its beam
Fell on me from a human brow
I would awake from that false dream
Which spell-binds every talent now

Why does not Reason firmly speak
And Pride thrust foolish Grief apart
Why does not courage rise and break
The chains whose rust corrodes my heart

Long may I weep-long cry for aid*

*This last line is written over top of two canceled lines which read:

They answer not--no impulse stirs
No strength will to the rescue come

Nos. **133-137** all point to the religious anguish her continued obsession with Zamorna was creating for Charlotte.

**136**

The poem occupies the bottom half of the manuscript page that contains the last twelve lines of the previous poem, dated May 30. A transcription by Nicholls at the Pierpont Morgan Library is signed "C. Brontë." Above the poem but separated from it appear two lines:

A woodland dream! a vision dim
With umbrage from depending tree

**137**

In a transcription at the Pierpont Morgan, Nicholls combines this poem with the previous one, but the speakers are different; the first is male, the second female. Alexander (EW, pp. 147-48) suggests 1836 as the date of composition, but 1837 is more likely (see comment for No. **132**).

**138**

Nicholls' transcription at the Pierpont Morgan is signed "C Brontë."

**139**

See comment for No. **193**.

**140**

The poem is printed on both sides of a half-sheet of the same paper and in the same ink as the group of seven items (see No. **132**); it may originally have been part of that manuscript group. The speaker would seem to be Zamorna's wife after her death during Zamorna's exile. From Charlotte's line numbers at the end of the poem it is clear that she linked this poem with others, but I have not been able to determine which.

**141**

See comment for No. **194**.

**142**

See comment for No. **195**.

**143**

The poem occupies the last page of a thirty-six page manuscript. The Angrian prose narrative on the previous thirty-five pages is signed "C. Brontë--June 29, 1837," but seems unrelated to the poem. However Nicholls' transcription of the poem in the Brotherton Collection, Leeds, is dated 1837. For "Beulah" (1. 9), see Isaiah 62:4.

**144** and **145**

The first two of five poems and fragments (Nos. **144-47**; **149**) on a leaf of blue-gray paper, with black ink print writing, folded to make four pages. Both of these items are undated and unsigned, but the third (No. **146**) is signed and dated C. Brontë, July 11, 1837. Nicholls' transcription of No. **145** in the Brotherton Collection, Leeds, is signed "C. Brontë--1837." The poem would seem to describe Mary on the eve of battle--perhaps the Battle of Evesham fought June 30, 1837 (Alexander EW, p. 158).

**146**

See comment for No. **196**.

**147**

These would seem to be a series of trial lines and fragments, the last two lines giving rise to No. **149.**

**148**

The first of three poems (see also Nos. **149** and **150**) in a twenty-eight page prose narrative by Charles Townshend, signed C. Brontë, July 21, 1837. The text used here is C. W. Hatfield's transcription at the BPM. There is also a transcription by Nicholls in the Brotherton Collection, Leeds, dated 1837, but the comparative lack of punctuation in the Hatfield transcription would suggest it is the more accurate. The song is a serenade by Thornton who is "exalted to the seventh heaven by the united influence of wine and love," but his advances are not reciprocated.

**149**

See comment for No. **197.**

**150**

This poem completes the manuscript described in No. **148.** Adrian H. Joline in **Meditations of an Autograph Collector** (New York, Harper & Bros., 1902), p. 72, provides a facsimile reproduction of the first 31 lines; the last 21 are again based on Hatfield's transcription at the BPM. Nicholls' transcription in the Brotherton Collection at Leeds is also signed "C. Brontë July 21$^{st}$ 1837."

**151**

Charlotte and her father both contributed poems to the album of Miss Sarah Thomas of Haworth.

**152**

Nos. **152** and **153** are related poems. Both are on half-sheets of the distinctive blue-gray paper and in the same black ink print writing. Also No. **152** is preceded by seven trial lines clearly related to No. **153:**

A single word so seen at such a time
Opens a hundred chambers in the heart
And there from every land and shore an[d] clime
Memory has stored her gathered wealth apart

A single word so seen, will bring
    Oppression to the heart
So waked, regrets

Given these factors and the date for No. **153**, late 1837 would seem a
more likely date of composition than the 1836 date Alexander suggests
(see item 402). However, the last stanza of No. **152** is in pencil
script, suggesting it was added at a later date. On the recto of the
half-sheet containing No. **152** is a prose passage of about 400 words
in which Charlotte comments on a letter she had received a week previously from Branwell, "containing a most exquisitely characteristic
epistle from Northangerland to his daughter," written by Percy on his way
into exile after his defeat by Zamorna. The poem, therefore, would seem
to be spoken by the Duchess in response to the letter:

"About a week since I got a letter from Branwell containing a most
exquisitely characteristic epistle from Northangerland to his daughter--
It is astonishing what a soothing and delightful tone that letter seemed
to speak--I lived on its contents for days, in every pause of employ-
ment--it came chiming in like some sweet bar of music--bringing with it
agreeable thoughts such as I had for many weeks been a stranger to--Some
representing scenes such as might arise in consequence of that unexpected
letter some, unconnected with it referring to other--events, another set
of feelings--these were not striking & stirring scenes of incident--no
they were tranquil & retired in their character such as might every day
be witnessed in the inmost circles of highest society--A Curtain seemed
to rise and discover to me the Duchess as she might appear when newly
risen, and lightly dressed for the morning--discovering her fathers
letter in the contents of the mail which lies on her breakfast table--
there seems nothing in such an idea as that--but the localities of the
picture were so graphic--the room so distinct the clear fire--of
morning--the window looking upon no object but a cold October sky."

Alexander suggests a date of October 1837 for this passage (item 26).


**153**

The poem was bound in green morocco for Wise by Rivière and wrongly
attributed to Emily on the binding. The speaker is Charlotte and the
thoughts expressed here are clearly linked to the prose passage in the
previous comment; the poem is a sequel to No. **106**.

**154**

This is the first of eleven poems and fragments (Nos. **154–60**; **163–64**; **167–68**) and one prose passage all in the same print writing on the same distinctive blue-gray paper. Unfortunately, when Wise had these items bound in red morocco by Rivière, the leaves were cut and inlaid, so one cannot tell if all the items were originally in precisely the same order. However, from the distribution of lines on pages it is clear that Nos. **154–58**; **160**, **163–64**; **167–68** form three distinct groupings within which the items must be in the order used here. The last three poems are dated January and July 1838, suggesting that the earlier items date from late 1837 and January 1838.

**155**

Although published as a single piece in SHB C and B, these lines would seem to be four separate fragments.

**157**

See comment for No. **198**.

**158**

These two fragments, divided in the manuscript only by the space of a stanza division, would seem to have been intended as parts of one poem. Only (b) has previously been published. Lowood was the name of Napoleon's prison-house on St. Helena.

**159**

This fragment occurs at the top of a leaf; the rest of the leaf contains an unrelated prose passage.

**160**

See comment for No. **199**.

**161**

See comment for No. **200**.

**162**

Part of a prose narrative by Charles Townshend, signed at the end
"Haworth 1838 C. Brontë Jan$^y$ 17$^{th}$." The Duchess of Zamorna turns
up unexpectedly at the house of Zamorna's mistress, Mina Laury, while
Zamorna is there. He goes into the drawing-room to meet his wife and
finds her reading these lines written by him on the fly-leaf of a book,
recalling his early love for Mina.

**163**

Lord Hartford is deeply in love with Mina, but she will not have him. In
the January 17$^{th}$ manuscript (see previous comment) he is shot by
Zamorna for his attempts to win Mina, and at the end of the manuscript is
dying. This poem would seem to be a direct follow-on, perhaps originally
intended to be part of the **Mina Laury** manuscript (see Alexander, item
103). Nicholls' transcription in the Brotherton Collection at Leeds
dates the poem 1838.

**164**

See comment for No. **201.**

**165**

Part of an untitled prose narrative dated June 28, 1838, this is "an
heroic song" sung by Jane Moore, recalling the bravery of Zamorna's supporters in the war after Zamorna's return.

**166**

This revised version appears in Charlotte's "Copy-Book" at the Pierpont
Morgan containing ten autograph transcriptions of poems from earlier
manuscripts of which this is the only one not used in the 1846 volume of
poems (see Alexander item 11). It is not possible to determine when
Charlotte began the Copy Book, although it was at least as early as 1841,
probably earlier (see comment for No. **192**). Possibly, therefore,
chronologically this poem should appear later in this volume, but it is
impossible to say where. There is an earlier version in the June
28$^{th}$ manuscript at the BPM (see previous comment) sung by Jane Moore,
also recalling Angria's civil war:

> Deep the Cirhala flows
> And Evesham o'er it swells
> The last night she shall smile upon
> In silence round her dwells!

All lean upon their spears                          5
All rest within around
But some shall know to-morrow night
A slumber far more sound!

The summer dew unseen
On tent & turret shines                            10
What dew shall fall when battle's voice
Is heard along the lines!

Trump & triumphant drum
The conflict won shall spread
Who then will turn aside & say                      15
We mourn the noble dead!

Strong hands, heroic hearts
Shall homeward throng again
Redeemed from battle's bloody grasp
Where will they leave the slain?                    20

Beneath a foreign sod
Beside an alien wave
Watched by one martyr's holy God
Who guards the martyrs grave!

## 167-72

On July 21, 1838 Charlotte completed an untitled manuscript, in the first
half of which Charles Townshend provides recollections of "the far
departed past," principally of "the wicked Aristocracy of the West"
(Alexander, item 58). Although not part of the manuscript (see comment
for No. **154**), Nos. **167** and **168** seem closely related to it.
Charles comments upon a recollection in a letter of the three-year-old
Douro: "Is it not odd . . . to think that that unthinking animal (all
laughing selfishness even then) should be now a big man--riding forth in
the middle of a General Staff to review ten thousand troops at Gazemba."
In l. 10, "Manoah's son" is Samson. The poem is preceded by five trial
lines:

Ten thousand to Gazemba are gone to meet the King

Fast, fast as snow-flakes flock the legions
And the heart throbs the blood runs fast
As gathering in from many regions
Returns the scattered, faded Past

No. **168** would seem to be a recollection of Lady Helen Victorine,
Douro's first wife, who like Marian Hume died after being deserted. Nos.

**169-72** are part of the July 21 manuscript; the text is based on a transcription made by Davidson Cook in 1925, now in the Symington Collection. Zamorna tells Percy he heard Caroline Vernon sing the words of No. **169** to herself in his study. She told him she found the poem in an old magazine and memorized it because it had her father's name in it. Caroline is Percy's daughter by his mistress Louisa Vernon (Dance), and Zamorna's ward. Nos. **170** and **171** are sung by Zamorna to Percy, who accuses Zamorna of having had too much brandy. No. **172** is part of Townshend's imaginative reconstruction of the death of Augusta di Segovia, Northangerland's mistress.

**173**

From an untitled prose narrative dated March 26, 1839, these lines are part of Elizabeth Hasting's musings over Sir William Percy.

**174**

See comment for No. **202**.

**175-76**

Both poems are from an untitled, undated manuscript [Caroline Vernon] composed, according to Gérin, between July and December 1839. No. **175** is part of the introduction to the second part of the manuscript, in which the author explains why she writes this sort of narrative:

> reader, these things don't happen every day. it's well they don't,
> for a constant renewal of such stimulus would soon wear out the
> public stomach & bring on indigestion--But surely one can find some-
> thing to talk about, though miracles are no longer wrought in the
> world--battle-fields, it is true, are now growing corn-- according
> to a paragraph in a westland newspaper which I had a while since in
> my hand. "Barley & Oats are looking well in the neighbourhood of
> Leyden & all the hay is carried from the fields about Evesham, and
> they tell us the Navigation of the Cirhala is about to be improved
> by a canal which will greatly facilitate the conveyance of goods up
> the country, & that subscriptions are on foot for erecting a new &
> commodious Piecehall in the borough of Westwood." What then, is all
> interest to stagnate because blood has ceased to flow--? has Life
> no variety now? is all crime the child of war? Does Love fold his
> wings--when victory lowers her pennons?--Surely not--it is true a
> tone of respectability has settled over society--a business-like
> calm--many that were wild in their youth have grown rational &
> sober.

No. **176** is from a letter by Quashia to Northangerland asking for the hand of Caroline Vernon.

**177**

Presumably a valentine sent to the Rev. William Weightman, Mr. Brontë's curate, by the Brontë sisters and Ellen Nussey. The text used here is that in the **Whitehaven News**, February 17, 1876, p. 4, under "Local Intelligence" from the Appleby Correspondent. The correspondent (A. H. Saltaire according to Gérin CB) writes:

Thirty-six years ago the verses were written by the celebrated authoress whose name appears at the foot of them, and addressed to a clergyman, a native of Appleby, and educated at the Appleby Grammar School, who was then officiating in the West Riding of Yorkshire. The original is now in my possession, and is signed by the authoress and three of her friends and relatives.

**178**

See comment for No. **203**.

**179**

Although the poem is undated and unsigned, it is clearly in Charlotte's hand, printed in pencil. It probably refers to the death of Martha Taylor in Brussels on October 12$^{th}$, 1842. Charlotte, hearing Martha was ill on the 12$^{th}$, hurried to see her on the morning of the 13$^{th}$ only to find that she was already dead. According to Gérin (CB, pp. 211-12), "what weighed most heavily on her [Charlotte's] heart both at the time and years afterwards was the fact that Martha had to lie in foreign soil." "I have seen Martha's grave--the place where her ashes lie in a foreign country," Charlotte wrote to Ellen Nussey on November 10, 1842 (SHB LL I, 282).

**180**

The manuscript, in pencil, is undated and unsigned, but in Charlotte's hand. The poem obviously reflects Charlotte's post-Brussels anger and anguish. From the evidence available, she wrote no poems in 1844, but by the end of that year was very distraught at Heger's failure to answer her letters and convinced that Madame Heger was her real enemy. On January 9, 1845, Charlotte wrote the angriest of all her letters to Heger and this poem seems to be an outgrowth of that letter (see pp. xl-xli above). Thus January 1845 would seem a plausible date of composition.

435

**181**

See comment for No. **185.**

**182**

See comment for No. **205.**

**183** and **184**

The third and fourth items of verse (for the first two see Nos. **181** and **182**) in an exercise book brought back from Brussels by Charlotte, entitled **Cahier d'Translations from English to German**, Bruxelles, May 1843. The first four of six pages of translations have been torn out. The remaining one and two-thirds are in ink, then the early draft of **Gilbert** (No. **181**) begins in pencil immediately after the last line of translation, indicating that the **Gilbert** lines were begun after the exercise book was no longer in use. Items **182, 83,** and **84** are also in pencil with **182** and **83** separated by two blank pages. All four items would seem to have been composed in the Spring of 1845 (see p. xl above).

**185 (181)**

For "Jonah" (l. 223) see Jonah 2. There is manuscript material for ll. 177-408 in an exercise book at the BPM brought back from Brussels (see previous comment and pp. xl-xli above). Those lines, in pencil script, with many alterations and variant readings, were probably composed early in 1845, soon after No. **180.**

**(181)**        Alas that misery should come
            In such an hour as this
        Why could she not this quiet home
            A little longer miss
       _But she is now within the door          5
            Her steps to Gilbert glide
        Her cloud-like shade has crossed the floor
            And pauses at his side

His earthly frame indeed is here
    But not his spirit now--                10
Read but the signs of dreadful fear
    Imprinted on his brow
His wife towards the children looks
    She does not note his mien
The children bending o'er their books          15
    His terror have not seen

In his own home by his own hearth
    He sits in solitude
And circled round with light and mirth
    Cold horror chills his blood           20
He sees--but scarce can language paint
    The tissue fancy weaves
For words oft give but the echo faint
    Of thoughts the mind conceives

Noise--tumult strange, and darkness dim     25
    Efface both light and quiet
No shape is in those shadows grim
    No voice in that wild riot
Sustained and strong a wondrous blast
    Above & round him blows          30
A greenish gloom dense over-cast
    Each moment denser grows

But Gilbert is not guarded yet
    Not from himself secured
The same thoughts o'er his spirit flit      35
    He when alone endured
His cushioned chair shakes with the start
    That shook the leafless tree
And fast and anxious throbs his heart
    With the secret agony *          40

The mother risen from her seat
    Towards her children gazed
Her eyes with Gilbert's do not meet
    With Gilbert's wild upraised
In his own home--by his own hearth       45
    He sits in solitude
And circled round with light and mirth
    -------------------------- mood

                Delivered up to untold strife
                    His frame seems sunk and crushed                    50
            _   'Twixt him and his another life
                    Another world has rushed
                'Twixt him and his a wondrous blast
                    Deep-tones and hollow blows
            _And through [t]his awful region fast                       55
                    A sound of water flows

                That air erewhile--all calm & light
                    Is turbid tossed and dim
                A greenish gloom beclouds his eyes
                _   A long roar fills his ear                           60
                Nor gloom nor roar can recognize
                    His tyrant sense of fear

                He nothing knows nor clearly sees
                    Resistance checks his breath
                _The high impetuous ceaseless breeze                    65
                    Blows on him cold as death
                And still the undulating gloom
                    Mocks sight with formless motion
                Was such sensation Jonah's doom
                _   Gulphed in the depths of ocean                      70

                Streaking the air--this nameless vision
                    Fast driven deep sounding flows
                Oh whence its source and what its mission
                    How will its terrors close
                _Long-sweeping--rushing--vast & void                    75
                    The universe it swallows
                And still the black devouring tide
                    A dreamy tempest follows

                More slow it rolls--its furious race
                _   Sinks to a solemn gliding                           80
                The stunning roar, the winds wild chase
                    To stillness are subsiding
                And slowly borne along a form
                    The shapeless chaos varies
                _Poised in the eddy of the storm                        85
                    Before the eye it tarries

                A woman drowned sunk in the deep
                    On a long wave reclining
                The waters clear and limpid sweep
                _   Like glass her shape enshrining                     90
                Her pale dead face to Gilbert turned
                    Seems as in sleep reposing
                A feeble light now first discerned
                    The features well disclosing

                            438

_Dark streamed the hair--the gleaming arms          95
   At times waved with the billow
In death's serene and marble charms
   She pressed her ocean pillow
The long curled wave arrested there
_  Stood stirless with its                          100

Dark streams the hair--white floats the dress
   The arms wave with the billow

It lifeless rolls as rolls the wave

Her face is young and lily pale
_  She seems a rain-drenched blossom               105
 No sun will e'er again avail
   To warm her snow-cold bosom

No effort from the haunted air
   The awful scene could banish
_That hovering wave arrested there                  110
   Rolled, throbbed but did not vanish
If Gilbert upward turned his gaze
   He saw the ocean shadow
If he looked down, the endless seas
_  Lay green as summer meadow                        115

And turned to him the pallid face
   The tresses long and streaming
Still in the vision held their place
   Before his eyesight gleaming
_His mind had failed beneath the weigh[t]           120
   Oft its own dark creation
Had not at length relenting fate
   Ordained the dream's cessation

The storm that to the tortured sea
_  A transient truce had given                       125
 Returned with doubled energy
   In roughest impulse driven
And yielding to the mighty sway
   Of storm upon the billows
_The corse was swept &                               130

And straight before the corse was stretched
   So near--his hand extending
He could the lifeless limbs have reached
   Or touched the wave impending
_He saw the arms uplifted wave                       135
   With movement of the billow
The face lay sad and pale and grave
   Upon its cold ocean-pillow

439

All moved--a strong returning blast
    The whole great deep upraising             140
Bore wave and passive carcase past
    While Gilbert yet was gazing
Deep in her isle-conceiving womb
    It seemed the Ocean thundered
And soon by realms of rushing gloom       145
    Were seer and phantom sundered

Then swept some timbers from a wreck
    On following surges riding
Then sea-weed by the turbid rack
    Uptorn, went slowly gliding          150
The horrid shade by slowly degrees
    A beam of light divided
And then the roar of raving seas
    Fear--faint and fast subsided

And all was gone--gone like a mist        155
    Corse, billows--sounding breeze
Three children close to Gilbert prest
    And eager climbed his knees
Good-night--good-night the prattlers said
    And kissed their fathers cheek      160
'Twas now the hour, their quiet bed
    And placid rest to seek

The mother with her offspring goes
    To hear their evening prayer
She nought of Gilbert's vision knows    165
    And nought of his despair
But pitying God abridge the time
    Of anguish now his fate
Though haply great has been his crime
    Thy mercy too is great         170

Gilbert at length uplifts his head
    Bent for some moments low
And there is neither grief nor dread
    Upon his hardy brow
For well can he his feelings task      175
    And well his looks command
His face has taken on a marble mask
    Unmoved serene and bland

Gilbert has reasoned with his mind
_    He says 'twas all a dream                    180
He strives his inward sight to blind
     Against truth's inward beam
He pitied not that shadowy thing
     When it was flesh and blood
_Nor now can pity's balmy spring                  185
     Refresh his arid mood

"And if that dream has spoken truth"
     Thus musingly he says
"If Elinor be dead in sooth
_    Such chance the shock repays                 190
A net was woven round my feet
     I scarce could further go
Ere shame had forced a fast retreat
     Dishonour brought me low

_Conceal her then deep silent sea                 195
     Give her a secret grave
She sleeps in peace and I am free
     No longer Terror's slave
And homage still from all the world
_    Shall greet my spotless fame                 200
Since surges break and waves are curled
     Above its threatened shame

Above the city hangs the moon
     Some clouds in boding rain
_Gilbert--erewhile on journey gone               205
     This night comes home again
Ten years have passed above his head
     Each year has brought him gain
His prosperous life has swiftly sped
_    Without or tear or stain                     210

'Tis somewhat late the city clocks
     Twelve deep vibrations toll
As Gilbert at that mansion knocks
     Which is his journey's goal
_The street is still and desolate                 215
     The moon hid by a cloud
Gilbert impatient, will not wait
     His second knock peals loud

The clocks are hushed--there's not a light
    In any window nigh                              220
And not a single planet bright
    Looks from the clouded sky
The air is raw the rain descends
    A bitter north wind blows
His cloak the traveller scarce defends              225
    Will not the door unclose?

He knocks the third time and the last
    The summons now they hear
Within a footstep hurrying fast
    Is heard approaching near                        230
The bolt is drawn the clanking chain
    Falls to the floor of stone
And Gilbert to his heart will strain
    His wife and children soon

The hand that lifts the latch upholds               235
    A candle to his sight
And Gilbert on the step beholds
    A woman clad in white
Lo! water from her dripping dress
    Runs on the streaming floor                      240
From every dark and clinging tress
    The drops unceasing pour

There's none but her to welcome him
    She holds the taper high
And motionless in form and limb                     245
    Stands cold and silent nigh
There's sand and sea-weed on her robe
    Her hollow eyes are blind
No pulse in such a frame can throb
    No life is there defined                         250

Gilbert turned ashy white but still
    His lips vouchsafed no cry
He spurred his strength and master-will
    To pass the figure by
But moving slow it faced him straight               255
    It would not flinch nor quail
Then first did Gilbert's strength abate
    His stony firmness fail

442

He sank upon his knees and prayed
  The shape stood rigid there            260
He called aloud for human aid
  No human aid was near
An accent strange did thus repeat
  Heaven's stern, but just decree
The measure thou to her dids't mete    265
  To thee shall measured be"

Gilbert sprang from his bended knees
  By the pale spectre pushed
And wild as one whom demons seize
  Up the hall-staircase rushed        270
Entered his chamber--near the bed
  Sharp steel and fire-arms hung
Impelled by maniac purpose dread
  He chose those stores among

Across his throat a keen-edged knife    275
  With reckless hand he drew
The wound was wide--his outraged life
  Rushed rash & redly through
And thus died by a shameful death
  A wise & worldly man         280
Who never drew but selfish breath
  Since first his life began

[early 1845]

Text:  ll. 16-24:  are penciled vertically in the margin opposite a canceled stanza
ll. 33-40:  the asterisk is Charlotte's.  There are four lines penciled vertically in the margin:
  She lays her hand upon his heart
    It bounds with agony
  His fireside chair shakes with such start
    As shook the garden tree
l. 57:  "erewhile" penciled above "All glow"; neither is canceled
        "&" penciled above "all"; neither is canceled
l. 62:  "Tyrant" and "sense of" penciled above an uncanceled line that reads "His inward panting fear"
l. 77:  uncanceled original reading:  "the visionary and dreamy tide"
l. 100:  left unfinished
l. 118:  uncanceled original version:  "Held fixed and motionless a place"
l. 119:  uncanceled original version:  "Amid the waters gleaming"
l. 130:  left unfinished
l. 138:  "ocean" penciled above "sea"; neither is canceled

l. 142: "Gilbert yet" canceled but no alternative provided
ll. 143-46: penciled vertically in the margin opposite two canceled lines in the text
l. 151: "slowly" penciled above "rapid"; neither is canceled
ll. 151-54: penciled vertically in the margin
l. 156: "sounding breeze" penciled above "tumultuous seas"; neither is canceled
l. 202: "its" penciled above "my"; neither is canceled.

At the end of the manuscript are 21 trial lines:

And oh so near the pale corpse lay
   Upheld by air or billow
It seemed he could have touched the spray
   That churned around its pillow
The hollow anguish of the face
   Had moved a fiend to sorrow
No calm of death could raise the trace
   Of suffering's* deep-worn furrow

Dishevelled streamed the brine-drenched hair
And sad it was to see a form
   So young and early-broken
Of mental <woes> and inward storm
   Reveal so sure a token
Far more than sudden wrench from life
   Was in that brows expression

Around how pale and wan a brow
   The brine drenched hair was streaming
How sunk and quenched with weary woe
   The eyes were dimly gleaming
The lifeless head hung heavy back
   And every limb shewed token

*uncanceled alternative: "Of long Afflictions"

ll. 1-8: an alternative version of ll. 131-38 above
ll. 9-21: an alternative version of ll. 95-107 above

## 186 and 187

There are no known manuscripts for these two poems, nor any concrete evidence for when they were composed. They seem to reflect a determination on Charlotte's part to control and put behind her, her anguish over Heger, suggesting that they were composed in late 1845 (see p. xli above). However, No. **186** has unmistakable Angrian overtones, and may well be a revision of an earlier poem, the manuscript of which has been lost. No. **187** sounds remarkably like St. John Rivers in **Jane Eyre**. For "Jephta" (l. 43), see Judges 11:30-40.

While there is no known manuscript, the poem is definitely of Angrian
origin (Charlotte's footnote notwithstanding), closely related to Mina
Laury's comments in a prose narrative, composed in December 1836 or
January 1837, on how she accompanied Zamorna during his exile in France
(SHB Misc II, pp. 298-99). In all likelihood, the lost first draft was,
therefore, composed in late 1836 or early 1837. It is one of four revisions of Angrian poems in the 1846 volume--see also **Apostasy,**
**Regret,** and **The Wife's Will**--in which Charlotte changed the name
of the male character to William.


**189** (**125**)

Seven trial lines for the second stanza of **Pilate's Wife's Dream**
occur on a manuscript fragment immediately below No. **124** (see the
comments for Nos. **124** and **125**).

(**125**)        How far is Night advanced?--oh when will day
                 Reveal the vanished outlines of my room?
                 I fear not yet--for not a glimmer grey
                 Steals through the formless blank and solid gloom
                 Which shuts me in--would I could sleep away
                 The hours--till skies all flushed with mornings bloom
                 Shall open clear and red and cheer with light


                                             [early 1837]

For the source of the poem, see Matthew 27:19; for "Moriah" (l. 141), see
II Chronicles 3:1.


**190** (**127**)

The final version of **Frances** seems to have been composed in early
1845 (see pp. xl-xli above), but there is an early draft of ll. 213-
227 which dates from early 1837 (see comments for Nos. **124** and
**126**):

(**127**)        New forms and faces passing ever
                 May hide the one I still retain
                 Defined and fixed and fading never
                 Stamped deep on vision heart and brain

                 'And we might meet--time may have changed          5
                 Chance may reveal the mystery
                 The secret influence which estranged him
                 Love may restore him yet to me


                          445

```
        False thought--false hope--in scorn be banished
        Loved I am not, nor loved have been                        10
        Recall not then the dreams scarce vanished
        Traitors--delude me not again

        To words like yours I bid defiance
        'Tis such my mental wreck have made;
        Of God alone and                                           15
```

Text:  l. 14:  "mental" written above "inward"; neither is canceled

These lines are pencilled on half of a half-sheet, with the bottom half torn away, suggesting there may have been more.  Thus while the final version of the poem was undoubtedly shaped by Charlotte's feelings about Heger, its origins were Angrian, perhaps an expression of Mary's despair over the loss of Zamorna.  Lines 53-56 were taken over directly from the first stanza of **Reason** (No. **111**).  In l. 155 "Sodom's lake" is the Dead Sea.


## 191 ( **131** and **132**)

Charlotte used two separate manuscript fragments in composing **The Teacher's Monologue** for the 1846 volume.  The first of these, which formed the second half of the poem, is the last item of the manuscript group described for No. **128**.  Lines 42-56 are entirely in pencil script (in contrast to the ink printing of the rest), and on a separate page suggesting they may have been added at a later date:

( **131**)         'Tis not the air I wished to play
                     The strain I wished to sing
                  My wilful spirit slipped away
                     And struck another string
                _I neither asked for smile nor tear             5
                     For joy nor bitter woe
                  But just a song that soft & clear
                     Though haply sad might flow

                  A quiet song to solace me
                _    When sleep refused to come                 10
                  A strain to chase despondency
                     When sorrowful for home
                  A note such as a bird might sing
                     Its last & sweetest lay
                _Before its weak weary wing                     15
                     Was folded for the day


                              446

```
    In vain I try I cannot sing
       All feels so cold & dead
    No deep distress, no gushing spring
  _    Of tears in anguish shed                          20
   But all the impatient gloom of one
       Who waits a distant day
    When some great task of suffering done
       Repose shall toil repay
  _For youth departs, & pleasure flies                   25
       And life consumes away
    And youth's rejoicing ardour dies
       Beneath this drear delay
    And patience weary with her yoke      May 12^th 1837
  _    Is yielding to despair                            30
   And health's elastic spring broke
       Submits to tyrant care
       --Beneath the strain of care


    And wild repining fills the time
  _    That should be given to sleep                      35
   While conscience speaks of sin & crime
       Because so long I weep
    I have no want, I know no pain
       Without the sun shines bright
  _But O! I feel again, again                             40
       Within a starless night!


    Life will be gone e'er I have lived
       Where now is life's first prime
    I've worked & studied long and grieved
  _    Through all that rosy time                         45
   To toil to think to long to grieve
       Is such my future fate?
    The morn was dreary must the eve
       Be also desolate?


  _God give me patience give me faith                     50
       Vouchsafe me strength to bear
    'Tis but some years then gentle Death
    Will


    Well such a life as this makes Death
       <At least a> wished for <fear>                     55
    So aid me, Reason, Patience Faith
       To suffer to the end
```

The second fragment, used to form the first half of the 1846 poem, is the
first in a group of seven poems and fragments (see No. **133**) bound
together with thread by Charlotte. As in the case of No. **131**, it
contains many pencil alterations made in preparation for the 1846
edition:

( **132** )

The room is quiet thoughts alone
People its mute tranquility
The yoke put off, the hard toil done
I am, as it is bliss to be,
_Still and untroubled, now I see                                    5
For the first time, how soft the day
O'er waveless water and stirless tree
Silent & sunny wings its way
Now as I watch that distant hill
_So faint so blue so far removed                                   10
Sweet dreams of home my heart may fill
That home where I am known & loved
It lies beyond, that azure brow
Parts me from all earth holds for me
_And morn & eve my yearnings flow                                  15
Thither ward tending, changelessly
My happiest hours aye all the time
I love to keep in memory
Lapsed among moors ere youth's first prime
_Decayed to dark anxiety                                          20

Sometimes I think a narrow heart
Makes me thus mourn those far away
And keeps my love so wide apart
From friends & friendships of to-day
_Sometimes I think 'tis but a dream                                25
I treasure up so jealously
All the sweet thoughts I live on seem
To vanish into vacancy
And then this strange coarse world around
_Seems all that's palpable & true                                  30
And every sight & every sound
Combine my spirit to subdue
To aching grief, so void & lone
Is Life & earth, so worse than vain
_The hopes that in my own heart grown                              35
And cherished by such sun & rain
As joy & transient grief may shed
Have ripened to a harvest there
But now I hear it darkly said
_Thy golden sheaves, are empty air                                 40

448

All fades away, my very home
I think will soon be desolate
I hear at times a warning come
Of bitter partings at its gate
_And if I should return & see                        45
 The hearth-fire quenched, the vacant chair
And hear it whispered mournfully
That farewell's have been spoken there
And look around on a house of gloom
_And listen for a voice in vain                       50
 And feel that never ev'en at home
My heart shall bound to joy again
What shall I do?--

May 15<sup>th</sup> 37

What shall I do, and whither shall I turn
Where look for life? When cease to mourn?

Text:   1. 13:   "that azure brow" written above "what parts me so";
        neither is canceled
        1. 55:   "life" written above "peace"; neither is canceled
        11. 54-55:   in pencil, written vertically in the margin


**192 ( 134 )**

There are two manuscript versions of this poem, both dated May 29, 1837.
The earlier one, at the BPM, has very few revisions:

**( 134 )**        Confession of my christian faith
                      Thou solemn priest hast heard
                   Though now upon my bed of death
                      I call not back a word
                _Point not to thy Madonna priest              5
                      Thy sightless saint of stone
                   She cannot from this burning breast
                      Wring one repentant moan

                   Thou say'st that when a sinless child
                _     I duly bent the knee                     10
                   And prayed to what in marble smiled
                      Cold radiant, mute on me
                   I did but, listen! children spring
                      Full soon to riper youth
                _And I for this encircling ring               15
                      Have sold my early truth


449

'Twas not a grey bare head like thine
    Bent o'er me when I said
That land, that Heaven, that faith are mine
_   For which thy Father's bled                          20
‾I see thee not my eyes are dim
    But well I hear thee say
O Daughter cease to think of him
    For he is far away


_And did I need that thou should'st tell                 25
‾   How long the green deep sea
Has rolled between our last farewell
    How long! how wearily!
And did I need that thou should'st taunt
_   My dying hour at last                                30
‾By bidding this worn spirit pant
    No more for what is past


Priest must I cease to think of him?
    How hollow rings that word
_Can time can tears, can distance dim                    35
‾   The memory of my lord!
I said before I saw not thee
    Because an hour agone
Over my eye-balls heavily
_   Sank dow[n] the lids like stone                      40


But how my soul's mysterious sight
    Beholds his image glow
So fixed so clear so burning bright
    Thou father cans't not know!
_Speak not of thy last sacrament                         45
‾   Tell not thy beads to me
Both rite & prayer are vainly spent
    As thin dews on the sea


To him my childhood's faith is given
_   Beyond the wild deep's swell                          50
‾I own no God, I hope no heaven
    I die an infidel
O say no more of bliss above
    Of rest from sin's alarms
_My bliss was in my bridegroom's love                    55
    My rest was in his arms

```
            Yet will I kiss the sacred sign
               Thy faltering hand lifts now
            I claim it mine as thou dost thine
      _        O trace it on my brow                            60
            As the priest lowered the cross she died
               Without one prayer for grace
            The monk with solemn accent cries
               "Pass spirit to thy place

      _     "'Tis done & thou hast ceased to live           65
      _        A sad farewell to thee
            An awful God will not forgive
               Such dark apostasy"
            I saw the bud unclose as fair
      _        As ever flower might bloom                        70
            The fruit lies crushed & trampled there
               How sorrowful her doom!"
```

May 29<sup>th</sup> 1837

The second version, although also dated May 29, is in Charlotte's Copy-Book at the Pierpont Morgan. Nine of the ten poems in the Copy-Book were used for the 1846 volume. Just when she began to copy these poems one cannot tell; it was not earlier than July 1838, the date of the second poem (No. **166**) in the volume--the first is not dated. The dates of the poems range from May 1837 to December 1841, but two are noted as having been copied at Brussels in 1843, and one at Haworth in August 1845. Thus the Pierpont Morgan version of **Apostasy** was, in fact, prepared much later than May 29, 1837, and is heavily amended in pencil in preparation for the 1846 version:

**Apostacy**

```
            This last denial of my faith
               Thou, solemn priest, hast heard
            And though upon my bed of death
               I call not back a word
            Point not to thy Madonna--priest               5
               Thy sightless saint of stone;
            She cannot from this burning breast
               Wring one repentant moan

            Thou say'st that when a sinless child
               I duly bent the knee                          10
            And prayed to what, in marble smiled
               Cold--placid, mute, on me.
            I did--but listen! children spring
               Full soon to riper youth,
            And for Love's vow and Wedlock's ring           15
               I sold my early truth
```

451

'Twas not a grey, bare head like thine
    Bent o'er me, when I said
"That land--and God and Faith are mine
    "For which thy fathers bled"                          20
I see thee not, my eyes are dim
    But well I hear thee say
"O daughter, cease to think of him
    Who led thy soul astray!"

And did I need that thou should'st tell                   25
    How long the green, deep sea
Has rolled between our last farewell?
    How long! how wearily!
Between you lies both space and time
    Let leagues and years prevail                         30
To turn thee from the path of crime
    Back to the church's pale
And did I need that thou shouldst tell
    What mighty barriers lie

And did I need that thou should'st taunt                  35
    My dying hour at last
By bidding this worn spirit pant
    No more for what is past?

Priest--must I cease to think of him?
    How hollow rings that word!                           40
Can time--can tears--can distance dim
    The memory of my lord?
I said before I saw not thee
    Because an hour agone
Over my eye-balls heavily                                 45
    The lids fell down like stone

But still my spirit's inward sight
    Beholds his image beam
As fixed, as clear, as burning bright
    As some red planet's gleam.                           50
Talk not of thy last Sacrament
    Tell not thy beads to me
Both rite and prayer are vainly spent
    As dews upon the sea

Speak not one word of heaven above                    55
    Rave not of Hell's alarms
Give me but back my Williams love
    Restore me to his arms.
Depress again the sacred sign
    Thy faltering hand lifts high                     60
Lay down the cross thou deem'st divine
    Its virtue I deny

May 29<sup>th</sup> Roe-Head
1837

Now go--for at the door there waits
    Another stranger guest
--I come my weak pulse scarcely beats                 65
My heart fails in my breast
Again that voice--how far away
How dreary sounds that tone
And I methinks am gone astray
In trackless wastes and lone                          70

I'll rest till daybreak comes again
    However black the night
There is, we know, a moment when
    God speaks and all is light
I'll rest--I'll sleep--she murmuring spoke            75
    Then still and voiceless lay
The slumber from which none ever woke
    Had wrapt her soul away

"I come--I come"--in haste--she said
    'Twas William's voice I heard                     80
Then up she sprung--but fell back dead
    His name her latest word

Text:  1. 24:  originally read "For he is far away!"; neither version is
       canceled
       ll. 29-32:  penciled vertically in the margin
       ll. 33-34:  penciled vertically in the margin on the next page of
       the manuscript
       l. 35 ff.:  the brackets are Charlotte's, also added in pencil
       ll. 55-58:  contain many uncanceled readings, and read in full:
                   Speak not one word
                   O say no more of heaven above
                       Rave not of Hell's
                       Of rest from Sin's alarms!
                   Give me but back my Williams love
                   My bliss was in my husband's love
                       Restore me to his arms
                       My rest was in his arms

453

l. 62: originally read "And watch a woman die!"; neither version
is canceled
ll. 63-82, following the date and signature, are penciled inside
the front cover of the Copy-Book and were likely added at a later
date
l. 65: "weak" penciled above "faint"; neither is canceled
l. 75: "spoke" penciled beneath "spake"; neither is canceled
l. 77: "slumber" penciled above "sleep"; "ever" penciled above
"awake"; neither is canceled
Above ll. 63-68 appears an earlier version, also in pencil:

    Now go--for at the door there knocks
        Another stranger guest
    I come--three wild strange and fearful shocks
        Now passed through brain & breast

    I come O Death! drag me not hence
        With mien so fierce and fell
    What night is this? what <blackness dense>
    World--Life <Light Sense> farewell!
    Thus wild she spoke <eer>


**193 (139)**

The earliest version of this poem is at the BPM:

(139)      If thou be in a lonely place
               If one hour's calm be thine
           As evening bends her placid face
               O'er this sweet day's decline
           If all the earth & all the heaven          5
               Now look serene to thee
           As o'er them shuts the summer even
               One moment think of me

           Pause in the lane, returning home
               'Tis dusk, it will be still              10
           Pause near the elm & sacred gloom
               Its breezeless boughs will fill
           Look at that soft & golden light
               High in th' unclouded sky
           Watch the last bird's belated flight        15
               As it flits wandering by

```
Hark for a sound amid the hush
    Wait for it earnestly
Amid the stillness feel a rush
    Of happy thoughts of me                             20
If thy love were like mine how sweet
    That twilight hour would be
Which saw our severed spirits met
    In magic memory

If thy love were like mine how wild                     25
    Thy longings even to pain
For sunset soft & moonlight mild
    To bring that hour again
But oft' when in thy arms I lay
    I've seen thy dark eye shine                         30
And deeply felt its haughty ray
    Spoke other love than mine

My love is almost anguish now
    It beats so strong & true
'Twere rapture could I think that thou                   35
    Such anguish ever knew
I have been but thy transient flower
    Thou were my God divine
Till Death the victor claim his hour
    This heart must throb for thine                      40

And well my dying hour were blest
    If life's expiring breath
Should pass as thy lips gently prest
    My forehead cold in death
And peacefully my corse will                             45
    Beneath its guardian tree
If sometimes through thy warm veins leap
    One pulse still true to me
```

May 14<sup>th</sup> 37

Text: l. 45: "sleep" "rest" at the end of the line; both canceled

The date is confusing, for the poem is the last in the manuscript group
described in No. **133**, with earlier poems dated May 15 and 30.   One
can only surmise, therefore, that Charlotte made a mistake in her dating
or that there was an even earlier version no longer extant.   On August
30, 1845 Charlotte copied the poem into the Pierpont Morgan Copy-Book,
and made many pencil alterations in preparation for the 1846 edition:

## Stanzas.

If thou be in a lonely place
    If one hour's calm be thine,
As Evening bends her placid face
    O'er this sweet day's decline;
If all the earth and all the heaven        5
    Now look serene to thee
As o'er them shuts this summer even,
    One moment--think of me!

Pause in the lane, returning home;
    'Tis dusk, it will be still:        10
Pause near the elm, a sacred gloom
    Its breezeless boughs will fill.
Look at that soft and golden light,
    High in the unclouded sky,
Watch the last bird's belated flight        15
    As it flits silent by.

Heark for a sound upon the wind
    A murmur, whisper--sigh
If all be still then yield thy mind
    Unchecked to memory        20
If thy love were like mine how blest
    That twilight hour would seem
When back from the regretted past
    Returned our early dream.

If thy love were like mine, how wild        25
    Thy longings, even to pain
For Sunset soft and Moonlight mild
    To bring that hour again
But oft', when in thy arms I lay
    I've seen thy dark eye shine,        30
And deeply felt its changeful ray
    Spoke other love than mine.

My love is almost anguish now,
    It beats so strong and true;
'Twere rapture, could I think that thou        35
    Such anguish ever knew.
I have been but thy transient flower
    Thou wert my God divine
Checked by death's congealing power
    This heart must throb for thine.        40

456

And well my dying hour were blest,
    If life's expiring breath
Should pass as thy lips gently prest
    My forehead, cold in death.
Sweet my sleep would be and sound                45
    Beneath is the cypress tree
If sometimes in thy breast should bound
    One pulse, still true to me.

Written May 14 1837 at Roe-Head
Copied at Haworth August 30<sup>th</sup> 1845

Text: l. 16: "silent" penciled above "wandering"; neither is canceled
Stanza 3: many alternative readings penciled in; it reads in
full:

Heark for a sound upon the wind
Heark for a sound amid the hush
    A murmur, whisper--sigh
    Wait for it earnestly;
If all be still then yield thy mind
Amid the stillness feel a gush
                            rush
    Unchecked to memory
    Of happy thoughts of me.
If thy love were like mine how blest
                            sweet
    That twilight hour would seem
When back from the regretted past
Which saw our severed spirits meet
    Returned our early dream
    In magic memory.

l. 39: originally read "Till Death the victor claims his hour";
neither version is canceled

ll. 45-48: many alternative readings penciled in; they read:
    Sweet my sleep would be and sound
And peacefully my corse would sleep
                        the cypress tree
    Beneath is guardian tree,
                        breast should bound
If sometimes in thy bosom leap
    One pulse, still true to me.

Penciled in the margin to the left of the last four lines are the
following lines:
    And sound my sleep will be & sweet
    Beneath the churchyard tree
    If sometimes in thy bosom beat
    One pulse still true to me

457

The manuscript version would seem to be Angrian material, probably the Duchess of Zamorna writing to her husband in exile.  The title was added later in pencil, one of Charlotte's many revisions for the 1846 edition. Lines 23-24, 26, 36 are entirely in pencil as are all the bracketings:

(**141**)          **The letter**

    What is she writing? watch her now
       How fast her fingers move
   How eagerly her youthful brow
       Is bent in thought above
  Her long curls drooping shade the light         5
       She puts them quick aside
  Nor knows that band of crystals bright
       Her hasty touch untied
   It slips adown her silken dress
       Falls glittering at her feet        10
  Unmarked it falls for she no less
       Pursues her labour sweet

   The very loveliest hour that shines
       Is in that deep blue sky
  The golden sun of June declines        15
       It has not caught her eye
  The cheerful lawn & unclosed gate
       The white road far away
   In vain for her light footsteps wait
       She comes not forth to-day        20
  The[re] is an open door of glass
       Close by that lady's chair
  From thence on soft lawns of mossy grass
       Descends a marble stair.

  And flowers of bright & fragrant bloom    25
       Around the threshold &lt;blow&gt;
   Their clustered blossoms shade the room
       From that sun's radiance deep
  Why does she not put forth her hand
       And gather one red rose        30
  And cast one glance on that rich land
       Before the day-light close?
  O look again, still fixed her eye
       Unsmiling earnest, still
  And rapidly fingers fly        35
       Urged by her eager will

        Her soul in the absorbing task
            To whom then doth she write
        Nay watch her still more closely, ask
            Her own eyes' ardent light                        40
        Where do they turn, as now her pen
            Hangs o'er the unfinished line
        Whence fell the tearful gleam which then
            For something seemed to give
        The summer parlour looks so dark                      45
            When from that sky you turn
        And from the glow of that green park
            You scarce may aught discern

        But o'er the piles of porcelein rare
            And o'er the couches soft                          50
        Sloped forward from the cornice fair
            A picture frowns aloft
        'Tis there she turns, you may not see
            Distinct each pencilled trace
        The mass looks dark & shadowy                          55
            Those gilded mouldings grace
        But still some feelings vague descend
            Of youth wild & warm
        That strengthen as you longer bend
            Your gaze upon that form                           60

        There seems a glossy flush of curls
            The eyes you well might deem
        A wild hawks & like even pearls
            The teeth of ivory seem
        And then so broad & white a brow                       65
            And features grandly cast
        In such a mould as tells us now
            Of times & heros past
        Is that her God? I cannot tell
            Her eye a moment met                               70
        The impending picture, then it fell
            Darkened & dimmed & wet

        A moment more, her task is done
            And sealed the letter lies
        And now toward that setting sun                        75
            She turns her tearful eyes
        Those tears flow over wonder not
            For by the inscription see
        In what a strange & distant spot
            Her heart of hearts must be                        80
        The name the place, this all revealed
            You feel how lone she dwells
        Though round her park or grove & field
            So rich in radiance swells

                        459

```
 ┌──
 │ _You feel those clustering flowers may fade          85
 │      Unwatched unplucked unmourned
 │      You feel unmarked, the Twilight shade
23        May close where sunset burned
_4    You know that ever in her ear
92  _    The sound of waves will be                      90
 │    For all her youthful heart holds dear
96 │       Is far beyond the sea
 │  ──

      And neither hope that silver dove
         Nor Fear that carrion slave
       _Nor wildest wish inspired by love              95
         Can cross the rolling wave
```

          606                              June--1837

Text:  The line numbers in the left-hand margin are Charlotte's
       1.  11:   "Unmarked" penciled beneath "Unheard"; neither is
       canceled
       1.  37:   "absorbing" penciled above "appointed"; neither is
       canceled
       11. 57-68: canceled in pencil
       1.  71:   "impending" penciled beneath "glorious"; neither is
       canceled
       11. 93-96: canceled in pencil
       Opposite the final stanza penciled vertically in the margin:
              remote colonial wilds detain
              th' adventurer dark & stern


## 195 (142)

The 1846 version was based on a poem at the end of a thirty-five page
untitled and undated manuscript in the library of Sir Alfred Law, transcribed by Davidson Cook (see SHB Misc II, p. 281). The transcription is
now in the Symington Collection. Although Charlotte initially accepted
the death of the Duchess of Zamorna in Branwell's plot development, she
could not long abide the death of one of her favorites and revived her in
December 1836 by rewriting the history of events (see Alexander EW, p.
156). The prose tale preceding this poem describes Zamorna's triumphant
return from exile, and has Mary still alive, rushing out to meet him and
become his wife again. However the poem itself does not seem to be
closely linked to the prose narrative:

(142a)      Arranging in long-locked drawers, and shelves
            Of cabinets shut up for years
            What a strange task we've set ourselves
            How still the lonely room appears


                              460

And is this chamber just the same                         5
As when the last Ancestress died
As when that rumoured deed of shame
Tarnished the baron's crested pride
Yes all round looks cold and white
     As it looked Forty years ago                         10
When stretched in state that solemn night
She lay as pale and cold as snow
A generation's passed since then
And leaves have fallen and bloomed again
     Many O! many a time                                  15
In this wild woodland place that sees
Such constant change of flowers and trees
     And hears th' unaltered chime
Of one Church-bell--a mile away
Tolled every hour of every day                            20
But you are young and scarcely know
How things went forty years ago
I was by when you were born
Early one soft and pleasant morn
Of a mild day in spring                                   25
You were a pretty child and grew
Like a young rose-bud washed with dew
     How oft I used to sing
Beside your cradle while you slept
And never western zephyr crept                            30
To softer cheek or brighter curls
Or rosier lips, enclosing pearls
Than yours young lady--but a tear
Rises as if you grieved to hear
Of those first days--your after fate                      35
Has left you somewhat desolate


Open that casket--look how bright
Those bracelets glitter in the light
The jewels have not lost a ray
Of lustre since her wedding day                           40
But look upon that pearly chain
How black lies time's discolouring chain [stain]
I've seen that in her daughter's hair
Sweet sylvan flower so soft and fair
Ere either she or it had faded                            45
To years that since have deeply shaded
The shine of each. You saw the hour
That trampled that unspotted flower
The sacred marble hides her place
In aisles and chancels sanctified                         50
That's a fair form whose sculptured face


461

Smiles on the line which tells she died
Her picture as you well may see
Is now hung in the gallery
_Looks bright in sun and sad in gloom                          55
Like all which fill that haunted room

That little ring which lies among
Those tangled chains, I found one day
On yonder toilet--She was young
_Who left it in her girlish play                               60
Ere she went bright in hope away
Almost a child but still a bride
Her name was high, her lands were wide
A scion of this noble line
_And flushed with all its radiant shine                        65
Of pure but passing beauty, made
    Like all her ancestry
To be in moulds sepulchral laid
    Before maturity
_I stood a moment by that chair                                70
    The morn she went away
The room was freshened with the air
    Of early summer day
Her white dress on that toilet laid
_   Hung soft as silver cloud                                  75
Fresh flowers that but too soon would fade
    Were strewn as o'er a shroud
The mirror where her hair was drest
    Clear, dark, and silent gave
_Each object from its placid breast                            80
    Like stream unstirred by wave
She was not there the room was lone
    Down in the open hall
Was many a hurrying step and tone
_   And many a hasty call.                                     85
The carriage stood with harnessed steeds
    Beside the gates flung wide
O'er all the manor's woods and meads
    The word was "mount and ride!"

_And as I stood and watched the gloom                          90
    And sunshine check the wall
I heard her in a distant room
    Singing farewell to all
A wild half-sad half-playful strain
_   Which closed at every line                                95
"O! shall I e'er come back again
    To these old haunts of mine?"
She never did--the winter snow


                          462

```
          Lay white on every glade
 _It melted and each aged bough                          100
    In April sunshine swayed
 Then she too closed her gentle eyes
    Serene on all below
 And she too watched those golden skies
 _   In dreary glimpses go                               105
 And now she has no other home
    Than those monastic piles
 With crypt beneath--and arch or dome
    Above their darkened aisles


 _This graven seal was his whose hand                    110
    As fire-side tales have said
 One moonless night, by secret light
    With guiltless blood was red
 Years lapsed--and then they found him laid
 _   When crime for wrath was ripe                       115
 Dead, with the suicidal blade
    Clutched in his desperate gripe
 'Twas on the threshold of that hut
    Where now my age decays
 _The fierce axe struck his giant root                   120
    And lopped his bloody days
 You know the spot where three vast trees
    Entwine their arms on high
 And moan to every passing breeze
 _   This voice "We saw him die!"                        125
 Blackened and mouldering rest his bones
    Where holier ashes lie
 But doubt not that his Spirit groans
    In Hell's eternity!
```

                    [June-July 1837]

Text: l. 42: "stain" added in pencil, but not in Charlotte's hand

Another version, at the BPM, also undated and unsigned, in pencil script
on a single sheet folded over to make four pages, is quite different:

( **142b** )        Arranging long-locked drawers and shelves
                    Of cabinets, shut up for years
                    What a strange task weve set ourselves,
                    How still the lonely room appears!
                  _ How strange this mass of relics old             5
                    In sullied pearl and tarnished gold
                    These volumes clasped with costly stone


                            463

With print all faded gilding gone
Now stored with cameos--china--shells
In this old closet's dusty cells                               10
Why do the rich thus lay up treasures
Which they forget or seldom see?
They only think of present pleasures
And rarely turn to memory
Thus Lady Frances leaves her home                             15
These English woods--this ancient tower
And better loves abroad to roam
Than live where she has land and power
'Tis strange that she so little loves
Her own hereditary groves                                      20
'Tis strange her bosom does not warm
To this old mansion's stately charm
But if you saw as I have seen
With what a sad and restless mien
She looks round on each panelled room                         25
And seems to fear its pleasant gloom
When at far intervals returning
She in her birth-place reappears
Passes a single week of mourning
Then leaves again her home for years                          30
Surely there is some old distress
Some sorrow lingering here, for her
I scarce know what--yet partly guess
When to past times my thoughts recur--

These thoughts can thirty years retrace                       35
Passed in the self-same scene and place
So long my life has bounded round been
By Acton's park & woodlands green
The house and forest seem the same
As the first day I hither came                                40
Old were they then--old are they now
More moss upon the trees may grow
More ivy round the gables cling
With each returning quickening spring
But axe has never felled an oak                               45
Nor change nor tillage scared a rook
Nor Art one old carved chair displaced
Nor stolen one cup or vase enchased
Nor one small ornament defaced
No diamond latticed-frame unhinged                            50
No plant removed, around it fringed
Woodbine and brier about them grew
And age since just as now they do--
But 'tis not so with living things

464

        _To them warm suns and genial springs                   55
         Bring no renewal--they decay
         Even in the arms that seek to cherish
         When each one has fulfilled his day
         'Tis written he must pass and perish
        _Full soon the grave remembrance swallows               60
         The heir succeeds--a new race follows--

         This house is void and desert now
         'Twas peopled thirty years ago
         Master & Mistress--youthful heir
        _Daughters both young, one passing fair                  65
         Servants and guests and lordly cheer
         Made all things gay & joyous here
         Clara and Frances were my care
            To teach in childhood and in youth
        _To tend--each whim with mildness bear                   70
            When gay to guard--when sad to soothe

         Clara had beauty from her birth
            Always fine eyes and flowing hair
         Her mother knew that beauty's worth
        _    And cultured it with constant care                  75
         It prospered--she became each day
            More perfect in her symetry
         Her eyes acquired a brighter ray
         Her face a sweeter harmony
        _She was at length her parents' pride                    80
            And seldom left their fostering side

                        [June-July 1837]

Text:   l. 9:   "china" written above "vases"; neither is canceled
        l. 12:  "or" written above "and"; neither is canceled
        l. 16:  "ancient" written above "grey old"; neither is canceled
        l. 55:  "suns" written above "rains"; neither is canceled
        l. 78:  "brighter" written above "softer"; neither is canceled


**196 ( 146)**

There are two manuscript versions of this poem.  In the earlier one at
the BPM, the last stanza was added later in pencil, at the bottom of the
next manuscript page, after some intervening stanzas of another poem:




                              465

Sister you've sat there all day
    Come to the hearth a while
The wind so wildly sweeps away
    The clouds so darkly pile
_That open book has lain unread                         5
    For hours upon your knee
You've never smiled nor turned your head
    What can you Sister see?


Come hither Jane--look down the park
_    A thick mist shuts the scene                        10
See how like night it closes dark
    Around those alleys green
Aslant and small and sharp the showers
    Are driven by cold, wild gales
_Through all our walks in all our bowers               15
    A saddening whisper wails


How desolate how lonely spread
    The long & sweeping glades
No ring-dove's flight no roe-buck's tread
_    Awakes their shrouded shades                        20
How thin the rustle of the leaves
    Sounds now from every tree
The latest day of Autumn grieves
    In wan despondency


_Have you forgot how different shone                    25
    The Summer past away
Have you forgot how bright the sun
    Rose smiling every day?
How still and beautiful its beams
_    Went calmly down at night                           30
And woke in us, such glorious dreams
    Who watched their dying light?


Yes Emma I remember well
    Those skies--those suns divine
_Yet mourn I not, for every dell                        35
    Shall see again their shine
And every flower again shall blow
    And every tree unfold
Its foliage to the softest glow
_    Of summer skies of gold                             40




466

Hope Jane as you were born to hope
    Live out your destiny
But dearest sister heaven's blue cope
    Shall shine no more for me
_Forgive these tears, forgive the thought          45
    That brings that strange forebode
I know my task is almost wrought
    My path is well-nigh trode

            * * * * * * * * * *

Emma the very pride of June
_    Burns high in heaven again                     50
A thousand birds their sweetest tune
    Pour forth in choral strain
Emma the tranquil world asleep
    On evening's bosom lies
_Thy father's lake blue calm & deep                55
    Reflects unclouded skies

Full low in twilight's purple zone
    The moon set full & mild
Shines glorious as she ever shone
_    Smiles as she ever smiled                      60
And Jane sits on an old oak's root
    Her feet on flowers repose
The wild birds round her playful shoot
    The deer unstartled browze

_She's thinking of one winter's day               65
    A few short months ago
When Emma's corpse was borne away
    O'er wastes of frozen snow
She's thinking how that drifted snow
_    Dissolved like thought or shade               70
And how her sister's memory now
    To fade as blossoms fade
Fades even &

                    C Bronte July 11
                         1837

The Snow will whiten earth again
_    But Emma comes no more                         75
She left mid Winter's sleet & rain
    The earth for Heaven's far shore
On Beulah's hills she wande[r]s now
    On Eden's tranquil plain
_To her shall Jane hereafter go                    80
    She never shall come to Jane

                    467

Text:  l. 71:  "how" written above "left"; neither is canceled
       l. 73:  left unfinished
       The final stanza was added later in pencil script

Charlotte then transferred the poem, with revisions, to her Pierpont
Morgan Copy-Book sometime between July 1838 and December 1841.  The date
of May 1837 is puzzling, as the earlier BPM version is clearly dated July
11, 1837.  She used both manuscripts in preparing the 1846 version.


## Presentiment

"Sister you've sat there all the day
    "Come to the hearth awhile
"The wind so wildly sweeps away
    "The clouds so darkly pile
"That open book has lain unread                          5
    "For hours upon your knee;
"You've never smiled nor turned your head,
    "What can you Sister see?"

"Come hither Jane--look down the park,
    "A thick mist shuts the scene;                        10
"See, how like night it closes dark
    "Around those alleys green.
"Aslant, and small, and sharp, the showers
    "Are driven by cold, wild gales;
"Through all our walks, in all our bowers,               15
    "A saddening whisper wails.

"How desolate, how lonely spread
    "The slopes, the sweeping glades;
"No ring-dove's voice, no roe-buck's tread
    "Awakes their shrouded shades.                        20
"How thin the rustle of the leaves
    "Sounds now from every tree;
"The latest day of Autumn, grieves
    "In wan despondency.

"Have you forgot how different shone                      25
    "The Summer past away?
"Have you forgot how bright the Sun
    "Rose smiling every day?
"How flamed in fire its burning beams
    "In sunset pomp at night                              30
"And stirred to life such glorious dreams
    "In us who watched that light?"

"Yes Emma, I remember well
    "Those skies, those suns divine
"Yet mourn I not--for every dell                         35
    Shall see again their shine
"And every flower again shall blow;
    "And every tree unfold
"Its foliage to the softest glow
    Of summer skies of gold"                             40

"Hope Jane, as you were born to hope;
    "Long be your life and free,
"But Sister neither bower nor slope
    "Shall smile again for me.
"Forgive these tears, forgive the thought                45
    "Which brings that strange forbode;
"I know my task is almost wrought
    "My journey well-nigh trode"

              ————————————————————
              ————————————————————


Emma! the very pride of June
    Burns high in heaven again                           50
A thousand birds their sweetest tune
    Pour forth in choral strain
Emma! the tranquil world--asleep
    On evening's bosom lies;
The rivers breast blue, calm and deep                    55
    Reflects unclouded skies

Full low in "twilights purple zone"
    The moon set large and mild
Shines softly as she ever shone
    Since first in heaven she smiled                      60
And Jane sits at an old tree's foot
    Her feet on flowers repose
The wild-birds round her playful shoot
    The sheep unstartled browze

She's thinking of one winter's day                       65
    A few short month's ago,
When Emma's corpse was borne away
    O'er wastes of frozen snow.
She's thinking how that drifted snow
    Dissolved like thought on shade,                     70
And how her sister's memory now
    Fades, even as blossoms fade.

```
            The Snow will whiten earth again
               But Emma comes no more
            She left mid Winter's sleet and rain          75
               This world, for Heaven's far shore.
         On Beulah's hills she wanders now,
               On Eden's tranquil plain;
         To her shall Jane hereafter go
               She ne'er shall come to Jane!             80


                          May--1837

Text:   1. 55:   "The rivers breast" penciled above "Thy father's lake";
        neither is canceled
        1. 64:   "sheep" penciled above "deer"; neither is canceled
```

**197 (149)**

The 1846 version is based on the text in the Pierpont Morgan Copy-Book:

### Lament

```
         Long ago I wished to leave
         The house where I was born
         Long ago I used to grieve
         My home seemed so forlorn
         In other years its silent rooms            5
         Were full of gloom to me
         Now their very memory comes
         O'ercharged with ecstasy

         Life and Marriage I have known
         Things that seemed so bright;              10
         Now, how utterly has flown
         Every ray of light!
         Mid the unknown sea of life
         I, no blest isle have found
         At last through all its wild wave's strife  15
         My bark is homeward bound

         Farewell--dark and rolling deep!
         Farewell--foreign shore!
         Open--in unclouded sweep--
         Thou glorious realm before!                20
         Yet though I had safely past
         That weary, vexed main
         Still one voice--through surge and blast
         Could call me back again
```

Though the soul's bright morning rose                    25
O'er paradise for me
     William even from heaven's repose
I'd turn--invoked by thee!
Storm nor surge should e'er arrest
My soul exulting then
All my heaven was once thy breast;
Would it were mine again!

                    Haworth   July 1837

Text:   Title:   "Regret" added in pencil; neither is canceled
        l. 5:   "rooms" penciled above "wood"; neither is canceled
        l. 6:   "Were" penciled above "Was"; neither is canceled
        ll. 7-8:   originally read:
                    Saw I now that shadow brood
                    How happy I should be!
        Neither version is canceled
        ll. 25-27 have many alterations; they read in full:
                    Though the soul's bright morning rose
                    Clear though sung the heavenly breeze
                    In o'er
                    Of paradise for me
                         William even from heaven's repose
                    Even from Eden's bowers and trees

The Copy-Book text is based in turn on a manuscript dated July 21, 1837
(see Nos. **148** and **150**), where it is the second of three poems in
a twenty-eight page prose narrative. C. W. Hatfield transcribed that
version in the BST, 1920 as follows:

(**149**)          Long ago I wished to leave
                       'The house where I was born';
                   Long ago I used to grieve,
                       My home seemed so forlorn.

                   In other years its silent wood                    5
                       Was full of gloom to me;
                   Saw I now its shadow brood
                       How happy should I be!

                   Life and marriage I have known:
                       Things that seemed so bright;                 10
                   But now utterly has flown
                       Every ray of light.

                   When my childhood's hopes were fled,
                       Brighter hopes arose;
                   Now the last is vanished:                         15
                       It set in clouds of woes.

```
        Mid the unknown sea of life
          I no blest isle have found;
        At last, through all its wild waves' strife,
          My bark is homeward bound!                                    20

        Farewell, dark and rolling deep!
          Farewell, foreign shore!
        Open, in unclouded sweep,
          Thou glorious realm before!

        But, though I had over-gone                                     25
          That weary, vexed main,
        Through its tempest speaks a tone
          Could call me back again!

        Though clearly sung the heavenly airs
          In Paradise for me,                                           30
        From the softest smile it wears,
          I'd turn, invoked by thee!

        Storm nor surge should e'er arrest
          My soul, exulting then!
        All my heaven was once thy breast:                              35
          Would it were mine again!
```

In this manuscript the words are sung by the Duchess of Zamorna. There is an even earlier, undated version of lines 1-16 at the BPM; the lines would seem to have been written in the summer of 1837 (see comment for No. **134**):

```
        Long ago, I wished to leave
          The house where I was born
        Long ago I used to grieve
          That house seemed so forlorn.
        Long ago its silent wood
          Was full of gloom to me
        Saw I now its shadow brood
          How happy should I be!

        Life and marriage I have known
          Things that seemed so bright
        Now how utterly has flown
          Every ray of light
        Mournful 'tis for hours to wait
          And listen for a tread
        Then to lie down desolate
          On a lonely bed
```

**198 (157)**

The manuscript version at the BPM is preceded by three trial lines:

O never, never leave again

> O! never, never leave again
> The land that holds thy father's bones.

Although the manuscript contains no revisions, the text of the 1846 version is quite different; it provides a good example of the sort of changes Charlotte had to make to remove the Angrian substance and language of the original:

(157)       Sit still--a breath, a word may shake
              The calm--that like a tranquil lake
              Falls settling slowly o'er my woes
              Perfect, unhoped-for, sweet repose
             _O leave me not--forever be              5
              Thus more that Heaven--than God for me
              An hour ago how lone I lay
              Watching the taper's pallid ray
              As struggling through the night it shed
             _A light upon that statue's brow         10
              To the cold, rigid marble head
              Giving a strange half life-like glow   -
              That startled sleep--and oftimes brought
              Terror of night and dread of thought
             _I scarce that dread may now recall      15
              For thou are here myne own, my all!

              Let me now in the silence tell
              What I have felt when far away
              The Ocean's wide and weltering swell
             _Parted us further day by day          20
              And scarce as thou wert wandering on
              Could I in thought those lands pourtray
              Where wrapt perchance in slumber lone
              My lord mid foes and dangers lay
             _Confused the dream of stormy waves     25
              And battle-fields and gory graves
              And woods untrodden-wildering ways unknown
    28    Still round my midnight couch was thrown

```
         If the soft evening star arose
        _To seal some cloudless day's repose                    30
         And would bring peace with tranquil ray
         Where pain had tortured many a day
         Would touch the heart that yearned for thee
         With a kind balm like sympathy
        _How following in that glimpse of rest                  35
         Redoubling anguish racked this breast
         Anguish because no          eye
         Could see the light of that sweet sky
         And as to my wide halls I turned
        _How dim the torch, and hearth-light burned             40
         Beneath their gilded domes there fell
         The gloom of lonely hermit's cell
   15    And music if awakened died
         As if wild gales repining sighed
        _Through vaulted crypt, through columned aisle           45
         Threading some old religious pile

         Is it so now? O nearer still
         Clasp me and kiss the tear away
         That starts--as that remembrances chill
        _Crosses with clouds my radiant day                     50
         Close not thy dark eyes, for divine
         To me, their full and haughty shine
         Do I repent that long-past hour
         Of moon-light-love and mystery
        _When the wide forest's arching bower                   55
         Heard me vow lasting faith to the[e]?
         Suffering and loneliness and wrong
         Are nothing to a heart like mine
         They only firmer knit the strong
        _The ties that twine its strings with thine             60
         I might reproach and chide the[e] now
         For days when coldness dimmed thy brow
         But only burning love will speak
         In tears for words are all too weak
```

Text:  The numbers in the left hand margin are Charlotte's
       l. 6:  Charlotte obviously intended "than" instead of "that"
       l. 37:  a blank space in the manuscript


**199** (**160**)

The 1846 text is based on the Pierpont Morgan Copy-Book version:

We take from Life one little share,
 And say that this shall be
A space redeemed from toil, and care;
 From tears, and sadness free.
And haply Death unstrings his bow     5
 And Sorrow stands apart;
And for a little while we know
 The Sunshine of the heart.

Existence seems a summer eve,
 Warm, soft and full of peace:     10
Our free, unfettered feelings give
 The soul its full release
A moment then, it takes the power
 To call up thoughts, that throw
Around that charmed and hallowed hour   15
 This life's divinest glow.

But Time, though viewlessly it flies
 And slowly, will not stay;
Alike through clear, or clouded skies,
 It cleaves its silent way     20
Alike the bitter cup of grief,
 Alike the draught of bliss;
Its passage leaves but moment brief,
 For baffled lips to kiss

The sparkling draught is dried away;   25
 The hour of rest is gone;
The urgent voices round us say;
 Ho lingerer! hasten on.
And dying dreams of light, are sealed
 In marble urns, to be     30
No more to ear or eye revealed
 Save Memory, by thee!

Thou, with soft eyes, and shadowy hair
 Shalt watch the sacred shrine;
And in some hour of dead despair,    35
 Unveil perchance its shine
And then when faithless Hope is gone,
 And glowing Love is cold
Shall thine, and Heaven's pure stores alone
 The last, sweet thought unfold!    40

There is an earlier undated draft (late 1837 or early 1838) at the BPM
that, in addition to some differences in punctuation, has the following
differences in wording:

l. 6:  "apart" written above "aside"; neither is canceled
l. 17: "silently" instead of "viewlessly"
l. 23: "swift flight" instead of "passage"
l. 31: "sense or thought" instead of "ear or eye"
l. 39: "Shall thy pure holy stores alone"


**200 (161)**

The only extant manuscript of this poem is in the Pierpont Morgan Copy-
Book and undated. The "Haworth" signature suggests that it was initially
composed either in the summer of 1837 or during the following Christmas
vacation, when Charlotte was home from Roe Head. The similarity of subject, language, and stanza form to **Winter Stores** (No. **199**) suggests the two were companion poems. As all the poems in the manuscript
group containing **Winter Stores** date from late 1837 or early 1838 (the
next poem in the group is dated January 29, 1838), the Christmas vacation
1837-38 seems the most likely time of composition:

(**161**)      **Remembrance**

The human heart has hidden treasures
In secret kept--in silence sealed
The thoughts, the hopes, the dreams, the pleasures
Whose charm were broken if revealed
And days may pass, in gay profusion                          5
And nights in rosy riot fly
While lost in Fame's or Wealth's illusion
The memory of the past--may die

But there are hours of lonely musing
Such as in evening silence come                             10
When, soft as birds their pinions closing
The heart's best feelings gather home
When around our heart there seems to languish
A tender grief that is not woe
And thoughts that once wrung groans of anguish              15
Now cause but some mild tears to flow

And feelings once as strong as passions
Come softly back--a faded dream;
Our own sharp griefs--and wild sensations
The tale of others' sufferings seem                          20
Oh when the heart is freshly bleeding
How longs it for that time to be,
When through the mist of years receding
Its woes but live in reverie!

And it can dwell on moonlight glimmer                        25
On evening shade and loneliness
And while the sky grows dim, and dimmer
Feel no untold and strange distress
Only a deeper impulse given
By lonely hour and darkened room                             30
To solemn thoughts that rise to heaven
Seeking the life & world to come

Haworth

Text:   ll. 13-16 contain many uncanceled variants.  The lines given above
        are penciled vertically in the margin.  In the main body these
        lines read (with the second, fourth, and sixth lines in pencil):
            And then, we tell our treasures over
            Thoughts of lost friends and early days
            Recall the past hours fled away
            And griefs that once wrung tears of anguish
            And then, doth Memory's hand discover
            Now scarce with dimness cloud our gaze
            His own dim realm of twilight grey
        l. 30:  originally read "By darkened room and lonely hour"
        l. 31:  originally read "To thoughts that rise like stars in
        heaven
        l. 32:  originally read "With solemn shine and mystic power"


**201 (164)**

The 1846 text is based on the Pierpont Morgan Copy-Book version, which
Charlotte copied at Brussels in 1843:

### Parting

There's no use in weeping,
Though we are condemned to part;
There's such a thing as keeping
A remembrance in one's heart.

There's such a thing as dwelling                                  5
On the thought, ourselves have nurst,
And with scorn and courage telling
The world, to do its worst!

We'll not let its follies grieve us,
We'll just take them as they come,                               10
And then every day will leave us
A merry laugh for home.

When we've left each friend and brother,
When we're parted wide and far,
We shall think of one another                                    15
As much better than we are.

Every glorious sight above us,
Every pleasant sight beneath,
We'll connect with those that love us,
Whom we, truly love till death.                                  20

In the evening, when we're sitting
By the fire,--perchance alone,
Then shall heart with warm heart meeting
Give responsive tone for tone.

We can burst the bonds which chain us,                           25
Which cold human hands have wrought
And where none shall dare restrain us
We can meet again, in thought.

So there's no use in weeping;
Bear a cheerful spirit still,                                    30
Never doubt that Fate is keeping
Future good, for present ill!

Written at Haworth 1838.  Copied at Bruxelles 1843.

There is an earlier version at the BPM dated January 29, 1838 which is
preceded by the lines:

A little while

A bell tolled and I woke--I had been dreaming
By daylight, not the broken dreams of sleep
But a strange waking vision--

and followed by:

Sigh no more--it is a dream
So vivid that it looks like life

478

The BPM version (No. **164**) differs from the later text in that:

(a) it has an additional stanza as its fifth which reads:
    We'll nurse romantic notions
      Of our superior sense
    And despise the world's commotions
      As devoid of pith or sense
(b) its last two lines read:
    I could swear the Future's keeping
    A reward for all that ill.

Since Charlotte returned to Miss Wooler's school on 30 January 1838, both versions may have been composed on the $29^{th}$, and reflect her reluctance to resume her teaching duties.

## 202 ( **174** )

The 1846 text is identical to the text in the Pierpont Morgan Copy-Book (except for minor variations in punctuation) also copied at Brussels in 1843. An earlier version concludes the **Henry Hastings** manuscript, dated March 26, 1839:

( **174** )
    Life believe is not a scene
      So dark as sages say
    Oft' a little morning rain
      Will bring a pleasant day
    _Sometimes there are clouds of gloom        5
      But these are transient all
    If the shower will make the roses bloom
      O why lament its fall?
      Merrily--rapidly
   _   Our sunny hours flit by        10
      Then gratefully--cheerily
      Enjoy them as they fly.

    What though Death at times steps in
      And calls our best away?
    _What though sorrow seems to win        15
      O'er Hope a heavy sway?
    Yet Hope again elastic springs
      Unconquered, though she fell.
    Still buoyant are her golden wings
   _   Still strong to bear us well.        20

```
        Then manfully, fearlessly
      The day of trial bear
        For gloriously victoriously
      Can Courage quell Despair!

    Charles Townshend--March 26^th 1839
```

These words are sung in the drawing room by either the Duke or Duchess of
Zamorna--the manuscript does not indicate which.


**203 ( 178 )**

The 1846 text is a revision of the text in the Pierpont Morgan Copy-Book,
dated December 1841:

( 178 )          **Passion**

```
        Some have won a wild delight
        By daring wilder sorrow;
        Could I gain thy love to-night
        I'd hazard death to-morrow.

        Could the battle-struggle earn              5
        One kind glance from thine eye
        How this withering heart would burn
        The heady fight to try!

        Welcome nights of broken sleep
        And days of carnage cold                   10
        If I thought that thou would'st weep
        To hear my perils told.

        Tell me, if with wandering bands
        I roam full far away--
        Wilt thou to those distant lands           15
        In spirit ever stray?

        Wild, long a trumpet sounds afar
        Bid me--bid me go
        Where Gaul & Briton meet in war
        By southern Douro's flow                   20

        Blood has dyed the Douro's waves
        With scarlet stain--I know
        Spain's Sierras yawn with graves
        Yet--command me, go--
```

480

```
 _Bid me do some wilder thing!                               25
  Angel! bid me be
  False to country--false to king--
  True--alone to thee!

  If hot from war I seek thine arms
 _Dar'st thou turn aside?                                    30
  Dar'st thou then withdraw thy charms
  In scorn and maddening pride?

  No my will shall yet control
  Thy will so high & free
 _And love shall tame that haughty soul,                     35
  Yes, tenderest love for me!

  I'll read that victory in thine eyes
  Behold & prove that change
  Then leave perchance my noble prize
 _Once more in arms to range                                 40

  I'd die when all the foam is up
  The bright wine sparkling high
  Nor wait till in the exhausted cup
  Life's dull dregs only lie

 _And Love thus crowned with sweet reward                    45
  Hope--blest with fulness large
  I'd mount the saddle--draw the sword
  And perish in the charge!
```

Finished at Upperwood    Dec^{br} 12^{th} 1841

Text: l. 17:  the uncanceled original line reads:
                "A trumpet sounds--remote and wild!"
       l. 19:  the uncanceled original line reads:
                "Where tents are pitched and arms are piled"
       l. 20:  "By" penciled above "On"; neither is canceled
       l. 22:  "scarlet" penciled above "crimson"; neither is canceled
       Between lines 28 and 29 there is a "4" in pencil

Charlotte was governess at Upperwood House in Yorkshire from March 2 to
December 24, 1841. The version she completed there has distinct Angrian
overtones; stanzas 5 and 6 refer to Wellington's campaign against the
French in the Peninsular War (1809-13) for which he was knighted Baron
Douro of Wellesley. In the 1846 version she revised the stanzas to refer
to Wellington's Indian campaign (Second Maratha War, 1803-05) to remove
the Angrian connection. Either the poem was begun before her leave-
taking of Angria in 1839, or more likely that leave-taking was not as
definite as her declaration suggests. In a letter to Branwell from

Brussels, May 1, 1843, Charlotte wrote, "in the evening when I am in the great dormitory alone, having no other company than a number of beds with white curtains, I always recur as fanatically as ever to the old ideas, the old faces, and the old scenes in the world below."

## 204

These lines are inscribed on the fly-leaf of a 1776 Bible Charlotte presented to Emily. Immediately following the lines are the words:
> I wrote this dear Emily, directly
> I rose from bed on Christmas morn.
> C. B.

There is a note with the Bible suggesting 1845 as the year of presentation, but no evidence in support of such a date; it may have been suggested by Henry Yates Thompson who donated the Bible to Newnham College in May 1909. Alexander suggests it may be a forgery (item 387); but the hand, especially the initials "C. B." seem to me to be Charlotte's.

## 205 (182)

Because the novel was published posthumously, the text given here is that in the fair copy of the manuscript, dated June 27, 1846 at the end. There is an earlier version (No. **182**) in an exercise book at the BPM, probably dating from early 1845 (see pp. xl-xli above) which is partially adapted from No. **180**. Aside from punctuation, the differences in the two versions are slight; in the earlier version:

l. 21: "stopped" instead of "stayed"
l. 32: "returning" instead of "responsive"
After l. 36, eleven trial lines:
> And half a smile sufficed to cheer
>                                    school
> I once again returned to bear
>     Tuitions ------------------------rule
>
> It was a genial summer day
> The sun the lattice lit
> Bees humming in the ardent ray
> O'er garden buds did flit

```
            A gentle breeze as fresh as sweet
               In through the window blew
            I weary of the schoolroom heat
               Aside the curtain drew
     l. 60:   "trees" instead of "bees"
     l. 91:   "notice" instead of "quail to"
     l. 92:   "So strong was" instead of "Upheld by"
     l. 96:   "weary" instead of "throbbing"
     l. 103:  "gaping" instead of "bleeding"
```

The novel was originally entitled **The Master**; Charlotte changed that title to the present one sometime after she began the fair copy, for it has the present title on a strip of paper glued over the original title.


## **206** and **207**

These undated poems are in pencil script on a single leaf. Because there is an early draft of the last stanza of Rochester's song in **Jane Eyre** after No. **207**, these poems would seem to be contemporaneous with the writing of the novel, which Charlotte began in late August 1846 and completed in August 1847.


## **208**

The text here is that of the Clarendon edition, 1969. Alexander (item 301) dates the poem 16-19 March, 1847, the date Charlotte prepared a fair copy of the novel. However, as Charlotte began the novel in August 1846, the poem was likely composed sometime that fall.


## **209**

The text is that of the Clarendon edition, 1969. The final version was probably completed sometime in the spring of 1847. Stanzas 1-10 were adapted from No. **189**. There is an early draft of stanza 12 at the BPM (see comment for No. **206**):

```
     My love has vowed with smile & kiss
        The holy bond to tie
     I have at last my nameless bliss
        As I love loved am I
```

```
Text:   l. 1:   "vowed with" written above "pledged me"; neither is
        canceled
        l. 2:   "holy bond" written above "eternal knot"; neither is
        canceled
```

For an interesting discussion of the interrelationship of Nos. **180,** **205** and **209,** see "Charlotte Brontë and Mr. Rochester," **Brontë Facts and Brontë Problems** by Edward Chitham and Tom Winnifrith, London: Macmillan, 1983.


**210**

The poem is clearly related to Charlotte's feelings for Heger, but seems to view the whole episode from a distance. It is in pencil on the verso of a draft of a letter to W. S. Williams, dated December 14, 1847, suggesting a composition date of late December 1847.


**211**

Written in the margin vertically opposite these lines are the words "O that word never." The handwriting, the ink, and the format, especially the distinctive form of dating, are identical to the manuscript of Charlotte's well-known poem on Emily's death, dated "Dec 24." These lines, then, were very likely written on December 23, 1848, the day after Emily's funeral.


**212**

The many uncanceled variants in the manuscript suggest that Charlotte wrote the lines in a state of agitation. She never returned to them to prepare a final draft. The editors of the SHB C and B chose to use the earliest of the alternative readings; this version gives the latest.


**213**

Again the many uncanceled variants suggest the poem was written in a state of agitation. Charlotte never returned to it to prepare a final draft.


**214**

Bound like one of the many little books of 1830, the manuscript has a brown paper cover inscribed:

```
           THE first book of Voltaire's
                    HENRIADE
                   TRANSLATED
                      INTO
                  ENGLISH VERSE
                       BY
                              ..
              CHARLOTTE BRONTE
                               th
                 August 11
                     1830

                 _____
                 _____
```

and a title-page that reads:

```
           A TRANSLATION INTO ENGLISH
                      VERSE
              OF THE FIRST BOOK OF
                  VOLTAIRES

                   HENRIADE

                    FROM
                 THE FRENCH.

                    BiiiY

                 CHARLOTTE
                          ..
                 BRONTE

                 AUGUST THE
                  eleventh
                  18     30
                    1830

                 _____
                 _____
```

For a discussion of Charlotte's competence as a translator see Enid L.
Duthie, BST, 1959 and her book **The Foreign Vision of Charlotte Brontë,**
1975.    According  to  Duthie,  Charlotte  bought  a  copy  of  **La  Henriade**
in May 1830 (see also Alexander EW, p. 67).

**215**

A translation of Louis Belmontet's "Les Orphelins."    The text here is
that published in **The Manchester Athenaeum Album,** 1850.    The manuscript in the Bonnell Collection at the Pierpont Morgan reads:

## The Orphans

The summer days are passed away;
 The fields are frozen o'er;
How 'reft of hope, and far from aid,
 Woe to the houseless poor!
By cold hearts spurned, how hard their fate,    5
To die unpitied, desolate!

'Twas New-Year's night; the joyous throng
 Of guests from banquet rose,
And lightly took their homeward path
 Across the drifted snows.    10
That night, e'en to the peasant's shed
Some little gleam of gladness spread.

That night, beside a chapel-door,
 Two lonely children stood;
In faltering tone, with utterance faint    15
 They asked a little food;
Careless, the laughing guests passed by,
All heedless of the orphan's cry.

A lamp that lit the sacred shrine
 The children's white cheeks shewed;    20
The elder stretched his trembling hand
 For what was not bestowed;
The younger sung a plaintive strain,
Oft dropped, then feebly raised again.

"Two friendless, helpless children we,    25
 "Our mother's death we weep
"Together, in one narrow grave,
 "She and our father sleep.
"We too of cold and want must die,
"If none will help or hear our cry.    30

His voice was lost; the <u>winter</u> wind
 Bore off its tones subdued,
And soon the merry feasters gone
 Left all in solitude:
Oh none had looked towards the church,    35
Or marked the orphans in its porch!

Then turned they to the chapel-door;
 Their mother oft had said,
That God will shield the friendless poor,
 When other aid is fled.    40
They knocked; an echo mocked the ear;
They waited; Death alone drew near.

```
            Time speeds; the lamp shines faintly still,
              The chimes of midnight sound;
            Hear now from far, a chariot's wheels                45
              Ring o'er the frozen ground.
            Rise orphans! call! No--hushed their cry,
            Unchecked the chariot thunders by.

            A priest his matins came to say
              When dawn first lit the skies;                     50
            He found them on the threshold laid
              He called, they would not rise.
            The icy steps of stone their bed,
            The white snow for their covering spread.

            Clasped closely in each others arms                  55
              As if for warmth, they lay;
            But perished was the fire of life
              And stilled the pulses play
            Mute, motionless, and ashen pale
            They slept no more to wake or wail                   60

            The elder pressed the younger's lips,
              As if to check a prayer;
            As if to say:  "'Tis vain to ask,
              Compassion dwells not here."
            And half he screened his brother's form              65
            To hide him from the frozen storm.

            Lulled thus in everlasting sleep
              The orphan babes are laid;
            Now these their piteous fate may weep
              Who would not give them aid;                       70
            Crowds thronged the church by morning light,
            But none came near that winter night.

                Louis Belmontet.  Bruxelles Fevrier 1843

Text:  1. 4:  "there" penciled above "not"; neither is canceled
       1. 14:  "lonely" penciled above "naked" which is canceled in
       pencil
       1. 18:  "All heedless of" penciled above "Too gay to mark" which
       is canceled
       1. 20:  "The children's white cheeks" penciled above "Their pallid
       faces" which is canceled
       Between stanzas five and six is a canceled stanza which reads:
              "The stranger said; my children's bread
                "I cannot give the poor;
              "Go elsewhere, I must feed my own.
                "He sternly closed the door,
              "His daughter wept, he saw her grief,
              "Yet deigned not to bestow relief"

                            487
```

l. 31:  "The orphan's" penciled above "His voice," but canceled
l. 35:  "Oh" penciled above "And" which is canceled
l. 43:  "faintly" penciled above "feebly" which is canceled
l. 57:  "perished was" penciled above "quenched is now" which is canceled
l. 58:  "stilled" penciled above "checked" which is canceled
l. 59:  "Mute" penciled above "All" which is canceled
l. 60:  "slept" penciled above "sleep" which is canceled
l. 62:  "a" penciled above "the" which is canceled
l. 69:  originally read:  "Now the proud rich their doom may weep"; neither version is canceled
l. 69:  "bitter" penciled beneath "piteous" but canceled

**216**

A translation of Auguste Barbier's "L'Idole" from **Iambes**, 1831. There are various trial lines, undated, on both sides of a single sheet at the BPM.  The recto reads:

Thy France O straight-haired Corsican
   How bold and bright was she
When the broad sun of Messidor
   Woke her full energy

She was a young rebellious steed               5
   That rein or bridle spurned
Foaled of a wild and fiery breed
   Her veins with lava burned

Her veins still hot with kingly blood
Gave not their strength to toil                10
Wild with the joy of liberty
Her free hoof struck the soil

   Tyrant check of thong or spur
   The touch of violence or force
   To her was yet unknown              15
   And o'er her loins had foreign foe
   The shameful harness thrown

   She trampled generations in her course
   For fifteen bloody years

On the verso appears:

O Corsican thou of the stern contour
   Thy France how fair when free
When the broad ardent Sun of Messidor
   At length beheld her free
Then like a horse, unbroke to servitude                         5
   Bridle She scorned & rein
Still on her hot flanks smoked the recent blood
   Of kings on scaffolds slain

Proudly her free hoof struck the ancient soil
   Insult wrong or force                                        10
She knew not--never hand of outrage vile
   Had passed on that wild horse
Never had her deep flanks the saddle borne
   Or harness of the foe
All virgin she he[r] heavy mane unshorn                         15
   Wantoned in vagrant flow

reared up erect She the whole world dismayed with her wild neigh

L je n'ai pas achevé --parceque je craignais de faire
le Devoir trop long

Text: 1. 1: "stern contour" written above "straight dark hair"; neither
        is canceled
      1. 2: "when free" penciled above "was she"; neither is canceled
      1. 17: penciled in the margin opposite two canceled lines
      ll. 18-19: penciled vertically in the margin
      At the bottom of the page are parts of five lines--trial lines for
      stanza three of the final version--incomplete because the bottom
      right hand corner has been torn away.

In the manuscript of **Shirley** (volume III, chapter 26), but subsequently deleted, Charlotte quotes the first verse of Hugo's "Une nuit
qu'on entendait la mer sans la voir" and the opening lines of Barbier as
examples of poems Louis Moore would have enjoyed (see p. 559 of the
Clarendon edition).


**217** and **218**

These translations of poems by Schiller are in an exercise book of German
translations done at Brussels.  The exercise book is dated on the cover
April 25, 1843.

The first of these translations is bound with an unpublished devoir of Charlotte's entitled **L' Immensite De Dieu**; the other five in a volume entitled **William Wallace and Other Essays in prose and verse** (the title is Wise's, who had both volumes bound). The volumes both consist of pages cut out of an exercise book of the kind Charlotte used in Brussels; in fact, from the similarity of paper, ink, lining, and handwriting, it is likely that all the pages come from the same exercise book. Although the first volume is dated c 1842-43, and the second 1842, by Wise, there are no dates on any of the manuscripts. Charlotte pursued her study of German in particular during her second year in Brussels, and an exercise book of translations of Schiller into English at the BPM is dated April 25, 1843 (see Nos. **217** and **218**). It would seem, therefore, that spring of 1843 is a likely date for these translations. The poems translated are Scott's "Coronach" from Canto III, stanza 16 of **The Lady of the Lake,** Schiller's "Des Mädchens Klage," "Der Alpenjäger," "Ritter Toggenburg," "Nadowessische Totenklage," and Byron's **Childe Harold's Pilgrimmage,** Canto IV, stanzas 140-41. The four Schiller translations contain corrections and annotations by Heger. In **Villette,** chapter XXVI, Lucy Snow notes that in their German lessons, she and Paulina de Bassompierre enjoyed reading and translating Schiller's Ballads, and that "Des Mädchens Klage" was one of Paulina's favorites.

# Index of Titles and First Lines

492

494